THE CFO PLAYBOOK

Mastering Risk Management in FP&A

Hayden Van Der Post

Reactive Publishing

To my daughter, may she know anything is possible.

CONTENTS

FOREWORD

It is with great pleasure and a profound sense of responsibility that I write this foreword for "The CFO Playbook", meticulously penned by the esteemed Hayden Van Der Post. At the very outset, let me express my deep appreciation for the work that has gone into crafting this essential piece of literature in the domain of financial planning and analysis.

Risk management has grown ever more complex and integral for Chief Financial Officers (CFOs) across the globe. We live in a dynamic world where financial landscapes are continuously influenced by global events, changing regulations, technological advancements, and market volatility. It is within this context that Van Der Post's guide emerges not just as a timely resource, but as a beacon of expert guidance through the multifaceted challenges CFOs are bound to encounter.

The significance of this book lies in its comprehensive nature; it is an exhaustive exploration of risk management strategies and practices specifically tailored for financial professionals tasked with steering their organisations through the turbulent waters of economic uncertainty. As someone who has spent decades in the field, I can attest to the fact that this guide is not just theoretical—it is practical, incisive, and replete with real-world applications.

What sets this book apart is its remarkable depth in covering not only traditional risk management tools, but also blending them with cutting-edge insights into analytics, forecasting, and strategic financial planning. Van Der Post's robust discussion on leveraging technology and big data analytics to identify, mitigate, and manage risk will undoubtedly resonate with forward-thinking finance leaders seeking to arm themselves against the unforeseen.

More than just strategies and tools, "The CFO playbook" is suffused with the author's rich experience, put into context with case studies and anecdotes that bring the abstract into stark, relatable focus. Hayden Van Der Post demonstrates time and again why understanding the nuances of risk is a non-negotiable aspect of the CFO's role in the modern enterprise.

My personal recommendation of this book is etched from seeing first-hand how the absence of robust risk management frameworks can unravel even the most astute financial strategies. The content herein is not simply useful —it is indispensable for professionals committed to not only preserving but growing value for their stakeholders amidst a landscape replete with potential threats and opportunities.

As readers delve into these pages, I trust they will find a trusted guide—a torchbearer to illuminate the ever-evolving path that financial leaders must tread. This book is a testament to Van Der Post's expertise and a must-read for those who aspire to excel in the art and science of financial leadership and risk management.

Sincerely,

Johann Strauss

INTRODUCTION

In the high-stakes world of business, where unpredictable tides of the economy could shift the fortunes of an entire organization overnight, the role of the Chief Financial Officer (CFO) has evolved into that of a master strategist and visionary. "The CFO Playbook" is the definitive manifesto tailored for the forward-thinking financial leaders who refuse to be caught unprepared.

Like the experienced captain of a ship who navigates through tumultuous seas, an adept CFO must steer a company's financial course with precision and foresight. This book is your compass and your chart; it is both theoretical framework and practical playbook. As you turn these pages, you will be drawn into a world where risk is not a threat, but an opportunity—a complex puzzle that, when solved, grants you the key to ongoing success and financial durability.

We commence on a journey through the multifaceted landscape of risk management, scrutinizing the subtle threads that weave the fabric of financial planning and analysis. From the intricacies of market volatility to the enigma of regulatory compliance, from the puzzle of liquidity to the challenge of strategic investment—all these themes are examined through the seasoned lens of the CFO.

But this is no ordinary guide. You will be engaged, not just with theories and concepts, but with practical, actionable strategies that are the product of years of expertise and proven results. You'll delve into advanced methodologies, equipped with case studies, analytical tools, and simulation techniques that will elevate your understanding and application of risk management to unparalleled heights.

As you grip this tome in your hands, know that it is more than a book—it is the silent ally and confidant whispering the secrets of risk management excellence. Prepare to be challenged, enlightened, and transformed. Welcome to the ultimate journey of mastering risk management for FP&A. Welcome to the indispensable reserve of wisdom for the contemporary CFO. Welcome to a future where you are the beacon of assurance in a landscape riddled with uncertainty.

And so, without further ado, let's step into the crucible of finance, armed with the knowledge that will shape not just the future of your organization, but the very essence of your legacy as a financial leader.

PART 1: FUNDAMENTALS OF RISK MANAGEMENT IN FINANCIAL PLANNING & ANALYSIS (FP&A)

CHAPTER 1: UNDERSTANDING THE RISK ENVIRONMENT

In the panorama of financial planning and analysis (FP&A), recognizing the risk environment forms the cornerstone of any robust strategy. It is the canvas upon which CFOs and financial professionals paint their forecasts and plans. The risk environment encompasses the myriad uncertainties that can affect an organization's financial health and operational efficacy. To navigate this terrain, one must be as much a cartographer as a strategist, mapping out the terrain of potential pitfalls and windfalls with equal acumen.

The financial risk environment is a kaleidoscope of variables, each shifting in response to global economic tides, market volatility, regulatory changes, and technological advancements. In the intricate web of modern finance, these factors interlace, creating a complex matrix of potential outcomes. Understanding this environment is not about predicting the future with unwavering precision; it's about preparing for a spectrum of possibilities.

At its core, the risk environment is defined by the dual

forces of volatility and uncertainty. Volatility captures the frequency and extent to which prices fluctuate over a period, while uncertainty refers to the unpredictability inherent in financial markets and economic conditions. Together, they create a dynamic landscape that FP&A professionals must traverse with a balance of caution and opportunity.

To understand the risk environment, one must first categorize the risks. Market risks, encompassing interest rate, equity, currency, and commodity risks, reflect the changes in market conditions that can adversely affect an organization's financial instruments. Credit risks arise from potential defaults by borrowers or counterparties, while operational risks are linked to the internal processes, systems, and human factors within an organization. Lastly, strategic risks stem from decisions that affect an organization's long-term goals and objectives.

A nuanced understanding of these risk categories allows financial leaders to anticipate adverse events and capitalize on favorable conditions. The FP&A function, therefore, involves continuously monitoring the external market conditions and internal company metrics to identify early signs of risks that can impact financial performance.

Technological advancements have armed financial professionals with sophisticated tools to analyze and interpret vast amounts of data, leading to more informed decision-making. Predictive analytics, for instance, can help in identifying patterns and correlations in historical data, allowing for better anticipation of market movements and potential risk events.

Simultaneously, the risk environment is not static; it evolves with each new financial product, each geopolitical shift, and each technological breakthrough. This constant evolution demands that FP&A professionals remain lifelong learners, agile in their approach and innovative in their thinking.

Understanding the risk environment is thus a multifaceted challenge. It requires a blend of analytical rigor, awareness of market dynamics, and a proactive stance towards risk management. This understanding is not an endpoint but a continuous journey of adaptation and strategic foresight. As we delve deeper into specific risks and their management in subsequent sections, we will build upon this foundational knowledge to arm FP&A professionals with the tools needed for navigating the uncertain waters of financial risk.

Types of Risks Impacting FP&A

The domain of financial planning and analysis (FP&A) is complex and multifaceted, requiring a nuanced understanding of the various risks that can impact an organization's financial stability and strategic objectives. These risks are not merely abstract concepts but tangible factors that can materially influence the financial outcomes and dictate the need for astute risk management strategies.

Market Risks

Market risks in FP&A require careful monitoring and strategic management due to their potential to disrupt the financial landscape of organizations. These risks arise from the unpredictable nature of the market, leading to fluctuations that have the power to impact a company's balance sheets and fiscal forecasts. To safeguard corporate strategies, FP&A professionals must remain vigilant, continuously evaluating and adapting their approaches to navigate these risks effectively. By understanding market dynamics, analyzing trends, and implementing risk mitigation strategies, organizations can work towards mitigating the impact of market risks and maintaining stability in their financial planning and analysis.

A deep dive into the anatomy of market risks reveals several core elements that FP&A professionals must grapple with:

Equity Risk:

Equity risk is the volatility attached to stock market investments, where the value of equities may plunge due to market dynamics, affecting the asset side of the balance sheet. FP&A analysts must keep a pulse on market sentiment, industry trends, and the financial health of companies within their investment portfolios to anticipate such fluctuations. Hedging strategies using derivatives or reallocating assets to defensive stocks are among the tactical responses to this form of risk.

Interest Rate Risk:

Interest rate risk speaks to the vulnerability of an organization's financial position to the fluctuations in interest rates. An increase can mean higher borrowing costs and a decrease in the value of fixed-income investments. FP&A teams address this by constructing interest rate sensitivity analyses and utilizing interest rate swaps or futures to mitigate exposure.

Currency Risk:

Globalization has heightened the exposure to currency risk.

Adverse shifts in foreign exchange rates can impact the value of international transactions and affect the multinational company's earnings. To combat this, FP&A functions employ currency hedging instruments like forwards, options, and swaps, alongside natural hedging through currency diversification and matching currency flows.

Commodity Risk:

For companies in sectors reliant on raw materials—such as manufacturing, energy, or agriculture—commodity risk is a significant concern. Price volatility of commodities can affect cost structures and profitability. FP&A units must employ commodity derivatives like futures and options contracts to hedge against such risks, locking in prices to stabilize cost projections.

Market risks are inextricably linked to macroeconomic indicators and geopolitical events, which can surface with little warning. The interconnected nature of global finance means that these risks are not siloed but can cascade across sectors and regions, affecting economic actors large and small. FP&A departments, therefore, employ sophisticated financial models that incorporate various market risk scenarios, ensuring that the organization can weather potential market storms.

Enhanced by the power of simulation techniques and predictive analytics, FP&A specialists are increasingly adept at forecasting the potential impacts of market risk on an organization's fiscal health. They craft scenarios ranging from the mundane to the cataclysmic, each informing a diverse set of strategies formulated to sustain the organization's capital and operational agility.

Credit Risks

Credit risk, an ever-present specter in the realm of FP&A, arises from the potential for default on a debt that may arise from a borrower failing to make required payments. In the intricate financial ecosystem, credit risk emerges as a pivotal consideration that impacts lending decisions, portfolio management, and even the broader economic stability.

Let us delve into the nuances of credit risk and its implications within the FP&A landscape:

Counterparty Risk:

At its core, counterparty risk refers to the likelihood that the other party in an investment, or a financial contract, may not fulfill their end of the transaction. This form of risk is of particular concern in over the counter (OTC) derivatives markets wherein the bilateral nature of transactions lacks a centralized clearinghouse. The mitigation of counterparty risk involves meticulous creditworthiness assessments, the use of collateral arrangements, and engaging in netting agreements to offset reciprocal exposures.

Sovereign Risk:

Sovereign risk encompasses the uncertainty tied to investments in government bonds or other securities issued by a nation. It is the risk that a foreign central authority will default on its obligations or that political instabilities will lead to payment failures. FP&A strategists address sovereign risk by diversifying investment geographically, analyzing political and economic indicators, and employing sovereign credit default swaps as a form of insurance against such eventualities.

Settlement Risk:

Settlement risk occurs during the lag time between transaction execution and settlement—the risk that a counterparty may default after the other party has upheld their part of the trade. This risk is especially pertinent in foreign exchange markets, where time zone differences add layers of complexity. Real-time gross settlement systems (RTGS) and delivery versus payment (DvP) mechanisms are employed to reduce settlement risk.

Concentration Risk:

This risk materializes when there is a lack of diversification in an investment portfolio or when a financial institution has substantial exposure to a single counterparty or economic sector. Such concentration can amplify the impact should a significant credit event occur. FP&A teams counter this risk through portfolio diversification strategies and setting exposure limits based on credit ratings and sector analyses.

Credit Spread Risk:

Credit spread risk refers to the risk borne from the variability in the difference between interest rates of corporate bonds and risk-free securities. This spread reflects the market's perception of credit risk. The FP&A function must be attuned to the dynamics that influence credit spreads, such as changes in economic conditions or entity-specific news, and hedge interest rate risk through credit derivatives.

Effectively managing credit risk is not merely about avoidance but about informed acceptance and management. FP&A professionals use a blend of predictive analytics, historical data analysis, and scenario planning to assess the level of credit risk that an organization is exposed to at any given time. They incorporate credit risk considerations into financial models to simulate various economic conditions and default probabilities, ensuring that the organization's credit policies are robust and responsive.

Through active credit monitoring and regular reviews of credit policies, the FP&A department remains vigilant, adapting to the shifting sands of creditworthiness in the marketplace. The subsequent sections will dissect the tools and frameworks that FP&A experts deploy to assess, monitor, and mitigate credit risk, ensuring the financial fortitude of the organization they safeguard.

Operational Risks

Operational risks are the hazards and uncertainties rooted in the day-to-day functional aspects of a business that can lead to financial losses or disruptions. These risks originate from internal processes, people, systems, or external events —each thread intertwining to form the complex fabric of an organization's operational risk profile.

Within the FP&A domain, operational risk management demands a proactive stance. Let's explore the various subcategories of operational risks and the strategies employed to mitigate their potential impact:

Process Risks:

Process risks arise from inadequate or failed internal procedures. These might include transaction processing errors, data entry mistakes, or the breakdown of workflow systems. To manage these risks, FP&A professional's advocate for robust process designs, regular audits, and the implementation of automated systems to minimize human error. Continuous process improvement methodologies, such as Six Sigma, are often applied to refine operational efficiency and reliability.

Human Risks:

Human risks stem from actions taken by employees, management, or even third-party consultants that could negatively affect the company. This encompasses both deliberate actions, such as fraud or theft, and unintentional errors due to lack of training or oversight. FP&A addresses this risk by enforcing stringent internal controls, promoting a culture of integrity and ethical behavior, and conducting thorough staff training and development programs.

Systems Risks:

The FP&A function relies heavily on information technology systems for data analysis, reporting, and strategic planning. Systems risks include software malfunctions, hardware failures, or cybersecurity breaches that can compromise the integrity of financial data. Regular system updates, comprehensive IT security protocols, and disaster recovery plans are critical in safeguarding against systems risks.

External Risks:

External operational risks are those that arise from outside the organization, such as natural disasters, political instability, or regulatory changes. While these are often beyond the direct control of the FP&A team, scenario planning and stress testing can help prepare for such contingencies. Additionally, maintaining comprehensive insurance coverage and forging strong supplier relationships can provide buffers against external operational shocks.

Model Risks:

In FP&A, financial models are pivotal tools for forecasting and decision-making. Model risks occur when these models are based on incorrect assumptions or when they fail to accurately represent the underlying financial dynamics. To mitigate model risks, FP&A professionals perform regular model validations, sensitivity analyses, and engage in peer reviews to ensure the models' soundness and relevance.

The holistic approach to operational risk management in FP&A involves not only identifying and mitigating risks but also embedding a risk-aware culture throughout the organization. It's about fostering open communication channels where employees at all levels are encouraged to report potential risks or inefficiencies. By doing so, companies can harness the collective vigilance of their workforce to detect and address operational risks more swiftly.

To further empower the FP&A function, advanced data analytics tools and risk management software can provide real-time surveillance of operational risk indicators. By leveraging these technologies, FP&A professionals can anticipate potential issues and deploy preemptive measures, thereby fortifying the organization against the unpredictable nature of operational hazards.

Strategic Risks

Strategic risks are the potential adverse effects on an organization's long-term goals and overall strategic direction. These risks can be rooted in shifts within the market landscape, competitor actions, changes in consumer preferences, regulatory adjustments, or even misaligned internal strategies. For the FP&A professional, strategic risks require an in-depth understanding of both the macro and micro-environmental factors that could influence the organization's trajectory.

Let's delve into the facets of strategic risks:

Market Evolution Risks:

The market's continuous evolution can render a company's products or services obsolete. FP&A practitioners keep a vigilant eye on market trends, consumer behaviors, and technological advancements to anticipate these shifts. Strategic foresight tools like PESTLE analysis (Political, Economic, Social, Technological, Legal, Environmental) enable the identification of potential market evolution risks and the formulation of contingency plans.

Competitive Landscape Risks:

Competitors' strategies and their potential impact on market share and profitability are always a concern. FP&A teams utilize competitive intelligence and frameworks like Porter's Five Forces to assess the competitive dynamics and the potential for new entrants, substitute products, or shifts in supplier and buyer power. By understanding these factors, companies can adapt their strategies to maintain a competitive edge.

Technological Disruption Risks:

The rapid pace of technological innovation can disrupt established business models and value chains. FP&A

professionals must stay abreast of emerging technologies and assess their implications for operational efficiency, customer engagement, and product development. Strategic partnerships with tech firms or investments in research and development may be necessary to mitigate the risks associated with technological disruptions.

Regulatory Changes Risks:

Regulatory changes can have significant implications for strategic planning and financial performance. Compliance risks must be factored into strategic decision-making, with FP&A teams working closely with legal and compliance departments to monitor legislative changes and assess their potential impact. Proactive engagement with policymakers and regulatory bodies can also help to anticipate and influence regulatory developments.

Alignment and Execution Risks:

Strategic risks may also arise from within an organization if its corporate strategy is not well-aligned with its operations or if there is a failure in strategic execution. FP&A must ensure that strategic plans are grounded in realistic financial projections and that resources are appropriately allocated to strategic initiatives. Performance management systems and balanced scorecards can aid in tracking the execution of strategic objectives and identifying any misalignments early on.

The FP&A function plays a pivotal role in the mitigation of strategic risks by facilitating a tight alignment between strategic initiatives and financial planning. Through rigorous scenario planning and stress testing, FP&A can explore the financial implications of various strategic alternatives and identify the most viable paths forward in the face of uncertainty.

Moreover, developing a dynamic strategic planning process that allows for agility and quick responses to external and internal changes is crucial. This includes fostering an organizational culture that is receptive to change and innovation, encouraging cross-departmental collaboration, and promoting transparency in decision-making.

The Role of a CFO in the Risk Environment

The following outlines the quintessential responsibilities and strategic interventions that embody the modern CFO's role within the risk environment:

As the executive torchbearer of financial integrity, the CFO crafts a vision that integrates risk management into the corporate ethos. Risk leadership entails championing a risk-aware culture and articulating a clear narrative on how managing risks is integral to achieving the organization's strategic objectives. The CFO's remit includes spearheading the development of an enterprise-wide risk management framework that aligns with the organization's risk appetite and strategic goals.

Financial and Strategic Risk Analysis:

The CFO, armed with a profound grasp of financial intricacies and an analytical acumen, scrutinizes the horizon for potential financial risks that could destabilize the organization. This involves a continuous assessment of credit risks, market volatility, liquidity constraints, and the impact of fluctuations in foreign exchange rates and interest rates. By leading a robust financial and strategic risk analysis, the CFO ensures that risk considerations are embedded within strategic planning and decision-making processes.

Governance and Policy Development:

Governance is a cornerstone of effective risk management, and the CFO is pivotal in establishing stringent policies that govern risk-taking activities. In concert with the board of directors and various committees, the CFO helps to develop and enforce governance standards that ensure compliance and ethical conduct. These policies serve as the bedrock upon which risk management practices are built and sustained.

Risk Communication and Advocacy:

As a communicator par excellence, the CFO ensures that risk-related insights are disseminated across the enterprise and to external stakeholders, including investors and regulatory bodies. This involves translating complex risk scenarios into actionable intelligence that can be understood and acted upon by non-financial managers. Furthermore, the CFO advocates for risk management priorities in board meetings, ensuring that risk considerations are given the weight they deserve in strategic deliberations.

Integrating Risk and Financial Planning:

The CFO synthesizes risk management with financial planning by embedding risk assessments within budgeting, forecasting, and financial reporting processes. This integration allows for a more nuanced financial planning that accounts for potential risk scenarios, thereby enhancing the reliability of financial projections and enabling a proactive rather than reactive approach to risk management.

Nurturing Risk Management Talent:

Acknowledging the importance of human capital in

managing risks, the CFO plays a pivotal role in nurturing a pool of talent adept in risk management disciplines. This entails overseeing the development of training programs, mentoring emerging leaders in finance, and fostering a learning environment where financial acumen and risk intelligence are valued and developed.

In sum, the CFO's role in the risk environment is one of orchestration—harmonizing the various strands of risk management into a coherent whole that safeguards the organization's assets and propels it towards its strategic aspirations. The next section will unveil the strategic imperatives for the CFO to effectively steer the organization through the tumultuous seas of risk and uncertainty, ensuring its continued prosperity and resilience.

By translating risk management from an abstract concept into a tangible strategic function, the CFO not only fortifies the financial foundations of the organization but also shapes its destiny in the ever-evolving business milieu.

Leadership and Governance

Leadership within the CFO's domain transcends traditional boundaries, infusing every layer of the organization's operations with a strategic vision and a commitment to robust governance. This leadership is not a static trait but a continuous journey of influencing and steering the organization towards its objectives while navigating the intricacies of financial risk.

The CFO's leadership extends into governance by enforcing

frameworks that are designed to ensure accountability, transparency, and ethical business practices. Herein lies the strategic governance role of the CFO, which intertwines with leadership to form a comprehensive approach to steering the organization. This section delves into the intricate theoretical underpinnings of the CFO's role in leadership and governance.

Cultivating Strategic Influence:

Leadership for a CFO is characterized by the ability to cultivate strategic influence across all organizational levels. This involves engaging with various stakeholders, from board members to operational teams, and aligning them with the enterprise's financial and risk management vision. The CFO acts as an influencer who can clearly articulate the financial implications of strategic decisions and encourage a shared commitment to the organization's fiscal health.

Ethical Governance as a Strategic Imperative:

Governance is not merely a compliance obligation but a strategic imperative that the CFO champions. By embedding ethical considerations into decision-making processes, the CFO fosters a governance culture that reinforces the organization's reputation and stakeholder trust. This ethical governance extends to ensuring the integrity of financial reports, overseeing regulatory compliance, and setting the tone for corporate conduct.

Risk Governance Integration:

In today's complex risk environment, the CFO's leadership role is significantly tied to the integration of risk governance. This involves aligning risk management with corporate governance structures to ensure that risks are adequately identified, assessed, and managed. The CFO ensures that governance mechanisms are responsive to the changing risk landscape, thus enabling the organization to remain agile and resilient.

Frameworks and Controls:

Under the leadership of the CFO, governance frameworks and internal controls are established and continuously refined. These frameworks act as the scaffold for operationalizing the governance policies, setting up a system of checks and balances that protect the organization's assets. The CFO oversees the development of control mechanisms that detect and prevent errors, fraud, and financial misstatements, thereby reinforcing financial control and accountability.

Board Engagement and Reporting:

The CFO's leadership is pivotal in engaging with the board of directors, ensuring that governance and financial oversight functions are effectively carried out. Through regular reporting and communication, the CFO provides the board with critical financial insights that inform governance decisions. This process involves presenting complex financial data in a manner that is accessible and actionable, enabling the board to fulfill its oversight responsibilities with greater efficacy.

Navigating Governance Challenges:

The CFO is often at the frontline of navigating governance challenges, from regulatory changes to evolving stakeholder expectations. By staying ahead of these challenges, the CFO ensures that the organization's governance practices are robust and can withstand external pressures. This proactive stance on governance challenges is a testament to the CFO's strategic foresight and leadership acumen.

As we dissect these aspects of leadership and governance, it becomes evident that the CFO's role is integral to weaving a strong governance fabric that supports the organization's strategic framework. Strong leadership coupled with governance excellence empowers the CFO to pilot the organization towards financial sustainability, steering through the currents of risk and regulatory demands with unwavering commitment and strategic insight. The subsequent sections will delve deeper into the various dimensions of the CFO's leadership and governance role, further illuminating the theoretical and practical aspects of financial stewardship in the modern enterprise.

Risk Appetite and Tolerance

Risk appetite refers to the level of risk that an organization is willing to accept in pursuit of its objectives. It reflects the organization's willingness to take on risks and its strategic outlook regarding potential rewards. Risk tolerance, on the other hand, describes the organization's capacity to withstand and absorb the impact of risks without compromising its financial stability or strategic goals. While risk appetite sets the direction and boundaries for risk-taking, risk tolerance determines the organization's ability to bear the consequences of those risks.

Both risk appetite and risk tolerance play crucial roles in shaping a company's risk management strategy. They guide decision-making at all levels, from the CFO to departments and individual employees. By articulating and defining risk appetite and tolerance, organizations can align their risk management efforts, establish risk thresholds, and implement appropriate risk mitigation measures. A clear understanding of these concepts helps organizations strike a balance between taking on strategic risks and maintaining resilience in the face of uncertainties, thereby fostering a proactive and informed approach to financial planning and analysis.

Defining Risk Appetite:

Risk appetite is the level of risk that an organization is prepared to accept in pursuit of its strategic objectives before action is deemed necessary to reduce it. It reflects a company's attitude towards risk-taking, encapsulating its willingness to balance potential losses with opportunities for gain. The CFO plays a critical role in articulating the risk appetite, ensuring it is congruous with the company's strategic ambitions and shareholder expectations.

Articulating Risk Tolerance:

While closely related, risk tolerance is the granular specification of the risk appetite. It refers to the acceptable level of variation the company is willing to accommodate in relation to specific risks. Risk tolerance sets quantifiable boundaries that determine the thresholds for risk-taking in various activities. The CFO is tasked with defining these thresholds in alignment with the risk appetite, translating broad statements into actionable criteria.

Risk Appetite Statement:

The risk appetite statement is a formal declaration that encapsulates an organization's appetite for risk. Drafted with the involvement of the CFO and the board, this statement serves as a strategic guidepost for decision-making across the organization. It aligns risk-taking with corporate strategy and provides a framework for risk-based decision-making. The CFO's insights into financial implications play a critical part in shaping a nuanced and informed risk appetite statement.

Aligning Risk Appetite with Corporate Strategy:

Risk appetite cannot exist in isolation; it must be tightly interwoven with the company's strategic planning processes. The CFO ensures that the organization's risk-taking capabilities are aligned with long-term strategic goals, growth plans, and capital allocation. This entails a dynamic process of calibration, where the risk appetite evolves in response to internal developments and external market conditions.

Measuring Risk Tolerance:

Operationalizing risk tolerance involves developing a suite of metrics that can effectively measure the degree of risk being taken in various business activities. These metrics may include financial ratios, earnings volatility, cash flow projections, and capital adequacy. The CFO is responsible for establishing these metrics and ensuring they are integrated into performance reports, dashboards, and regular reviews.

Risk Appetite in Governance:

The governance role of the CFO encompasses embedding the risk appetite within the organization's culture and governance structures. This involves creating policies and procedures that reflect the established risk appetite and tolerance levels. By doing so, the CFO ensures that risk management is not a siloed function but a pervasive aspect of the organizational ethos.

Communicating Risk Appetite:

Effective communication of the risk appetite and tolerance levels is vital to ensuring that they are understood and implemented throughout the organization. The CFO leads this communication effort, providing clarity and guidance to ensure that all stakeholders, from the boardroom to the front lines, are aligned with the organization's risk perspective.

Adjusting Risk Appetite and Tolerance:

Market conditions, competitive dynamics, regulatory changes, and organizational growth can all necessitate adjustments to the risk appetite and tolerance levels. The CFO must maintain a forward-looking view, anticipating changes that may affect the organization's risk profile and adjusting the risk parameters accordingly to maintain strategic alignment.

Risk appetite and tolerance are not static concepts to be set and forgotten. They require continuous reassessment and recalibration, with the CFO as the steward of this iterative process. By effectively managing these critical aspects of risk, the CFO enables the organization to pursue its objectives with a clear understanding of the risks it is prepared to take, and the capacity it has to absorb potential variations. The nuanced approach to risk appetite and tolerance underpins a robust financial strategy that balances ambition with prudence, driving the organization towards sustainable growth and resilience in an ever-evolving financial landscape.

Communication and Reporting

Effective communication and reporting within financial

planning and analysis (FP&A) serve as the arteries through which critical information flows, delivering the lifeblood of data that informs strategic decision-making. This section offers a comprehensive overview of the foundational elements that constitute proficient communication and reporting practices in the context of FP&A, with a particular emphasis on the pivotal role these elements play in risk management.

At its core, FP&A communication involves a strategic synthesis of complex data into coherent narratives that support executive decision-making. The CFO, in tandem with FP&A teams, orchestrates this process, ensuring that financial insights and risk implications are presented in a digestible format. Effective communication hinges on the ability to translate intricate financial concepts into actionable intelligence, enabling stakeholders to grasp the strategic implications of the data presented.

Reporting mechanisms are not simply a reflection of historical performance but also a prognostic tool that can illuminate potential future trajectories. Reports must encapsulate a blend of retrospective analysis, current performance metrics, and forward-looking projections. By incorporating elements such as trend analyses, variance reports, and predictive indicators, reporting transforms into a dynamic instrument that guides risk management strategies and informs business agility.

A one-size-fits-all approach to communication is ineffectual in the nuanced realm of FP&A. Different stakeholders require varying levels of detail and complexity. The CFO must adeptly tailor communications to meet these needs, ranging from high-level summaries for the board of directors to granular data sets for operational managers. This targeted approach ensures that relevant information is accentuated, fostering informed decision-making across all levels of the organization.

Risk reporting is an integral component of comprehensive FP&A reporting. It must provide a transparent overview of the organization's risk profile, highlighting areas of concern and emerging threats. The CFO is charged with crafting risk reports that not only outline current risk exposures but also forecast potential vulnerabilities. This transparency is crucial in building trust among investors, regulators, and internal stakeholders.

Advancements in technology have revolutionized communication and reporting methodologies. Data visualization tools, real-time dashboards, and interactive reporting platforms have elevated the accessibility and impact of financial information. The CFO must be at the vanguard of integrating these technological solutions, ensuring that data dissemination is efficient, engaging, and aligned with the organization's technological infrastructure.

In an era marked by stringent regulatory oversight, the CFO must navigate a complex landscape of compliance requirements. Reporting practices must adhere to established standards such as GAAP, IFRS, or industry-specific guidelines. The CFO ensures that communication and reporting fulfill these regulatory obligations, while also serving the strategic needs of the organization.

An often-overlooked aspect of FP&A communication is the incorporation of feedback loops. The CFO must establish channels through which stakeholders can provide input on the reports and communications they receive. These feedback mechanisms enable a continuous improvement process, refining the relevance and effectiveness of financial communication over time.

In moments of crisis, such as market downturns or operational challenges, the way the CFO communicates and reports financial information can significantly influence the organization's response. Crisis communication must be clear, timely, and decisive, offering a stabilizing force that guides the organization through turbulent periods. The CFO is responsible for maintaining this clarity and directing a cohesive narrative that aligns the organization's actions with its overarching risk management strategy.

Communication and reporting in the domain of FP&A are not merely administrative tasks but are strategic imperatives that underpin the organization's ability to navigate risk and pursue its objectives. Through meticulous attention to detail, a commitment to clarity and transparency, and an embrace of technological innovation, the CFO ensures that these practices enhance the organization's strategic capabilities. By doing so, the CFO elevates FP&A from a support function to a strategic advisor, integral to the organization's enduring success.

Integration with Strategic Planning

The integration of financial planning and analysis (FP&A) within the broader canvas of strategic planning is akin to interweaving the threads of financial foresight into the fabric of an organization's long-term vision. This vital process calls for a harmonious alignment between the monetary pulse of the enterprise and its strategic objectives, ensuring that every financial decision is a step toward the realization of overarching goals.

Strategic planning initiates with a clear articulation of the company's vision, mission, and long-term objectives. FP&A integration begins here, as the financial team molds the raw data of current performance and market dynamics into a coherent financial narrative. This narrative must resonate with the strategic aspirations, serving as both a reflection of current realities and a scaffold for future ambitions.

Robust FP&A practices empower strategic planning through precise financial modeling and projections. These forward-looking insights allow an organization to craft strategies that are both ambitious and financially viable. By simulating various scenarios, FP&A provides a spectrum of potential outcomes, equipping strategists with the foresight to navigate uncertainties and seize opportunities.

The budgeting process is the crucible where strategy is tempered with fiscal discipline. Here, FP&A integration ensures that resource allocation is in staunch alignment with strategic priorities. Budgets become more than mere financial constraints; they transform into strategic enablers that channel investment into initiatives with the highest potential for strategic advancement.

FP&A integration brings a nuanced understanding of risk to strategic planning. By assessing the potential financial impacts of strategic choices, FP&A functions as a strategic compass, guiding the organization through the risk-return landscape. Strategic risk assessment involves not only identifying potential hazards but also evaluating the financial ramifications of strategic risks and opportunities.

Performance metrics serve as signposts on the path to strategic fulfillment. FP&A integration ensures that these metrics are not only tailored to measure financial health but are also aligned with strategic milestones. This creates a cohesive framework where performance tracking becomes a multi-dimensional exercise, encapsulating both financial results and strategic progress.

FP&A stands as a pillar of support for strategic decision-making. With a vantage point that surveys the financial horizon, FP&A offers insights that shape strategic decisions, from mergers and acquisitions to market expansions and product development. The integration of FP&A within this realm ensures that every strategic decision is supported by a rigorous financial analysis.

The integration of FP&A into strategic planning necessitates effective communication channels that ensure the seamless flow of financial insights to strategic decision-makers. This involves creating dashboards, reports, and briefings that are tailored to the informational needs of the strategy team, ensuring that financial intelligence is both accessible and actionable.

Strategic planning is not a static process; it requires constant re-evaluation in response to internal and external changes. FP&A integration provides a financial lens through which the organization can continually reassess and recalibrate its strategy. By regularly reviewing financial performance in the context of strategic goals, FP&A maintains the agility of the strategic planning process.

The integration of FP&A with strategic planning is a dance of numbers and visions, where financial acumen and strategic insight waltz in lockstep. It is a dynamic interplay that ensures the organization's financial heartbeat is synchronized with its strategic pulse. This confluence of foresight and strategy is not merely about aligning budgets with goals but is an ongoing dialogue—a conversation that shapes the destiny of the enterprise through every financial nuance and strategic turn. Through this seamless integration, FP&A transcends its traditional role, becoming a linchpin in the machinery of strategic evolution and a catalyst for the organization's sustainable growth.

Regulatory Frameworks and Standards

The labyrinthine world of financial regulation is a testament to society's pursuit of stability, transparency, and fairness in financial activities. For professionals navigating the FP&A domain, a deep dive into regulatory frameworks and standards is not merely an academic exercise but a practical necessity.

The Basel Accords

In the grand theatre of global finance, the Basel Accords stand as a trilogy of regulatory frameworks, each act building upon its predecessor to strengthen the bulwarks against financial instability. These accords, emanating from the Swiss city of Basel, are the brainchild of the Basel Committee on Banking Supervision (BCBS) and have been adopted by banking institutions worldwide.

The first of the accords, Basel I, emerged in 1988 as a response to the burgeoning need for international convergence on capital standards. Its primary focus was credit risk, setting the minimum capital requirements that banks should hold against their assets. This groundbreaking agreement introduced the concept of risk-weighted assets, which fundamentally changed how banks assessed and managed their risks.

Basel II, adopted in 2004, expanded the scope by introducing three pillars: minimum capital requirements, supervisory review process, and market discipline. This accord delved deeper into the sophistication of risk management, encouraging banks to develop and use better risk assessment models, particularly for credit, market, and operational risks. Basel II's nuanced approach recognized the diversity of banking operations and the varying degrees of risk they present.

The crisis of 2007-2008 laid bare the inadequacies of the existing framework, catalyzing the development of Basel III. This iteration, which began implementation in 2013, sought to fortify the banking sector against the types of liquidity crises that underpinned the global financial meltdown. Enhanced requirements for capital adequacy, stress testing, and liquidity management are hallmarks of Basel III, all designed to promote greater resilience within financial institutions.

For those in the realm of FP&A, the Basel Accords represent more than a regulatory yardstick; they serve as a beacon guiding the long-term financial strategy. The accords compel FP&A professionals to ensure that their organizations not only meet the minimum regulatory capital ratios but also manage their capital planning and stress testing processes with an eye toward the dynamic nature of the regulatory environment. The implications extend to the valuation of assets, the structuring of investment portfolios, and the management of balance sheet composition—all under the watchful eye of the Basel standards.

Adopting the Basel Accords is not without its challenges. Translating the complex and often technical requirements into practical strategies requires a blend of regulatory expertise and strategic acumen. FP&A professionals are tasked with interpreting how these global standards manifest within different jurisdictions and financial environments, thus ensuring compliance while still pursuing optimal financial performance.

As the financial landscape evolves with technological advancements and emergent risks, so too must the Basel Accords adapt. The ongoing refinement of these regulations ensures they remain relevant and equipped to address the challenges of modern finance. This iterative process signifies the importance of regulatory agility within FP&A functions, as they must remain vigilant and responsive to the shifting sands of banking supervision.

In synthesis, the Basel Accords are a foundational element in the structure of financial risk management and strategic planning. FP&A's engagement with these regulations is indicative of a broader commitment to financial stability and prudent risk-taking. Through diligent application of the Basel standards, FP&A can contribute to the overarching goal of preventing systemic crises, thus ensuring the enduring health and competitiveness of the banking sector.

SOX Compliance

The enactment of the Sarbanes-Oxley Act of 2002, known as SOX, was a defining moment that signalled a seismic shift in corporate governance and financial practice within the United States. The legislation was a direct response to the high-profile financial scandals that eroded public trust in the financial markets, most notably Enron and WorldCom. SOX aimed to restore confidence by introducing rigorous regulatory standards for all publicly traded companies.

At the heart of SOX lies the commitment to transparency, accountability, and internal controls within corporations. The act sets stringent requirements for financial reporting, including the implementation of robust internal controls to detect and prevent fraudulent activities. SOX mandates that senior corporate officers take personal responsibility for the accuracy and completeness of corporate financial reports.

For FP&A professionals, SOX compliance is not merely a legal obligation but a strategic imperative that permeates various aspects of financial operations. FP&A teams play a critical role in ensuring that financial reports accurately reflect the company's fiscal health and that the processes leading to these reports are sound and verifiable. Compliance with SOX also means that FP&A must closely collaborate with internal audit departments to test and strengthen internal controls.

Under SOX, the importance of detailed documentation cannot be overstated. FP&A teams are required to maintain meticulous records that support financial entries and decisions. This diligence extends to documenting the design and efficacy of internal controls and procedures that influence financial reporting, a critical component of SOX Section 404.

Quarterly and annual financial reports have come under increased scrutiny due to SOX. These reports now include an internal control report stating that management is responsible for establishing and maintaining an adequate internal control structure, along with an assessment of the effectiveness of the internal control structure for financial reporting. This requirement has a profound influence on the FP&A function, which must ensure that the data feeding into these reports is rigorously vetted and supported by solid controls.

SOX also introduced protections for whistleblowers, recognising their role in uncovering financial misconduct. FP&A professionals are often in a unique position to identify discrepancies or irregularities in the company's financials. As such, they must be aware of their rights and protections under the act, ensuring that they can report concerns without fear of retribution.

FP&A's commitment to SOX compliance is not a one-time event but an ongoing process of improvement and adaptation. The dynamic nature of business necessitates continuous monitoring of internal controls and periodic updating of compliance practices. FP&A professionals must stay apprised of evolving interpretations and best practices in SOX compliance to maintain the integrity of financial reporting.

SOX compliance is an integral part of the FP&A landscape, underpinning the commitment to ethical and accurate financial reporting. The act's stringent requirements have embedded a culture of accountability, which FP&A upholds through its dedicated efforts in maintaining financial integrity. As regulatory environments continue to evolve, FP&A's proactive approach to SOX compliance will remain a cornerstone of corporate trustworthiness and financial stability.

International Financial Reporting Standards (IFRS)

The global finance landscape is a mosaic of diverse practices and regulations, yet a common thread that aims to harmonize these differences is the International Financial Reporting Standards (IFRS). Conceived and issued by the International Accounting Standards Board (IAS, IFRS serves as a universal financial language for business affairs, enabling transparent and comparable reporting across international boundaries.

IFRS emerged from a need to create a global framework that would allow investors and other market participants to make informed economic decisions. Prior to IFRS, the lack of comparability between financial statements prepared under different countries' accounting standards was a substantial barrier to investment and economic growth. The adoption of IFRS has been instrumental in reducing this barrier, fostering trust and confidence in the global markets.

For FP&A professionals, IFRS presents both challenges and

opportunities. The transition from local GAAP (Generally Accepted Accounting Principles) to IFRS requires a comprehensive understanding of the differences between the two systems and the implications for financial reporting and analysis. FP&A plays a vital role in navigating this transition, ensuring that financial statements are compliant, and that the resulting figures are used effectively for planning, analysis, and strategic decision-making.

The standards set forth by IFRS cover a wide range of accounting activities, from the recognition of revenue and the valuation of financial instruments to the presentation of financial statements and disclosures about operations. FP&A must not only ensure that the accounting treatments are accurate but also that they reflect the underlying economic reality of the company's operations.

With the widespread adoption of IFRS in over 140 jurisdictions, the standards have played a pivotal role in the cross-border consistency of financial reporting. This is particularly beneficial to multinational corporations that operate in multiple countries, as it simplifies the consolidation process and fosters greater comparability for investors and analysts. FP&A professionals working within such corporations must possess a global mindset and the capability to report in line with IFRS while understanding its impact on the company's financial position and performance.

IFRS is not static; it evolves to address emerging issues and improve the clarity and relevance of financial reports. FP&A professionals must, therefore, commit to continuous learning and professional development to stay abreast of new and amended standards. This ongoing educational journey ensures that FP&A teams remain capable of implementing the necessary changes to financial processes and controls, maintaining the integrity of financial reporting.

Beyond compliance, IFRS offers strategic implications for FP&A. The principles-based nature of IFRS encourages a focus on the economic substance of transactions over their legal form. This approach aligns closely with the strategic perspective of FP&A, which seeks to inform management and stakeholders about the financial implications of business decisions and to contribute to value creation.

IFRS represents more than a set of accounting procedures; it's a strategic tool that enhances the credibility of financial information, providing a consistent foundation for financial planning and analysis across the globe. FP&A's expertise in IFRS is not just about adherence to reporting standards but is also a critical element in shaping a company's global financial strategy, ensuring that financial statements truly reflect the company's operational and financial reality, thus enabling better decision-making and fostering investor confidence.

Local Financial Reporting Standards

Local financial reporting standards are the bedrock of fiscal accountability and transparency within any given nation's borders. Serving as the codified embodiment of a region's economic ethos, these standards govern how companies record and communicate their financial activities to stakeholders, including investors, regulators, and the public.

The genesis of local financial reporting standards stems from the unique economic, legal, and cultural landscapes of each country. These standards are tailored to address the specific needs and expectations of local markets and regulatory bodies. They provide a framework that, while similar in purpose to IFRS, is often more closely aligned with domestic business practices and regulatory requirements.

Financial planning and analysis (FP&A) professionals operating within the confines of local standards bear the responsibility of ensuring their organization's compliance with these regulations. Mastery of local standards is imperative, as they affect everything from tax obligations to the recognition of revenue. FP&A teams use these standards as a baseline for budgeting, forecasting, and strategic planning, ensuring that all financial activities are consistent with local regulatory expectations.

Local financial reporting standards can vary considerably from one jurisdiction to another. This variance poses a significant challenge for FP&A professionals, especially in organizations that operate in multiple countries with different reporting requirements. FP&A must navigate the complexities of each set of local standards, understanding nuances such as the valuation of assets, the treatment of pensions, or the recognition of government grants.

Despite the specificity of local standards, there is an ongoing effort toward harmonization with international standards like IFRS. This is particularly prevalent as economies become more interlinked and companies seek to attract foreign investment. FP&A professionals play a critical role in this harmonization process by bridging the gap between local standards and IFRS, ensuring that financial statements are both locally compliant and globally comprehensible.

Local financial standards are subject to change, often in response to economic events or shifts in regulatory philosophy. FP&A teams must therefore maintain an adaptive stance, ready to respond to legislative amendments and regulatory updates that could affect reporting processes and financial outcomes. This agility ensures that an organization can swiftly align its financial strategy with the evolving landscape of local reporting requirements.

While compliance is a key concern, local financial reporting standards also offer strategic value by providing insights into the fiscal health and operational efficiency of an organization. FP&A leverages these insights to advise on performance improvements, cost management, and risk mitigation, tailoring strategies to the local business environment and contributing to sustainable growth.

In conclusion, local financial reporting standards represent a critical component of a comprehensive FP&A framework. These standards facilitate a nuanced understanding of a company's financial narrative as viewed through the lens of local business practices and regulatory demands. For FP&A professionals, excellence in navigating local standards is not merely about compliance; it's an opportunity to enhance organizational resilience, foster strategic agility, and drive value creation within the specific context of each market in which they operate.

Building a Risk-Aware Culture

The architecture of a risk-aware culture is foundational to the resilience and competitiveness of any organization. It is a matrix within which each decision is scrutinized through the prism of risk and reward—a culture that infuses every level of the enterprise with the acumen to not only identify potential hazards but to also embrace risk as a catalyst for innovation and growth.

The endeavor to build a risk-aware culture begins with education. It involves the dissemination of risk knowledge across all departments, ensuring that each employee, from the executive suite to the front lines, understands the implications of risk in their daily responsibilities. A risk-aware culture is underpinned by a shared vocabulary of risk, allowing for coherent communication and collective vigilance against potential threats.

FP&A professionals hold the vanguard in championing this culture. They are the sentinels, armed with the financial foresight to foresee market turbulences and the sagacity to guide strategic responses. By integrating risk assessment into financial planning, FP&A serves as a nexus between financial stability and strategic risk management, fostering an organizational mindset where risk considerations are not an afterthought but a prerequisite.

A risk-aware culture demands that risk management be embedded into the DNA of organizational processes. This integration spans from the inception of a project to its culmination, from the allocation of capital to performance evaluations. It is a comprehensive approach that ensures risk considerations are an intrinsic part of the decision-making process, rather than a peripheral checkmark.

Empowering a workforce with the tools to identify and assess risk is paramount. This arsenal includes risk metrics, dashboards, and scenario planning applications that enable employees to quantify and visualize the impact of risks. By equipping staff with such tools, an organization not only democratizes risk management but also encourages proactive identification and mitigation of risks.

A culture that prizes open communication facilitates a free flow of information regarding potential risks without fear of recrimination. It encourages whistleblowing mechanisms, where employees can safely report concerns, and ensures that such reports are taken seriously and acted upon. This transparency is pivotal in catching the ripples of risk before they swell into waves of crisis.

A risk-aware culture is not just about avoiding negative outcomes; it also recognizes and rewards risk-aware behavior. Incentives for employees who demonstrate prudence in risk-taking or who innovate risk mitigation strategies reinforce the value the organization places on intelligent risk management. Such positive reinforcement promotes a shared sense of ownership over risk and its management.

Building a risk-aware culture is akin to constructing a lighthouse on a rocky shoreline. It serves as a beacon that guides the organization through the fog of uncertainty, alerting it to hidden dangers and illuminating pathways to safe harbor. For FP&A professionals, the task is clear: to be the architects of this culture, laying down the keystone of risk awareness that will uphold the structural integrity of the organization's financial and strategic endeavors.

Risk-Focused Training for Employees

Risk-focused training is the compass by which organizations navigate the treacherous waters of the financial landscape. For employees to contribute effectively to the mitigation and management of risk, they must be equipped with the skills and knowledge to identify, assess, and respond to potential threats. Such training elevates the collective risk intelligence of the workforce, turning each member into an active participant in the organization's risk management strategy.

Customized training programs are essential to address the specific risk profiles associated with different roles within the organization. A procurement officer's risk exposure differs vastly from that of a financial analyst or a database administrator. Therefore, designing role-specific training that addresses the unique risk factors of each position ensures that employees are not only aware of the risks inherent to their functions but are also prepared to manage them effectively.

The foundation of risk-focused training is establishing a baseline level of risk literacy that all employees, irrespective of their role, must possess. This baseline includes an understanding of the types of risks the organization faces, the potential impact of these risks, and the general protocols for reporting and responding to risk scenarios. Ensuring this common knowledge base creates a unified front against the myriad risks that can affect the organization.

The effectiveness of risk-focused training hinges on the

delivery method. Interactive workshops, gamified learning modules, and real-world simulations make the acquisition of risk management skills more engaging and memorable. Employees are more likely to internalize and apply their knowledge when they can actively participate in their learning through case studies, hypothetical scenarios, and hands-on activities that mimic the complexity of real-life risk situations.

Risk landscapes are perpetually shifting, so risk-focused training cannot be a one-off event. It requires ongoing education to keep pace with emerging threats, such as changes in market conditions, technological advancements, and regulatory updates. Regular refresher courses, updates on the latest risk management techniques, and lessons learned from past risk events all contribute to a workforce that remains vigilant and adaptive to the evolving risk environment.

To ensure the training programs are achieving their intended objectives, organizations must implement mechanisms to evaluate their effectiveness. This could include pre- and post-training assessments, feedback surveys, and monitoring the application of risk management principles in day-to-day operations. Such evaluations allow for a continuous improvement approach, tweaking training modules as necessary to address any identified gaps in knowledge or skills.

Embedding a culture of continuous risk education requires leadership to champion the cause and resources to maintain momentum. It involves recognizing and supporting risk management as a critical aspect of every employee's professional development. By creating formal avenues for employees to deepen their risk expertise—such as sponsoring certifications or providing access to industry conferences—organizations underline the importance of staying ahead of risks.

Risk-focused training for employees is the bedrock upon which a robust risk management framework is built. It transforms theoretical understanding into practical action, enabling the organization to not just confront risks, but to leverage them into opportunities for strategic advantage. The FP&A department, as the standard-bearer of such training, empowers individuals to take ownership of risk, fostering a risk-savvy workforce that is an invaluable asset in the pursuit of the organization's long-term objectives.

Encouraging Open Communication

In the intricate mosaic of an organization's risk management framework, the thread that weaves through its very core is open communication. It is the catalyst that promotes transparency, fosters trust, and cultivates a responsive and agile environment where risks can be reported, discussed, and mitigated with collective insight.

To encourage open communication, organizations must first dismantle the hierarchical barriers that often stifle the free flow of information. Open-door policies and flat communication structures empower employees to voice their concerns and report potential risks without fear of repercussion. Leaders must actively listen and respond to these concerns, demonstrating that every employee's input is valued and plays a critical role in safeguarding the organization.

Risk is not confined to departmental silos; it permeates every aspect of an organization. Cross-functional risk dialogues enable diverse perspectives to converge, providing a more holistic understanding of potential threats and vulnerabilities. These dialogues often uncover interdependencies and risks that might otherwise go unnoticed in isolated conversations.

Effective communication is not inherent; it is a skill that can be developed with proper training. Organizations should invest in communication workshops that focus on the articulation of risk-related issues. Skills such as active listening, clear and concise expression, and non-verbal communication cues are all essential for the cultivation of a workforce adept at discussing complex risk topics.

In today's digital age, technology serves as a powerful enabler of open communication. Platforms that allow for real-time reporting, discussion forums, and collaborative risk assessments can bridge the geographical and temporal divides that may exist within an organization. Digital tools also enable the logging and tracking of risk communications, ensuring that no concern goes unaddressed.

One of the most significant barriers to open communication about risk is the stigma that can be associated with raising alarms. Normalizing these discussions requires a shift in mindset, where employees are encouraged to view risk communication as a proactive and positive action. Regularly scheduled 'risk roundtables' or 'safety moments' at the start of meetings can set the precedent that discussing risks is not only acceptable but expected.

To reinforce the value placed on open communication, organizations can implement recognition and reward systems for those who contribute valuably to risk discussions. Whether through formal awards, acknowledgment in company communications, or tangible incentives, these rewards signal to all employees that active participation in risk management is crucial and appreciated.

Encouraging open communication is a vital component of a forward-thinking risk management strategy. It involves a deliberate and concerted effort to create an environment where every voice can be heard and each concern is addressed with equal gravity. With open channels of communication, the FP&A function can more effectively predict, prepare, and pivot, transforming risk management from a reactive obligation to a proactive strategic lever.

Implementing a Whistleblower Policy

In the labyrinthine world of financial planning and analysis, a whistleblower policy stands as a sentinel against misconduct and unethical behavior. Its implementation marks a decisive step towards integrity and accountability within an organization's risk management framework.

The first stride in implementing a whistleblower policy is to delineate its scope clearly. It must encompass all forms of reportable conduct, from financial malfeasance and legal violations to breaches of company policy and ethical standards. A comprehensive policy ensures that employees are not left uncertain about what constitutes reportable behavior.

Accessibility is key to a robust whistleblower policy. Multiple, secure, and confidential channels should be available to employees for reporting concerns. These might include dedicated hotlines, secure web portals, or direct access to a designated ombudsman. Anonymity must be preserved to protect whistleblowers from potential retaliation and to encourage candid reporting.

A policy that fails to offer protection is merely a hollow promise. A cornerstone of any whistleblower policy is a firm commitment to the non-retaliation clause. This clause assures employees that they will not face dismissal, demotion, or any form of discrimination for raising concerns in good faith. Legal protections should also be incorporated, aligning with applicable whistleblower legislation.

Beyond the written policy, fostering a culture that values transparency and ethical behavior is vital. Leadership must lead by example, championing the policy and demonstrating a zero-tolerance stance towards retaliation. Trust is cultivated not by words on paper, but by consistent actions and demonstrable support for those who raise concerns.

Regular training sessions should be mandatory to familiarize all employees with the whistleblower policy and procedures. From recognizing the signs of potential misconduct to understanding the process of reporting, such education ensures that employees are not only aware but also equipped to act responsibly.

The policy must outline clear procedures for the receipt,

investigation, and follow-up of reports. An independent body or committee should assess whistleblower reports to ensure impartiality. Timeliness is crucial; delays can exacerbate risks and diminish trust in the system. Feedback loops and updates to the whistleblower, where possible, can also affirm that their report is being taken seriously.

As the business environment evolves, so too should the whistleblower policy. Regular reviews are necessary to refine its effectiveness and to adapt to new risks or changes in legislation. By maintaining the policy as a living document, an organization demonstrates its unwavering commitment to ethical standards and continuous improvement.

Implementing a whistleblower policy is a strategic imperative in the domain of risk management. Such a policy is not merely a compliance measure but a reflection of an organization's dedication to ethical operation. It serves as an underpinning for a risk-averse culture that prizes vigilance and responsibility, empowering each employee to be a custodian of integrity. In the FP&A landscape, where financial foresight is paramount, a sound whistleblower policy is the bulwark that safeguards against the unseen dangers that may compromise an organization's fiscal prudence and reputation.

Rewarding Risk-Sensitive Behavior

An effective risk management strategy in FP&A goes beyond policies and procedures, emphasizing the importance of the human element. Cultivating an organizational culture that fosters risk awareness and encourages risk-sensitive behavior is crucial. This entails creating an environment where employees at all levels actively contribute to identifying, assessing, and mitigating risks.

By recognizing and rewarding risk-sensitive behavior, organizations can incentivize employees to prioritize risk management in their day-to-day activities. This includes promoting open communication channels, encouraging collaboration, and establishing mechanisms for reporting and addressing risks. Through training programs and awareness campaigns, employees can be equipped with the necessary skills and knowledge to effectively identify and manage risks within their respective roles.

The integration of the human element into the architecture of risk management ensures that risk-awareness becomes embedded in the organizational DNA. This approach not only strengthens the overall risk management framework but also facilitates a proactive and resilient approach to financial planning and analysis, contributing to the long-term success and sustainability of the organization.

Rewarding risk-sensitive behavior is a nuanced concept that seeks to acknowledge and incentivize actions that contribute to risk awareness and mitigation. This approach is instrumental in reinforcing a proactive risk culture, where employees are motivated not just by the completion of their tasks, but by the manner in which they navigate risk.

The incentives offered must be intricately aligned with the organization's risk management goals. These incentives could be financial, such as bonuses or stock options, or non-financial, such as recognition programs or career advancement opportunities. The key is that they should be structured in such a way that they promote decision-making that balances risk and reward effectively.

Each department within an organization faces unique risks, necessitating tailored reward programs. For instance, in the FP&A department, an analyst who identifies a potential risk in a financial model and takes steps to address it might be recognized for their diligence. In contrast, a sales manager who opts out of a potentially lucrative but risky deal might be rewarded for prudence.

A critical aspect of rewarding risk-sensitive behavior is establishing clear metrics for measurement. These metrics might include reduction in incident reports, successful completion of risk management training, or demonstration of risk-averse decision-making in high-stakes scenarios. Transparency in how these metrics are measured and rewarded is paramount to gaining employee trust.

To embed a culture of risk sensitivity, the value of such behavior must be effectively communicated throughout the organization. This involves storytelling and sharing examples where risk-aware behavior led to positive outcomes, thereby setting a precedent and inspiring others to emulate such behavior.

While individual rewards are important, fostering team-based incentives can encourage a collective approach to risk management. Group rewards for departments or project teams that exemplify risk-sensitive behavior can enhance collaboration and create a shared sense of responsibility for risk management.

As with any policy, the reward system should undergo

regular reviews to ensure its continued relevance and effectiveness in promoting risk-sensitive behavior. This includes seeking feedback from employees on the reward system's performance, and making necessary adjustments to ensure that it remains in line with evolving risk landscapes and organizational objectives.

In FP&A, where financial outcomes are intricately linked to risk, fostering an environment that rewards risk-sensitive behavior is more than a strategic advantage—it is a necessary safeguard. By recognizing and rewarding employees who demonstrate a keen understanding of risk and a commitment to the organization's risk management protocols, a company can fortify its defenses against potential financial uncertainties and secure its competitive edge in the marketplace. The result is a robust, risk-aware culture where caution and foresight are valued as cornerstones of strategic financial planning.

CHAPTER 2: RISK IDENTIFICATION AND PRIORITIZATION

The process of risk identification and prioritization is as critical as it is complex. It forms the bedrock upon which all subsequent risk management actions are built. Without an accurate and thorough identification of potential risks, efforts to mitigate them may be misguided or ineffective. Similarly, failing to prioritize these risks can lead to a misallocation of valuable resources. This section delves into the theoretical underpinnings of this crucial step in the risk management process.

Risk identification is the process of pinpointing potential events that might jeopardize an organization's ability to meet its objectives. In theory, this involves a systematic and exhaustive exploration of all possible sources of risk, whether internal or external. Theoreticians in risk management underscore the need for a multidisciplinary approach, tapping into insights from economics, behavioral science, and organizational theory to uncover not just the obvious risks but also those that are latent or emerging.

A battery of tools and methodologies is employed to surface these risks. These range from the traditional—such as SWOT analysis (Strengths, Weaknesses, Opportunities, Threats) and PESTLE analysis (Political, Economic, Social, Technological, Legal, and Environmental factors)—to more sophisticated techniques like Delphi method consultations with experts and horizon scanning for nascent trends. Each tool has its strengths and can uncover different layers and types of risks.

Once risks have been identified, they must be prioritized. Theoretical models suggest a variety of frameworks for prioritizing risks, often involving the assessment of each risk's likelihood and potential impact. The Risk Matrix, for example, is a common tool that plots risk on two axes— probability and severity—to help visualize priority. However, the practice of prioritization is as much an art as it is a science, as it requires a nuanced understanding of the organization's risk appetite and strategic goals.

The organization's risk appetite—the amount of risk it is willing to accept in pursuit of its objectives—plays a pivotal role in the prioritization process. Risks that fall within the appetite are managed differently from those that exceed it. Similarly, risk tolerance levels dictate the threshold of variations in risk levels that the organization can withstand. Both concepts are key in determining how risks are ranked and addressed.

Given the ever-changing business landscape, risk identification and prioritization is not a one-time exercise but a dynamic, ongoing process. It requires vigilance and adaptability, with regular updates to the risk register—a document that records all identified risks along with their prioritization and ownership. This fluidity ensures that the organization's risk management efforts are responsive to the evolving environment.

For risk identification and prioritization to be effective, it must be deeply integrated into the organization's processes and not siloed within the risk management function. This means embedding risk awareness into daily operations, strategic planning, and decision-making at all levels. Theoretical perspectives suggest that when risk considerations are part of the organizational DNA, the identification and prioritization of risk become more informed, nuanced, and reflective of the true risk landscape.

In conclusion, risk identification and prioritization is a foundational element of FP&A that demands a blend of theoretical understanding and practical application. It requires an organization to employ various tools and techniques for uncovering risks, assess them through the lens of their risk appetite and tolerance, and constantly recalibrate their priorities considering new information. By approaching this process with rigor and foresight, financial leaders can steer their organizations through uncertain waters with confidence, ensuring that risks are managed proactively and strategically.

Risk Assessment Methodologies

Risk assessment within the realm of FP&A is a complex and intricate process that showcases the discipline's dedication to accuracy and future planning. Financial professionals utilize various methodologies as compasses to navigate through the unpredictable waters of uncertainty. These methodologies encompass a range of theoretical and practical tools that aim not only to predict potential challenges but also to equip the organization with the means to mitigate and address them effectively.

By employing risk assessment methodologies, FP&A teams can systematically identify and evaluate risks specific to their organization's financial landscape. These methodologies may involve quantitative analyses, such as statistical modeling and scenario analysis, as well as qualitative assessments that consider factors like industry trends, regulatory changes, and macroeconomic conditions. The goal is to gain a comprehensive understanding of the potential risks that the organization may face and their potential impact.

Armed with this knowledge, financial navigators can develop appropriate risk mitigation strategies and allocate resources effectively to address identified risks. The objective is to proactively protect the organization's financial stability, capitalize on opportunities, and make informed decisions that contribute to its long-term success.

At the core of risk assessment lies a dual objective: to quantify the potential for loss and to articulate strategies for the effective management of that risk. Diverse methodologies offer a spectrum of lenses through which risks can be viewed, analyzed, and prioritized. The choice of methodology often hinges on the type and complexity of risk, the data available, and the specific contours of the organization's industry.

Methodologies bifurcate into qualitative and quantitative paths. Qualitative techniques hinge on expert judgment and scenario analysis, allowing for a narrative understanding of risks and their implications. These methods are particularly beneficial when quantitative data is scant or when assessing intangible risks such as reputational damage. In contrast, quantitative approaches deploy numerical analysis, utilizing statistical models to predict probability and impact. This data-driven pathway provides a perceived objectivity and is potent when abundant historical data is available.

A keystone in risk assessment is scenario analysis, which weaves narratives of possible futures. This methodology involves creating detailed scenarios of events that could significantly impact the organization—both positively and negatively—allowing planners to test strategies against a variety of outcomes. By examining the effects of different scenarios, organizations can prepare contingency plans and maintain agility in the face of change.

Stress testing is a methodology borrowed from the crucible of financial institutions, designed to evaluate how certain stress conditions would impact the organization's financial health. This robust process involves simulating extreme market conditions or operational failures to assess the resilience of financial models and the adequacy of capital buffers. It's a rigorous exercise in hypotheticals, but one that delivers crucial insights into vulnerabilities.

The intricacies of sensitivity analysis lie in its ability to determine how changes in one or more independent variables affect a particular dependent variable under a given set of assumptions. This methodology is invaluable for FP&A professionals, as it aids in identifying which variables have the most influence on outcomes and where control efforts should be concentrated. Sensitivity analysis fosters a granular understanding of the financial model's responsiveness to change.

While the methodologies are steeped in analytical rigor, it's paramount to acknowledge the role of professional judgment and experience. Theoretical models are vital, yet they can only serve their purpose when complemented by the seasoned intuition of financial experts. This confluence of art and science ensures that risk assessments are not only methodologically sound but also grounded in the practical realities of the business world.

The methodologies of risk assessment in FP&A serve as a navigational grid for financial professionals. By deploying a blend of qualitative and quantitative techniques—enhanced by scenario analysis, stress testing, and sensitivity analysis—organizations can gain a multidimensional understanding of their risk profiles. It's through this sophisticated assessment that FP&A leaders can calibrate their strategies to not only withstand potential shocks but to emerge from them with competitive advantages solidly intact.

Qualitative vs. Quantitative Approaches

The methodologies employed to assess risk are as crucial as the compass to the mariner, guiding through the fog of economic uncertainties. Amongst the most critical decisions financial planners make is the choice between qualitative and quantitative approaches to risk assessment. Each path offers distinct insights and tools, and their judicious application can significantly enhance the precision of risk management strategies.

Qualitative risk assessment is an exploratory process, often narrative-driven, that relies heavily on the expertise and intuition of industry veterans. It does not seek to numerically score risks but to understand their nature, triggers, and potential impacts through a descriptive lens. Tools such as the risk register, expert interviews, and the Delphi method are often employed to gather and synthesize knowledge from experienced professionals. These tactics allow for a deep dive into risks that are difficult to quantify, such as legal changes, brand perception, or shifts in consumer behavior.

In using qualitative approaches, FP&A professionals can create risk profiles that feel more tangible and narrative, despite the lack of numerical data. For instance, a risk matrix can visually categorize and prioritize risks based on subjective criteria such as likelihood and severity, yielding a hierarchy of concerns that can shape policy and response planning.

Conversely, quantitative risk assessments hinge on measurable data and statistical methods to calculate the probability and potential impact of risks. These approaches, grounded in numerical evidence, strive for objectivity and are often favored in financial contexts where past data can reliably inform future predictions. Techniques such as Monte Carlo simulations, Value at Risk (VaR), and financial impact analysis provide structured, model-based forecasts that are indispensable in financial decision-making.

Quantitative methods excel in environments where risks are well-defined, and data is abundant. For instance, market risks—such as interest rate fluctuations or commodity price volatility—are prime candidates for quantitative analysis, which can use historical market data to forecast future trends and calculate potential losses.

The dichotomy between qualitative and quantitative is not

about choosing one over the other but rather understanding how to integrate both for a comprehensive risk assessment. Qualitative insights can inform the assumptions and scenarios used in quantitative models, while quantitative data can validate or challenge the assumptions made in qualitative assessments.

For example, in developing a new product line, a qualitative approach might identify the risk of changing consumer preferences as a major concern. Quantitative analysis can then assess the fiscal impact of this risk by looking at sales data from similar product launches. The interplay between the two creates a more nuanced and multi-faceted view of risk, allowing organizations to prepare and respond with greater agility.

FP&A cannot be relegated to a one-dimensional analysis; the complexities of the business environment demand a comprehensive approach. The blend of qualitative and quantitative methods in risk assessment provides a balanced perspective that leverages the strengths of both. It allows for a thorough examination of the business landscape, crafting strategies that are both informed by data and enriched by experience. As practitioners navigate through the uncertain waters of finance, it is this synergy of approaches that will empower them to make decisions with confidence and clarity, ensuring the organization's steadfast progression in the face of potential adversities.

Scenario Analysis

Scenario analysis plays a crucial role in risk management

as it allows FP&A professionals to thoroughly analyze a wide range of potential future outcomes. By creating and examining different scenarios shaped by various variables and conditions, organizations can proactively prepare for volatility and capitalize on opportunities that may arise.

Through scenario analysis, FP&A professionals meticulously explore and test potential scenarios, considering factors such as market conditions, economic trends, regulatory changes, and competitive landscapes. This rigorous examination enables organizations to identify and understand the potential risks and opportunities associated with each scenario. By doing so, they can develop strategic responses and allocate resources accordingly.

Scenario analysis serves as a crucible, providing a framework for assessing the potential impact of different future states on the organization's financial position and performance. With this knowledge, organizations can better position themselves to navigate through the often unpredictable and turbulent market forces. By embracing scenario analysis, FP&A professionals can enhance their strategic finesse, make informed decisions, and establish a resilient foundation for their risk management and financial planning efforts.

At its core, scenario analysis is about stretching the fabric of reality to cover the realm of 'what-ifs.' It involves constructing detailed narratives that paint a picture of various plausible futures. The scenarios often include a base case—reflecting expected outcomes—alongside optimistic and pessimistic alternatives, each underscoring varying degrees of variability from the central forecast.

These narratives are not mere flights of fancy but are

grounded in a mixture of data extrapolation, expert insight, and economic forecasting. They serve as a form of stress test for the organization's strategies, financial models, and investment decisions, allowing planners to assess the resilience and adaptability of their approaches in the face of unforeseen events.

The process of developing scenarios begins with the identification of key drivers that can significantly influence market conditions or business operations. These drivers could range from macroeconomic indicators, such as GDP growth rates or currency exchange fluctuations, to industry-specific trends, like technology disruptions or regulatory changes.

Once identified, these drivers are then woven into coherent storylines. For instance, a 'worst-case' scenario may extrapolate the consequences of a major recession, while a 'best-case' scenario might explore the ramifications of a sudden market expansion due to a groundbreaking product release. The narratives consider not only the initial shock of the driver event but also its secondary effects and the potential ripple across the business ecosystem.

Scenario analysis plays a pivotal role in FP&A by grounding financial strategies in a context that acknowledges uncertainty. It provides a structured approach to identifying key assumptions, sensitivities, and leverage points within financial models. By preempting a range of outcomes, financial planners can outline contingent actions, set aside contingency reserves, and develop hedging strategies that align with each anticipated scenario.

For example, in considering the launch of a new service,

FP&A teams might utilize scenario analysis to evaluate the financial impact under various customer adoption rates. This not only aids in setting realistic revenue targets but also in preparing for the capital and resource reallocations necessary should the service's popularity deviate from expectations.

While scenario analysis is deeply theoretical—relying on models and projections—its true value lies in its practical applications. The insights gleaned from examining different scenarios feed into tactical and strategic planning. They guide decision-makers in setting thresholds for action, inform policy development, and shape risk management practices.

A practical application of scenario analysis may involve the FP&A team regularly presenting their findings to the board of directors, allowing the leadership to make informed decisions on capital investments, market entry, or even divestments. These informed discussions ensure that when a scenario starts to unfold, the organization is not caught off-guard but is equipped with a premeditated course of action.

In an era defined by its unpredictability, scenario analysis stands as a testament to the forethought and preparedness that characterizes astute financial governance. By marrying the theoretical with the practical, FP&A practitioners can turn uncertainty into an operational framework for strategic agility. It is through these carefully crafted analyses that organizations can not just survive but thrive, turning potential disruptions into avenues for growth and innovation. As the financial landscape continues to evolve, scenario analysis will remain an indispensable element in the FP&A toolkit, providing a lens through which to view the future and a map to navigate the unknown.

Scenario Analysis Summary:

1. Define Objectives: Start by clarifying the goals of your business. Understand what you want to achieve and what success looks like. This sets the context for the scenarios you'll explore.

2. Identify Key Drivers: Determine the factors that have a significant impact on your business. These could be economic conditions, market trends, technological advancements, or regulatory changes. Understanding these drivers helps in creating realistic scenarios.

3. Develop Scenarios: Here's where your creativity and expertise shine. Based on the key drivers, develop a range of scenarios. Typically, you should create at least three: an optimistic (best case), a pessimistic (worst case), and a most likely scenario. Remember, these aren't predictions but plausible futures that could impact your business.

4. Analyze Impact: For each scenario, analyze how your business would be affected. Consider different aspects like revenue, market position, operational efficiency, and resource allocation. It's vital to think about both the direct and indirect impacts.

5. Plan Responses: Develop strategies to address each scenario. This involves identifying actions you would take to capitalize on positive outcomes or mitigate negative ones. It's like having a playbook ready for different versions of the future.

6. Implement Monitoring Mechanisms: Since the future is uncertain, it's important to keep an eye on the trends and indicators that might signal which scenario is becoming more likely. This means setting up a system to monitor key metrics and

market signals.

7. Review and Revise: The business environment is constantly changing, so regularly review and update your scenarios. This keeps them relevant and ensures your strategies are aligned with the latest market conditions.

Stress Testing

Stress testing is a critical component of financial risk management, serving as a meticulous rehearsal that examines extreme scenarios to evaluate the resilience of an organization's financial strength. FP&A professionals utilize stress testing to quantify the robustness of financial positions and assess the impact of severe yet plausible distress scenarios on the organization's balance sheet.

Through stress testing, organizations subject their financial portfolios and positions to rigorous analysis, simulating adverse events such as economic downturns, market shocks, or liquidity crises. This process enables them to gauge the potential vulnerabilities and exposures to different risk factors. By stress testing, organizations gain valuable insights into the potential impact on their financial metrics, risk levels, and capital adequacy in adverse circumstances.

The objective of stress testing is to ensure that institutions are well-prepared for financial shocks. By stress testing their financial fortitude, organizations can identify areas that may require additional resilience, develop appropriate risk mitigation strategies, and establish contingency plans to manage challenging scenarios. Stress testing is an integral part of a comprehensive risk management strategy, enabling organizations to go beyond mere survival and proactively prepare for potential adverse events.

Ultimately, stress testing empowers FP&A professionals to make informed decisions and enhance the organization's overall risk management framework, strengthening its ability to navigate through turbulent financial environments and safeguard its long-term stability.

Stress testing is akin to subjecting a ship to a tempest in controlled conditions; it is to anticipate how well the vessel can weather a real storm. In financial terms, it translates to simulating crisis conditions to evaluate how financial assets, portfolios, or entire business models withstand sudden and adverse changes. Stress tests are designed to expose vulnerabilities before they manifest into crises, offering an opportunity to reinforce the financial infrastructure accordingly.

The construction of stress test scenarios is both an art and a science, requiring an astute understanding of possible risk factors and their correlations. Scenarios may be based on historical events, such as past financial crises, or hypothetical situations, including geopolitical conflicts or pandemics. The variables manipulated in these scenarios often encompass a wide range of factors—interest rate spikes, stock market crashes, or liquidity droughts.

For FP&A, stress testing is a process deeply embedded in the strategic planning and capital allocation framework. It informs decision-making on aspects such as capital reserves, debt management, and investment strategies. Financial models are adjusted to reflect stress test outcomes, providing a spectrum of results that guide actions under various levels of duress.

A practical example of stress testing within FP&A is assessing the impact of a sudden drop in consumer demand on the company's cash flow and working capital requirements. The stress test helps in crafting strategies to manage cash reserves, adjust credit lines, and renegotiate payment terms with suppliers to maintain liquidity under such adverse conditions.

Increasingly, stress testing has not only become a voluntary exercise but a regulatory mandate, particularly within the banking sector. Regulatory bodies often prescribe specific stress testing exercises to ensure that institutions have sufficient capital buffers and risk management practices in place.

Best practices in stress testing involve not only conducting the tests regularly but also integrating the insights into the organizational risk appetite and tolerance levels. This ensures that the outcomes of stress tests are not merely academic exercises but are actively informing risk management frameworks and business continuity plans.

Stress testing stands as an indispensable tool in an FP&A professional's arsenal, equipping them to foresee the potential fissures within an organization's financial structure and enabling them to fortify it preemptively. It is a deliberate and rigorous approach that seeks to transform theoretical vulnerabilities into actionable insights. As businesses operate in an increasingly complex and interconnected financial ecosystem, stress testing will continue to be a cornerstone of sound financial planning, ensuring that organizations are not only insulated against shocks but are strategically positioned to respond and adapt with agility and insight.

Stress Testing Summary:

1. Identify Objectives: First, understand why you're conducting the stress test. Is it to evaluate financial resilience, operational capacity, or something else? Knowing the objective helps tailor the stress test to your specific needs.

2. Determine Key Variables: Identify the variables that significantly impact your business. This could include economic factors, market changes, supply chain disruptions, or technological shifts. These variables will be the focus of your stress tests.

3. Develop Stress Scenarios: Create hypothetical situations that challenge these key variables. These scenarios should be extreme but plausible, like a severe economic downturn, a major supply chain breakdown, or a drastic regulatory change. Think of it as preparing for the worst-case scenarios.

4. Quantify Impacts: Assess how these stress scenarios would quantitatively affect your business. This involves analyzing financial metrics such as cash flow, profitability, and liquidity under stress conditions. Use your business data and financial models to estimate the impacts.

5. Qualitative Assessment: Besides numbers, consider qualitative factors. How would these stress scenarios affect your brand reputation, customer relationships, or employee morale? This holistic view is crucial for comprehensive planning.

6. Develop Contingency Plans: Based on the insights from the stress test, develop strategies to mitigate the identified risks. This might include diversifying revenue streams, building a financial buffer, or strengthening operational flexibility.

7. Implement Monitoring Systems: Establish mechanisms to monitor the key indicators that signal the onset of a stress scenario. This helps in taking timely actions to mitigate risks.

8. Regular Reviews and Updates: The business environment is dynamic, so regularly review and update your stress testing scenarios and strategies. This ensures that your business remains prepared for evolving challenges.

9. Communication and Training: Ensure that your team understands the stress testing process and outcomes. Effective communication and training are key for quick and coordinated responses during actual stress situations.

10. Documentation and Compliance: Finally, document the process and outcomes of your stress tests, especially if you're in a regulated industry. This documentation can be vital for regulatory compliance and future reference.

Sensitivity Analysis

Sensitivity analysis, within FP&A, investigates how changes in underlying variables affect the outcome of a financial model. This analytical tool enables financial analysts to uncover the extent to which individual factors influence specific results, such as net income, cash flow projections, or asset valuations. By conducting sensitivity analysis, analysts gain valuable insights into the robustness of their models and enhance the precision of their financial planning.

Through sensitivity analysis, analysts systematically vary input parameters and observe the corresponding impact on the output. By assessing the degree of sensitivity to changes in variables, analysts can identify which factors have a significant influence on key financial metrics. This understanding allows them to prioritize their attention, allocate resources effectively, and identify potential risks and opportunities associated with specific variables.

Sensitivity analysis serves as a forensic tool, functioning like a microscope to scrutinize the reliability and accuracy of financial models. By evaluating the response of outcomes to changes in underlying variables, analysts can assess the potential range of outcomes and evaluate the reliability of their projections.

By integrating sensitivity analysis into the FP&A process, analysts can make more informed decisions, refine their models, and enhance the overall accuracy and precision of financial planning. This diagnostic tool enables organizations to evaluate the potential impact of different factors, identify key drivers of financial performance, and improve the reliability of their forecasts and projections.

Identifying the variables for sensitivity analysis is a strategic decision that hinges on the specific context of the financial model in question. Common variables include input costs, interest rates, exchange rates, and revenue growth. Selecting the right variables is crucial, as it determines the relevance and effectiveness of the analysis.

The process of sensitivity analysis typically involves fluctuating one variable at a time, holding all others constant, to isolate the effect of that single variable. This method, known as ceteris paribus, ensures clarity in understanding the cause-and-effect relationship between the variable and the outcome. Analysts create a sensitivity table that displays a range of possible outcomes based on different scenarios for each variable, which can be visualized in data dashboards for easy interpretation.

Sensitivity analysis is invaluable in strategic planning, as it provides a quantitative understanding of risk exposure. For example, a company considering expansion into a foreign market might use sensitivity analysis to gauge the impact of currency fluctuation on projected revenues. By understanding which variables have the most significant impact on financial outcomes, organizations can prioritize risk management efforts and make informed strategic decisions.

In a Vancouver-based exporting firm, sensitivity analysis could be crucial for understanding how fluctuations in the Canadian dollar might affect profit margins on goods sold internationally. The analysis would allow the company to develop strategies to mitigate negative impacts, such as currency hedging or adjusting pricing strategies.

While a powerful tool, sensitivity analysis is not without limitations. It does not account for the simultaneous movement of multiple variables or the interdependence between them, which can be a significant factor in complex financial systems. The interpretation of sensitivity analysis results requires a nuanced understanding of the business environment and a critical eye for the interplay of multiple risk factors.

Sensitivity analysis is more than an academic exercise; it is a strategic enabler that empowers FP&A professionals to anticipate fluctuations in key financial indicators and prepare for multiple fiscal landscapes. By rigorously applying this tool, organizations can refine their forecasting accuracy, bolster their strategic planning, and navigate the intricacies of financial decision-making with greater confidence. It is through such meticulous examination of potential outcomes that businesses can adapt to the ever-evolving dance of market dynamics, ensuring financial resilience and sustained profitability.

Sensitivity Analysis Summary:

1. Objective Identification: First, determine the specific objective of the sensitivity analysis. It could be to assess the impact of cost changes on profits, price fluctuations on sales volume, or interest rate changes on loan repayments.

2. Variable Selection: Identify the key variables you want to test. These are usually inputs that are uncertain or could significantly impact the business outcome. Common examples include costs, pricing, interest rates, market demand, or production capacity.

3. Baseline Establishment: Set a baseline or standard scenario. This is the current or expected situation, against which you'll compare the changes. The baseline should reflect the most likely set of conditions.

4. Range Determination: For each key variable, define a range of possible values. These ranges should reflect realistic extremes – both high and low – to understand the full spectrum of potential impacts.

5. Model Creation: Develop a model that illustrates the relationship between the independent variables (the ones you're testing) and the dependent variable (the outcome). This could be a financial model, a spreadsheet, or a statistical model.

6. Analysis Conducting: Run the model multiple times, each time altering the value of one key variable while keeping others constant. This helps in isolating the effects of each variable. Record how the changes in each variable impact the outcome.

7. Results Interpretation: Analyze the results to understand the sensitivity of the dependent variable to changes in each independent variable. Identify which variables have the most and least impact on the outcome.

8. Scenario Planning: Use the insights from the analysis for scenario planning. This can help in developing strategies to mitigate risks or capitalize on potential opportunities identified through the sensitivity analysis.

9. Reporting and Decision Making: Present the findings in an easily understandable format, often through charts or graphs that illustrate the impact of variable changes. Use these insights to inform decision-making processes.

Data-driven Risk Analysis

Data-driven risk analysis plays a crucial role in financial planning and analysis, providing a powerful defense against the unpredictable nature of uncertainty. It serves as a compass that guides modern financial professionals in navigating through the challenging waters of market unpredictability. By relying on data and advanced analytical methodologies, data-driven risk analysis helps uncover and understand even the most hidden and elusive fiscal risks.

The mechanics and methodologies underpinning data-driven risk analysis involve leveraging large datasets, utilizing statistical techniques, and employing sophisticated modeling approaches. Financial professionals use these tools to extract valuable insights and patterns from the data, enabling them to identify and assess potential risks across various financial dimensions. By examining historical trends, analyzing market indicators, and incorporating economic data, they gain a comprehensive understanding of the risks that the organization may face.

Data-driven risk analysis provides a systematic and objective approach to identifying and quantifying risks, empowering financial professionals to make informed decisions. By relying on data-driven insights, organizations can more effectively allocate resources, develop appropriate risk management strategies, and enhance their ability to respond to changing market conditions.

Grounding risk analysis in empirical data transmutes intuition into intellect. In the era of big data, FP&A professionals harness a wealth of internal and external data sources. Internal data might include historical financial results, operational metrics, and customer behaviors, while external data encompasses market trends, economic indicators, and competitive intelligence. The judicious integration of these data points sets the stage for a comprehensive risk profile.

Analytical Methodologies:

Data-driven risk analysis employs a suite of statistical techniques to extricate meaningful insights from the complex mosaic of raw data. Predictive analytics, for instance, utilizes historical data to forecast future trends, enabling organizations to preemptively identify potential risks. Correlation analysis might reveal unexpected dependencies between variables that could amplify risk exposure. Moreover, machine learning algorithms can sift through vast data sets, unveiling patterns that elude conventional analytics.

In an academic setting, one might draw parallels between data-driven risk analysis and the meticulous work of an archaeologist, where layers of sedimentary data are carefully excavated to uncover the relics of predictive insights that lie beneath.

The potency of data-driven risk analysis is amplified through adept data visualization. Dashboards and heat maps translate complex data sets into intelligible and actionable visual representations. Decision-makers can swiftly assimilate risk landscapes and adjust strategies accordingly. Visualization tools not only democratize data comprehension across organizational strata but also act as a catalyst for collaborative risk mitigation.

Consider a Vancouver real estate investment trust evaluating the risk of market volatility. A data-driven risk analysis might leverage housing sales data, demographic shifts, and economic forecasts to predict future property values. Visualizing this data through heat maps could rapidly convey areas of high risk and growth potential, enabling strategic investment decisions that balance risk and reward.

Data-driven risk analysis must be underpinned by a staunch commitment to ethical standards and data integrity. The integrity of data—its accuracy, completeness, and timeliness —is a linchpin of the analysis. Ethical considerations encompass data privacy, consent, and the avoidance of biases that could skew analytical outcomes. Organizations must navigate these considerations with diligence, ensuring that their risk analysis is both legally compliant and morally sound.

Data-driven risk analysis, an intellectual lodestar in the financial firmament, equips FP&A professionals with the foresight to avert fiscal calamities and seize opportunities amidst market convulsions. It is a testament to the power of data to not only inform but to transform; a testament to the alchemy that transpires when quantitative precision meets strategic acumen. As businesses continue to sail through the digital age, their success will increasingly hinge on the capacity to integrate and interrogate vast data repositories, ensuring that decisions are not left to the capricious winds of fate but are steered by the rudder of informed analysis.

Use of Big Data and Analytics

The adoption of big data in FP&A is not merely a trend but a paradigm shift, augmenting the financial acumen of organizations. Big data, characterized by its volume, velocity, variety, and veracity, propels organizations into a new epoch of data-driven decision-making. The potent combination of extensive datasets and advanced analytics is reshaping how organizations forecast growth, manage risk, and optimize their financial strategies.

Advanced analytics, the cerebral cortex of big data, is the methodological alchemy that transforms raw data into strategic gold. Through techniques like predictive analytics, machine learning, and complex algorithms, FP&A teams can discern patterns and insights that were once veiled by the sheer scale and complexity of information. These insights inform strategic decisions, from investment to cost savings, allowing companies to maneuver with agility and confidence.

Consider, for example, the power of predictive analytics within FP&A. By scrutinizing past financial performance and external market variables, predictive models can provide a probabilistic view of future outcomes. This foresight enables organizations to brace for potential headwinds or pivot towards emerging opportunities with a precision that traditional forecasting methods could not offer.

The application of big data and analytics also extends to

risk management—a cornerstone of FP&A. By leveraging risk analytics, organizations can quantify and categorize risks, translating uncertainty into a structured form amenable to analysis. This quantification is crucial, as it underpins the risk mitigation strategies that guard an organization's financial well-being.

However, the nirvana of big data does not come without its challenges. The deluge of data points can easily morph into a treacherous quagmire for the uninitiated. Data governance and data quality emerge as pivotal elements—ensuring that the data is accurate, timely, and relevant. This stewardship of data is a critical endeavor, for the insights gleaned from analytics are only as sound as the data from which they are derived.

To further compound the complexity, the integration of big data into FP&A necessitates a robust technological infrastructure—systems that can handle the ingestion, processing, and analysis of large datasets at breakneck speeds. Moreover, FP&A professionals must be adept at utilizing these tools, necessitating a culture of continuous learning and adaptation within financial teams.

In Vancouver, the convergence of big data and FP&A is vividly illustrated in its thriving tech scene. One anecdote is that of a local startup that adeptly utilized big data analytics to pivot its business model in the face of fluctuating market conditions during a period of economic downturn. The insights derived from big data were instrumental in steering the company towards a more sustainable and profitable trajectory.

The sophisticated use of big data and analytics in FP&A is

akin to charting a course through the vast ocean of financial uncertainty. It is about harnessing the power of vast datasets and cutting-edge analytical techniques to illuminate the path forward, steering clear of pitfalls, and capitalizing on the winds of opportunity. As FP&A continues to evolve, the synergy of big data and analytics will undoubtedly remain at its vanguard, a lodestar guiding the strategic course of enterprises toward a prosperous horizon.

Predictive Modeling

As the linchpin of modern financial intelligence, predictive modeling stands as a stalwart ally to financial planning and analysis (FP&A) professionals. It is the quintessence of harnessing historical data to anticipate future events, a process that melds statistical techniques with machine intelligence to foresee and shape financial destinies.

Predictive modeling, in its essence, is a form of financial clairvoyance, offering a glimpse into the myriad possibilities that the future holds. By analyzing patterns within large sets of historical financial data, predictive models enable FP&A teams to craft scenarios that reflect potential financial outcomes. This capacity to predict and prepare for likely future scenarios is indispensable in navigating the complex waters of corporate finance.

Deploying predictive modeling involves a series of methodical stages. Initially, data is meticulously collected and cleansed, ensuring its purity and relevance to the models to be constructed. The next phase is feature selection, a critical step where variables that significantly influence outcomes are identified. Here, domain expertise intertwines with data science, as financial professionals pinpoint the metrics that matter most.

After feature selection, model construction begins. Using algorithms ranging from regression analyses to neural networks, FP&A professionals train models on historical data sets. This training is a delicate dance, where the model learns to detect the nuanced interplay between financial variables and outcomes. It's a process akin to a sommelier deciphering the subtle notes and undertones in a complex vintage.

Once trained, these models are tested against unseen data —a rigorous validation process that ensures their predictive prowess holds up beyond the confines of the training dataset. The true test of a predictive model lies in its accuracy and reliability when exposed to novel data, a benchmark that can determine the fate of strategic financial decisions.

In practical terms, predictive modeling can illuminate a host of financial applications, from cash flow forecasting and revenue prediction to bankruptcy risk assessment and customer lifetime value estimation. For instance, in the realm of credit risk, predictive models can evaluate the likelihood of default, enabling financial institutions to manage credit portfolios with surgical precision.

The versatility of predictive modeling is further showcased in its contribution to investment strategies. By forecasting market trends and asset performance, these models empower FP&A teams to optimize asset allocation, hedge against market volatility, and enhance the robustness of investment portfolios.

Yet, the power of predictive modeling is not solely vested in its technical capabilities. Its strategic value unfolds when intertwined with human insight. In the hands of a seasoned FP&A professional, predictive modeling becomes an instrument of strategic artistry. It is the synthesis of algorithmic calculation and human judgment that forges the strongest financial strategies.

The city of Vancouver has borne witness to the transformative impact of predictive modeling in its dynamic business landscape. In vivid illustration, a Vancouver-based renewable energy company leveraged predictive models to optimize its investments in clean technologies, resulting in substantial cost savings and a fortified market position.

Predictive modeling, however, is not without its caveats. The models are, after all, constructs of the data they feed on—subject to biases and anomalies inherent within the data. Complacency can lead to over-reliance on models, a pitfall that can be mitigated by maintaining a critical eye and a readiness to adapt models as new data and market conditions evolve.

As we continue to drive financial strategizing into the future, predictive modeling will undoubtedly remain a cornerstone in the edifice of FP&A. It is a discipline that demands both respect for its computational acumen and an understanding of its limitations. For those who wield it wisely, predictive modeling is a beacon that lights the way to informed decisions and strategic foresight in the ceaseless quest for financial excellence.

Data Visualization Techniques

Data visualization, a crucial facet of financial analytics, serves as an optical conduit through which complex data narratives are conveyed with clarity and precision. In the realm of FP&A, data visualization is not simply about presenting data; it is about storytelling, bringing to life the intricate tales woven by financial figures.

The art and science of data visualization lie in its ability to translate the abstract into the tangible. By employing graphical representations of data, FP&A professionals can illustrate trends, patterns, and outliers that might otherwise remain obscured within tabulated numbers. This practice is pivotal in making informed decisions, as it allows stakeholders to grasp sophisticated financial concepts and data-driven insights briefly.

The techniques of data visualization are manifold, each with a specific purpose and applicability. Line charts, for instance, are adept at showcasing trends over time, making them ideal for tracking revenue growth or share price movements. Bar charts offer a comparative view of categorical data, such as the sales performance across different regions or product lines.

Pie charts, although sometimes criticized for their limitations in representing complex data sets, still hold value in depicting proportions, such as market share or expense breakdowns. Stacked bar charts extend this functionality by allowing for the comparison of multiple variables simultaneously, providing a richer, layered understanding of financial distributions.

More sophisticated visualization techniques include heat maps, which can display the concentration of financial activity across various regions, and scatter plots, which identify correlations between two quantitative variables, such as customer acquisition costs and customer lifetime value.

An advanced form of data visualization is the use of dashboards—a composite interface that integrates various data visualizations into a cohesive narrative. These dashboards are tailored to provide real-time insights, enabling FP&A teams to monitor key financial metrics and respond to changes with agility.

Effective data visualization also involves an understanding of color theory and design principles. The choice of color schemes can significantly impact the readability and interpretability of visualized data. For example, using a gradient of colors can denote the intensity or magnitude of financial variables, while contrasting colors can highlight differences or emphasize specific data points.

The choice of aesthetics must be guided by the principle of simplicity. Overly complex or cluttered visualizations can confuse rather than elucidate. Therefore, FP&A professionals must strike a balance between comprehensiveness and cognitive ease, ensuring that visualizations remain user-friendly and accessible to all stakeholders.

Let us consider a local anecdote from Vancouver's burgeoning tech sector. A software start-up used an interactive treemap visualization to unmask revenue streams from various subscription tiers. This allowed the management team to identify high-growth segments and adjust their marketing strategies accordingly, thereby enhancing the startup's profitability and customer engagement.

However, as powerful as data visualization can be, it is imperative to acknowledge its limitations. Misrepresentation of data through improper scaling, selective omission of data points, or inappropriate visualization choices can lead to misinterpretation and misinformed decisions. Vigilance and ethical consideration are paramount in ensuring that visualizations accurately reflect the underlying data and its context.

In the ever-progressing field of FP&A, data visualization techniques continue to evolve, spurred by technological advancements in data analytics platforms. The integration of artificial intelligence and machine learning into visualization tools is set to revolutionize the way financial data is interpreted and presented. As these technologies mature, they will equip FP&A professionals with even more powerful mechanisms for extracting and communicating valuable insights from financial data.

Data visualization blends the empirical with the experiential, transforming the abstract machinations of financial data into visual narratives that resonate and inform. As a cornerstone of modern financial communication, it empowers financial leaders to chart a course through the complexities of data, steering their organizations toward informed decision-making and strategic clarity.

Integrating External and Internal Data Sources

In the intricate web of financial planning and analysis, integrating external and internal data sources is akin to conducting an orchestra of diverse instruments, each contributing unique tones to the symphony of strategic insights. This integration is a multi-layered process that requires a harmonious blend of technological prowess, data governance, and analytical acumen.

At its core, the integration of external and internal data sources aims to provide a comprehensive view of an organization's financial landscape. Internal data sources typically include financial statements, transactional records, operational metrics, and customer data housed within an organization's enterprise resource planning (ERP) systems, customer relationship management (CRM) systems, and other internal databases.

External data sources, however, present a plethora of rich information that can significantly enhance the depth of analysis. These may encompass market data, economic indicators, competitor benchmarks, regulatory updates, and social media trends. The value of such data lies in its ability to offer contextual insights that inform an organization's performance and strategic positioning within the broader industry landscape.

The convergence of these data streams presents several challenges. Firstly, the sheer volume and variety of data can be overwhelming, necessitating robust data management strategies to ensure accurate and efficient processing. Secondly, the disparate nature of data formats and sources demands a flexible integration architecture that can reconcile differences for seamless analysis.

To address these challenges, the use of middleware and data integration tools is paramount. Middleware serves as an intermediary layer that facilitates communication between different software applications and databases, streamlining data flow and transformation. ETL (Extract, Transform, Load) tools are instrumental in this process, enabling the extraction of data from various sources, its transformation into a consistent format, and its loading into a central repository for analysis.

Once integrated, the data must be subjected to rigorous quality checks to ensure its accuracy and reliability. Data governance policies need to be established to define standards for data quality, security, and usage rights. These policies not only safeguard the integrity of the data but also ensure compliance with privacy regulations and intellectual property laws.

The integration process also demands a keen understanding of the data's relevance and timeliness. Historical internal data, when combined with current external market signals, can yield predictive insights that guide future financial strategies. For instance, the analysis of historical sales data alongside current consumer sentiment indicators can help forecast future demand and inform inventory management decisions.

Consider the example of a Vancouver-based renewable energy company that leverages climate and weather data, combined with its production metrics, to optimize its energy output forecasts. By integrating these external and internal data streams, the company can better anticipate production fluctuations and adjust its financial models to account for seasonal variability.

Technological advancements, such as cloud-based data warehouses and data lakes, have further revolutionized data integration. These solutions offer scalable storage and processing capabilities that accommodate the growing influx of data. Moreover, cloud platforms often come equipped with built-in analytics and machine learning tools that can unearth patterns and relationships within the integrated data.

The integration of external and internal data sources is not merely a technical endeavor but a strategic imperative. By weaving together the internal narrative of an organization's financial performance with the external mosaic of market dynamics, FP&A professionals can craft a holistic view of risks and opportunities. This integrated approach enables the crafting of resilient financial strategies that are attuned to both the heartbeat of the organization and the pulse of the market.

Through meticulous orchestration, financial leaders can ensure that the integration of data sources is not just an exercise in data aggregation but a transformative process that fosters informed decision-making, anticipates future scenarios, and propels the organization toward strategic objectives with confidence and foresight.

The Importance of Accurate Forecasting

Accurate forecasting in financial planning and analysis is the linchpin that secures the present to the future, laying the groundwork for strategic maneuvers and mitigating the risk of unfortunate financial surprises. Within the realm of FP&A, forecasting acts as a navigational tool, providing a directional compass for an organization's journey through the tumultuous seas of economic volatility.

The art and science of forecasting are driven by the careful synthesis of historical data, analytical models, and market intelligence. Historical data offers a rear-view mirror perspective, illustrating patterns and trends that may continue. Analytical models serve as the theoretical underpinnings that translate data into predictive insights, while market intelligence injects a dose of realism, ensuring that forecasts are not ensconced in a vacuum but are reflective of the dynamic business environment.

In the pursuit of accuracy, FP&A professionals employ various forecasting methodologies. Quantitative methods, such as time-series analysis, leverage mathematical formulas to predict future values based on historical data trends. Conversely, qualitative forecasts incorporate expert opinions and market research to anticipate outcomes where historical data may be sparse or irrelevant due to changing market conditions or new business ventures.

The accuracy of forecasting is paramount for several reasons:

1. Budgetary Alignment: Accurate forecasts enable alignment between an organization's budget and its strategic plans. By predicting future revenues and expenses correctly, companies can allocate resources efficiently, avoiding the pitfalls of underfunding or overfunding certain areas.

2. Cash Flow Management: Forecasts of cash flow are vital for maintaining liquidity and solvency. Accurate cash flow forecasting allows for prudent investment decisions, ensuring that there is sufficient capital to cover liabilities and invest in growth opportunities.

3. Risk Management: Forecasting is an essential component of risk management. By anticipating potential downturns or disruptions, organizations can devise contingency plans and set aside reserves to cushion against such events.

4. Investor Confidence: Stakeholders demand transparency and accuracy in an organization's financial projections. Precise forecasting builds trust among investors, as it demonstrates a command over the business levers and market dynamics that influence performance.

5. Strategic Planning: Long-term forecasts are critical for strategic planning, providing the foresight needed to make informed decisions about product development, market expansion, and capital investments.

To bolster the accuracy of forecasts, organizations are increasingly leaning on technological innovations. Machine learning algorithms, for example, can digest vast amounts of data, learning from the nuances to improve predictive accuracy over time. Similarly, simulation techniques, such as Monte Carlo simulations, offer a way to account for uncertainty by generating a range of potential outcomes based on variable inputs.

Despite advancements in forecasting methods and tools, it's important to acknowledge and plan for the inherent uncertainty. Scenarios and sensitivity analyses become critical exercises, enabling organizations to understand the impact of various assumptions and potential external shocks on their forecasts.

In a case drawn from the bustling corridors of Vancouver's financial district, a prominent investment firm harnessed the power of advanced analytics to refine their market forecasts. By integrating both global economic indicators and granular transactional data from their diverse investment portfolio, the firm was able to create a multi-dimensional forecast that accounted not only for the expected market movements but also for the volatility that could sway their positions.

The commitment to accurate forecasting is not just a technical imperative but a strategic one, underpinning the entire spectrum of financial decision-making. It demands a careful blend of empirical data, sophisticated modeling, and an acute awareness of the broader economic context. As FP&A professionals harness this trifecta, they transform forecasting from an esoteric exercise into a cornerstone of financial strategy, driving their organizations towards growth, stability, and long-term success.

Common Forecasting Pitfalls

Delving into the intricacies of forecasting within the sphere of financial planning and analysis reveals a landscape riddled with potential missteps. Common forecasting pitfalls can significantly distort the financial outlook of an organization, leading to misguided strategies and suboptimal decision-making. Navigating these treacherous waters requires not only a keen analytical mind but also an awareness of the hidden shoals that threaten the integrity of forecasting endeavors.

One such pitfall is overreliance on historical data without due consideration for change. While past performance can offer valuable insights, it is not always a reliable predictor of future outcomes. Market conditions evolve, consumer behaviors shift, and competitive landscapes transform—all factors that can render historical patterns obsolete. For example, the rapid rise of e-commerce has dramatically impacted retail forecasting models that were previously anchored in brick-and-mortar sales data.

Another common hurdle is the anchoring effect, where initial estimates or data points unduly influence subsequent forecasts. This cognitive bias can lead to a lack of adjustment in the face of new information or a tendency to underweight recent trends in favor of entrenched beliefs. Anchoring can be exacerbated by confirmation bias, where forecasters selectively acknowledge information that reaffirms their preconceptions while discounting contradictory evidence.

Moreover, the complexity of creating forecasts can lead to model overfitting, a scenario where the forecasting model is tailored too closely to historical data, capturing noise rather than the underlying trend. Such models may appear impressively accurate in hindsight but fail to generalize to future conditions. This situation is often compounded by the temptation to include an excessive number of variables, resulting in a convoluted model that is more difficult to interpret and validate.

A further pitfall lies in the misalignment of forecasting horizons. Short-term forecasts may not account for long-term strategic objectives, while long-term outlooks might ignore imminent threats or opportunities. This lack of alignment can lead to a disjointed approach to planning and resource allocation.

Underestimating the impact of external factors is yet another forecasting oversight. Global economic shifts, regulatory changes, technological advancements, and geopolitical events can all exert significant influence on an organization's financial trajectory. An FP&A team that neglects to integrate external data into their forecasting models may find themselves blindsided by external shocks.

A poignant example from Vancouver's real estate market illustrates the consequences of ignoring externalities. When new housing regulations were introduced to cool the overheated market, forecasters who failed to adjust their models accordingly found their predictions of continued growth to be wildly inaccurate.

To mitigate these pitfalls, FP&A professionals must foster a culture of vigilance and adaptability. They must be willing to challenge assumptions, seek out diverse perspectives, and continually refine their models in response to emerging data and trends. This includes the regular backtesting of forecasts against actual outcomes to identify systematic biases or inaccuracies.

Additionally, embracing advanced analytics can equip forecasters with the tools to navigate these pitfalls more effectively. Techniques such as rolling forecasts and probabilistic modeling allow for a more dynamic approach to prediction, incorporating the latest data and more accurately reflecting the uncertainty inherent in any forecast.

Common forecasting pitfalls represent a minefield for FP&A practitioners. However, by recognizing and actively addressing these challenges, forecasters can greatly enhance the accuracy and reliability of their projections. This proactive stance not only safeguards an organization's financial health but also ensures that its strategic vision is grounded in a robust and forward-looking financial analysis.

Best Practices for Reliability in Forecasting

In the pursuit of precision within the realms of financial planning and analysis, the establishment of reliability in forecasting stands as a paramount objective. The best practices for reliability are not mere suggestions but foundational pillars that uphold the integrity of the forecasting process. They serve to fortify the analytical ramparts against the incursions of uncertainty and the capricious nature of future events.

Central to fostering reliability is the principle of methodical rigor. This entails the careful selection of forecasting methods that align with the specific nature of the data and the strategic context of the analysis. For instance, time-series models may be appropriate for stable and historical data-driven forecasts, whereas causal models could be better equipped to account for known influencing factors, such as marketing campaigns or product launches.

Another cornerstone is the calibration of models to strike a balance between simplicity and explanatory power. While complex models can capture a broad array of nuances, they can also be susceptible to overfitting and fragility in the face of data volatility. Therefore, the application of Occam's razor —a principle advocating for simplicity—is often advisable, where the simplest model that adequately captures the trend should be favored.

The practice of triangulation also contributes significantly to reliability. By utilizing multiple forecasting methods and comparing their results, one can identify convergences that reinforce confidence in the projections. This approach draws strength from the diversity of perspectives, much like how the convergence of multiple sightlines enhances depth perception.

Regular re-evaluation and updating of forecasts are imperative. As new data emerges, existing forecasts should be revisited and revised to reflect the most current information. This dynamic process echoes the concept of rolling forecasts, which continuously extend the forecasting period to incorporate the latest data, rather than being fixed to a specific time frame.

Sensitivity analysis is a vital tool for assessing the reliability of forecasts. By systematically varying key inputs and assumptions, analysts can gauge the impact of changes on forecasted outcomes. This practice not only highlights the most influential variables but also maps out a range of plausible scenarios, enabling better preparation for different eventualities.

Engagement with subject matter experts across various departments can unearth insights that quantitative models may overlook. The qualitative input derived from these interactions can enrich the forecasting process, ensuring it is rooted in on-the-ground realities. For instance, insights from sales teams can provide invaluable context for demand forecasts, capturing nuances unobservable in historical sales data alone.

A best practice that is often underestimated is the clear documentation and communication of the forecasting process, assumptions, and uncertainties involved. This transparency allows for peer review and collective scrutiny, thereby bolstering the credibility of the forecasts. Moreover, it ensures that the rationale behind decisions is well understood by all stakeholders, facilitating informed strategic discussions.

In the context of Vancouver's diverse economy, which spans from natural resources to cutting-edge technology sectors, a best practice example would be the incorporation of regional economic indicators into forecasts. Local housing market trends, port activity, and tourism fluctuations all provide FP&A teams with vital, sector-specific data points that are crucial for crafting reliable forecasts.

The essence of reliability in forecasting is the relentless pursuit of accuracy, tempered by the humility of recognizing the limitations inherent in any attempt to predict the future. By adhering to these practices, financial professionals construct a robust framework upon which sound, strategic decisions can be made, steering their organizations toward a future of sustained success and resilience amidst the ever-shifting economic currents.

Short-term vs. Long-term Forecasting

When navigating the intricate landscape of financial forecasting, a critical distinction must be drawn between the methodologies and implications of short-term and long-term forecasts. Each serves a distinct purpose, tailored to accommodate the varying temporal scopes they encompass. This section delves into the theoretical underpinnings that differentiate these two forecasting horizons, articulating their unique roles in the strategic mosaic of FP&A.

Short-term forecasting, often spanning a period of up to one year, is characterized by a higher degree of accuracy due to the proximity of the forecasted timeframe to present conditions. The primary focus lies in operational efficiency, liquidity management, and immediate tactical decision-making. Short-term forecasts are pivotal for budgetary control, cash flow management, and the coordination of day-to-day activities. The granularity of short-term forecasts allows for a detailed breakdown of revenues and expenses, often on a monthly or quarterly basis, providing a clear picture of the company's imminent financial health.

In contrast, long-term forecasting, which may extend beyond one year to several decades, embraces a broader vision. Its essence lies in capturing the company's strategic trajectory, encompassing capital investments, market expansions, and product development cycles. Long-term forecasts are essential for assessing the viability of strategic initiatives, aligning with the overall corporate vision, and steering the organization towards its long-range objectives. These forecasts inherently embody a greater level of uncertainty, given the extended time horizon, and thus incorporate wider confidence intervals and scenario planning to accommodate potential variability.

The methodological approach to short-term forecasting typically involves extrapolative techniques, such as moving averages and exponential smoothing. These methods rely heavily on historical data, if past patterns will continue into the near future with relative stability. The use of quantitative methods is more prevalent in short-term forecasting, given the availability of recent, higher-frequency data and the lesser impact of external disruptive forces within a truncated timeframe.

Conversely, long-term forecasting often requires a blend of quantitative and qualitative methods. Given the extended horizon, qualitative inputs—such as expert opinion, market research, and an understanding of macroeconomic trends— become invaluable. Techniques such as the Delphi method, which harnesses the collective wisdom of experts, and trend analysis, which projects current trends into the future, are commonly employed. The incorporation of these qualitative assessments ensures that the long-term forecasts are not solely anchored in historical data but are informed by a forward-looking perspective that accounts for emerging trends and potential paradigm shifts.

It is pivotal to acknowledge the inherent variability and uncertainty that accompany long-term forecasting. To mitigate these challenges, scenario analysis and sensitivity testing are employed to explore a range of possible futures.

These techniques allow FP&A professionals to assess the impact of different assumptions and external factors, providing a more robust and resilient strategic planning process.

In application, consider a Vancouver-based renewable energy firm assessing its expansion plans. Short-term forecasting might focus on the immediate impact of policy changes and energy prices on its cash flow, crucial for operational decision-making. In contrast, the long-term forecast would need to account for technological advancements, shifts in global energy demand, and environmental regulation trends that could alter the industry landscape significantly over the coming decades.

The delicate interplay between short-term precision and long-term vision is a dance of analytical finesse. Each type of forecasting plays an integral role in the financial planning process, with short-term forecasts acting as the guiding light for immediate actions and long-term forecasts serving as the compass for strategic direction. The judicious use of both, coupled with a keen understanding of their distinct methodologies and purposes, equips FP&A professionals with the tools necessary to navigate the temporal spectrum of financial planning with acuity and insight.

Utilizing AI and ML for Enhanced Accuracy

The advent of artificial intelligence (AI) and machine learning (ML) has signified a paradigm shift, offering unparalleled precision and insight. This section elucidates the theoretical framework underpinning AI and ML, and how their integration within FP&A workflows revolutionizes the accuracy of financial forecasts, propelling businesses into a new era of data-driven decision-making.

Artificial intelligence, in its broadest sense, refers to the simulation of human intelligence within machines. These systems are designed to perform tasks that typically require human intellect, such as pattern recognition, learning from experience, and problem-solving. Machine learning, a subset of AI, is particularly vital in forecasting as it involves the development of algorithms that can learn and improve from data over time without being explicitly programmed.

The core objective of integrating AI and ML into financial forecasting is the enhancement of predictive accuracy. Traditional statistical models rely on fixed parameters and historical data to project future outcomes. However, given the dynamic nature of financial markets, these models often fall short in capturing complex, nonlinear relationships within the data. AI and ML algorithms excel in this environment by continuously refining their predictions as new data becomes available.

A cornerstone of ML's capability is its ability to process and analyze vast quantities of data—ranging from historical financial statements to real-time market feeds—at speeds and depths unattainable by human analysts. For instance, deep learning, an advanced form of ML, uses neural network architectures inspired by the human brain. These networks can unearth intricate patterns and dependencies across multiple data layers, making them particularly adept at forecasting financial time series with a high degree of volatility.

An example of ML's practical application in FP&A is in the domain of credit risk assessment. By leveraging a multitude of variables, including transaction history, market indicators, and even unstructured data such as news articles or social media sentiment, ML models can provide real-time risk scoring. These scores enable financial institutions to dynamically adjust their credit portfolios, minimizing exposure to bad debt and optimizing capital allocation.

Another innovative application is in anomaly detection. AI systems can be trained to identify irregularities within financial data that may signal fraudulent activity or accounting errors. By sifting through the intricacies of transaction records, these systems provide an additional layer of scrutiny, ensuring the integrity of financial reports and safeguarding against potential financial malfeasance.

Implementing AI and ML in FP&A also demands a thoughtful approach to data governance and model management. The quality and granularity of the input data directly influence the model's output. Therefore, building a robust data infrastructure, with rigorous preprocessing and validation protocols, is indispensable. Additionally, as these models learn and evolve, there must be a framework in place for continuous monitoring and recalibration to avoid model drift and ensure sustained performance over time.

In Vancouver's vibrant tech landscape, where startups and established firms alike are at the forefront of innovation, the application of AI and ML in FP&A is not just theoretical but a tangible competitive advantage. Local anecdotes describe how tech companies leverage these technologies to forecast customer demand, optimize pricing strategies, and manage inventory with unprecedented precision—transforming the bustling city into a hotbed of financial ingenuity.

The integration of AI and ML into financial forecasting represents a leap forward in analytical capabilities. By harnessing their power to process and interpret complex datasets, FP&A professionals can achieve a level of accuracy and nuance in their forecasts that was once beyond reach. As businesses continue to adopt these technologies, the landscape of financial planning is reshaped, offering a glimpse into a future where strategic decisions are informed by AI-driven insights, sculpting a more resilient and prosperous financial ecosystem.

Prioritization of Risks in FP&A

In the multifaceted discipline of Financial Planning & Analysis (FP&A), identifying risks is merely the initial step; the subsequent and more nuanced challenge is the prioritization of these risks. This section delves into the theoretical constructs and practical strategies employed to prioritize risks, optimizing the FP&A functions and fortifying the financial fortitude of an organization.

Risk prioritization in FP&A serves as the compass by which organizations navigate the treacherous waters of financial uncertainty. It involves evaluating and ranking risks based on their potential impact on the organization's financial objectives, as well as the likelihood of their occurrence. This bifocal assessment allows FP&A professionals to allocate resources effectively, tackle high-priority risks, and make informed strategic decisions that align with the company's overall risk appetite.

A theoretical underpinning of risk prioritization is the Risk-Return Tradeoff, a fundamental concept that posits that higher returns are generally associated with higher risks. In FP&A, this tradeoff must be carefully balanced to ensure that the pursuit of financial gain does not unduly expose the organization to catastrophic losses. Hence, the prioritization process involves a meticulous evaluation of the potential upside of a risk against its possible downsides.

The Impact vs. Probability Matrix is a cogent tool utilized in the prioritization process. This matrix plots risks on a grid based on their potential impact (financial, reputational, operational) and their probability of occurrence. Risks that are both highly likely and carry significant impact are prioritized for immediate attention, while those with lower likelihood and impact may be monitored or accepted as part of the ordinary course of business.

Resource allocation to high-priority risks is a critical step in the risk management process. It involves not only financial capital but also the dedication of human expertise and technological resources to develop robust mitigation strategies. FP&A teams must be adept at justifying investments in risk management initiatives to the executive leadership and the board, illustrating how these efforts align with the strategic objectives and protect the organization's value.

Monitoring and revising priorities is a continuous process. As the business environment and internal organizational dynamics evolve, so too must the risk management priorities. FP&A professionals must remain vigilant, reassessing risks regularly, and adjusting their strategies to reflect the ever-changing landscape. This dynamic approach ensures that the organization remains resilient in the face of new challenges and opportunities.

An anecdotal illustration of this lies in the bustling port of Vancouver, where supply chain disruptions present a tangible risk to businesses reliant on international trade. FP&A teams in these companies prioritize risks such as delays, tariffs, and currency fluctuations, and develop hedging strategies to mitigate their impact. This local context provides a microcosmic view of the global complexities that FP&A professionals navigate daily.

The prioritization of risks within FP&A is a disciplined process, guided by theoretical frameworks and honed by practical application. It demands a strategic mindset, a deep understanding of the organization's operational context, and an unwavering commitment to safeguarding the organization's financial health. As FP&A professionals master the art of risk prioritization, they empower their organizations to thrive amidst uncertainties, driving strategic growth and ensuring long-term sustainability.

Risk-return Trade-off

The risk-return trade-off concept is a cornerstone of financial theory, an axiom dictating that the potential return on an investment is commensurate with the level of risk undertaken. Within the domain of FP&A, this concept is not merely theoretical—it is an operational imperative that infuses every facet of financial decision-making, from capital budgeting to strategic forecasting.

Understanding the risk-return trade-off involves dissecting the very fabric of financial risk—its genesis, its potential to erode value, and its paradoxical ability to generate substantial rewards. It demands of FP&A professionals an acuity for discerning which risks may yield commensurate returns and those that could precipitate a fiscal plummet.

In the intricate dance of financial analysis, the risk-return spectrum spans a continuum from government bonds, often perceived as 'risk-free', to speculative ventures, where the chance of default is counterbalanced by the lure of substantial gains. FP&A's role is to position an organization's portfolio within this spectrum where the expected returns align with the company's strategic aspirations and risk appetite.

The practical application of this trade-off in FP&A is multifaceted. First, it shapes the design of an investment portfolio. The FP&A team must determine the suitable mix of high-risk, high-reward investments and more conservative assets that can buffer against market volatility. This balancing act is paramount in steering the organization towards its financial objectives while insulating it from shocks.

Second, the risk-return paradigm underpins capital budgeting decisions. When evaluating potential projects, FP&A analysts deploy models that forecast expected returns and incorporate the cost of capital, which reflects the risk level of the investment. These models become the crucible within which investment opportunities are distilled —analyzed for their essence of risk versus reward.

Third, the concept is instrumental in setting risk management policies. The FP&A function advises on the degree of risk that the organization is willing to accept to achieve its targets, crafting guidelines that ensure that risks are neither recklessly embraced nor excessively avoided. This policy becomes a beacon that guides the organization's journey through the uncertain terrain of business.

An illustrative example can be drawn from the tech sector in Vancouver, where emergent companies grapple with the decision to invest in groundbreaking but uncertain R&D projects. The potential returns are significant, promising market disruption and substantial financial gain. However, the inherent risks of failure and sunk costs are formidable. FP&A must weigh these factors, advising on a path that balances the exciting possibilities with prudent financial stewardship.

The risk-return trade-off, thus, is far more than a theoretical construct—it is the essence of strategic financial planning. It demands diligence, foresight, and a nuanced understanding of the market dynamics that influence risk and potential returns. FP&A professionals wield this concept as a strategic tool, harmonizing the desire for growth with the imperative of financial stability, driving the company forward with a keen eye on the horizon of possibilities and perils alike.

Impact vs. Probability Matrix

The impact versus probability matrix is an indispensable tool in the arsenal of financial planning and analysis, providing a visual and strategic approach to risk assessment. This matrix allows FP&A practitioners to map out potential risks based on two dimensions: the likelihood of occurrence and the severity of impact on the organization's financial health.

To construct this matrix, one axis represents probability, ranging from low to high, while the perpendicular axis quantifies impact, also scaling from low to high. Each risk event is plotted within this framework, providing a straightforward method to prioritize risks and inform decision-making processes.

In deploying the matrix, FP&A teams undertake a rigorous analysis of potential risk events, drawing on historical data, predictive models, and industry insights. Consider the example of a Vancouver-based shipping company assessing the risk of a labor strike. The probability is determined by factors such as current labor relations, historical incidence, and industry trends. The impact is quantified by considering potential lost revenues, increased costs, and reputational damage.

The true value of the impact vs. probability matrix lies in its ability to simplify complex risk profiles into an accessible format that facilitates dialogue and strategic planning. It serves as a guide for resource allocation, ensuring that the most significant threats—those with a high probability of occurrence and substantial impact—are addressed with appropriate risk mitigation strategies.

For risks that reside in the quadrant of high impact but low probability, such as catastrophic natural disasters, contingency plans are put in place, often involving insurance coverage or disaster recovery protocols. Conversely, risks that are high in probability but low in impact may require monitoring and incremental management efforts rather than exhaustive resources.

Moreover, the matrix is not a static tool but a dynamic part of the FP&A function's ongoing risk management cycle. It requires regular updates as new risks emerge and existing risks evolve. The advent of new technologies, shifts in regulatory landscapes, and geopolitical developments are all factors that can influence the position of risks within the matrix.

A practical application of the matrix can be observed in the financial services industry, where companies must assess a myriad of risks, ranging from credit defaults to cybersecurity threats. By employing the matrix, FP&A teams can visualize where each risk falls and how it compares to others, aiding in the development of a comprehensive risk management framework tailored to the company's specific circumstances.

The impact vs. probability matrix empowers FP&A professionals to present risk assessments in a manner that is both analytically sound and intuitively comprehensible to stakeholders. Through its utilization, they can navigate the complexities of risk with a methodical and strategic approach, underpinning the organization's financial strategies with a robust foundation of risk awareness and preparedness.

Impact vs. Probability Matrix Example

Impact					
	Trivial	Minor	Moderate	Major	Extreme
Rare	Low	Low	Low	Medium	Medium
Unlikely	Low	Low	Medium	Medium	Medium
Moderate	Low	Medium	Medium	Medium	High
Likely	Medium	Medium	Medium	High	High
Very likely	Medium	Medium	High	High	High

Resource Allocation to High-Priority Risks

When confronted with a constellation of potential threats, the discerning allocation of resources to high-priority risks stands as a critical undertaking within the discipline of financial planning and analysis (FP&A). It entails a strategic distribution of the organization's arsenal—both financial and operational—towards mitigating risks that pose the greatest threat to the enterprise's objectives.

Intrinsic to this strategic allocation is the practice of risk prioritization, which often utilizes the aforementioned impact versus probability matrix as a starting point. Once the matrix has illuminated the landscape of risks according to their severity and likelihood, the process of resource allocation can commence with a clear directive to neutralize or mitigate the most significant threats.

The elegance of this approach lies in its pragmatic focus. For instance, an FP&A team at a multinational corporation with exposure to various currency markets might identify exchange rate volatility as a high-priority risk. The allocation of resources in this scenario might involve setting up hedging positions through forward contracts or options, thereby employing financial instruments as a shield against adverse currency movements.

Resource allocation is not merely about diverting funds; it encompasses the mobilization of human capital as well. Skilled personnel are assigned to develop and execute risk mitigation strategies, underscoring the need for a well-equipped team that can navigate the intricacies of risk management. For example, an organization might allocate its best data analysts to scrutinize market trends and signals that could preempt financial tumult, thus deploying its human resources to fortify its risk assessment capabilities.

In the realm of high-priority risks, timing and proportionality are of the essence. Resources must be allocated swiftly to address imminent threats, and in a scale commensurate with the risk's potential impact. To illustrate, the introduction of stringent new regulations in each industry might necessitate immediate investment in compliance infrastructure to avert the high-impact risk of legal penalties or operational disruption.

The allocation process is also an exercise in foresight and adaptability. FP&A professionals must continually reassess risk priorities in response to an ever-evolving business environment. For instance, the increasing prominence of cyber threats requires a dynamic reallocation of resources to bolster cybersecurity measures, reflecting the shifting nature of high-priority risks.

A judicious allocation of resources involves not only defending against risks but also capitalizing on the potential upside of risk-taking. Therefore, FP&A teams must balance the resources devoted to risk mitigation with those reserved for seizing growth opportunities that arise from calculated risks. This dual focus ensures that the organization does not become overly risk-averse but rather embraces a balanced perspective where risk management and strategic ambition converge.

Resource allocation to high-priority risks is a sophisticated dance, orchestrated with meticulous precision. It necessitates a harmonious blend of analytical rigor, strategic acumen, and the agile deployment of an organization's resources. As such, it is an indispensable component of FP&A, a function that underwrites the financial fortitude and strategic agility of any forward-looking enterprise.

Monitoring and Revising Priorities

The dynamic theatre of business is underpinned by an ever-changing script, where the roles of risks are fluid and the plot twists of the market are unpredictable. In this setting, FP&A professionals must not only be adept at identifying and prioritizing risks but also at the perpetual task of monitoring these risks and revising their priorities as the business narrative unfolds.

Monitoring is an ongoing observatory process, functioning akin to a lighthouse, casting a vigilant beam over the murky waters where financial hazards may lurk. This process is continuous and iterative, ensuring that the organization's risk profile is accurately maintained in real time. The goal is to detect alterations in the risk landscape, be they subtle shifts or tectonic changes, that could necessitate a recalibration of priorities.

Advanced data analytics serve as the core instrument in this process, with FP&A teams leveraging an array of sophisticated tools to analyze risk indicators. The use of predictive modeling and real-time risk dashboards enables a proactive response to emerging risks. For example, a sudden fluctuation in commodity prices might be instantly flagged by the monitoring system, prompting an immediate review of the organization's exposure to this risk and the adequacy of its current mitigation strategies.

The revision of priorities is an equally strategic endeavor, one that requires not just vigilance but also vision. As market conditions evolve, so too must the organization's focus. FP&A teams must discern which risks have grown in magnitude and warrant a shift in resource allocation, and which have diminished and can be scaled back in terms of attention and assets.

A practical example of this would be the market entry of a disruptive new competitor, a development that might compel an urgent reshuffling of strategic priorities and a reallocation of resources to bolster competitive positioning. Similarly, post-incident reviews of risk events provide invaluable insights that can drive revisions in the risk management strategy. Incidents that were once deemed as low-probability, high-impact may, after review, be categorized differently, leading to a reordering of risk priorities.

The revision process is also an opportunity to review the organization's risk appetite—its willingness to take on certain risks to achieve its strategic objectives. As the economic climate changes, FP&A teams must align the risk management strategy with the organization's evolving risk tolerance, ensuring that it remains congruent with the overall business strategy.

FP&A's role in monitoring and revising priorities is thus not a passive one; it is active and anticipatory. It is not enough to chart a course through familiar waters; the financial navigator must also be prepared to adjust the sails when the winds of change blow. This adaptability ensures that the organization remains resilient and that its risk management strategy is both relevant and robust.

Monitoring and revising risk priorities demands a confluence of analytical expertise, strategic dexterity, and a thorough understanding of the business landscape. In an environment where change is the only constant, this iterative process of monitoring and adjustment is vital, safeguarding the organization's assets and ambitions against the caprices of an unpredictable world.

CHAPTER 3: FINANCIAL MODELING FOR RISK MANAGEMENT

Financial modeling for risk management emerges as an indispensable discipline—a compass in the hands of the FP&A navigator, charting courses through the stochastic seas of market volatility. The essence of financial modeling lies in its ability to crystallize complex economic variables into tangible, quantifiable entities that can be manipulated, tested, and understood.

At the heart of such models is the imperative to encapsulate the multifaceted nature of risk, transforming it from abstract concept to concrete analysis. The models constructed by FP&A experts are intricate frameworks, often resembling living organisms, which breathe and shift in synchrony with the organization's financial ecosystem. These models serve as simulacra of the real world, enabling the exploration of financial outcomes under varying scenarios of stress and uncertainty.

To craft a robust financial model, one begins with the architecture—a blueprint that dictates the structural integrity of the model. This architecture must be both resilient and malleable, capable of withstanding the rigors of scrutiny while adaptable to the evolving contours of the business landscape. The inclusion of a myriad of financial inputs—revenues, expenses, capital costs, and cash flow streams—is just the beginning. Beyond these basics lie the subtleties of assumptions and dependencies, which form the connective tissue of any financial model.

The essential components of a model for risk management include but are not limited to:

- Projected financial statements: Balance sheets, income statements, and cash flow statements projected forward, capturing the anticipated fiscal health of the enterprise.

- Sensitivity analysis: A systematic exploration of the model's response to changes in key variables, offering insights into potential vulnerabilities.

- Scenario planning: Models must be designed with the flexibility to simulate a range of strategic scenarios, from the most optimistic to the most pessimistic, providing a spectrum of possible futures.

- Risk quantification: Assigning numerical probabilities to risks and their potential impacts, thereby converting qualitative assessments into quantitative metrics.

- Mitigation strategies: Incorporation of financial strategies aimed at hedging or insuring against identified risks.

The process of financial modeling is not merely about the

synthesis of data; it is fundamentally an act of foresight and hypothesis. The FP&A professional, acting as both architect and oracle, employs these models to gaze into the fiscal future—to anticipate, plan, and prepare for the myriad paths the company might travel.

A well-constructed financial model for risk management enables the distillation of the chaotic cacophony of market noise into harmonious, dissectible frequencies. It allows decision-makers to parse through the cacophony, extracting the signals that inform strategic decisions, such as investment in growth initiatives or the divesture of underperforming assets.

Moreover, regulatory compliance and the need for transparency in reporting dictate the meticulous construction of these models. They must be defensible and auditable, with each assumption, each variable, each equation subject to validation and verification.

In an era where the pace of change is relentless, the financial model remains a potent tool for the FP&A professional. It is a dynamic artifact, constantly iterated upon to reflect the latest market intelligence and strategic insights. By embracing the rigorous discipline of financial modeling for risk management, organizations arm themselves with the predictive power and analytical clarity necessary to thrive amidst the uncertainties that define the modern economic landscape.

In conclusion, financial modeling for risk management is the alchemy through which raw data is transmuted into strategic gold. It is a discipline that demands precision, creativity, and an unyielding pursuit of insight—a discipline at the very core of effective financial planning and analysis.

Building Robust Financial Models

The construction of robust financial models stands as a pillar within the domain of financial analysis, underpinning the strategic endeavors of organizations as they navigate the treacherous waters of economic uncertainty. A model's robustness is reflected in its resilience to fluctuations and its dexterity in adapting to new data, ensuring reliability in the face of an ever-changing financial landscape.

Building a robust financial model is akin to engineering a vessel designed to weather financial tempests. It requires a meticulous blend of precision and flexibility, allowing for the accurate portrayal of an organization's financial dynamics while accommodating the inevitable shifts in market conditions and corporate strategies.

Accuracy in financial modeling is the cornerstone of trust and credibility. It necessitates a rigorous approach to data collection and validation, ensuring that the inputs reflect the true state of affairs. The model must be founded on realistic assumptions that are carefully documented and justified, with clear links to empirical data or credible projections. The precision of a financial model is often measured by its ability to replicate past performances and predict future outcomes with minimal deviation.

Flexibility, on the other hand, is the model's ability to evolve. As new information emerges and circumstances change, the model must be agile enough to incorporate adjustments without necessitating a complete overhaul. This adaptability is achieved through thoughtful design, where variables are clearly defined, and relationships between them are logically structured, allowing for smooth and straightforward modifications.

An essential feature of a robust financial model is its capability to perform scenario planning. By constructing a series of 'what-if' situations, analysts can explore the potential ramifications of various strategic decisions and external factors. Scenario planning allows for the examination of best-case, worst-case, and most likely outcomes, providing a comprehensive view of potential financial trajectories. It is through this lens that companies can preemptively gauge the impact of their choices and the external economic environment, aligning their strategies with both their risk appetite and market opportunities.

Robust financial models are equipped with sensitivity analysis tools that enable analysts to determine how different variables' changes impact the model's outcomes. This involves varying one input at a time to observe the effect on key outputs, which helps identify the most sensitive aspects of the model. Sensitivity analysis is indispensable in risk management as it highlights areas where the organization is most vulnerable to fluctuations, allowing for the development of targeted mitigation strategies.

For a financial model to serve its full purpose, it must be seamlessly integrated with the organization's forecasting and budgeting processes. This integration allows for the model to draw on the most current financial data and projections, ensuring that the analysis is rooted in the company's operational reality. Budgeting scenarios, with their associated income and expense projections, can be fed into the model to simulate future financial states and facilitate the alignment of short-term operational decisions with long-term strategic goals.

A robust financial model is not an end but a means to an end—an analytical tool that informs decision-making with a depth of insight and a breadth of perspective. It is a living document that is continually refined and calibrated, embodying the dynamic nature of financial analysis. To build such a model is a task that demands not only technical expertise but also a deep understanding of the organization's strategic objectives, the volatility of the markets in which it operates, and the interplay of various financial and non-financial factors.

Through the diligent application of these principles, FP&A professionals can craft financial models that stand as bastions against uncertainty—models that not only withstand the scrutiny of stakeholders but also serve as beacons, guiding the organization toward financial stability and strategic success.

Ensuring Accuracy and Flexibility in Financial Models

The twin pillars of any effective financial model are its accuracy and flexibility. These attributes form the bedrock upon which confident and informed strategic decisions are made.

Accuracy in financial modeling is paramount—an unerring compass that guides the financial ship through the murky waters of uncertainty. It begins with the collection and curation of data, where thoroughness and precision are non-negotiable. Each data point must be scrutinized, cleansed of anomalies, and validated against reliable sources, ensuring that the model's foundation is solid and uncontaminated by error.

Next is the calibration of the model to align with historical data, offering a litmus test against known outcomes. This retrospective analysis not only enhances the credibility of the model but also fine-tunes its predictive capabilities. Accuracy is further sharpened using standard industry benchmarks and peer comparisons, which provide an external frame of reference and enable the model to mirror the competitive landscape accurately.

Flexibility is intertwined with accuracy; a model that cannot adjust to new information is as rigid as it is fallible. To attain flexibility, the model must possess a modular structure, permitting individual components to be altered without necessitating widespread changes. This compartmentalization enables the swift adaptation to shifting scenarios without the loss of overall integrity.

The architecture of a flexible model incorporates key drivers as adjustable inputs, which can be easily manipulated to explore various outcomes. These drivers are connected through transparent and logical formulas, allowing for the cascade of changes that flow from altered assumptions. Furthermore, the model should be equipped with toggle switches or drop-down menus to test different scenarios and stress conditions, fostering a dynamic and responsive tool.

The relevance of a financial model hinges on its evolution;

it must live and breathe the temporal rhythm of the business it reflects. This necessitates a regimen of regular updates, where the model ingests new data, reflects the latest business developments, and incorporates emerging market trends. It calls for an ongoing dialogue between the model and the mutable world it seeks to capture—a commitment to perpetual refinement.

Regular updates also involve revisiting the assumptions underpinning the model, questioning their continuing validity, and adjusting them considering new insights. This process is not merely mechanical but analytical, demanding a keen understanding of the business's internal dynamics and the external factors that sway its fortunes.

Accuracy and flexibility in financial modeling are not fixed states but continuous pursuits. They demand a vigilance that is ever-watchful and an adaptability that is unyielding. Through meticulous data analysis, a modular and adjustable structure, and a commitment to ongoing updates, financial models can achieve the resilience and responsiveness necessary to serve as reliable instruments of financial insight and foresight.

Scenario Planning Features in Financial Models

Scenario planning stands as a testament to a financial model's robustness, offering a multi-lensed view into potential futures. It's a feature that transforms static figures into a vivid narrative of possibilities, a vital tool for any FP&A professional.

The essence of scenario planning lies in its capacity to imagine diverse futures. The baseline scenario—often the most likely outcome—serves as a reference point. From there, a spectrum of alternate realities is constructed: the optimistic scenario envisages a world awash with favorable conditions, while the pessimistic scenario paints a picture of challenges and downturns. But the utility of scenario planning does not stop at the probable; it extends to the extreme. Stress scenarios push the model to its limits, probing the resilience of financial structures against high-impact, low-probability events.

Effective scenario planning is not confined to altering a single variable. Instead, it weaves together multiple factors—economic indicators, market trends, operational changes—creating rich, multidimensional landscapes. Each scenario is crafted with meticulous attention to the interconnectedness of variables, ensuring that changes in one area naturally ripple through to others. This interplay is vital for capturing the complexity of real-world dynamics and providing a comprehensive view of potential impacts on the financial model.

To bring scenarios to life, financial models employ interactive dashboards that present a cohesive and digestible view of each alternative future. These dashboards act as a control center, allowing users to toggle between scenarios and observe corresponding changes in financial outcomes. Sensitivity analysis complements this by identifying which inputs have the most significant effect on key outputs, helping to pinpoint areas of vulnerability or opportunity.

The true power of scenario planning is realized when it informs strategic decision-making. Each scenario is paired with a set of potential actions, creating a playbook of responses that can be rapidly deployed as future events unfold. This forward-thinking approach breeds a proactive rather than reactive stance, equipping leaders with the knowledge to navigate uncertainty with confidence.

In conclusion, scenario planning is a feature of financial modeling that brings depth, nuance, and foresight to FP&A. By encompassing a range of outcomes, considering multidimensional shifts, employing interactive tools, and linking scenarios to strategic action, it becomes an indispensable component of any financial model, turning uncertainty into a landscape of explored opportunities.

Sensitivity Analysis Tools in Financial Models

Sensitivity analysis is a pivotal tool in financial modeling, designed to unravel the layers of uncertainty that cloak every assumption. It is the dissection of a financial model's responsiveness to changes in its key variables, a systematic exploration of "what-ifs." By adjusting one input at a time, sensitivity analysis uncovers which levers have the power to pivot the model's outcomes, shedding light on the financial forecast's fragility or robustness.

The core objective of sensitivity analysis tools is to articulate the degree of risk and influence embedded within each variable. These tools allow for an in-depth examination of how input fluctuations—interest rates, growth assumptions, cost variances—can sway the model's projections. The outcome is twofold: firstly, it isolates the inputs with the highest impact, spotlighting areas that require meticulous monitoring and secondly, it generates a hierarchy of influences, enabling prioritization in risk management efforts.

The navigation of sensitivity analysis is facilitated by a suite of dynamic tools. Sliders provide an interactive means for adjusting inputs and instantly observing the effects ripple through financial projections. Data tables offer a structured matrix that outlines the results of various combinations of two variables at once, furnishing a panoramic view of potential outcomes. Spider charts graphically represent the sensitivity of an output to multiple inputs simultaneously, illustrating the relative impact of each factor in a radar-like display.

The integration of sensitivity analysis into strategic financial planning is crucial. It enables decision-makers to anticipate potential scenarios and craft strategies that are resilient under a range of conditions. By understanding the bounds of variability, a financial model not only serves as a predictive tool but also as an instrument for strategic flexibility, guiding investments, and operational decisions that are attuned to the volatility of the economic landscape.

Looking ahead, the evolution of sensitivity analysis tools is intertwined with advancements in machine learning and predictive analytics. The incorporation of these technologies promises to enhance the precision of sensitivity analysis, allowing for more sophisticated modeling of complex, non-linear relationships between variables. Predictive uncertainty measures, derived from machine learning algorithms, will offer deeper insights into the potential variability of outcomes, fostering a new era of financial foresight.

Sensitivity analysis tools are indispensable in the arsenal of financial modeling. They provide clarity amidst uncertainty, guide strategic decision-making, and bring a measured understanding of the influence of each financial variable. As technology advances, these tools will become ever more integral to the craft of financial planning and analysis, sharpening the acumen with which financial professionals navigate the uncertain waters of economic change.

List of Sensitivity analysis tools

1. **Microsoft Excel**: One of the most accessible tools for sensitivity analysis. Excel can perform scenario and sensitivity analyses through built-in features like data tables, scenario manager, and Solver.

2. **@RISK (Palisade Corporation)**: Integrates with Microsoft Excel and provides advanced capabilities for performing risk analysis using Monte Carlo simulation, allowing for more detailed sensitivity analyses.

3. **Crystal Ball (Oracle)**: Another Excel add-in, Crystal Ball offers sophisticated modeling for risk analysis and predictive modeling, including sensitivity analysis.

4. **Sensitivity Analysis Library (SALib)**: A Python library designed for global sensitivity analyses, suitable for a wide range of applications from environmental modeling to financial forecasting.

5. **MATLAB**: Offers robust tools for mathematical modeling and simulation, with capabilities to perform sensitivity analysis in a variety of scientific and engineering contexts.

6. **Simul8**: Primarily used for simulating business processes, Simul8 allows for sensitivity analysis in the context of process improvement and operational efficiency.

7. **GAMS (General Algebraic Modeling System)**: A high-level modeling system for mathematical programming and optimization, GAMS is used in economic and scientific research, which also includes tools for sensitivity analysis.

8. **Tableau**: While primarily a data visualization tool, Tableau can be used for sensitivity analysis by visually representing data and allowing for interactive scenario exploration.

9. **SAS (Statistical Analysis System)**: Offers advanced statistical capabilities, including regression analysis and other techniques that can be used for sensitivity analysis in complex datasets.

10. **ModelRisk**: A comprehensive risk modeling software, which includes detailed sensitivity analysis capabilities, integrating with Excel for ease of use.

Forecasting and Budgeting Integration

Forecasting and budgeting are twin pillars in the edifice of financial planning, each serving a distinct yet complementary function. Forecasting is the art of peering into the financial future, using historical data, statistical algorithms, and market insights to predict upcoming trends and cash flows. Budgeting, on the other hand, is the process of allocating financial resources, setting spending limits, and establishing financial targets. The integration of these two disciplines is essential for creating a synergistic financial strategy that aligns short-term actions with long-term objectives.

Effective integration of forecasting and budgeting begins with the recognition of their symbiotic relationship. Forecasting informs the budgeting process with nuanced projections, enabling a data-driven approach to resource allocation. Conversely, the budget acts as a benchmark for forecasts, providing a structured framework within which expectations must be tempered and strategies refined. This interplay ensures that financial plans are both ambitious in their vision and grounded in practicality.

The methodological fusion of forecasting and budgeting is epitomized by rolling forecasts and iterative budgeting practices. Rolling forecasts extend the time horizon continuously, adapting to new information and market changes, thereby ensuring that the budget remains relevant throughout the fiscal year. Iterative budgets adopt a flexible stance, allowing for regular adjustments in response to the evolving insights provided by the rolling forecasts. This dynamic approach fosters agility within the organization, enabling rapid response to unforeseen financial developments.

Technology plays a pivotal role in uniting forecasting and budgeting processes. Advanced software solutions offer integrated platforms where real-time data feeds, predictive analytics, and scenario modeling converge, providing a cohesive view of the organization's financial trajectory. These systems enable seamless collaboration across departments, ensuring that every stakeholder contributes to a unified financial plan that resonates with both the forecasted realities and the strategic budgetary constraints.

Beyond methodologies and tools, the successful integration of forecasting and budgeting demands a cultural shift within the organization—a move towards a forward-looking financial mindset. This ethos values proactive analysis encourages cross-functional dialogue, and champions the use of forecast-driven insights to inform budgetary decisions. It is a culture where financial vigilance is habitual, where every team member is attuned to the organization's fiscal health and is empowered to act as a custodian of its financial future.

The confluence of forecasting and budgeting is not merely a procedural endeavor but a strategic imperative. It represents a commitment to financial excellence, where every dollar is spent with purpose, and every fiscal forecast is a beacon guiding the organization's journey. As we delve deeper into the mechanics and philosophy of this integration, we uncover a landscape where precision meets prudence, and where financial stewardship becomes synonymous with strategic acumen.

Advanced Techniques in Financial Modeling

Financial modeling stands as the cornerstone of evaluating economic variables and forecasting financial performance. Advanced techniques in financial modeling transcend traditional static models, offering a glimpse into a multifaceted future laden with uncertainties. These sophisticated methodologies are the cartographers' tools, mapping the contours of financial possibilities and enabling businesses to navigate through the treacherous waters of economic unpredictability.

At the forefront of advanced financial modeling is the Monte Carlo simulation—an analytical technique that utilizes randomness to simulate a range of possible outcomes. By running thousands of scenarios, each drawing from a distribution of variables, the Monte Carlo simulation provides a probabilistic landscape of potential futures. This technique is particularly invaluable when assessing financial instruments or investment portfolios, offering insights into risk and return profiles that are not evident through traditional deterministic approaches.

Real options analysis applies the principles of financial options to the valuation of choices available in investment projects or business strategies. It treats managerial flexibility and strategic decision-making as explicit options that have intrinsic value under uncertain conditions. By valuing these options, analysts can better understand the worth of deferring, expanding, contracting, or abandoning projects. This approach injects a layer of strategic foresight into financial models, reflecting the true potential of business decisions in dynamic markets.

Value at Risk (VaR) and Cash Flow at Risk (CFaR) are pivotal in quantifying the risk inherent in financial positions and cash flows. VaR measures the maximum loss expected over a given time horizon and at a specific confidence level, providing a clear metric for financial risk exposure. CFaR extends this concept to the volatility of expected cash flows, allowing for a more comprehensive view of liquidity risk and operational resilience. These metrics are integral to the risk management framework, aiding in the strategic allocation of capital and the mitigation of financial threats.

Sensitivity analysis and scenario analysis are twin techniques that analyze the impact of variable changes on the outcome of a financial model. Sensitivity analysis isolates each variable to determine its individual effect on the model's results, providing clarity on which drivers have the most influence. Scenario analysis, however, crafts detailed narratives—from optimistic to pessimistic—each encompassing a set of variable assumptions, allowing businesses to prepare for a spectrum of potential futures. Together, these analyses provide a robust understanding of the model's responsiveness to shifts in the external and internal environment.

The integration of artificial intelligence (AI) and machine learning (ML) within financial modeling is revolutionizing the analytical landscape. These technologies enable the processing of vast amounts of data, identifying patterns and trends that are imperceptible to the human analyst. AI and ML can also adapt and improve models over time through continuous learning, offering increasingly accurate and sophisticated forecasts. This technological prowess is transforming the very fabric of financial analysis, ushering in an era of predictive acumen that is unprecedented.

Advanced techniques in financial modeling serve as the navigational instruments for modern-day financial analysts, projecting a vision of the enterprise's financial trajectory with greater clarity and foresight. As we explore these methodologies further, we unravel the nuances of their application and the profound impact they have on strategic decision-making. The advanced modeler is not merely a number cruncher, but a visionary—a strategist who leverages sophisticated tools to envision the future of finance and steer the organization towards prosperity.

Monte Carlo Simulations

Monte Carlo simulations emerge as a pivotal technique for analysts seeking to illuminate the impact of risk and uncertainty on their financial forecasts. These simulations, rooted in statistical mechanics and named after the famed Monte Carlo Casino due to their inherent stochastic nature, provide a rigorous methodology for modeling the probability of various outcomes in a process that cannot easily be predicted due to the intervention of random variables.

At the crux of Monte Carlo simulations lies the law of large numbers, which posits that the results of a random event will, given enough trials, tend towards the expected value. To conduct a Monte Carlo simulation, an analyst constructs a mathematical model of the financial scenario in question, incorporating random inputs for each uncertain variable. The model is then computed repeatedly, each time using a fresh set of random values drawn from predefined probability distributions. The outcomes of these numerous iterations converge to form a probability distribution of potential results, offering a spectrum of insights that extend beyond the limitations of deterministic analysis.

In financial forecasting, Monte Carlo simulations are used to assess the risk associated with investment portfolios, project cash flows, and capital budgeting decisions. They are particularly powerful in situations where future outcomes are highly uncertain, such as in the valuation of complex financial derivatives or the assessment of project viability in volatile markets. By simulating thousands or even millions of scenarios, analysts can explore the full range of possible outcomes and the probabilities associated with each, thus equipping decision-makers with a more nuanced understanding of risk.

One of the key benefits of using Monte Carlo simulations is the ability to identify and analyze tail risk—the risk of extreme outcomes that lie outside the realm of normal day-to-day variations. Traditional risk models often focus on the mean or median outcomes, but Monte Carlo simulations allow analysts to look at the tails of the distribution curve, where the risk of substantial loss or gain resides. This feature is crucial in the planning of risk mitigation strategies and stress testing financial systems against rare but potentially catastrophic events.

The selection of appropriate probability distributions for the input variables is a critical step in constructing a Monte Carlo simulation. Financial analysts must draw upon historical data, market analysis, and expert judgment to determine the most suitable distributions—be it normal, log-normal, triangular, or any other form that reflects the behavior of the underlying financial variables. This careful calibration ensures that the simulation outputs remain as realistic and informative as possible.

The advent of high-powered computing and sophisticated software has greatly enhanced the feasibility and accuracy of Monte Carlo simulations. Modern technology enables the rapid processing of large-scale simulations, providing a depth of analysis that was previously unattainable. Furthermore, with the integration of AI and ML algorithms, simulations can become more adaptive, capable of adjusting their parameters in response to new information and improving the precision of their forecasts over time.

Monte Carlo simulations form an essential part of the advanced financial modeler's arsenal, providing a dynamic and robust approach to understanding and managing financial risk. As we delve into the nuances of this powerful technique, we reveal its vast potential to shape financial strategy in an unpredictable world. With each iteration and simulation, the Monte Carlo method helps demystify the complex dance of risk and uncertainty, guiding businesses towards informed decisions and strategic agility.

Monte Carlo Simulation Summary

1. Define the Problem or Decision: Identify what you want to model. This could be forecasting sales, estimating the risk of an investment portfolio, or any other situation where you need to assess uncertainty.

2. Identify Input Variables: Determine the key variables that will impact your model. In financial models, these could be factors like sales volume, price, cost, interest rates, etc. These variables should have uncertainty and significantly impact the outcome.

3. Assign Distributions to Inputs: For each input variable, assign a probability distribution (e.g., normal, log-normal, uniform). This distribution represents the range and likelihood of potential values each variable can take. The choice of distribution should be based on historical data or expert judgment.

4. Develop a Computational Model: Create a mathematical model that represents the relationship between your inputs and the outcome

you're interested in. This is typically done using a spreadsheet or specialized software.

5. Run Simulations: Using a random number generator, draw values from the distributions of your input variables and feed them into your model. This process is repeated many times (e.g., 10,000 or more iterations) to simulate a wide range of possible scenarios.

6. Collect Results: Record the result of each iteration. You will end up with a large dataset of possible outcomes.

7. Analyze the Results: Analyze the dataset to understand the probability distribution of your outcome. Key metrics to look at include the mean, median, standard deviation, and percentiles. You might also create histograms or other charts to visualize the distribution of outcomes.

8. Interpret and Apply Insights: Use the results of your analysis to inform decision-making. For example, if you're modeling financial risk, you might focus on the worst 10% of outcomes to understand potential losses in a worst-case scenario.

9. Validate and Test the Model: Validate your model by checking its assumptions and comparing its outputs with known data. You may need to adjust your model based on this feedback.

10. Report and Communicate Findings: Prepare a report or presentation that explains your model, methodology, assumptions, and findings in a way that's understandable to your stakeholders.

Real Options Analysis

Within the multifaceted world of financial decision-making, real options analysis stands as a testament to the value of strategic flexibility. As a progressive extension of the options theory traditionally applied to securities, real options analysis affords us the tools to evaluate investment opportunities where the future is rife with volatility and uncertainty. It is akin to holding a compass in the uncharted waters of corporate investments, where each potential path could lead to varying degrees of success or failure.

This analytical approach integrates the concept of options pricing into investment decisions, recognizing that the management team's ability to adapt strategies in response to evolving market conditions holds intrinsic value. Just as a financial option confers the right, but not the obligation, to buy or sell an asset at a predetermined price within a specified timeframe, a real option encapsulates similar decision-making powers within the realm of real assets, such as the development of a new product line, the expansion into emerging markets, or the acquisition of a strategic partner.

Real options come in various forms, each corresponding to the strategic maneuvers a firm might undertake. Expansion options allow a company to grow its operations in response to market demand, while contraction options provide the leeway to downsize or abandon projects to curtail losses. There are also options to defer, which grant the firm the latitude to postpone major capital investments until more information becomes available, thus reducing the risk of premature commitment.

Valuing real options involves sophisticated financial models that emulate the methodologies used for financial options, such as the Black-Scholes model or binomial lattices. These models require inputs regarding the underlying asset's value, the volatility of that value, the time to expiration of the option, the risk-free rate, and the option's strike price—the level at which management would choose to exercise the option. By simulating various scenarios and applying these inputs, the analyst can estimate the value that strategic flexibility adds to the investment decision.

A significant aspect of real options analysis is the nuanced treatment of risk. Traditional discounted cash flow (DCF) methods might undervalue or fail to capture the strategic options available to management, particularly in the presence of significant uncertainty. Real options analysis, with its roots in options pricing theory, adjusts for the riskiness inherent in the investment by using the risk-neutral valuation principle, which reflects the probabilistic distribution of future payoffs.

In practice, real options analysis can profoundly influence strategic planning and capital budgeting. It equips decision-makers to better gauge the value of investing in R&D, to determine the optimal timing for launching a new technology, or to assess the viability of resource extraction projects where future commodity prices are speculative. It fosters a mindset that is not rigidly anchored to static plans but is resilient and responsive to the ebbs and flows of the marketplace.

As we forge ahead into an era where agility and adaptability are paramount, real options analysis is poised to become an increasingly vital component of strategic financial management. It empowers organizations to navigate the vicissitudes of a global economy with informed confidence, to leverage uncertainty as an ally rather than a foe, and to meticulously orchestrate their investment symphonies with a conductor's precision.

In synthesizing the technical underpinnings and practical implications of real options analysis, we capture its essence as not merely a theoretical construct but as an indispensable framework for dynamic and forward-thinking financial planning. Its application is a declaration that in the unpredictable theater of business, the option to choose is among the greatest assets of all.

Real Options Analysis Summary

1. Identify the Project or Investment: Start by pinpointing the project or investment under consideration, focusing on the risks and uncertainties it faces.

2. Define the Real Option: In risk management, real options might include the option to delay, scale up/down, abandon, or switch strategies in response to market changes or other risks. Determine which type of real option is relevant to your project.

3. Collect Data and Identify Risk Factors: Gather all necessary data, including cost estimates, expected revenues, market conditions, etc. Identify key risk factors that could significantly impact the project, such as market volatility, regulatory changes, or technological advancements.

4. Calculate the Underlying Asset's Value: This is typically the present value of expected cash flows from the project, adjusted for risks. Use discounted cash flow (DCF) analysis, incorporating risk-adjusted discount rates.

5. Estimate Volatility of the Underlying Asset: Assess the uncertainty or risk in the value of the project. This involves estimating the volatility of cash flows or other relevant metrics, which can be based on historical data or sector-specific risks.

6. Choose an Appropriate Options Pricing Model: The Black-Scholes model and the binomial model are common choices. The selection depends on the complexity and nature of the option and the project.

7. Input Parameters for the Model: Enter data into the model, including the value of the underlying asset, exercise price (cost related to the option, e.g., cost of delaying or expanding the project), duration of the option, risk-free rate, and estimated volatility.

8. Calculate the Option Value: Use the model to determine the value of the real option. This value reflects the worth of having strategic flexibility in the face of project risks.

9. Incorporate Option Value into Risk Assessment: Analyze how the option value influences the project's risk profile. The value of flexibility can sometimes offset the risks, making a seemingly risky project more viable.

10. Conduct Sensitivity Analysis: Given the uncertainties involved, it's crucial to understand how changes in underlying assumptions impact the option value and the overall risk profile of the project.

11. Document Assumptions and Methodology: Clearly articulate your assumptions, the modeling approach, and the findings. This step is vital for transparency and for stakeholders to understand the risk analysis.

12. Risk-Based Decision Making: Use the insights from ROA to make decisions that effectively balance potential rewards against the risks, taking into account the value of strategic flexibility.

Value at Risk (VaR)

In the realm of risk management, Value at Risk (VaR) emerges as a pivotal benchmark—a metric that attempts to encapsulate the potential loss in value of a risky asset or portfolio over a defined period for a given confidence interval. It is the financer's yardstick, quantifying the market risk that a firm's investment portfolio is exposed to under normal market conditions. The essence of VaR lies in its ability to provide a probabilistic forecast, a numerical depiction of financial risk that managerial minds can decipher and act upon.

The calculation of VaR can be approached through three distinctive yet intertwining methodologies: the historical method, the parametric (analytical) method, and the Monte Carlo simulation. The historical method examines past market changes to estimate future risk, if history might echo into the future. The parametric method, rooted in statistical models, assumes that asset returns are normally distributed and calculates VaR using the mean and standard deviation of those returns. Monte Carlo simulation, the most computationally intensive, employs random sampling and statistical modeling to forecast potential losses across a spectrum of hypothetical scenarios.

Within the financial industry, VaR has been widely adopted by trading firms and investment banks not merely as a compliance measure but as an integral part of their risk management arsenal. It offers a succinct measure for traders to assess their exposure and to align their positions with their risk tolerance. Regulators often mandate VaR measurements for financial institutions to ensure they possess sufficient capital reserves to absorb potential losses, thereby safeguarding the economic fabric from systemic risk.

VaR is commonly expressed with a confidence level— typically 95% or 99%—and a time horizon, which might range from a single day to a couple of weeks. A 1-day 95% VaR of $1 million suggests that there is only a 5% chance that the portfolio will lose more than $1 million in a single day. This probabilistic boundary enables firms to brace for adverse financial tides and, if necessary, reposition their sails before the storm.

Despite VaR's widespread utilization, it is not without detractors. Critics argue that VaR, while adept at capturing risk under normal market conditions, falls short during turbulent times when the correlation between asset classes can dramatically alter. It also fails to specify the actual loss beyond the VaR threshold—the so-called "tail risk." Thus, it may understate extreme risk, leading to an underpreparedness for unlikely but catastrophic events.

To address these limitations, refinements such as Conditional VaR or Expected Shortfall have emerged. These metrics seek to provide additional insights into the tail of the loss distribution, accounting for the severity of loss in the worst-case scenarios. The financial world continues to advance, and with it, VaR evolves, incorporating not just market risk but also credit risk, operational risk, and liquidity risk into more comprehensive risk assessment frameworks.

Cash Flow at Risk (CFaR)

In the ebb and flow of financial management, Cash Flow at Risk (CFaR) stands as a lighthouse for navigating the uncertain waters of cash flow volatility. Akin to its progenitor Value at Risk (VaR), CFaR is a risk assessment tool; however, it diverges in its focus on predicting the variability of future cash flows rather than asset values. CFaR gauges the extent to which future cash flows can be expected to deviate from their forecasts within a specific confidence interval over a given time horizon.

The methodology underpinning CFaR entails meticulous historical analysis, statistical modeling, and simulation techniques. By appraising the company's cash flow history, CFaR identifies patterns and relationships between cash flows and various risk factors, such as interest rates, foreign exchange rates, or commodity prices. Advanced analytical methods, including Monte Carlo simulations, project a range of possible future cash flow outcomes, thus enabling firms to measure the potential impact of market variables on their liquidity positions.

CFaR is particularly salient for corporations in their financial planning and treasury management, serving as a beacon to guide capital allocation, investment decisions, and financing strategies. By forecasting the worst-case cash flow scenarios within a specified confidence level, a firm can formulate contingency plans, maintain adequate liquidity buffers, and optimize its capital structure to withstand cash flow volatility.

Time frames and confidence intervals are pivotal in the CFaR framework. A firm may calculate CFaR over various horizons—be it monthly, quarterly, or annually—tailoring the assessment to its operational cycle and strategic needs. A 95% confidence level may be standard, suggesting that the company is 95% confident that its cash flows will not fall below the CFaR estimate within the defined period.

As with any risk metric, CFaR has its limitations. It may not fully capture tail risks or the precise timing of cash flows, which is crucial for short-term liquidity management. Furthermore, CFaR assumes a certain stability in historical relationships between cash flows and risk factors, which may not hold in rapidly changing environments. To mitigate these constraints, firms often complement CFaR with stress testing, scenario analysis, and liquidity cushions to ensure a more comprehensive approach to risk management.

CFaR is instrumental in holistic risk management, synergizing with other financial risk metrics to provide a three-dimensional view of the company's risk profile. By integrating CFaR with VaR, Earnings at Risk (EaR), and other risk measures, financial leaders can attain a granular understanding of their exposure across different dimensions, steering the company towards a more resilient financial future.

Looking ahead, Cash Flow at Risk will continue to be a vital tool for finance professionals, evolving with advancements in data analytics and predictive modeling. It equips decision-makers with foresight in an uncertain economic landscape, enabling proactive rather than reactive management of financial challenges. The continuous refinement of CFaR methodologies will further enhance its precision and predictive power, solidifying its role in safeguarding corporate financial stability amidst the vagaries of global markets.

Model Validation and Stress Testing

As an essential practice in financial modeling, model validation and stress testing serve as the bulwarks against the unpredictable storms of market turbulence. These processes are designed to ensure that financial models are not only built on robust foundations but also that they remain sturdy when faced with economic gales. In the realm of risk management, the adequacy of a model's construction and its resilience under duress are critical in forecasting and decision-making accuracy.

Model validation is akin to subjecting a vessel's blueprint to meticulous scrutiny before it braves the open sea. It is a systematic and ongoing scrutiny process that assesses the quality and effectiveness of financial models. This includes verifying the accuracy of data inputs, the appropriateness of assumptions and methodologies, and the correctness of computational algorithms. The process ensures congruence between the model's output and the financial reality it aims to represent.

Stress testing complements model validation by simulating a model's performance under extreme but plausible economic scenarios. This involves altering key variables to extreme values and observing the model's response, revealing vulnerabilities and providing insights into potential financial exposure. Stress tests can range from hypothetical market crashes to geopolitical events, enabling firms to anticipate their impact on operations and liquidity.

Model validation and stress testing are not one-off events but parts of a dynamic feedback loop that requires regular recalibration. As financial markets evolve and new data emerges, models need to be adjusted and fine-tuned to maintain their relevance and accuracy. This ongoing calibration ensures that models continually reflect the present economic climate and maintain efficacy in risk prediction.

The governance of model risk management extends beyond validation and stress testing. It encompasses a framework of policies, procedures, and controls that oversee the model lifecycle from inception to decommission. A robust governance structure ensures that model risks are identified, assessed, monitored, and managed effectively, aligning with the organization's broader risk management objectives.

Independent reviews and audits are vital components of the model validation process. External experts or internal teams not involved in the model's development undertake these reviews. They provide an objective assessment of the model's design and performance, highlighting areas for improvement and ensuring that the model meets regulatory and industry standards.

Advancements in technology continuously shape the landscape of model validation and stress testing. The incorporation of artificial intelligence, machine learning, and complex algorithms offers powerful tools for enhancing model robustness. These innovations enable the processing of vast datasets, uncovering hidden patterns, and refining predictive accuracy, fortifying financial models against an ever-changing economic horizon.

Model validation and stress testing are indispensable navigational tools in the financial modeling arsenal. They provide assurance in the integrity of financial models and prepare organizations for potential crises. As fiscal stewards of their enterprises, financial professionals rely on these processes to pilot their organizations through the uncertainties of economic environments, ensuring that the ship of finance remains seaworthy amid the unpredictable waves of market dynamics.

Independent Reviews

Independent reviews stand as a non-negotiable counterbalance—a sentinel of objectivity in a field where complexity and subjectivity can cloud judgment. The independent review process is a thorough examination by an impartial entity, which can be an external firm or an internal department unrelated to the model's development. This meticulous scrutiny is critical to maintaining the integrity of financial models and, by extension, the financial health of institutions relying on them.

At the core of independent reviews is a relentless pursuit of objectivity. Reviewers are tasked with dissecting financial models to validate their structural soundness, uncover any biases, and ensure that the models perform as intended. They serve as a diagnostic tool, providing a comprehensive health check that reveals whether a model is fit for its purpose or if it harbours potential risks that could metastasize into significant financial damage.

The scope of an independent review is expansive, delving into every aspect of a model's architecture. It starts with a verification of data integrity, assessing the sources and methodologies employed in data collection and processing. The review then interrogates the assumptions and theoretical underpinnings of the model, questioning their relevance and robustness considering historical data and future projections. It also examines the computational algorithms, ensuring they are not only accurate but also compliant with relevant regulations and industry practices.

Independent reviews are anchored in a set of standards and benchmarks that define the quality and reliability expected of financial models. These standards consider regulatory requirements, industry best practices, and the specific risk profile of the organization. They ensure that the review process is not arbitrary but grounded in established criteria that hold models to a uniformly high standard of excellence.

The culmination of an independent review is a set of recommendations that feed into the continuous improvement cycle of financial modelling. These suggestions aim to fortify the model against identified weaknesses and future-proof it against potential market shifts. The implementation of these recommendations is crucial as it marks a model's evolution from a static tool to a dynamic asset, capable of adapting to new challenges and information.

While independent by nature, the review process is not conducted in isolation. It necessitates a collaborative approach with model developers, fostering an open dialogue about findings and improvement strategies. This ensures that recommendations are not only insightful but also actionable, aligning with the practical realities and constraints that the model development team may face.

The impact of independent reviews extends beyond individual models, influencing the broader risk management culture within organizations. They underscore the importance of accountability and transparency, setting a precedent for diligence and detail-oriented practices across the financial modelling landscape. The ripple effect is a heightened awareness of risk and a more robust approach to financial decision-making.

Independent reviews are a lynchpin in the machinery of financial modelling. By providing an impartial perspective, they help ensure the accuracy and reliability of models, bolstering the confidence of stakeholders who depend on them. As we navigate the intricate interplay of risks and returns, independent reviews stand as vigilant overseers, ensuring that the financial frameworks guiding our decisions are not only crafted with expertise but also with an unwavering commitment to truth and precision.

Backtesting Against Historical Data

The Retrospective Lens: Essential Insights from History

Peering into the rear-view mirror of finance, backtesting stands as an invaluable exercise in fiscal retrospection. It is the methodical process of testing a financial model against historical data to gauge its predictive prowess. In this empirical rehearsal, the model's rules and parameters are applied to past market events to ascertain how accurately it would have forecasted outcomes or uncovered risks.

The cornerstone of backtesting is its reliance on historical accuracy. This method anchors a model's hypothetical predictions in the concrete reality of what has already transpired. By doing so, it offers a robust framework for assessing a model's effectiveness. A model that aligns closely with historical data provides confidence that its future projections might hold water.

Backtesting does more than just validate predictions; it reveals the character of a model under stress. By simulating past periods of volatility, upheaval, or economic downturns, backtesting exposes a model's resilience—or lack thereof—to turbulent market conditions. This stress test acts as a trial by fire, ensuring the model is not just a fair-weather framework but one that can withstand the gales of financial storms.

The insights garnered from backtesting are instrumental in calibrating and refining financial models. This process is an iterative one, where the lessons of the past are used to fine-tune the model's algorithms and assumptions. It is a cycle of continuous improvement that sharpens the model's foresight, enhancing its ability to anticipate and navigate the complexities of the financial landscape.

In backtesting, the temporal range selected for historical data is a significant factor. The chosen timeframe must be expansive enough to capture a variety of market conditions, yet specific enough to remain relevant to the model's intended use. This temporal mosaic weaves together short-term fluctuations with long-term trends, offering a comprehensive view of market behaviour over time.

A critical caveat of backtesting is the danger of overfitting —a scenario where a model is so finely tuned to historical data that it becomes inflexible, failing to adapt to future conditions. Backtesting must be conducted with a discerning eye, wary of introducing biases that could skew the model's predictive accuracy. It is a delicate balance to maintain, ensuring that historical fidelity does not compromise future applicability.

Backtesting's true value is realized when theory meets practice—when the insulated confines of financial models confront the messy reality of real-world data. This confluence is a test of a model's robustness, demanding not just theoretical soundness but also practical viability. It is here, in the crucible of empirical validation, that backtesting proves its mettle as an indispensable tool in the arsenal of risk management.

Through the meticulous application of backtesting, financial professionals can cultivate a more intimate understanding of their models, illuminating strengths and weaknesses alike. It empowers them to make informed decisions, backed by the weight of historical evidence, and to face the future with a model that has been honed by the hard-earned lessons of the past.

Stress Testing Assumptions

In the domain of financial planning and analysis, stress testing emerges as a pivotal exercise, one that probes the resilience of financial models against tumultuous market conditions. This section delves into the theoretical underpinnings of stress testing, an indispensable tool in the FP&A arsenal, which empowers organizations to anticipate and prepare for potential financial adversities.

Stress testing operates on the principle of counterfactual analysis. It is the rigorous evaluation of financial models under extreme but plausible scenarios, designed to reflect a spectrum of adverse conditions. These conditions could range from sudden economic downturns and geopolitical crises to market liquidity shortages and catastrophic industry-specific events. The objective is to assess how financial variables and institutional portfolios might behave under strain, thereby revealing vulnerabilities that may not be evident under normal circumstances.

The theoretical constructs supporting stress testing are grounded in the notion of stochastic financial modeling, where variables are subjected to random fluctuations to simulate unpredictable market behavior. This randomness is applied to the assumptions underpinning a financial institution's projections, such as interest rates, exchange rates, commodity prices, or default rates, which are integral to the organization's risk exposure. By altering these parameters in line with historical or hypothetical extremes, the institution can assess its capacity to withstand shocks.

For instance, consider a financial model predicting a firm's cash flow based on current economic indicators. A stress testing scenario might involve a substantial interest rate hike, which could significantly impact the firm's debt servicing costs and, consequently, its liquidity. By testing this assumption, the firm can gauge the potential impact on its cash flow and make preemptive adjustments to its financial strategy, like securing fixed-rate financing or bolstering its cash reserves.

Another example could be the modeling of credit risk in a loan portfolio, where the default probability is a critical assumption. Stress testing would involve scenarios where the default rates are much higher than expected due to an economic recession or a sector-specific downturn, allowing the financial institution to evaluate the robustness of its capital adequacy and provision for bad debts.

The assumptions chosen for stress testing are not arbitrary; they must be relevant to the institution's specific context, derived from a blend of historical data analysis, expert judgment, and consideration of forward-looking indicators. It's here that qualitative judgment entwines with quantitative rigor, a dance of numbers and intuition choreographed to prepare for the unforeseen.

Additionally, stress testing should not be an isolated exercise but integrated into the broader risk management framework. It requires collaboration across departments, offering a holistic view that encompasses market, credit, liquidity, operational, and strategic risks. When conducted effectively, it informs not only risk mitigation strategies but also business planning and capital allocation decisions.

The intricate theoretical detail of stress testing lies in its dual nature: it is both an art and a science. It combines empirical data with creative scenario construction to generate insights that fortify financial models against potential crises. For FP&A professionals, stress testing is not just about compliance with regulatory mandates; it is a strategic foresight tool that enhances the resilience and agility of their organizations.

Industry Benchmark Comparisons

In the quest to maintain a competitive edge within the financial planning and analysis (FP&A) landscape, industry benchmark comparisons emerge as a crucial strategic tool. They serve as a compass, guiding FP&A practitioners as they navigate through the complex waters of market competitiveness and operational efficiency.

An industry benchmark is essentially a standard or point of reference against which a company's performance can be measured. Benchmarks are rooted in the aggregation of data from a defined set of competitors or market leaders, providing a snapshot of the industry's best practices and performance standards. These comparisons aid in gauging an entity's standing relative to its peers—be it in terms of profitability, cost management, investment returns, or risk metrics.

The theoretical foundation of industry benchmark comparisons is anchored in the concept of relative performance evaluation. This involves the application of various financial ratios and operational metrics that are pertinent to the industry in question. Common financial benchmarks might include return on assets (ROA), return on equity (ROE), or the debt-to-equity ratio, while operational benchmarks could encompass cost per unit, inventory turnover, or customer acquisition costs.

For illustrative purposes, consider a retail banking institution aiming to optimize its loan portfolio's performance. It might utilize benchmarks such as the average interest margin across the industry or the percentage of non-performing loans (NPLs) relative to total loans. By comparing its figures against these benchmarks, the bank can identify areas where it excels or lags, thus informing its strategy for risk management and capital allocation.

However, the benchmarking process transcends mere numerical comparison. It involves a deep dive into the qualitative factors that contribute to those quantitative outcomes. For instance, if a company finds its operating margin falling short of the industry average, the next step would be to analyze the drivers behind this variance. Is it due to higher production costs, less efficient processes, or perhaps a less favorable product mix?

Moreover, FP&A professionals must consider the dynamic nature of benchmarks—they are not immutable. As industry standards evolve with technological advancements, regulatory changes, and shifting consumer preferences, so too must the benchmarks. Therefore, continuous monitoring and updating of benchmarks are critical to retain their relevance and utility.

Implementing industry benchmark comparisons also requires a nuanced understanding of the specific context within which a company operates. Benchmarks must be tailored to reflect the size, geography, and market segment of the company, ensuring that the comparisons made are apples-to-apples. Overly broad or poorly defined benchmarks can lead to misleading conclusions and counterproductive strategies.

In practicing benchmark comparisons, FP&A teams should strive for a balance between external competitiveness and internal goal-setting. While external benchmarks provide insight into where a company stands in the larger industry context, internal benchmarks—historical performance, internal targets—remain pivotal in tracking progress towards the company's strategic objectives.

Industry benchmark comparisons are more than a performance yardstick; they are a catalyst for strategic reflection and action. They compel companies to look beyond their operational silos and measure their achievements in the broader market context. By integrating these comparisons into their analytical repertoire, FP&A teams can foster a culture of continuous improvement and strategic agility that is crucial for thriving in today's ever-changing financial environment.

Pitfalls and Best Practices in Financial Modeling

Financial modeling, an indispensable tool in FP&A, is akin to to the artistry of a sculptor—meticulous, deliberate, and nuanced in execution. However, even the most seasoned financial architects can encounter pitfalls that, if overlooked, can lead to the erosion of a model's integrity and usefulness. In this analysis, we delve into the common pitfalls and delineate best practices to sculpt financial models that stand robust against the scrutiny of decision-making.

One of the primary pitfalls in financial modeling is the over-reliance on assumptions. Financial models are, by nature, built on a foundation of assumptions about future market conditions, growth rates, and other variables. When these assumptions are not grounded in empirical data and rigorous analysis, the model's projections can become distorted—veering from carefully charted predictions to the realm of financial fantasy.

Consider the case of a technology firm launching a new product. The company's financial model might assume a steady market share growth rate without accounting for the intense competition and rapid innovation that characterize the industry. Such oversight can lead to overly optimistic revenue projections and the misallocation of resources.

To mitigate this, best practice mandates that financial modelers must apply due diligence in vetting and validating assumptions. Sensitivity analysis—a technique that models how changes in one or more input variables affect the outcome—can be deployed to understand the impact of uncertainty and to stress-test assumptions.

Another pitfall is the lack of flexibility in financial models. A static model, which does not accommodate changes in underlying variables or economic conditions, is a brittle tool in the hands of a strategist. The financial landscape is dynamic, and a model that cannot adapt to shifts in this landscape is of limited utility.

To illustrate, a model forecasting the profitability of an airline may not account for fluctuating fuel prices, a significant cost driver for the industry. When fuel prices deviate from the model's static assumption, the projected profitability becomes unreliable. Thus, a best practice is to build flexibility into models using dynamic formulas and scenario planning tools that allow users to adjust inputs and observe corresponding outcomes.

Complexity is a double-edged sword in financial modeling. While detailed models can offer depth, they can also become intractable labyrinths for users, obscuring insights rather than elucidating them. This complexity can stem from a myriad of intertwined projections and calculations that strain comprehension and auditability.

In practice, the maxim of parsimony should govern model construction—simplicity without sacrificing necessary detail. The principle is to make the model as simple as possible, but no simpler. This entails structuring the model in a modular fashion, where each component or worksheet serves a clear, distinct purpose, and the logic flows intuitively from one module to the next.

Documentation and transparency represent the bulwarks against the pitfall of opacity in financial models. Without clear documentation, models become cryptic repositories of knowledge, accessible only to their creators. The inclusion of a 'model map' or index, articulating the purpose and interconnection of various sections, and comprehensive notes elucidating the rationale behind key formulas and assumptions, enhance the model's longevity and utility.

Financial model validation is an often-overlooked practice, yet it serves as a critical line of defense against errors. Regularly scheduled model audits, conducted by independent parties, serve to unearth inaccuracies and inconsistencies. Backtesting the model against historical data provides an empirical check, anchoring the model.

Common Errors and How to Avoid Them

In financial modeling, precision is paramount; a single misstep can cascade into substantial miscalculations. This segment examines the most prevalent errors that beset financial models and elucidates strategies to circumvent them, thus fortifying the model's reliability.

Oversights in cell referencing rank among the most common of errors, particularly when models grow in complexity. An example of this would be a modeler inadvertently linking to a previous year's financial data cell when forecasting future earnings. This could result in a significant underestimation of potential revenue, adversely affecting strategic investment decisions. To stymie such errors, modelers are encouraged to employ relative and absolute cell references judiciously and utilize Excel's auditing tools to visualize and verify cell dependencies.

Another frequent error is the misapplication of financial formulas, which often stems from a misunderstanding of their underlying financial theory. For instance, utilizing an average weighted cost of capital (WACC) formula without adjusting for the tax shield on debt can overstate the cost of capital, potentially deterring viable investment opportunities. To negate such pitfalls, modelers must not only possess a robust understanding of financial concepts but also consistently review and cross-check calculations against established financial principles.

Hardcoding numbers directly into formulas, rather than using referential cells, can create opaque and inflexible models that are resistant to alterations and updates—an ill-advised practice in a fluctuating financial environment. For example, hardcoding the interest rate into a loan repayment model precludes easy adjustments should the rate change. Best practice encourages the use of input cells for all variables, ensuring models are adaptable and transparent.

Circular references, where a formula refers to its own cell directly or indirectly, can spawn calculation errors and iterative loops, leading to imprecise or non-converging results. For example, a model calculating interest expense based on a level of debt that, in turn, depends on the interest expense itself, creates a circularity that Excel struggles to resolve. Careful planning of the model's structure and the use of goal seek or iterative calculation options can resolve such circularities.

Error propagation is another treacherous pitfall. An initial, minor error can exponentially distort outcomes as it propagates through a cascade of linked calculations. For instance, a small rounding error in the initial cost of goods sold (COGS) calculation can inflate through subsequent layers of the model, skewing profitability analyses. Rigorous error checks, peer reviews, and the implementation of control totals at various stages of the model are efficacious in curbing the spread of such errors.

Modelers must also be vigilant of date-related errors, particularly in time-series forecasting models. Overlooking leap years or mixing up calendar and fiscal year ends can introduce subtle but impactful temporal discrepancies. Attentiveness to date conventions and the use of date functions can eliminate such temporal misalignments.

Lastly, a failure to adequately test and validate the model against extreme but plausible scenarios can leave decision-makers ill-prepared for outlier events. Stress testing a model by applying atypical values to key inputs—like sudden market downturns or spikes in material costs—enables the identification of vulnerabilities within the model and allows for the development of contingency strategies.

In summation, the meticulous construction of a financial model demands vigilance against these common errors. By fostering a disciplined approach to referencing, formula application, variable input, circularity management, error tracking, temporal accuracy, and comprehensive stress testing, financial modelers craft robust tools that serve as trustworthy navigational aids in the turbulent seas of financial decision-making. Through these practices, financial models become not merely reflective lenses but also predictive beacons, guiding enterprises towards prosperous horizons.

Documentation and Transparency

In the architecture of robust financial models, documentation and transparency are the foundational pillars that uphold the structure's integrity and utility. These principles are not mere embellishments but essential elements that engender trust and facilitate comprehension among stakeholders. Within this section, we delve into the strategic practices that ensure documentation and transparency are thoroughly embedded in financial modeling.

Documentation serves as a roadmap, elucidating the logic, assumptions, and data sources underpinning the model. It provides context and rationale for the model's framework, allowing users to navigate its complexities with clarity. For instance, a well-documented financial model might include an 'assumptions sheet' where all key inputs—such as growth rates, cost of capital, and tax rates—are clearly defined and sourced. This practice not only streamlines future updates as new data becomes available but also supports robust auditing procedures.

A comprehensive approach to documentation encapsulates various facets, including the recording of data origin. When a model relies on external market data, such as commodity prices or exchange rates, the source should be explicitly cited, and the retrieval method documented. This transparency assures users of the data's reliability and enables consistent updates from the same source, ensuring continuity and accuracy.

Version control is another critical aspect of documentation. Financial models are living documents, subject to revisions and updates to reflect changing circumstances. Each iteration of the model should be cataloged with a standard naming convention, detailing the version number, date, and brief description of changes made. This meticulous record-keeping avoids confusion over which model is the most current and provides an audit trail of the model's evolution.

The practice of 'annotating formulas'—embedding comments within the model that describe the purpose and parameters of complex calculations—is also invaluable. This is particularly beneficial in models with intricate formulas or bespoke calculations, where a user might otherwise be perplexed by the formula's intent. For example, a comment explaining the logic of a non-standard depreciation calculation not only clarifies its function but also aids in validation and error-checking processes.

Transparency, the second bedrock principle, is closely related to documentation but extends beyond it to encompass the model's overall accessibility and readability. A transparent financial model is one that invites scrutiny and facilitates understanding, even for those without intimate knowledge of its construction. It is characterized by a clear and logical layout, intuitive navigation, and consistent formatting.

The deployment of a 'user guide' or 'instruction manual' within the model is an effective tool for achieving transparency. This guide might detail the step-by-step methodology for inputting data, running scenarios, and interpreting outputs. For instance, a user guide might direct a user to first input baseline financial data into a designated 'input sheet,' then proceed to a 'calculations sheet' where operational metrics are derived, and finally review the 'output sheet' for financial projections and key performance indicators.

To exemplify the significance of transparency, consider a model developed for assessing the profitability of a new product line. Without clear documentation, users might overlook the assumptions made about market penetration rates or the calculation of incremental costs, leading to inaccurate interpretations of the model's projections. But with detailed documentation and a transparent structure, the model allows for informed decision-making and reliable strategic planning.

In summary, documentation and transparency are not optional extras but the cornerstones of sound financial modeling. They enhance the model's credibility, foster user confidence, and ensure the model's findings are interpreted accurately and utilized effectively. By adhering to the best practices outlined in this section, financial modelers can create comprehensive tools that not only withstand the rigors of scrutiny but also shine with the clarity of their meticulous construction.

Continuous Improvement and Updates

The journey of financial modeling is unending, charting a course that demands vigilance and a commitment to perpetual refinement. Continuous improvement and updates are not merely best practices—they are the lifeblood of a model's relevance and accuracy over time. This section elucidates the processes that foster iterative enhancement and the incorporation of fresh insights into financial models.

Continuous improvement in financial modeling is akin to the principles of kaizen in Japanese business philosophy, which focuses on constant, incremental advancement. It's an acknowledgment that economic conditions, regulatory landscapes, and business strategies are in flux, and that financial models must evolve accordingly to remain pertinent.

A model that remains static is one that rapidly becomes obsolete. As such, the process of continuous improvement begins with the establishment of a 'feedback loop.' This involves regular reviews of the model's performance against actual financial results, as well as soliciting input from a diverse array of users. For example, a quarterly review process might be instituted wherein the model's projections are compared with the company's reported financials, discrepancies analyzed, and adjustments made to improve forecasting accuracy.

The updating process is multi-faceted, encompassing not just the refinement of inputs and assumptions, but also the evolution of the model's structure to incorporate new business segments, products, or revenue streams. Consider an international corporation that acquires a new subsidiary; the financial model must be updated to integrate the subsidiary's financials, which may involve adding new currency exchange calculations or tax considerations.

In the realm of technology, the advent of new software tools or data sources also necessitates updates to financial models. Adapting a model to harness more granular data from enterprise resource planning (ERP) systems or integrating advanced analytics can dramatically enhance the model's predictive power. For instance, the introduction of machine learning algorithms to project customer churn rates could provide a more nuanced view of future revenue streams.

Continuous improvement also includes the regular updating of regulatory requirements. In an environment where financial legislation can shift with geopolitical tides, it's imperative that models reflect current compliance mandates. An update might involve adjusting the model to accommodate changes in tax law or the introduction of new financial reporting standards.

One illustrative example of continuous improvement is the iterative enhancement of a model used for capital budgeting. Initially, the model may have used a static discount rate for net present value (NPV) calculations. Over time, sensitivity analysis reveals that the discount rate is a primary driver of NPV variability. Consequently, the model is updated to include a dynamic discount rate that adjusts based on the weighted average cost of capital (WACC), recalculated with each iteration to reflect changing market conditions.

Equally important is the need to document each update comprehensively, ensuring that the model maintains its integrity and that users can track its evolution. This may involve maintaining a change log that records each update, the rationale behind it, and the individual responsible for its implementation.

Continuous improvement and updates are not tasks to

be undertaken sporadically, but principles to be woven into the fabric of financial modeling practices. They are the mechanisms by which a financial model retains its relevance, accuracy, and utility in the face of an ever-changing business landscape. By committing to a structured process of review, feedback, and revision, financial modelers can ensure that their models remain at the cutting edge, providing stakeholders with insights that are both timely and reliable.

Model Audit and Control Procedures

In the domain of financial modeling, the twin sentinels of integrity and precision stand guard over the vast citadels of data and calculations that form the complex network of any robust financial model. Model audit and control procedures serve as the critical apparatus for ensuring that these models are not only scrupulously accurate but also steadfastly reliable. This section delves into the intricacies of the audit and control mechanisms that safeguard the sanctity of financial models.

The concept of a model audit is grounded in a systematic review process that seeks to verify the model's mathematical correctness, the appropriateness of its assumptions, and the soundness of its logic. This rigorous examination is conducted to ensure models are adeptly crafted to withstand the scrutiny of both internal stakeholders and external regulators. A model audit can be visualized as a meticulous dissection, where each component of the model is isolated, examined, and tested against a checklist of best practices and compliance requirements.

Control procedures, meanwhile, are the predefined protocols that manage the input, handling, and modification of the model's data and structure. These procedures are put in place to prevent unauthorized changes, reduce the risk of human error, and provide a traceable history of adjustments—akin to a finely tuned symphony of checks and balances that harmonizes the model's ongoing operations.

An example of an audit procedure is the use of 'walkthroughs,' where auditors trace the flow of data from its entry point to its final impact on the model's outputs. Imagine a financial model designed to forecast cash flows for a chain of retail stores. During a walkthrough, the auditor examines how sales data is captured, the conversion of this data into revenue figures, the treatment of seasonal adjustments, and the eventual influence on projected cash flows.

Control procedures often involve the implementation of 'version control' systems. These systems manage the release of model updates, ensuring that only authorized versions are in use. For instance, a model that predicts inventory requirements might have a version control system that logs each update to the formulas that forecast inventory turnover, with each iteration being reviewed and approved before deployment.

Another critical aspect of model audit and control is the 'sensitivity analysis,' which evaluates how variations in input values impact the model's outputs. It is a diagnostic tool to identify the model's most susceptible variables. For example, a sensitivity analysis on a financial model assessing project viability could reveal that the model is highly sensitive to interest rate fluctuations, prompting closer scrutiny of the assumptions around interest rates and the incorporation of hedging strategies.

Control procedures also encompass the establishment of 'user access levels.' These levels dictate who can view, edit, or approve changes within the model, creating a hierarchy of permissions that aligns with organizational structures. In a scenario where a model determines capital allocation, user access levels ensure that only individuals with the requisite authority and expertise can adjust the algorithms that drive investment decisions.

A model audit might also include 'backtesting,' where the model's predictions are compared with actual historical outcomes to assess its predictive accuracy. For a financial model used in foreign exchange trading, backtesting would involve comparing the model's currency movement predictions against historical exchange rate data to evaluate the model's forecasting power.

To encapsulate, model audit and control procedures are not merely ancillary functions but are central to the governance and credibility of financial modeling. They provide a framework within which models can be trusted to perform with both consistency and conformance to the highest standards of financial rigor. It is through diligent application of these audits and controls that financial models can be deemed reliable tools, capable of guiding strategic decisions and withstanding the turbulent tides of market dynamics.

CHAPTER 4:
STRATEGIC
PLANNING AND
DECISION MAKING

Strategic planning and decision making form the backbone of robust financial planning and analysis, providing a structured approach to shaping an organization's future and navigating the myriad risks and opportunities that lie ahead. In this section, we will dissect the multifaceted process of strategic planning and elucidate the pivotal role of decision-making mechanisms that guide a company toward its long-term objectives.

Strategic planning in FP&A is an anticipatory exercise— a confluence of foresight, analysis, and projection that coalesces into a blueprint for the organization's aspirations. It is akin to charting a course through uncharted waters, using the stars of data and analytics as navigational aids. The strategic planning process begins with a comprehensive assessment of the company's current state, including its financial health, competitive position, and market dynamics. This assessment lays the groundwork for establishing clear, attainable goals and setting the direction for the business.

Let us illustrate this with a tangible scenario: a multinational corporation aiming to expand its footprint in the burgeoning Asian market. The FP&A team, in their strategic planning role, must evaluate the economic landscapes of potential countries, assess the regulatory hurdles, understand competitive forces, and forecast the demand for the company's products or services. Their analysis will culminate in a strategic plan that details entry points, growth targets, investment requirements, and risk mitigation strategies.

Decision making, the companion to strategic planning, is the process by which choices are made among alternative courses of action. It is not a singular event but a complex series of evaluations, deliberations, and resolutions that take place within the framework of the strategic plan. Decisions in FP&A are frequently shaped by financial modeling tools that simulate the potential outcomes of different strategies, incorporating variables such as cost structures, revenue streams, and capital investments.

Consider the strategic decision to acquire a competitor. The FP&A team will construct a financial model that simulates the acquisition's impact on market share, cost synergies, and revenue enhancement. They will conduct due diligence, engage in scenario planning, and perform a valuation analysis to determine the acquisition's viability. The decision-making process in this context is a meticulous blend of quantitative rigor and qualitative judgment—a balance between the numbers and the strategic fit with the company's long-term vision.

Incorporating risk into strategic planning and decision making is essential to ensure that FP&A activities are aligned with the company's risk appetite and provide a holistic view of potential challenges. The incorporation of risk-adjusted return on capital (RAROC) and risk-based performance indicators into strategic decisions allows for a more nuanced understanding of the trade-offs between risk and reward.

For instance, a company may be faced with the decision to invest in a new technology that promises operational efficiencies but carries significant upfront costs and implementation risks. By applying RAROC, the FP&A team can evaluate whether the potential returns justify the risks and align with the company's strategic objectives. This approach ensures that risk considerations are seamlessly integrated into the strategic planning process, enabling informed decision making that supports sustainable growth.

In conclusion, strategic planning and decision making in FP&A are complex, iterative processes that demand a thorough understanding of the business environment, a rigorous approach to data analysis, and an ability to translate insights into actionable strategies. By employing a systematic approach to these processes, FP&A professionals equip their organizations with the tools to make informed decisions, adapt to changing market conditions, and chart a course for success in an uncertain future.

Integrating Risk into Strategic Planning

In the realm of strategic financial planning, the integration of risk management is not merely an addendum but a fundamental component that must be woven into the very fabric of the strategic planning process. It is a preemptive measure, a crucial counterbalance to the ambitious strides an organization makes toward its future.

The fusion of risk considerations into strategic planning demands a comprehensive and dynamic approach. It requires the FP&A team to not only identify and assess potential risks but to also devise strategies that embed risk mitigation within the company's pursuit of its objectives. This integrated approach ensures that risk is not a hindsight consideration but a foresight-driven aspect of planning.

A profound example of integrating risk into strategic planning is the utilization of risk-adjusted return on capital (RAROC) – a metric that measures the trade-off between risk and return. RAROC is a compass that guides organizations through the treacherous waters of high-stakes investments and strategic endeavors. By calculating the expected rate of return on an investment adjusted for the associated risks, FP&A professionals can make strategic decisions that align with the organization's risk profile and financial goals.

Let's illustrate this with a scenario: a financial institution is considering a significant expansion of its credit portfolio by entering into a new, potentially lucrative market segment. The FP&A team, tasked with the strategic planning of this venture, would employ RAROC to evaluate whether the estimated returns from this expansion would justify the credit risk exposure. They would analyze historical default rates, market volatility, and economic forecasts to determine the risk-adjusted profitability of the new segment.

However, integrating risk into strategic planning is not limited to financial metrics alone. It encompasses a broader spectrum of potential uncertainties, including operational, reputational, regulatory, and strategic risks. Each of these risk categories must be meticulously assessed and accounted for in the strategic plan. For instance, in our scenario, the FP&A team would also need to consider the operational capacity to support the credit expansion, the reputational implications of entering a new market, and the potential regulatory changes that could impact the segment.

To manage these risks effectively, FP&A professionals leverage a variety of risk assessment methodologies. These methodologies enable them to prioritize risks based on their potential impact and likelihood. Such prioritization facilitates the allocation of resources to manage and mitigate the most significant risks proactively. Tools like the impact vs. probability matrix become invaluable in this context, helping to visualize and compare the array of risks that the strategic plan must address.

Furthermore, the integration of risk into strategic planning is an ongoing process. It is not a one-time assessment but a continuous loop of monitoring, evaluation, and adjustment. As the business environment evolves, new risks emerge, and existing risks change in nature and magnitude. A robust strategic plan remains flexible, adaptable to these shifting conditions. It requires the FP&A team to stay vigilant, regularly updating the risk assessments and adjusting the strategic plan accordingly.

In the final analysis, the integration of risk into strategic planning is a vital discipline that ensures the organization's strategic objectives are pursued with a clear understanding and management of the potential adversities. It is the keystone of a resilient FP&A approach, one that not only aspires to achieve growth but also to sustain it in the face of an ever-changing business landscape.

Aligning Risk with Business Objectives

Central to the strategic orchestration of an organization's vision is the alignment of risk with business objectives. Such alignment demands a nuanced understanding of the organization's mission, the strategic goals it pursues, and the external and internal risk environment that could impede progress. It is a dance of alignment, where the rhythm of risk management must be in step with the melody of organizational aspirations.

The alignment process commences with the articulation of clear business objectives that encapsulate the organization's vision and strategic direction. These objectives serve as the lodestars for the FP&A team's risk assessment efforts, guiding the identification and evaluation of risks that could potentially derail the organization's trajectory towards these goals.

For example, consider a manufacturing firm with the objective to expand its operations into emerging markets over the next five years. The FP&A team, in aligning risk with this objective, would diligently assess a multitude of factors such as geopolitical stability, currency fluctuation, supply chain reliability, and local market competition in the target regions. Each of these risk factors poses a potential threat to the successful achievement of the expansion objective and must be managed accordingly.

Once risks are identified, the next phase is to conduct a

rigorous analysis to ascertain the alignment between these risks and the organizational objectives. This involves the quantification of risks, where possible, and the assessment of their potential impact on specific business goals. Techniques such as sensitivity analysis play a pivotal role here, examining how changes in risk factors could influence the outcomes of business objectives.

Employing the manufacturing firm scenario, the FP&A team might use sensitivity analysis to understand how a 10% fluctuation in exchange rates could impact the profitability of the overseas expansion. Should the analysis reveal a substantial risk to profit margins, the team would then explore hedging strategies to mitigate this currency risk.

Alignment also extends to the measurement and prioritization of risks. Not all risks are created equal; some pose a more immediate threat to the achievement of business objectives, while others may be longer-term concerns. This prioritization is essential for effective resource allocation, ensuring that the firm's efforts and investments in risk management are directed towards the most significant threats.

Furthermore, aligning risk with business objectives requires a close collaboration between the FP&A team and other departments within the organization. This interdisciplinary engagement ensures that risk management strategies are infused with diverse perspectives and expertise, which is crucial for tackling multifaceted risks that span across various business functions.

Lastly, the alignment of risk with business objectives is not a static process but a dynamic one, necessitating continuous monitoring and recalibration. As the business environment evolves, new risks may surface while existing ones may dissipate or change in nature. The FP&A team must, therefore, maintain an adaptable risk management strategy that can respond to these changing conditions, adjusting the alignment of risk management efforts with the business objectives accordingly.

In conclusion, aligning risk with business objectives is a strategic imperative for FP&A. It involves a detailed and ongoing process of risk identification, analysis, prioritization, and management, with a focus on ensuring that risk management strategies are in harmony with the organization's pursuit of its strategic goals. By achieving this alignment, the organization can navigate the uncertain waters of business with confidence, steering towards its vision with resilience and determination.

Risk-Adjusted Return on Capital (RAROC)

In the realm of financial performance measurement, the concept of Risk-Adjusted Return on Capital (RAROC) stands as a beacon of insight, illuminating the true profitability of an undertaking when weighed against the risks incurred. Originating from the banking industry, RAROC has burgeoned into a universal metric that aids organizations in determining the economic value contributed by each unit of risk taken.

The quintessence of RAROC lies in its ability to provide a lens through which the returns on investment can be viewed in the context of the riskiness of those returns. It bridges the chasm between the realms of finance and risk management, fostering an environment where strategic decisions are made not solely on the potential for profit but also on the appetite for risk.

The RAROC metric is computed by dividing the expected return of an investment, adjusted for expected losses (such as credit losses or operational losses), by the economic capital allocated to absorb the uncertainty of these losses. The economic capital represents a buffer of funds set aside to endure potential adverse scenarios, ensuring the organization's solvency and stability.

To illustrate, let us consider a financial institution evaluating two distinct investment opportunities. Investment A offers a high return but is fraught with substantial credit risk, whereas Investment B provides a more modest return with considerably lower risk. An initial appraisal based purely on return might favor Investment A. However, when assessing the RAROC for each investment, the institution may discover that, after adjusting for the elevated risk, Investment B offers a more favorable risk-adjusted return.

Such revelations are pivotal in the strategic allocation of capital. They empower financial stewards to steer resources toward ventures that align with the organization's risk tolerance and strategic objectives. In this way, RAROC becomes not just a yardstick for performance but also a compass for strategic direction.

The implementation of RAROC within an organization necessitates a robust framework for risk assessment and quantification. This involves the development of sophisticated financial models that can accurately forecast expected returns and potential losses under various scenarios. Such models often incorporate elements of probability theory, financial analysis, and scenario simulation to achieve a holistic view of risk.

One of the prime challenges in the application of RAROC is the accurate determination of economic capital. This requires a deep dive into the intricacies of risk types—market, credit, operational, among others—and the potential for their confluence to create complex risk profiles. Organizations may employ advanced statistical techniques such as Monte Carlo simulations or stress testing to gauge the capital needed to absorb these risks.

Moreover, the RAROC metric must be interpreted within the broader context of the organization's strategic imperatives. A high RAROC value, while indicative of favorable risk-adjusted performance, must be balanced against the firm's growth ambitions, market positioning, and competitive dynamics. It is a tool for informed decision-making, not a standalone determiner of strategic action.

RAROC serves as a critical component in the financial leader's arsenal, enabling a calculated assessment of the trade-offs between risk and return. By embedding RAROC into the fabric of financial planning and analysis, organizations can cultivate a disciplined approach to capital allocation—one that respects the boundaries of risk tolerance while pursuing value creation. As markets continue to evolve and new risks emerge, the RAROC framework stands as a testament to the foresight and agility required to navigate the ever-changing landscape of financial risk management.

Risk-based Performance Indicators

In the intricate lattice that is financial governance, risk-based performance indicators (RBPIs) are the pivotal threads that connect risk management to business performance, enabling organizations to measure and monitor the effectiveness of their risk-taking activities against their operational outcomes. RBPIs are not merely metrics but are strategic tools that serve to align risk appetite with business objectives, thereby fostering a risk-aware culture across all levels of the organization.

At the core of RBPIs lies the principle of integrating risk into performance assessment. Traditional performance metrics often focus on financial outcomes without adequately factoring in the risks involved in achieving those outcomes. RBPIs, however, consider the volatility of returns, the likelihood of adverse events, and the impact of risk mitigation strategies, thereby providing a more comprehensive view of an organization's performance under the purview of risk.

To operationalize RBPIs, organizations first need to identify key risk drivers relevant to their strategic goals. These drivers could range from market volatility, credit exposure, and liquidity constraints, to regulatory compliance, cybersecurity threats, and reputational risks. Once identified, these risk drivers are then quantified and integrated into performance measurement systems, creating a multidimensional framework for evaluation.

For instance, a RBPI could be the 'Earnings at Risk' measure, which estimates the potential decrease in earnings over a specific time, given normal market conditions. It allows management to understand the extent to which unexpected market movements could affect the bottom line. Similarly, 'Value at Risk' (VaR) is a widely recognized RBPI that quantifies the maximum loss expected on an investment portfolio over a given time frame and at a certain confidence level.

Another example is the 'Operational Risk-Adjusted Performance Measure' (ORAPM), which adjusts operating income by the capital required to support operational risk. This measure provides insight into the performance of business units by accounting for the operational risks they are exposed to and the effectiveness of the operational risk management in place.

To illustrate the application of RBPIs in decision-making, consider a multinational corporation (MNC) with a diversified investment portfolio across various geographies. One of the RBPIs it employs is the 'Country Risk-Adjusted Return', which adjusts the investment returns from each country for the geopolitical and currency risks associated with that location. This RBPI informs the MNC's capital allocation decisions, ensuring that investments are directed towards regions where the risk-adjusted returns align with the company's risk tolerance levels.

Implementing RBPIs is not without challenges. One significant hurdle is ensuring that the data used to calculate these indicators is accurate, timely, and relevant. This necessitates robust data management and analytics capabilities. Moreover, tailoring RBPIs to the unique aspects of a business requires thorough understanding and expertise —not only of risk management concepts but also of the business's operational environment.

Finally, it is essential to communicate the significance of RBPIs across the organization effectively. This involves training and educating employees at various levels to understand and use these metrics in their day-to-day decision-making processes. By doing so, RBPIs can become an integral part of the organization's performance management system, steering it towards a more risk-aware operational strategy.

In summary, risk-based performance indicators serve as crucial navigational instruments in the vast ocean of corporate performance measurement. By anchoring risk squarely within the context of performance, RBPIs enable organizations to not just chase after ambitious financial targets but to do so with a clear understanding and management of the risks involved. These indicators are the beacons that guide the ship of enterprise toward achieving a balanced and sustainable trajectory of growth and profitability.

Scenario-based Strategy Development

The tumultuous seas of the business world necessitate a compass that not only guides through present uncertainties but also charts a course through the potential storms of the future. Within the strategic arsenal of financial planning and analysis, scenario-based strategy development stands out as a powerful tool that anticipates multiple futures and prepares organizations to navigate through them with foresight and agility.

Scenario-based strategy development is a systematic process that constructs various plausible future states of the world, considering a wide array of variables and their complex interplay. This methodology extends beyond traditional forecasting by challenging the usual assumptions and incorporating external factors that are often volatile and unpredictable, such as geopolitical shifts, economic disruptions, technological advancements, and social dynamics.

A well-crafted scenario-based strategy involves a multi-step approach. Initially, it begins with identifying critical uncertainties—those factors that are both highly uncertain and highly impactful to the organization's operations. These might include new regulatory landscapes, competitor innovations, or shifts in consumer behavior. The next step is to develop a set of diverse scenarios that represent different ways these uncertainties might unfold in the future.

For example, a banking institution may develop scenarios around the future of fintech, ranging from one where regulatory changes favor traditional banking to another where decentralized finance technologies dominate, rendering traditional models obsolete. Each scenario would describe a coherent narrative, including potential changes in market conditions, customer preferences, and technological ecosystems.

Once the scenarios are established, the institution would then analyze the strategic implications of each scenario. This entails understanding the risks and opportunities that each future state presents and formulating strategic responses. These responses might involve diversification of services, investment in technology, or partnerships with fintech startups.

The scenario planning process also demands that strategies be flexible and adaptable. A concept known as 'robust strategy' is often used in this context—it refers to a strategy that performs well across multiple scenarios. For instance, the banking institution might find that investing in digital infrastructure is a robust strategy, as it would serve them well in both a traditional banking-friendly future as well as one dominated by fintech.

Moreover, the process is iterative. As the external environment evolves, scenarios need regular updates to remain relevant, and strategies need recalibration in response to new insights. It's a dynamic process that fosters an organizational culture of continuous learning and adaptability.

An excellent example of scenario-based strategy in action is seen in the oil and gas industry. Companies in this sector often face high levels of environmental and political uncertainties. A leading oil and gas company might develop scenarios that range from a future with stringent climate policies leading to decreased demand for fossil fuels, to another with continued reliance on oil and gas due to slower adoption of renewable energy sources. In response to these scenarios, the company might decide to invest in renewable energy capabilities while also optimizing their existing oil and gas operations for efficiency.

In FP&A, scenario-based strategy development thus serves

as both a telescope to gaze into the future and a blueprint for constructing multiple strategic pathways. It provides a framework within which an organization can test its strategies against possible future events, ensuring preparedness and resilience. This forward-thinking approach allows financial leaders to make informed decisions, allocate resources prudently, and steer the organization confidently into the future amid the myriad possibilities that lie ahead.

Risk Communication and Reporting

In the labyrinthine world of FP&A, the threads that hold the fabric of financial strategy together are woven with the twin fibers of risk communication and reporting. These processes are crucial for elucidating complex risk landscapes and ensuring that all stakeholders grasp the financial narrative with clarity and insight.

Risk communication is an art—balancing transparency with discretion, it involves conveying the inherent uncertainties and potential impacts of financial risks to stakeholders in an understandable and actionable manner. Effective risk communication is proactive, engaging, and tailored to the informational needs of diverse audiences, from board members to investors, and from employees to regulators.

To illustrate, let us consider a financial institution facing the risk of loan defaults due to an economic downturn. The art of risk communication in this scenario involves not just stating the potential loss figures, but also explaining the broader economic context, the institution's exposure to various market segments, the anticipated default rates, and the mitigative actions being undertaken. The CFO plays a pivotal role, translating data into strategic insight, ensuring that the board can make decisions with a full understanding of the risk spectrum.

Reporting, on the other hand, is the science of risk communication. It is the structured and periodic dissemination of risk information through formal channels. Risk reports must be clear, concise, and consistent, enabling stakeholders to track changes in the risk profile over time and measure the effectiveness of risk management strategies. They often take the form of dashboards, executive summaries, and detailed risk analyses, containing both qualitative assessments and quantitative metrics.

A practical example of risk reporting can be seen in the annual reports of public companies, which include detailed sections on risk factors affecting the business. These sections are carefully crafted to provide shareholders with a transparent view of the challenges the company faces, ranging from operational risks to cyber threats, and from market volatility to regulatory changes.

Within the framework of risk communication and reporting, it is also vital to consider the frequency and channels of communication. Some risks warrant real-time alerts, while others may be discussed in quarterly risk reviews. Digitally savvy companies leverage intranets, corporate social networks, and even mobile apps to disseminate risk information, ensuring that it is accessible and timely.

The fusion of communication and reporting is not without its challenges. One must navigate the delicate balance between alarmism and complacency, ensuring that stakeholders are concerned enough to take necessary actions without inducing undue panic. Moreover, the evolving regulatory landscape demands that reporting standards adapt to ensure compliance with new requirements, such as those arising from changing privacy laws or sustainability reporting standards.

A case in point is the adoption of the Task Force on Climate-related Financial Disclosures (TCFD) recommendations by financial firms worldwide. These guidelines encourage companies to report on the financial implications of climate-related risks and opportunities. Adopting such frameworks not only enhances transparency but also positions the company as a leader in addressing global challenges.

Risk communication and reporting serve as the neural network of the FP&A function, transmitting vital signals that enable the organization to respond to risks with intelligence and agility. It is through these channels that financial leaders craft the story of risk—engaging, enlightening, and equipping stakeholders to partake in the stewardship of the company's financial voyage through uncertain waters.

Dashboarding and Executive Summaries

The consummate art of distilling complex data into cogent, digestible insights is epitomized in the creation of dashboards and executive summaries. These tools are indispensable for financial leaders who must swiftly convey the essence of an organization's risk profile to busy executives and decision-makers.

Dashboards are the epitome of this distillation process—a visual interface that presents the most critical risk metrics immediately. Imagine a digital mosaic, each tile displaying a key performance indicator (KPI), that collectively offers an immediate pulse on the organization's financial health. For instance, a risk dashboard for a multinational corporation may highlight currency exposure, credit default swaps spreads, and commodity price fluctuations, each color-coded to signify status relative to the risk appetite.

Executive summaries complement dashboards by providing a narrative that contextualizes the data. These high-level overviews interpret the graphical representations for stakeholders, allowing them to absorb pertinent information without wading through reams of detailed reports. An executive summary might describe the potential impacts of a newly identified geopolitical risk on the supply chain, summarized in a concise paragraph with bullet points highlighting actionable strategies.

Let's consider a case study of a retail giant that uses a sophisticated risk dashboard to monitor its global inventory exposure. The dashboard tracks real-time sales data, supplier risks, and inventory levels across continents, alerting the FP&A team to potential stockouts or overstock situations that could impact profitability. The executive summary accompanying this dashboard provides a succinct analysis of the data, flagging any areas that require immediate attention from the leadership team.

In the realm of FP&A, the utility of dashboards and executive summaries extends beyond mere presentation.

They serve as a strategic tool for risk management, enabling leaders to monitor risk trends over time, identify emerging threats, and assess the effectiveness of mitigation strategies. These summaries enable decision-makers to pivot quickly, reallocating resources or adjusting strategies in response to the dynamic financial landscape.

To craft a compelling dashboard, FP&A professionals must first identify the most relevant KPIs that align with the organization's strategic objectives and risk profile. For a financial services firm, these might include loan delinquency rates, market liquidity ratios, and yield curve spreads. The dashboard should be intuitive, allowing users to drill down for more details or to interact with the data to test various scenarios.

Similarly, an executive summary must be thoughtfully composed, with a clear structure that highlights key findings, implications, and recommended courses of action. It should anticipate the questions and concerns of its audience, providing them with the assurance that risks are being monitored and addressed competently.

In a rapidly advancing digital age, the integration of advanced analytics and machine learning into dashboarding can elevate the practice to new heights. For example, predictive analytics integrated into a dashboard can forecast potential risk scenarios based on historical data, allowing financial leaders to proactively manage risks before they materialize.

In conclusion, dashboards and executive summaries are not just reporting tools; they are instruments of strategic governance that empower financial leaders to steer their organizations through the intricate web of risks in the modern business environment. By harnessing the power of these tools, FP&A professionals can transform data into strategic foresight, fostering a culture of informed decision-making that is responsive to the ever-evolving mosaic of risk.

Communication Strategies for Stakeholders

Navigating the multifaceted landscape of stakeholder communication is akin to conducting an orchestra—each instrument, or in our case, each stakeholder group, requires a unique approach to harmonize with the overall symphony of organizational strategy. In the context of FP&A, the ability to articulate risk-related information effectively to diverse stakeholder groups is crucial for maintaining transparency, fostering trust, and facilitating informed decision-making.

Stakeholders in any organization span a broad spectrum, from internal teams such as employees and management to external entities like investors, regulators, and customers. Each group holds distinct concerns and levels of understanding regarding the organization's financial risks. Hence, the communication strategies employed must be tailored to address these variances while ensuring a cohesive and consistent message.

Consider an FP&A professional who must communicate the potential financial impact of a new regulatory change to different stakeholder groups. For the internal management team, the communication might involve a detailed analysis of the regulation's implications on financial projections and strategic initiatives. This could take the form of in-depth reports or presentations, supplemented by workshops to explore strategic responses.

In contrast, when addressing investors, the communication strategy might focus on how the regulatory change affects the investment thesis, emphasizing the long-term financial health of the organization and the measures being taken to mitigate any adverse effects. This might be conveyed through investor briefings, quarterly earnings calls, or targeted communications that align with the cadence of financial disclosures.

A poignant example can be drawn from a technology firm grappling with the introduction of stringent data privacy laws. The FP&A team might utilize a multi-channel communication strategy, comprising webinars for employees to understand the operational impacts, press releases for media and the public to ensure brand integrity, and investor fact sheets that outline the strategic adjustments to safeguard profitability.

Effective communication strategies also incorporate feedback mechanisms, enabling stakeholders to pose questions, express concerns, and provide input. This two-way dialogue is essential for building a risk-aware culture and can be facilitated through interactive Q&A sessions, surveys, or dedicated communication platforms.

For external stakeholders like regulators, the strategy may involve more formalized reporting structures. The communication must align with statutory requirements, ensuring compliance and avoiding misinterpretations. Regular meetings and updates may also be part of the strategy to maintain an open line of communication and address any regulatory feedback proactively.

Another dimension of stakeholder communication is crisis communication. In times of financial upheaval or significant risk events, FP&A professionals must be adept at swift and clear communication to prevent misinformation and panic. For example, during a market downturn that impacts the organization's financial stability, a well-crafted crisis communication plan would be activated, delivering timely updates to stakeholders through press statements, dedicated hotline numbers for investor queries, and social media updates to reach the broader public.

To underscore the importance of a tailored communication strategy, let's highlight the case of a global bank that faced credit risk exposure due to an economic downturn. The FP&A team devised a communication plan that included personalized emails to high-net-worth clients detailing the robustness of their portfolios, town hall meetings with employees to address job security concerns, and press conferences to reinforce the bank's stability to the market.

In crafting effective communication strategies for stakeholders, FP&A experts must consider the modality, frequency, and content of the messages. By leveraging various communication channels—such as reports, newsletters, social media, and face-to-face meetings—they can ensure that each stakeholder receives information in a manner that is both accessible and comprehensible.

In summary, communication strategies for stakeholders within the FP&A framework are not a one-size-fits-all proposition. They require a nuanced understanding of each group's informational needs and preferences. By adopting a stakeholder-centric approach and utilizing diverse communication tools and techniques, FP&A professionals can ensure that risk information is transmitted with clarity, accuracy, and strategic intent, thereby safeguarding the organization's integrity and reinforcing its position in the marketplace.

Regulatory Reporting Requirements

The granular intricacies of regulatory reporting form a critical lattice within the financial planning and analysis framework, ensuring accountability, transparency, and adherence to the established financial statutes. In depth, regulatory reporting is a meticulous process, one that demands both precision and strategic forethought, serving as a fiduciary compass that guides an organization's financial disclosures.

At this juncture, we turn our focus to the labyrinthine domain of regulatory reporting requirements—a bastion of compliance that FP&A professionals must navigate with adept proficiency. The pivotal role of regulatory reporting in safeguarding the integrity of financial markets cannot be overstated. It is a mechanism that enables regulatory bodies to monitor an institution's financial health, ensure market stability, and protect investors from undue risks.

The process of regulatory reporting is akin to a multi-tiered edifice, where each level corresponds to a different regulatory demand. FP&A professionals must first lay the foundation by identifying the relevant regulations that pertain to their industry and jurisdiction. This could range from the Sarbanes-Oxley Act (SOX) in the United States, which mandates stringent controls on financial reporting, to the Markets in Financial Instruments Directive (MiFID II) in Europe, which introduces robust requirements for financial instruments transactions.

Illustrating the practical application, let us consider a global bank that operates across multiple regulatory environments. Its FP&A team must compile comprehensive reports that satisfy the diverse requirements of the Federal Reserve, the European Central Bank, and other financial authorities. Each report is a mosaic of data, weaved from various business units and functions, and must be presented in formats conforming to the distinct regulatory standards, such as XBRL for electronic submissions.

In the sphere of securities, an FP&A team may be tasked with reporting on the organization's exposure to market risks. This involves compiling detailed information on asset valuations, investment portfolios, and risk management strategies. The reports must be meticulously structured to align with regulations such as the Securities and Exchange Commission (SEC) rules for listed companies, which demand regular disclosures of material financial information.

Evolving regulations also play a significant role in shaping reporting requirements. For instance, with the advent of the General Data Protection Regulation (GDPR), companies are now required to report any data breaches that may have financial implications. This necessitates a robust system to track and report incidents within the stringent timelines imposed by the regulation.

To breathe life into abstract concepts, take the case of a

multinational technology firm that must report its financial performance under the International Financial Reporting Standards (IFRS). The FP&A team collaborates with the legal and compliance departments to decipher the nuances of IFRS 9, which deals with financial instruments, ensuring that all relevant transactions are recorded, classified, and reported in compliance with the standard's expectations.

Moreover, the landscape of regulatory reporting is not static. It is continually reshaped by financial innovations and systemic global shifts. An FP&A professional must stay abreast of emerging regulations, such as those pertaining to cryptocurrency assets or sustainability reporting standards, which are rapidly gaining prominence in response to societal and environmental concerns.

Consider the scenario where a company is navigating the complexities of carbon credit trading and must report its transactions and holdings in line with the Task Force on Climate-related Financial Disclosures (TCFD) recommendations. The FP&A team must develop reporting processes that aggregate data on emissions, assess financial risks related to climate change, and communicate the findings effectively to stakeholders and regulators.

In the realm of practical execution, effective regulatory reporting requires a confluence of rigorous data management, astute analytical capabilities, and a comprehensive understanding of the legal frameworks. FP&A professionals often employ specialized software and reporting tools to aggregate data from across the organization, ensuring consistency, accuracy, and timeliness of the information reported.

Hence, regulatory reporting is not merely a statutory obligation but a strategic endeavour—one that demands meticulous attention to detail, a proactive stance on compliance, and an unwavering commitment to upholding the highest standards of financial transparency and integrity.

In conclusion, as this section of the book unfolds, it becomes evident that regulatory reporting is a veritable linchpin in the machinery of financial governance—a discipline that requires FP&A professionals to be vigilant custodians of fiduciary truth. Through a synthesis of examples and theoretical detail, we have illuminated the contours of this essential function, equipping the reader with the knowledge to excel in the stringent world of financial reporting requirements.

Real-time Risk Data Dissemination

In the pulsating nerve center of financial operations, the swift dissemination of risk data in real-time is a vital artery, carrying the lifeblood of information that enables proactive management and nimble strategic pivots. The real-time dissemination of risk data transcends conventional reporting frameworks, offering a high-resolution lens through which financial landscapes are scrutinized, and potential hazards are identified with immediacy.

Embarking on an exploration of real-time risk data dissemination, we delve into its core, understanding it as the rapid transmission of pertinent risk information across an organization's stakeholders. This process facilitates an instantaneous feedback loop, empowering decision-makers with the agility to respond to market dynamics and operational anomalies as they occur.

Picture an international trading floor where milliseconds can mean the difference between substantial gains and staggering losses. Here, real-time risk data flows seamlessly, alerting traders to sudden shifts in market sentiment, volatility spikes, or liquidity crunches. The use of sophisticated analytics platforms enables the distillation of complex datasets into actionable insights, which are then broadcast across digital dashboards, ensuring that every stakeholder from the junior analyst to the Chief Risk Officer (CRO) is synchronized in their awareness of the prevailing risk environment.

In an illustrative scenario, consider a financial institution that must monitor its credit exposure to various industries. The advent of an unforeseen event—such as a regulatory change or a geopolitical crisis—could rapidly alter the default risks associated with certain sectors. Real-time risk data dissemination allows the institution to detect these developments as they unfurl, enabling swift adjustments to credit limits and investment strategies.

This dynamic transmission of risk data is fueled by advancements in technology, notably through the integration of Internet of Things (IoT) devices, cloud computing, and advanced network protocols that ensure data integrity and security during transmission. For instance, an energy company with a distributed network of assets might rely on IoT sensors to relay real-time data on operational risks, such as equipment malfunctions or safety breaches, to a centralized risk management system.

The efficiency of real-time risk data dissemination is further amplified by the advent of machine learning algorithms, which can parse through vast troves of data, identifying patterns and correlations that might elude the human eye. These algorithms can forecast potential risk events, sending preemptive alerts and recommendations to portfolio managers, who can then take immediate action to mitigate risks.

In practical terms, the utility of real-time risk data dissemination can be observed in the realm of cyber security. Cyber threats pose a significant and ever-evolving risk to the financial sector. Through real-time monitoring and alert systems, an organization's cyber defense team can detect intrusion attempts, data breaches, or suspicious activities, enabling them to initiate countermeasures without delay, thereby safeguarding sensitive financial information and maintaining operational continuity.

The process of real-time risk data dissemination is not without its challenges. It requires a robust technological infrastructure, capable of handling large volumes of data with low latency. Furthermore, it necessitates a cultural shift within organizations, where data-driven decision-making becomes the norm, and where silos are dismantled to foster holistic risk awareness.

To illustrate how real-time risk data can create a transformative impact, we can look to the insurance industry. Here, telematics devices in vehicles convey real-time data to insurers, who can assess driver behavior and adjust premiums accordingly, virtually in real-time. This not only enhances risk assessment but also incentivizes safer driving practices among policyholders.

In closing, real-time risk data dissemination stands as a paragon of modern risk management—an essential component that equips financial professionals with the velocity and acumen required to navigate the turbulent seas of market uncertainty. As we progress through this textual voyage, readers will grasp the paramountcy of this capability in constructing a resilient and responsive financial planning and analysis function.

Capital Allocation Decisions

Seamlessly dovetailed into the fabric of fiscal governance, capital allocation decisions represent the strategic compass guiding an organization's voyage towards its long-term objectives. This intricate process involves the deliberate and meticulous deployment of financial resources into investments and projects that are anticipated to yield optimal returns, buttress competitive advantage, and ensure the enduring sustenance of the enterprise.

In the theatre of financial planning and analysis, capital allocation is akin to the experienced hand of a maestro, orchestrating a symphony of investment decisions, each note resonating with the potential for growth, innovation, and value creation. Capital allocation decisions are the fulcrum upon which an organization's financial stability and growth trajectory are balanced. They are the crucible within which risk and opportunity are melded to forge a resilient and dynamic portfolio.

To elucidate the theory underpinning capital allocation, let us consider the principle of resource scarcity. It is this scarcity that predicates the need for judicious investment choices. Organizations must evaluate a spectrum of projects, each vying for a slice of the finite pie of capital. The strategy employed in this evaluative process is multifaceted, incorporating financial models, forecasting techniques, and risk assessments to project the potential outcomes and returns of various investment opportunities.

Consider a global technology firm standing at the crossroads of innovation, deciding whether to invest in the development of a new line of consumer electronics or to expand its cloud computing services. The former promises immediate market impact and brand visibility, while the latter offers sustained revenue streams and strategic positioning in a burgeoning sector. The company must weigh these options, considering not only the expected financial returns but also strategic congruence with its overarching vision.

In practical application, capital allocation decisions often pivot on the concept of the risk-return trade-off. Organizations must navigate this trade-off by employing tools such as the risk-return matrix, which plots potential investments according to their expected yields and associated risks. This matrix serves as a navigational aid, directing capital towards ventures that align with the company's determined risk appetite and targeted returns.

One illustrative example of capital allocation in action is the deployment of funds towards research and development (R&D) within the pharmaceutical industry. Here, the decision to allocate capital to R&D projects is fuelled by the prospect of discovering breakthrough therapies that promise substantial returns. However, the inherently high risk of failure in drug development necessitates a rigorous evaluation of the potential drugs' success probabilities and the anticipated market demand.

Another facet of capital allocation is the consideration of opportunity costs—the benefits foregone by choosing one investment over another. An enterprise must contemplate the alternative uses of its capital, ensuring that the selected investments are not merely good but are the best among all possible options. This introspection often requires organizations to forego short-term gains in favor of long-term strategic benefits.

Capital allocation also intersects with the domain of corporate finance through the utilization of financial instruments such as debt and equity. An organization may, for instance, decide to issue corporate bonds to raise capital for a new manufacturing facility. The decision to use debt over equity or internal funding sources must be carefully calibrated, considering the cost of capital, the impact on financial leverage, and the prevailing market conditions.

In a world increasingly shaped by sustainability concerns, capital allocation decisions are also being scrutinized through an environmental, social, and governance (ESG) lens. Investors and stakeholders are placing greater emphasis on how an organization's investments contribute to social and environmental objectives, alongside financial performance. This shift has led companies to integrate ESG factors into their capital allocation frameworks, recognizing the long-term value of responsible investment.

The discipline of capital allocation is a testament to the intricate dance of financial strategy, requiring a blend of analytical rigor, foresight, and adaptability. As stewards of an organization's financial resources, FP&A professionals must hone their acumen in this discipline, balancing the scales of fiscal prudence and strategic ambition to chart a course for prosperity and growth.

Balancing Risk and Opportunity Costs

Within the grand strategy of financial stewardship, the balancing act between the risk inherent in any venture and the opportunity costs of foregone alternatives is the fulcrum upon which the financial fate of an organization might pivot. This delicate equilibrium requires a nuanced understanding of the complex interplay between prospective rewards and the ancillary roads not taken. A deep dive into this intricate theoretical landscape reveals the contours and nuances of decision-making that define the essence of prudent financial planning and analysis.

Let us deconstruct the concept of opportunity cost. It is the potential benefit an organization misses when choosing one alternative over another. The subtleties of this concept are not lost upon the financial maestro who must weigh the unseen against the seen, the future potential against the present choice. It is the path untrodden that is measured against the path that is chosen, and it is in this context that the organization must assess the inherent risk of any given investment.

An illustrative example of this principle at work could be drawn from a scenario faced by a burgeoning software company. The firm stands at a precipice, deciding whether to allocate significant capital towards the expansion of its current flagship product line or to invest in an ambitious new project that leverages emerging technologies. The decision is complex, with the risk associated with the new technology's developmental uncertainty contrasting sharply with the opportunity cost of not capitalizing on the established product's market presence and customer base.

To navigate these waters, the firm might employ decision trees or real options analysis to illuminate the potential outcomes of each path. These tools allow for a visual and quantitative representation of the different choices and their associated risks and benefits, offering a clear framework for decision-making.

In practice, the rigorous application of cost-benefit analysis serves as a cornerstone for evaluating opportunity costs. This analysis entails a systematic approach to estimating the strengths and weaknesses of alternatives, allowing for the comparison of the expected balance of benefits and costs, including foregone opportunities. For instance, in the case of a city government considering building a new park, the opportunity cost might be the alternative public works that could have been funded with the same resources, such as infrastructure improvements or educational programs.

Another dimension of balancing risk and opportunity costs is the concept of the time value of money. This principle posits that a dollar today is worth more than a dollar tomorrow due to its potential earning capacity. As such, the opportunity cost of investing capital in one project must be weighed against the potential earnings from alternate investments over the same time horizon. In the case of a multinational corporation deliberating whether to use excess cash to invest in a safe but low-yield bond or in a risky but potentially lucrative new market, the time value of money is a critical factor to consider.

Organizations also grapple with the opportunity cost of limited human resources. For instance, a talented project team could be tasked with enhancing the user experience for an existing product or diverted to innovate a new offering. Each option bears potential risks—either the risk of stagnation by not innovating or the risk of diluting the brand's core competencies with an unsuccessful new venture.

In strategic decision-making, the balance of risk and opportunity costs must also account for the broader macroeconomic and sector-specific trends. A telecommunications company, for example, must survey the landscape of technological advancements and regulatory shifts to determine whether investing in expanded network infrastructure is more advantageous than diverting funds into strategic acquisitions.

The art of balancing risk and opportunity costs is an exercise in foresight, strategy, and judgment. It demands that FP&A professionals not only analyze the present landscape but also anticipate future shifts in market dynamics, competitive pressures, and internal capabilities. By meticulously quantifying and qualifying these factors, organizations can make informed decisions that balance the scales of risk and return, paving the way for a future of financial robustness and strategic triumph.

Capital Budgeting under Uncertainty

Capital budgeting is a critical process—one that demands a rigorous analytical approach, especially under the shadow of uncertainty. It is the process by which an organization decides how to invest its scarce capital resources to achieve maximum return while navigating treacherous pathways of risk.

The theoretical bedrock of capital budgeting under uncertainty lies in the recognition that the future is a frontier marked by unpredictable events and shifting sands. Each investment decision, therefore, carries with it a specter of doubt about the accuracy of the projected cash flows, the stability of the economic environment, and the agility of the organization to adapt to unforeseen circumstances.

Let us consider, for example, a renewable energy company facing the decision to invest in a new wind farm project. The project requires significant upfront capital expenditure and promises a stream of future cash flows derived from the sale of electricity. However, the uncertainty is multifaceted: Will government subsidies for renewable energy persist? Will technological advances lower the cost of alternative energy sources, rendering the wind farm less competitive? What if climate patterns change, affecting wind consistency and, consequently, power generation?

This scenario encapsulates the inherent challenges in capital budgeting under uncertainty. To address these challenges, organizations employ several advanced theoretical models and frameworks that incorporate uncertainty into the decision-making process.

One such model is the Net Present Value (NPV) analysis

under uncertainty, which accounts for the time value of money and integrates probability distributions for cash flow variables. Instead of a single point estimate, the NPV model under uncertainty produces a range of possible outcomes, offering a probabilistic assessment of the project's value.

Another critical tool is the Monte Carlo simulation, which enables analysts to model the probability of different outcomes in complex, uncertain scenarios. This stochastic technique uses random sampling to generate a multitude of potential future cash flow paths, thus providing a distribution of NPVs based on the varying underlying assumptions. For the wind farm investment, a Monte Carlo simulation might reveal the probability distribution of returns, considering fluctuating energy prices, maintenance costs, and changes in government policy.

Real options analysis further refines capital budgeting for uncertainty by evaluating the investment as a series of options rather than a one-time decision. This approach acknowledges that management has the flexibility to make future decisions that can affect the outcome of the project. In our wind farm example, a real option might be the ability to expand the project if initial performance exceeds expectations or to abandon it if regulatory changes make it unviable.

Scenario analysis is another critical technique used to evaluate the impacts of different uncertainty factors on a project. It involves developing a small number of scenarios —typically a base case, an optimistic case, and a pessimistic case—and analyzing the outcomes for each. This method allows decision-makers to understand the range of possible outcomes and the impacts of specific variables.

A robust capital budgeting process under uncertainty will also include sensitivity analysis, which investigates how the change in one variable, while all others remain constant, affects the project's NPV. Sensitivity analysis helps identify the variables to which the project's success is most sensitive, offering a lens through which management can scrutinize key assumptions and prepare for potential variances in those factors.

In addition to these quantitative techniques, qualitative assessments play a complementary role. These might include evaluating the strategic fit of the investment with the company's long-term goals, the potential for synergy with existing projects, and the alignment with the company's risk tolerance and values.

Capital budgeting under uncertainty is a multifaceted exercise that intertwines financial theory with strategic thinking. It requires FP&A professionals to harness a blend of sophisticated analytical tools and shrewd business acumen. Through rigorous analysis and strategic foresight, they can illuminate the path forward, transforming the fog of uncertainty into a landscape of informed, strategic investment decisions that underpin the financial fortitude of their organizations.

Investment Portfolio Diversification

Investment portfolio diversification is akin to the deployment of an array of pieces, each moving with distinct capabilities, poised to protect the king—here, the investor's capital—from unexpected assaults. It is the strategic art of spreading investments across various assets to reduce exposure to any single risk or market fluctuation—a tactic as prudent as it is time-honored in the realm of investment management.

Diversification is rooted in the fundamental principle that different asset classes and securities do not move in perfect synchrony. When one asset experiences a downturn, another may hold steady or even appreciate, mitigating overall portfolio risk and smoothing returns over time. The theoretical underpinnings of this approach are encapsulated in Modern Portfolio Theory (MPT), introduced by Harry Markowitz in the 1950s, which posits that an investor can achieve an 'efficient frontier'—a portfolio offering the maximum possible expected return for a given level of risk.

To comprehend the practical implementation of portfolio diversification, let us envision an investor seeking to construct a diversified portfolio. The investor's starting point is asset allocation, deciding the proportional representation of various asset classes such as stocks, bonds, real estate, and commodities. Each asset class carries distinct characteristics in terms of risk, return, and correlation with other investments.

For instance, equities are known for their potential for high returns but come with significant volatility, while government bonds often provide steady, if modest, income streams, with lower risk levels. Real estate investments can offer a hedge against inflation and an alternative source of returns, whereas commodities such as gold often serve as safe havens during times of market stress.

Within each asset class, further diversification is achieved by spreading investments across sectors, industries, and geographies. Equities might be divided among tech innovators in Silicon Valley, healthcare providers in Europe, and consumer goods manufacturers in emerging markets. This geographic and sectoral dispersion insulates the portfolio from localized economic downturns or industry-specific disruptions.

Consider an example where a global pandemic impacts the tourism and travel industry; an investor with a diversified portfolio would likely suffer less than one heavily concentrated in airline and hotel stocks. Conversely, healthcare and technology sectors might experience a surge, offsetting losses and underscoring the virtues of diversification.

To elucidate, let's take a closer look at a practical application of this principle. A portfolio may include shares of a multinational tech corporation like Microsoft, which could benefit from increased demand for cloud services and remote work solutions. Simultaneously, it could hold stock in Procter & Gamble, a company with consumer staples that are essential regardless of economic conditions, thereby providing stability. By including both, the investor can balance the portfolio's risk and potential returns.

Another facet of diversification involves the temporal dimension—timing. By staggering investments across various maturities and investment horizons, investors can manage liquidity needs and interest rate exposure, a technique known as laddering. A bond ladder, for instance, consists of bonds that mature at different intervals, allowing the investor to reinvest proceeds at regular intervals and potentially capture higher yields as interest rates fluctuate.

While diversification can't eliminate risk entirely, it is an indispensable component in the investor's toolkit, particularly in an unpredictable landscape where change is the only constant. It requires a keen eye for correlation matrices, an understanding of the cyclical nature of economies, and a commitment to rebalance the portfolio periodically to maintain the desired risk-return profile.

Portfolio diversification is a dynamic process that evolves in tandem with market conditions, investor goals, and the global economic milieu. It is not a one-time set-and-forget strategy but a continuous endeavor—one that requires vigilance, adaptability, and an unwavering focus on the goal of safeguarding and growing the investor's wealth in the face of an uncertain future.

The Role of Hedging Strategies

Embarking on a journey through the nuanced landscape of financial security, one must not overlook the pivotal role that hedging strategies play in safeguarding an investment portfolio. Hedging—akin to an insurance policy in the realm of finance—is a meticulously crafted approach that protects an investment from adverse price movements, effectively reducing the risk of monetary loss.

The fundamental premise of hedging is not to eliminate risk altogether but to manage and control it strategically. It is a process wherein an investor takes an offsetting position in a related security, such as derivatives, to mitigate the potential loss in the holdings of the underlying asset. These financial instruments—futures, options, and swaps—serve as the bulwarks against the unforeseen and often unwelcome market fluctuations.

To illustrate, consider the investor who holds a substantial position in crude oil. Aware that a geopolitical event could precipitate a precipitous drop in oil prices, they may opt to hedge by taking a position in crude oil futures contracts that lock in a sale price. Should the market price decline, the gain from the futures contract would offset the loss in the value of the physical oil holdings.

Futures contracts are an archetype of hedging instruments where two parties agree to buy or sell an asset at a specified future date and price. The contract's value fluctuates with the underlying asset's price, providing a hedge against spot market volatility. For instance, an airline company may use futures to hedge against the volatility of jet fuel prices, thereby stabilizing their operating expenses and protecting their bottom line.

Options, another cornerstone of hedging, offer the holder the right, but not the obligation, to buy or sell an asset at a predetermined price before a specified expiration. A put option, for example, allows an investor to hedge against a potential decline in the stock price. If the stock price falls below the strike price, the put option's value increases, offsetting the loss in the stock investment.

Swaps, meanwhile, allow two counterparties to exchange cash flows or other financial instruments. Interest rate swaps, for example, enable companies to hedge against the risk of fluctuating interest rates by exchanging variable-rate interest payments for fixed-rate payments, thus ensuring predictability in their debt obligations.

A real-world application of hedging can be seen in the agricultural sector, where farmers hedge against the risk of price drops in their crops. By entering futures contracts, they secure a guaranteed price for their harvest, providing income stability regardless of market volatility. This financial maneuver allows for consistent budgeting and financial planning, irrespective of the whims of the market.

Hedging strategies are not solely the province of large institutions or wealthy individuals. Retail investors can also benefit from these techniques. For example, an investor worried about a market downturn might purchase index put options to hedge their equity portfolio. If the market falls, the increased value of the put options can help reduce the portfolio's overall losses.

It is imperative to note, however, that hedging is not a one-size-fits-all solution. The cost of implementing these strategies must be weighed against the potential benefits. Options contracts, for instance, come with premiums that can erode profits if the hedged risk does not materialize. Therefore, the decision to hedge must be made with a clear understanding of the trade-offs involved.

Hedging strategies are a sophisticated and essential component of modern investment portfolio management. They provide a buffer against financial storms, allowing investors to navigate the tumultuous seas of the market with greater confidence and serenity. By understanding and employing these strategies judiciously, investors can protect their assets, ensuring that their financial voyage remains on course towards the desired destination of growth and stability.

Linking Risk Management to Value Creation

Risk management and value creation are the twin pillars upon which the temple of corporate prosperity is built. Though seemingly disparate in their nature—one guards against potential downfall, and the other champions growth—they are inextricably linked in a symbiotic dance that, when choreographed with finesse, can elevate an organization to the pinnacle of fiscal success.

Risk management, traditionally viewed as a defensive mechanism to shield an enterprise from financial hazards, has evolved. No longer is it merely a bulwark against volatility; it has been reimagined as a strategic ally in value creation. This paradigm shift has brought forth a realization that managing risk, when executed with strategic forethought, not only preserves capital but also acts as a catalyst for unlocking opportunities that engender incremental value.

Consider the analogy of an alchemist, transforming base metals into gold. The modern Chief Financial Officer (CFO) assumes the role of this alchemist, with risk management being the crucible in which value is forged. A holistic, proactive approach to risk—anticipating, identifying, and mitigating potential threats—can pave the way for safe exploration and harnessing of lucrative avenues that might otherwise be shrouded in uncertainty.

A prime example lies in the realm of mergers and acquisitions (M&A). Here, rigorous risk assessment serves as the groundwork for identifying strategic fits—a precursor to value accretion. By meticulously analyzing the target entity's market position, financial health, and cultural compatibility, a company can mitigate the risks associated with integration, thereby smoothing the path towards realizing synergies and driving long-term shareholder value.

Innovation, too, is a beneficiary of adept risk management. By quantifying the risks associated with research and development (R&D) endeavors, firms can allocate capital judiciously towards projects with the most favorable risk-reward profiles. This measured approach does not stifle innovation; rather, it nurtures it, ensuring that resources are channeled into ventures that promise the greatest potential for market disruption and value augmentation.

Furthermore, an organization's risk management framework can enhance its value proposition by bolstering investor confidence. A transparent and robust risk management system signifies to shareholders and potential investors that the company is vigilant, well-prepared for contingencies, and poised for sustainable growth. It serves as an assurance that their capital is shepherded with prudence and strategic intent.

Yet, one must tread with care, for the relationship between risk management and value creation is delicate and nuanced. Overzealous risk aversion can hamper growth, while excessive risk-seeking can jeopardize stability. The key lies in balance—striking a harmonic chord between safeguarding assets and fostering innovation.

To encapsulate these concepts, let us consider a tech conglomerate venturing into the nascent field of quantum computing. The risks are manifold: technological complexity, market uncertainty, significant R&D expenditure. However, by delineating these risks—conducting scenario analyses, stress testing development timelines, and rigorously evaluating market potential—the conglomerate can prudently navigate this high-stakes venture. The result is a calibrated balance between the pursuit of breakthrough technology and the preservation of shareholder value.

Effective risk management is not a mere shield against the slings and arrows of outrageous fortune but a strategic sword wielded to carve out value and craft a legacy of growth. It is a testament to the alchemy of finance, where the careful stewardship of risk transmutes potential peril into excellent opportunity.

Enhancing Shareholder Value Through Risk Management

The complexities of risk management are often likened to a game of chess, where each move is calculated with precision and foresight, anticipating fluctuations in the market and safeguarding the company's assets. In this strategic interplay, the enhancement of shareholder value emerges as the endgame—the objective that gives purpose to every risk-mitigated maneuver on the corporate board.

Shareholder value is the litmus test of a company's success, reflecting the collective judgment of the market on its ability to generate profits and grow sustainably. It's a measure keenly observed by every stakeholder with vested interests, from the smallest retail investor to the largest institutional shareholder. As such, the integration of risk management into the broader corporate strategy becomes vital, not only to protect but also to increase the wealth of shareholders.

To delve into the theoretical underpinnings of enhancing shareholder value through risk management, one must examine the core tenets that govern this practice. The primary principle is the alignment of risk management with the company's strategic objectives and the expectations of its shareholders. This alignment ensures that risk is not merely avoided but is managed in a way that contributes to achieving the strategic goals and maximizing returns.

For instance, a multinational corporation might face currency fluctuation risks. The traditional risk-averse approach might lead to over-hedging, effectively locking in current rates and preventing the firm from benefiting from future favorable shifts. A more nuanced risk management strategy would employ selective hedging, allowing the firm to take advantage of positive currency trends while still protecting against severe devaluations, thus optimizing the outcome for shareholders.

Another aspect of enhancing shareholder value through risk management is the concept of risk-adjusted performance metrics. These metrics, such as Economic Value Added (EVA) or Risk-Adjusted Return on Capital (RAROC), introduce a dimension of risk consideration into the evaluation of the company's performance. By focusing on these metrics, management can make informed decisions that account for the cost of risk and the potential for value creation.

A practical application can be observed in the banking industry, where RAROC is employed to assess the performance of different business units. By adjusting for the risk of loans and investments, banks can identify which units are truly contributing to shareholder value and allocate capital accordingly, enhancing overall profitability and stability.

Communication also plays an indispensable role in the relationship between risk management and shareholder value. Transparent disclosure of risk management practices assures shareholders and potential investors of the company's commitment to prudent financial stewardship. This transparency can be achieved through detailed reporting in annual reports, investor presentations, and other regulatory filings that outline the company's risk profile, mitigation strategies, and the impact on financial performance.

To illustrate, a company facing supply chain vulnerabilities might openly discuss its risk mitigation initiatives, such as diversifying suppliers or investing in technology that enhances logistical efficiency. By doing so, it instills confidence in shareholders that management is actively addressing potential disruptions, thereby protecting—and potentially enhancing—shareholder value.

Lastly, the integration of a robust risk management culture into the organizational fabric is essential for sustained value creation. This culture should permeate all levels of the company, from the boardroom to the frontline employees. It encapsulates the principles of continuous risk assessment, proactive mitigation, and collective responsibility for risk oversight.

Consider a technology firm that is exposed to rapid obsolescence risks. By fostering a culture that encourages innovation and agility, the firm positions itself to anticipate market trends, adapt its product offerings, and maintain a competitive edge. Such a culture not only mitigates the risk of obsolescence but also drives the company's growth trajectory, contributing to an increase in shareholder value.

Enhancing shareholder value through risk management is a multifaceted endeavor that demands strategic integration, performance measurement, transparent communication, and cultural embracement. By weaving these elements into the fabric of corporate governance, companies can transform risk management from a defensive tactic into a strategic tool that propels shareholder value to new heights.

Risk and Reward Considerations in Mergers and Acquisitions

In the dynamic landscape of mergers and acquisitions (M&A), the scales of risk and reward are perpetually in flux, requiring acuity and nimbleness from the financial architects orchestrating these corporate transformations. M&A transactions are complex ventures fraught with potential perils but also ripe with opportunities for substantial gains—a dichotomy that must be meticulously navigated to secure success.

At the heart of any M&A transaction lies the strategic intent to create value that exceeds the sum of the individual entities. The theoretical framework for understanding risk and reward in M&A is predicated on the doctrine of synergistic advantage. Synergy—the notion that the combined entity's performance will outstrip the aggregate capabilities of the separate companies—is the promised land that deal-makers strive to reach.

However, the path to achieving synergy is strewn with risks, both overt and covert. Due diligence, the rigorous investigative process that precedes any M&A deal, serves as the bulwark against unforeseen hazards. It encompasses a thorough examination of the target company's financial statements, legal obligations, operational efficiencies, and cultural dynamics. The acquirer's ability to uncover and quantify these risks directly influences the transaction's reward potential.

For instance, in assessing a target company's financial health, the acquirer must probe beyond the surface-level indicators such as revenue and profit margins. A deep analysis of cash flow patterns, debt obligations, and contingent liabilities can reveal the actual financial robustness and the potential impact on the acquirer's balance sheet. One prominent example is the acquisition of Autonomy by Hewlett-Packard in 2011, where post-deal revelations of financial irregularities led to a write-down of nearly $9 billion—an exemplar of overlooked financial risks resulting in significant value destruction.

Legal and regulatory scrutiny is an aspect where risk can sharply incline, especially in cross-border transactions. Considerations must include compliance with antitrust laws, data protection statutes, and industry-specific regulations. A pertinent example is the proposed acquisition of MoneyGram by Ant Financial in 2018, which was halted due to concerns from the Committee on Foreign Investment in the United States (CFIUS). The inability to obtain regulatory approval nullified the potential rewards and led to a mutual termination of the deal.

Operational risks are equally critical, with compatibility and integration concerns at the forefront. The merging of distinct operational frameworks can be likened to the confluence of two different rivers—the smoothness of their union dictates the new stream's power and direction. The acquirer must evaluate the target's operational processes, supply chain robustness, and technology infrastructure. A failure to integrate these elements can lead to inefficiencies and erode the expected synergistic value. A prime example is the Daimler-Benz and Chrysler merger in 1998, where cultural clashes and operational misalignments resulted in a disappointing venture, culminating in a de-merger in 2007.

Cultural risk, often undervalued, can be a silent saboteur of M&A outcomes. A clashing of corporate cultures can undermine employee morale, stifle innovation, and lead to talent attrition—eroding the value that the acquisition sought to augment. A harmonious blend of organizational cultures, conversely, can create an environment ripe for collaborative growth. The Disney-Pixar merger in 2006 showcases a successful cultural integration, where the two companies managed to preserve their unique creative spirits while leveraging shared resources to dominate the animation industry.

From a reward perspective, the expected benefits of M&A are multifold. Synergies can manifest in revenue enhancement, cost reduction, market expansion, and accelerated innovation. The acquisition of Instagram by Facebook in 2012, for example, allowed the latter to capture a new demographic, tap into burgeoning mobile advertising revenue, and solidify its dominance in the social media space.

Risk and reward considerations in M&A are intrinsically linked, requiring a profound understanding of the intricacies involved in every facet of the deal. Through scrupulous due diligence, a judicious evaluation of operational and cultural integration, and a laser focus on achieving synergies, organizations can tip the scales in favor of reward and stitch together a narrative of M&A triumph that reverberates through the annals of corporate history.

Innovation Risk and Competitive Advantage

Navigating the waters of innovation carries an intrinsic dualism—the pursuit of breakthroughs that can bestow competitive advantage also engenders risk, the potential to erode existing value streams. As businesses vie for supremacy within their markets, the calculus of innovation risk becomes a pivotal factor in ensuring that the scales tip towards enduring success.

Innovation risk encompasses the uncertainties and potential losses that organizations face when they attempt to introduce new products, services, or processes. These risks can take many forms, from technological feasibility to market acceptance. The theoretical underpinning of innovation risk management is grounded in the strategic alignment of an organization's risk appetite with its pursuit of innovation-driven growth.

Consider the telecommunications sector, where the race

to develop and implement 5G technology is a potent illustration of innovation risk. Companies must invest heavily in research and development, infrastructure, and marketing. These investments carry the risk of uncertain returns, regulatory hurdles, and the potential for rapid obsolescence. Yet, the reward for successfully leading the 5G revolution is a substantial competitive edge in terms of network speed, efficiency, and the enablement of innovative applications like autonomous vehicles and smart cities.

A comprehensive approach to managing innovation risk begins with identifying the types of risks that can arise. Market risk involves misjudging customer needs or market trends, as exemplified by Kodak's late response to digital photography despite having developed the core technology. Technological risk is the danger of investing in a technology that fails to perform as expected, which was the case with the hoverboard craze, where safety issues led to recalls and reputational damage.

Operational risk in innovation pertains to the internal processes or resources that may be inadequate for new initiatives. An example is Boeing's 737 MAX, where design and development processes faced severe scrutiny after tragic incidents, leading to grounded fleets and significant financial fallout.

To harness innovation risk for competitive advantage, organizations must develop a robust framework that integrates risk management into the innovation process. This includes fostering a culture that encourages calculated risk-taking and values learning from failure. Google's 'X' division, for instance, is renowned for its 'moonshot' approach to innovation, where ambitious projects are pursued with an acceptance of failure as a stepping stone to revolutionary advancements.

Risk assessment tools such as scenario planning and sensitivity analysis can help organizations gauge the impact of various risk factors on their innovation projects. For example, pharmaceutical companies use scenario planning extensively to assess the potential outcomes of drug development pipelines, considering variables like clinical trial results, regulatory landscapes, and market competition.

In addition to risk assessment, strategies for mitigating innovation risk include diversification of innovation portfolios, strategic partnerships, and leveraging open innovation platforms. Tesla's open-sourcing of its patent portfolio is a strategic move that mitigates risk by encouraging industry-wide innovation, thereby expanding the electric vehicle market and reducing dependence on its own R&D outcomes.

Furthermore, establishing clear metrics to measure innovation performance, such as time to market, adoption rates, and return on innovation investment, allows organizations to monitor progress and make informed decisions about scaling or pivoting their initiatives.

The interplay between innovation risk and competitive advantage is a delicate balancing act. By embedding risk management into the innovation process, organizations can not only safeguard against potential pitfalls but also elevate their market position. Through strategic risk-taking, continuous learning, and the deployment of advanced risk assessment tools, businesses can fortify their competitive edge and steer the wheel of innovation towards a prosperous horizon.

Long-term Sustainability and Ethical Considerations

The notion of long-term sustainability is intrinsically linked to an organization's ethical compass. The intricate dance between enduring corporate success and moral responsibility is a contemporary challenge that demands a sophisticated blend of strategic foresight and ethical deliberation.

Long-term sustainability refers to the ability of an organization to maintain its operations and growth over an extended period, without depleting the environmental, social, and economic resources that future generations rely on. Ethical considerations, on the other hand, revolve around principles that govern the organization's decisions and actions, ensuring they are just, fair, and respect the rights and dignity of all stakeholders.

The theoretical framework for integrating long-term sustainability and ethical considerations into FP&A involves developing strategies that transcend short-term gains in favor of sustainable value creation. This requires organizations to adopt a holistic view of their impact on society and the planet, often referred to as the triple bottom line—people, planet, profit.

Take the example of a multinational corporation in the consumer goods sector that decides to source raw materials from fair trade suppliers. This decision, while potentially increasing costs in the short term, enhances the company's ethical stance and contributes to the social sustainability of the communities involved. Furthermore, it can strengthen the company's brand reputation, leading to increased customer loyalty and long-term profitability.

Ethical considerations also extend to governance and transparency. For instance, a financial institution that adopts stringent anti-money laundering practices and actively combats financial crime not only upholds legal and moral standards but also minimizes the risk of regulatory sanctions and reputational damage.

Additionally, the adoption of environmental, social, and governance (ESG) criteria has become a benchmark for evaluating a company's ethical and sustainable practices. Investors and consumers increasingly gravitate toward companies that score highly on ESG metrics, affecting the inflow of capital and market share. A case in point is the renewable energy industry, where companies like Vestas Wind Systems have gained a competitive edge by aligning their business models with the global transition towards sustainable energy sources.

FP&A professionals play a critical role in embedding long-term sustainability and ethical considerations into organizational strategy. By applying rigorous financial analysis to sustainability initiatives, they can quantify the benefits and costs, model potential scenarios, and provide insights into the financial implications of ethical decisions.

For example, scenario analysis can help estimate the fiscal impact of a move towards sustainable packaging materials over traditional plastics. While the cost may be higher initially, the analysis may reveal long-term savings from reduced waste disposal fees, compliance with regulatory requirements, and meeting consumer demands for eco-friendly products.

Furthermore, ethical considerations must be integrated into the incentive systems within an organization. Performance metrics and reward structures need to reflect not only financial targets but also ethical achievements, such as reducing carbon emissions, improving labor practices, or engaging in corporate philanthropy. This ensures that the pursuit of sustainability is ingrained in the organizational culture and decision-making processes.

In the context of Vancouver, a city known for its green initiatives, a local tech startup might gain competitive advantage by committing to carbon neutrality. By setting up its operations to adhere to stringent environmental standards and engaging in community-driven environmental programs, the startup can differentiate itself in a crowded market and attract both eco-conscious talent and investors.

The interwoven nature of long-term sustainability and ethical considerations within FP&A is a reflection of an evolving business paradigm. It calls for a nuanced approach that considers a broad spectrum of stakeholders and balances immediate financial performance with the imperative for a sustainable and ethical future. By championing sustainability and ethical conduct, organizations not only pave the way for enduring success but also contribute to the collective well-being of society and the planet.

PART 2: ADVANCED RISK MANAGEMENT TOOLS AND TECHNIQUES

Chapter 5: Technology in Risk Management

Technology is a lighthouse, guiding enterprises through the murky waters of uncertainty and complexity. The potent combination of innovative technology and risk management has transformed the landscape, empowering organizations with the tools to identify, assess, and mitigate the myriad risks they face in today's dynamic environment.

Modern risk management is no longer a reactive practice but a proactive doctrine, and technology serves as the cornerstone of this evolution. The adoption of sophisticated technology in risk management strategies heralds a new era where foresight, precision, and agility are not just ideals but tangible realities.

To delineate the role of technology in risk management, we must first understand that risk is omnipresent—entwined with every business decision and strategic direction. From market fluctuations to cyber threats, from regulatory compliance to reputational damage, the spectrum of risks is vast and varied. In response, technology offers an arsenal of solutions, each designed to tackle specific elements of risk within the financial planning and analysis domain.

The heart of this technological revolution lies in data— the fuel that powers risk management engines. Through advanced data analytics and big data processing capabilities, organizations can harness vast quantities of information, converting it into actionable insights. The ability to swiftly aggregate and analyze data across various sources and systems enables risk managers to paint a comprehensive picture of their risk profile.

Artificial intelligence (AI) and machine learning (ML) are the vanguard technologies redefining risk management. These intelligent systems can learn from patterns, predict potential risks, and provide strategic recommendations. By incorporating AI/ML into their risk management frameworks, organizations benefit from enhanced predictive capabilities, leading to more informed and timely decision-making.

Among the most pivotal contributions of technology to risk management is the development of Enterprise Risk Management (ERM) systems. These integrated platforms allow for a holistic approach to risk management by consolidating risk data, monitoring risk levels, and facilitating communication across the organization. ERM systems are instrumental in breaking down silos and fostering collaboration, essential for a unified risk management strategy.

Another technological ally in the realm of risk management is blockchain. With its decentralized ledger and immutable record-keeping, blockchain introduces a new level of transparency and security to transactions and processes. Its potential to mitigate fraud, streamline KYC procedures, and improve contract management through smart contracts is just beginning to be tapped.

As we advance further into the digital era, cybersecurity becomes a critical aspect of risk management. Organizations must protect their digital assets from a spectrum of cyber threats that evolve in sophistication. Here, technology plays a dual role—both as the subject of risk management initiatives and as the means to secure digital infrastructures.

In this intricate dance between risk and technology, one must not overlook the human element. The most advanced technology can only be as effective as the individuals wielding it. Thus, an integral part of employing technology in risk management is the continuous education and upskilling of the workforce, ensuring they are adept at leveraging these tools to the organization's advantage.

The interplay between technology and risk management is a complex yet harmonious one, where each advances the other's capabilities. As we delve deeper into this section, we will explore specific technologies reshaping risk management, from sophisticated ERM systems to the burgeoning field of AI and ML, and the profound implications they hold for FP&A professionals. The future of risk management is here, and it is deeply entwined with the technological marvels of our time.

Enterprise Risk Management (ERM) systems

In the dynamic theatre of enterprise risk, the implementation of Enterprise Risk Management (ERM) systems stands as a pivotal chapter in the annals of financial defense mechanisms. These systems serve as a digital bulwark designed to navigate the intricate nuances and multifarious nature of risk that organizations face in the fluid landscape of global commerce.

At their core, ERM systems are a symphony of methodologies, processes, and software—meticulously orchestrated to deliver a comprehensive view of the risks inherent within an enterprise's strategic and operational activities. These sophisticated systems enable organizations to transcend traditional risk management practices that often operate in isolation, instead advocating for an integrated approach that envelops the entire organizational structure in its protective fold.

The advent of ERM systems brought forth a paradigm shift from siloed risk management to a more holistic strategy. This shift was not merely procedural but philosophical, ushering in a culture where risk awareness permeates every level of the organization. With ERM, risk is not a distant concern for a dedicated department but a common thread that binds all facets of business operations.

ERM systems are built upon a foundation of identifying and cataloging risks across the enterprise, followed by a rigorous assessment of their potential impact and the likelihood of their occurrence. This comprehensive risk inventory becomes a living document within the ERM, constantly updated and refined through continuous monitoring and analysis.

The functionality of an ERM system extends into the realm of risk quantification, leveraging both qualitative and quantitative data to appraise the value at risk (VaR). This valuation is not confined to financial metrics alone but also assesses reputational risk, operational risk, and other intangible yet critical risk factors that can impact an organization's trajectory.

Once risks are identified and assessed, ERM systems facilitate the development of mitigation strategies. These strategies are not static; they are ever-evolving as they are tested against real-world scenarios and organizational changes. In this context, ERM systems enable businesses to be agile, adapting their risk management tactics in real-time as new threats emerge and old vulnerabilities are patched.

Beyond risk assessment and mitigation, ERM systems play a crucial role in risk reporting and communication. They act as a nerve center that collects risk intelligence and disseminates it throughout the organization in an accessible and actionable format. Through dashboards, alerts, and reports, ERM systems ensure that from the C-suite to the operational teams, every stakeholder is informed and equipped to act on the risk landscape before them.

To maintain relevance and efficacy, ERM systems must be seamlessly integrated with other business systems— financial, operational, and compliance frameworks. Such integration enables the ERM to not only draw upon a diverse set of data sources for risk assessment but also to operationalize risk management in the day-to-day activities of the enterprise.

The rollout of an ERM system is not without its challenges. It necessitates a careful orchestration of technology, processes, and people. The successful deployment hinges on executive sponsorship, cross-departmental collaboration, and a clear roadmap that aligns with the strategic objectives of the organization.

This section of the book will delve into the minutiae of ERM systems, exploring their architecture, the standards guiding their implementation, and the best practices that ensure their success. We will also look at case studies where ERM systems have been pivotal in steering organizations away from the precipice of risk and towards the harbor of stability and growth.

The narrative of ERM systems is one of constant evolution, driven by the relentless pace of technological innovation and the ever-shifting patterns of global risk. As we progress further into this discourse, it becomes evident that ERM systems are not just tools but strategic assets that, when effectively wielded, can secure a competitive edge in the uncertain waters of enterprise risk management.

Features of Leading ERM Software

Leading Enterprise Risk Management (ERM) software, a cornerstone of modern risk mitigation strategies, is characterized by a suite of features that empower organizations to preemptively identify, evaluate, and manage the multifaceted risks they face. The efficacy of an ERM software lays in its capacity to furnish decision-makers with the tools necessary for crafting a robust risk management ecosystem.

Key features of top-tier ERM software include:

a) Comprehensive Risk Assessment Tools: The software provides a framework for systematic risk identification across various business units, ensuring that no potential threat goes unnoticed. Advanced assessment modules facilitate the categorization of risks based on their nature, source, and potential impact, allowing for a nuanced risk profile.

Dynamic Risk Analysis: At the heart of leading ERM solutions lies the capability for dynamic risk analysis. This includes real-time data analytics, scenario planning, and predictive modeling, all of which coalesce to form a predictive lens through which organizations can anticipate risk events before they materialize.

c) Integrated Risk Intelligence: These systems are adept at integrating internal data with external intelligence, such as market trends, geopolitical events, and regulatory changes. This integration empowers businesses to contextualize their risk landscape within the broader economic and social milieu.

d) Customizable Dashboards and Reporting: ERM software typically offers customizable dashboards that provide a visual representation of an organization's risk posture. Users can tailor these dashboards to monitor specific KPIs and KRIs, and generate reports that suit the informational needs of different stakeholder groups, from operational teams to board members.

e) Workflow Automation and Remediation Tracking: Automating the workflows associated with risk management processes not only streamlines operations but also reduces the likelihood of human error. Leading ERM platforms include features for tracking remediation efforts, ensuring that mitigation plans are executed and progress is monitored against set timelines.

f) Policy and Compliance Management: These systems often include modules for managing policies and ensuring compliance with relevant regulations. They can trigger reviews of policies in response to changes in the regulatory landscape and provide audit trails for compliance activities.

g) Incident Management and Response Planning: Effective ERM software equips organizations with the tools to log incidents as they occur, analyze the root cause, and develop response plans. This proactive approach to incident management is crucial for minimizing the impact of risk events when they do occur.

h) Communication and Collaboration Facilities: Encouraging collaboration across departments and levels of hierarchy, leading ERM systems feature communication tools that facilitate the sharing of risk information and encourage a culture of collective risk ownership.

i) Scalability and Flexibility: As organizations grow and evolve, so too does their risk environment. Leading ERM software is designed with scalability in mind, ensuring that it can expand to accommodate new business units, geographies, and types of risk.

j) User-Friendly Interface and Training Support: Recognizing the diversity of users, top ERM solutions boast intuitive interfaces that minimize the learning curve. They often come with comprehensive training materials and support services to ensure that users can leverage the software to its full potential.

In the subsequent sections of this book, we will dive deeper into the operational nuances of these features, dissecting the ways in which they translate into tangible benefits for organizations. We will explore the innovative technologies that underpin these systems, such as artificial intelligence, machine learning, and blockchain, and how they are leveraged to enhance the capabilities of ERM software.

Through case examples and expert insights, we will illuminate the transformative impact that well-implemented ERM software can have on an organization's resilience to risk. The narrative will unfold to reveal not just the features of these powerful tools, but their strategic application in the relentless pursuit of enterprise robustness and agility.

Implementing an ERM System

The implementation of an Enterprise Risk Management (ERM) system is a strategic venture that requires meticulous planning, stakeholder engagement, and customized integration to align with the organization's unique risk profile and business objectives. This section will delve into the theoretical frameworks and practical steps involved in successfully deploying an ERM system.

Initiating the ERM Implementation Process:

To set the stage for a successful ERM system implementation, organizations must first establish clear objectives and outcomes for the initiative. This involves defining the scope, determining the risk appetite, and identifying specific risk categories relevant to the organization. Leadership buy-in is paramount, as is the formation of a cross-functional team responsible for overseeing the implementation process.

Strategic Alignment and Risk Assessment:

The next phase involves aligning the ERM system with the organization's strategic goals. A thorough risk assessment is conducted to create a baseline for future risk management efforts. This includes identifying existing and potential risks, as well as assessing their likelihood and impact. The assessment should be an inclusive process, spanning the breadth of the organization and incorporating insights from all levels.

System Selection and Customization:

Selecting the right ERM software requires a careful evaluation of the organization's specific needs and a comparison of various offerings in the market. The chosen system must be scalable and configurable to adapt to the organization's evolving risk landscape. Customization plays a critical role in ensuring that the ERM system reflects the organization's processes, reporting structures, and risk management methodologies.

Integration and Data Management:

A pivotal aspect of ERM system implementation is the integration with existing systems and data sources. Ensuring data consistency and accuracy is crucial for meaningful risk analysis. Organizations must address challenges related to data silos and establish protocols for data governance, quality control, and secure data handling.

User Training and Change Management:

For an ERM system to be effective, users across the organization must be adept at using it. A comprehensive training program, encompassing various learning styles and proficiency levels, is essential. Change management strategies must be employed to address resistance and foster a culture that embraces the ERM system as a vital tool for decision-making.

Testing, Validation, and Feedback Loops:

Before full-scale deployment, the ERM system should undergo rigorous testing to validate its functionality and ensure that it meets the predefined objectives. Feedback from early users should be incorporated to fine-tune the system and address any gaps in its capabilities or user experience.

Rollout and Ongoing Evaluation:

With testing and validation complete, the ERM system is ready for rollout. A phased approach is often recommended, starting with key areas of the organization that are most susceptible to risk. Continuous evaluation of the system's effectiveness is necessary, with periodic reviews and updates to ensure that it remains aligned with the organization's risk management needs.

Achieving ERM Maturity:

The goal of implementing an ERM system is to achieve a mature state where risk management is an integral part of the organization's DNA. This involves ongoing refinement of risk assessment methodologies, regular updates to risk intelligence, and proactive enhancements to the system's capabilities.

By methodically executing these steps, organizations can ensure that the implementation of their ERM system is not just a one-time project but a transformative journey towards a more resilient and risk-aware enterprise. The subsequent chapters will expand upon this foundation, offering in-depth explorations into advanced ERM functionalities and their application in a variety of industry contexts.

Customizing ERM to Fit Company Needs

Essential to the efficacy of an Enterprise Risk Management (ERM) framework is its harmonious integration with the entity's distinct operational fabric. Customizing an ERM system to suit the specific needs of a company stands as a non-negotiable prerequisite for the transmutation of raw data into strategic foresight. This segment shall dissect the intricacies of tailoring an ERM system to become the lifeblood of an organization's risk intelligence apparatus.

The initial undertaking in the customization process involves a granular evaluation of the company's risk environment, industry-specific challenges, and operational complexities. This diagnostic phase serves as the crucible within which the ERM system's configuration is meticulously refined. Factors such as company size, market dynamics, regulatory requirements, and internal workflow patterns emerge as the architects of the configuration blueprint.

The ERM system's architecture must be woven into the very fabric of the company's processes, ensuring seamless integration. This requires mapping out each business unit's risk management procedures with the ERM's capabilities, creating a synchronized network of workflows. The ERM system should augment, not disrupt, existing protocols, thus enhancing the overall risk management ecosystem.

Every company encounters a unique constellation of risks. Consequently, the ERM system must incorporate customized risk models that mirror the company's exposure spectrum. Variables such as market volatility, credit risk, operational disruptions, and strategic shifts are tailored within the ERM to mirror the firm's reality, thus ensuring the system's relevance and precision.

The usability of an ERM system is pivotal. A user interface designed with the end-user in mind—accessible, intuitive, and responsive—will foster higher engagement levels. Customizing the user experience based on employee feedback and usability studies guarantees that the system is not only functional but also embraced by those who are key to its daily operation.

Reports and dashboards are the visual epitome of an ERM system's utility. Customizing these elements to display pertinent risk metrics, tailored to the stakeholders' requirements, is imperative. The ERM must offer the flexibility to generate ad hoc reports and create dashboards that provide a real-time pulse of the company's risk landscape.

A static ERM system is an obsolete one. Customization includes planning for scalability and future growth. The system must be designed to accommodate new risk categories, evolving business models, and emerging technologies. This forethought ensures that the ERM system evolves in concert with the company it serves.

Instituting robust mechanisms for feedback and continuous improvement within the ERM framework allows the system to adapt and refine based on user experience and changing risk scenarios. This cyclical process of feedback, analysis, and modification stands as the cornerstone of a dynamic ERM system.

Customizing an ERM system to fit company needs is an exercise in precision engineering. It demands a deep understanding of the company's strategic vision, operational nuances, and risk profile. When meticulously executed, it assures that the ERM system serves as a powerful ally in the quest to navigate the treacherous waters of business risk, turning potential vulnerabilities into strategic opportunities. The ensuing chapters will build on this foundation, delving deeper into the advanced functionalities and industry-specific applications of a well-integrated ERM system.

Integrating ERM with Other Business Systems

The integration of Enterprise Risk Management (ERM) with other business systems is a strategic imperative that enables organizations to achieve a cohesive and comprehensive risk oversight. In the pursuit of enterprise-wide resilience, it is paramount that the ERM framework does not operate in isolation but rather as a nexus that draws insights from various business segments. This section elucidates the methodological approaches and technical nuances that underpin the successful amalgamation of ERM with other business systems.

At the onset, the ERM framework must be conceptually aligned with the overarching business objectives and strategies. This alignment ensures that risk management is not merely a compliance exercise but a strategic tool for advancing business imperatives. The integration process begins with the identification of key performance indicators (KPIs) and strategic goals across the organization, subsequently mapping them against risk factors that could impede their achievement.

Technological infrastructure is the backbone of integration. ERM systems should be engineered with the capability to interface with other core business systems such as enterprise resource planning (ERP), customer relationship management (CRM), and supply chain management (SCM) platforms. This interoperability is facilitated through application programming interfaces (APIs) or middleware that allow for real-time data exchange and process synchronization.

An integrated ERM system necessitates the aggregation of data from disparate corporate systems. It is crucial to ensure consistency in data definitions and formats across systems to provide an accurate and unified view of risks. Data warehousing techniques and the establishment of a common data model are instrumental in achieving this consistency, thereby enhancing the integrity of risk analysis and reporting.

ERM integration is inherently cross-functional. It requires collaboration among various departments, from finance and operations to IT and human resources. Establishing cross-functional teams and committees can aid in breaking down silos and fostering a culture of shared responsibility for risk management. These collaborative groups serve as forums for dialogue, issue resolution, and the continuous refinement of the integrated risk framework.

The integration of ERM with other business systems should yield operational efficiencies through automation of risk-related workflows. Automating risk assessments, controls, and response strategies within the company's business processes facilitates prompt decision-making and reduces the likelihood of human error. Decision support tools embedded within the ERM system can provide predictive analytics and scenario planning, thereby empowering management with actionable intelligence.

Given the complex regulatory landscape, ERM systems must be aligned with compliance management functions. Integrating the ERM with governance, risk, and compliance (GRC) modules ensures that regulatory requirements are factored into risk assessments and that compliance controls are an integral part of the risk mitigation toolkit.

An integrated ERM system thrives on continuous monitoring. Embedding risk monitoring capabilities within operational systems enables the detection of anomalies and emerging risks in real time. Additionally, the ERM system should be equipped with feedback loops to capture lessons learned and facilitate continuous improvement, ensuring that the system remains reflective of the dynamic business environment.

In conclusion, integrating ERM with other business systems is a multifaceted endeavor that hinges on strategic alignment, technological agility, data coherence, cross-functional synergy, process automation, and a commitment to continuous evolution. As we delve further into subsequent sections, we will dissect specific integration strategies, examine case studies, and explore the transformative impact of a fully integrated risk management approach on the organization's strategic agility and competitive edge.

Role of Artificial Intelligence (AI) and Machine Learning (ML) in Risk Management

The role of Artificial Intelligence (AI) and Machine Learning (ML) in the realm of risk management signifies a paradigm shift from traditional analysis to predictive and prescriptive analytics. This section ventures into the granular intricacies of how AI and ML are redefining the boundaries and capabilities of risk management within modern enterprises.

AI and ML stand at the forefront of computational

innovation, powering algorithms capable of recognizing patterns and making decisions with minimal human intervention. In the context of risk management, these technologies are leveraged to anticipate potential threats and optimize risk responses. Core applications of AI and ML in risk management include anomaly detection, risk classification, and predictive forecasting.

Anomaly detection, a critical function within AI-driven risk management, involves the identification of outliers within datasets that may indicate potential risks. ML algorithms are trained to discern patterns in vast quantities of transactional data, flagging transactions that deviate from established norms. Such capabilities are vital in detecting fraud, network intrusions, and operational inconsistencies.

AI systems excel at classifying risks based on historical data and correlating them with various risk factors. By ingesting and analyzing data from multiple sources, ML models can evaluate the likelihood and potential impact of different risks, assisting in the prioritization process. This classification extends to credit risk assessment, where AI models assess borrower profiles to predict creditworthiness and potential defaults.

Predictive models harness past and current data to forecast future risk scenarios. ML algorithms can sift through economic indicators, market trends, and company performance metrics to anticipate financial risks. Prescriptive analytics takes this a step further by not only predicting risks but also suggesting optimal risk management strategies based on the forecasts.

AI and ML are not stand-alone solutions; their true power

is unleashed when integrated with broader ERM systems. This integration allows for a dynamic risk management environment where AI-generated insights inform decision-making and risk response planning. The integration also facilitates the automation of routine risk management tasks, freeing human analysts to focus on more complex, strategic risk considerations.

As AI and ML become more pervasive in risk management, ethical considerations and the potential for algorithmic bias must be addressed. Organizations are implementing AI auditing practices to ensure algorithms do not perpetuate existing biases or inequalities. This involves regular reviews of AI decision-making processes and outcomes to maintain fairness, accountability, and transparency.

Despite the transformative impact of AI and ML on risk management, challenges persist, such as data quality and privacy concerns, the need for specialized talent, and the continuous evolution of AI algorithms. Looking ahead, the role of AI and ML in risk management is set to expand, with advancements in natural language processing and deep learning offering new avenues for risk identification and mitigation.

In summary, the integration of AI and ML into risk management processes heralds a new age of efficiency, precision, and anticipatory governance. Their role in augmenting human expertise with powerful computational intelligence is a testament to the transformative potential of these technologies. As we further explore the nuances of AI and ML in the proceeding sections, we will uncover the depth of their impact on the strategic foresight and adaptability of contemporary enterprises.

Predictive Risk Analytics

Predictive risk analytics, a sophisticated branch within the sphere of data science, stands as a formidable tool in the arsenal of risk management. This section delves into the theoretical underpinnings and practical applications of predictive analytics, aiming to equip financial professionals with the foresight necessary to navigate the labyrinthine complexities of risk.

Predictive risk analytics is rooted in statistical theory and machine learning methodologies. It involves the use of historical data, statistical algorithms, and machine learning techniques to identify the likelihood of future outcomes based on historical patterns. This form of analytics is particularly adept at managing market, credit, and operational risks by forecasting the probability of adverse events before they manifest.

The efficacy of predictive analytics is largely contingent on the robustness of statistical models and the sophistication of machine learning algorithms. Time series analysis, logistic regression, and Cox proportional hazards models are staple techniques for forecasting events over time. Machine learning algorithms such as neural networks, decision trees, and ensemble methods enhance the predictive accuracy by adapting to new data and uncovering non-linear relationships.

At the heart of predictive risk analytics lies the capability to pinpoint and quantify potential risks. By processing vast datasets from diverse sources, such as market feeds, transaction records, and social media, predictive models can discern subtle indicators of risk that may escape traditional analysis. Through quantification, these analytics transform abstract risk notions into tangible metrics that can be integrated into strategic planning.

Predictive analytics are instrumental in scenario analysis and stress testing, where multiple risk factors are simulated to assess their potential impact on financial outcomes. Scenarios ranging from economic downturns to geopolitical events are modeled to stress test the resilience of financial strategies against a spectrum of plausible future states.

The ultimate purpose of predictive risk analytics is to inform and enhance decision-making processes. By providing actionable intelligence, predictive models empower financial professionals to devise pre-emptive measures that mitigate risk. Decision trees and simulations offer a visual representation of risk-return trade-offs, aiding in the selection of optimal risk management strategies.

Predictive analytics is a natural complement to FP&A activities, where financial forecasting and budgeting are central to success. The forward-looking nature of predictive analytics dovetails with the projection of financial trends, revenue, and expenses—enabling a more proactive and informed approach to financial planning.

The domain of predictive analytics is continually evolving with the advent of big data technologies and advanced computational capabilities. The integration of real-time data streams and the adoption of cloud analytics platforms are expanding the horizon of predictive risk analytics.

Innovations such as deep learning and reinforcement learning present new frontiers for even more accurate and dynamic risk prediction models.

Predictive risk analytics represents a quantum leap from hindsight to foresight in the domain of risk management. It is a discipline that marries the empirical rigour of statistical analysis with the adaptive intelligence of machine learning, conferring upon financial practitioners the power to anticipate and navigate the uncertain waters of risk with greater confidence and precision. As the financial landscape grows increasingly complex, the demand for predictive risk analytics is poised to surge, cementing its role as an indispensable facet of modern financial strategy.

Algorithmic Decision-Making

In the intricate web of financial decision-making, algorithmic approaches have emerged as a pivotal force, driving efficiency and objectivity in risk-related resolutions. This section delves into the theoretical underpinnings and practical applications of algorithmic decision-making in risk management.

Algorithmic decision-making refers to the process by which computer algorithms analyze data sets to make predictions or decisions without human intervention. The theoretical backbone of this process rests on mathematical and statistical models that can process vast quantities of data far more rapidly and consistently than human counterparts.

The development of decision-making algorithms involves creating models that can learn from data and improve over time. Optimization techniques refine these models to minimize error and maximize predictive accuracy. Algorithms such as logistic regression, decision trees, and neural networks are commonly used, each with its strengths and considerations for specific types of risk analysis.

Algorithms can augment the risk assessment process by detecting subtle patterns and correlations that may elude human analysts. By continuously ingesting and processing new data, these algorithms stay current with the evolving risk landscape, thereby aiding in the early identification of financial, operational, or strategic risks.

One of the most visible applications of algorithmic decision-making is in the realm of algorithmic trading, where algorithms execute trades based on predefined criteria. Here, risk management becomes crucial as algorithms must factor in market volatility, liquidity, and the potential impact of trading strategies on market dynamics.

The rise of algorithms necessitates a discussion on ethics and regulation. Ensuring fair and unbiased decision-making, maintaining transparency, and safeguarding against the systemic risk posed by widespread use of interconnected algorithms are all paramount considerations in the deployment of these sophisticated tools.

To illustrate the practicality of algorithmic decision-making, this section will incorporate case studies from financial services. Examples include credit scoring algorithms that assess the likelihood of default and risk management systems that dynamically adjust portfolios in response to market shifts.

Despite their benefits, algorithmic systems are not without challenges. Key among these is the 'black box' problem, where the decision-making process is opaque, making it difficult to interpret or challenge algorithmic decisions. There are also risks of overfitting, where algorithms become too tailored to historical data and may not perform well when faced with new, unseen scenarios.

Looking forward, the evolution of algorithmic decision-making is poised to become increasingly sophisticated with the advent of quantum computing and next-generation AI techniques. As these technologies mature, their potential to transform risk management strategies is immense, promising unprecedented levels of analytical depth and foresight.

Algorithmic decision-making represents a frontier of innovation in risk management, offering the promise of enhanced precision and adaptability in an uncertain financial landscape. As organizations deploy these algorithms, they must navigate the attendant complexities with a balance of enthusiasm for technological advancement and a vigilant eye on the ethical and systemic implications of these powerful tools.

AI Auditing and Ethical Considerations

As artificial intelligence (AI) permeates the financial sector, the need for rigorous auditing and staunch ethical standards becomes ever more crucial. AI auditing is the systematic examination of AI systems to ensure accuracy, fairness, and compliance with regulatory and ethical standards. This section explores the granular aspects of AI auditing and the ethical considerations at play.

AI auditing encompasses a range of activities, including the validation of data quality, the assessment of algorithmic fairness, and the verification of model performance. The primary aim is to ensure that AI systems function as intended, without causing unintended harm or exhibiting bias. For financial institutions, this is particularly important given the potential for AI to influence credit decisions, risk assessments, and trading activities.

A robust AI audit involves a multi-faceted approach. It begins with an evaluation of the data used to train AI models, checking for quality, representativeness, and potential biases. Following this, auditors examine the model's design and the logic it employs to make decisions, ensuring that it aligns with ethical guidelines and business objectives. Stress testing and scenario analysis are also integral to gauge how the AI system performs under different conditions.

Algorithmic bias is a critical concern in financial AI systems. Auditors scrutinize algorithms for fairness, ensuring that they do not perpetuate existing inequalities or discriminate against any group. Techniques like adversarial testing and fairness-aware machine learning are employed to detect and mitigate biases.

A cornerstone of ethical AI is transparency. Auditors assess the explainability of AI decisions, which is essential for trust and accountability. Financial institutions are encouraged to adopt AI systems that provide clear rationales for their decisions, allowing for human understanding and oversight.

In the context of finance, regulatory compliance is non-negotiable. AI auditing ensures that AI systems adhere to existing laws and regulations, such as those concerning consumer protection and anti-discrimination. It also prepares institutions for emerging regulations aimed specifically at governing AI use.

Beyond legal compliance, AI systems in finance must align with broader ethical principles. These include respect for individual autonomy, privacy, and the avoidance of harm. Ethical considerations also extend to the societal implications of AI, such as the potential for job displacement and the concentration of power among those who control AI technologies.

Effective AI auditing involves engaging with a wide array of stakeholders, including regulators, customers, and employees. This engagement is crucial for understanding the diverse perspectives on AI's impact and for ensuring that the AI systems serve the interests of all parties involved.

In summary, AI auditing and ethical considerations form an indispensable part of responsible AI deployment in finance. By rigorously evaluating AI systems and upholding the highest ethical standards, financial institutions can harness the transformative potential of AI while mitigating its risks, ensuring that these powerful tools are wielded with integrity and foresight.

Big Data and Advanced Analytics

In the vanguard of finance's evolution stands the towering influence of big data and advanced analytics, a paradigm that has redefined the contours of financial planning and analysis. This section delves into the theoretical intricacies of big data's application and the transformative power of advanced analytics in the financial domain.

Big data refers to the vast expanses of structured and unstructured data that financial institutions accumulate—data that traditional processing software can no longer efficiently handle. It encompasses not only quantitative metrics but also qualitative information such as customer sentiments and market trends. The convergence of big data with finance marks a revolution in how financial entities glean insights, forecast trends, and forge strategies.

Advanced analytics, with its sophisticated algorithms and computational prowess, enables the deep interrogation of big data sets. Through techniques like machine learning, predictive modeling, and complex event processing, financial analysts can extract nuanced insights and foresights that were previously inaccessible.

A pivotal aspect of leveraging big data is the ability to parse both structured data, such as spreadsheets and databases, and unstructured data, which includes text, video, and social media content. Advanced analytics employs natural language processing (NLP) and sentiment analysis to distill relevant information from unstructured sources, enriching the financial decision-making process with a more holistic view of the data landscape.

In the realm of FP&A, the capacity to analyze and monitor risk in real time has become a sine qua non. Advanced analytics platforms are capable of processing and visualizing data streams instantaneously, thereby allowing financial professionals to identify and respond to potential risks with unprecedented speed and accuracy.

With great power comes great responsibility—maintaining the integrity of data is paramount. Effective data governance frameworks establish policies and standards for data management, ensuring quality and mitigating the risk of errors that could lead to suboptimal financial decisions.

The reliance on big data also introduces heightened cybersecurity risks. Financial institutions must implement robust security measures to protect sensitive data against breaches and cyber threats. Advanced analytics contributes to cybersecurity efforts by identifying patterns indicative of fraudulent activities, thereby bolstering the institution's defenses.

The ethical utilization of big data is a topic of increasing significance. Financial entities must navigate the delicate balance between data-driven opportunity and the ethical implications of data collection, usage, and privacy. Transparency with stakeholders and adherence to ethical standards is essential to maintain trust and comply with regulatory requirements.

Big data and advanced analytics are not siloed technologies but integral components of modern FP&A practices. They enhance forecasting accuracy, optimization of financial models, and strategic planning, ultimately driving superior financial performance.

In summation, the intricate theoretical framework presented herein encapsulates the vital role of big data and advanced analytics in the financial landscape. As the bedrock of data-driven decision-making, their judicious application promises not only to elevate FP&A practices but to redefine the very fabric of financial strategy for the near future.

Leveraging Structured and Unstructured Data

In the multifaceted sphere of Financial Planning & Analysis, data stands as the bedrock upon which all discerning analysis is built. Structured data, with its highly-organized and quantifiable nature, readily integrates into traditional databases and is amenable to straightforward analysis. Unstructured data, by contrast, is more akin to the unruly wilds of untapped knowledge—emails, social media posts, videos, and other forms of content that defy conventional data models but hold a wealth of untold insight.

The challenge and, indeed, the art of FP&A lie in the fusion of structured and unstructured data into a coherent, actionable whole. Structured data offers the comfort of familiarity —financial statements, transaction histories, and customer databases. Yet, it is in the marriage with unstructured data where the true potential for competitive advantage is unlocked. This unstructured data requires sophisticated tools for its extraction and interpretation, often utilizing NLP, text mining, and semantic analysis to render its raw complexity into a structured form.

Advanced analytics platforms stand at the ready to assist in this endeavor, brandishing an arsenal of tools designed to parse and integrate diverse data types. Machine learning algorithms excel in identifying patterns within unstructured data, gradually improving their accuracy as more data is processed. Data mining techniques reveal hidden correlations and associations, while semantic analysis deciphers the intent and meaning behind words and sentences.

The coalescence of structured and unstructured data within these platforms yields predictive insights that are of paramount importance to FP&A professionals. It enables a panoramic view of the financial landscape, considering not just historical performance but the subtleties of market sentiment, consumer behavior, and emerging trends. Predictive analytics thus provides a forward-looking lens, informing strategies that are proactive rather than reactive.

To fully realize the potential of both structured and unstructured data, it is essential to establish robust data governance and management practices. This ensures the quality and integrity of data, facilitating its seamless integration and analysis. It also necessitates a concerted effort to maintain the privacy and security of data, in line with regulatory requirements and ethical standards.

The practical applications of leveraging structured and unstructured data are extensive within FP&A. It informs risk management by providing a more nuanced risk profile that feeds into more resilient financial models. It shapes budgeting and forecasting by factoring in a broader array of variables and influences. Moreover, it enriches strategic planning with a depth of market intelligence that can prove decisive in an increasingly competitive environment.

The intricate art of leveraging structured and unstructured data represents a cornerstone of contemporary FP&A. The synthesis of these data types through advanced analytics heralds a new era of insight-driven finance, one that is primed to navigate the complexities of today's economic landscape with agility and foresight.

Real-time Risk Analysis and Monitoring

The era of real-time risk analysis and monitoring has dawned, heralding a transformative shift in how Financial Planning & Analysis (FP&A) departments preempt and respond to potential threats. As markets evolve at a breakneck pace, the ability to analyze and act upon risk-related information instantaneously has become indispensable.

The incorporation of real-time analytics into the FP&A toolbox is a leap forward from traditional periodic reviews, which are often retrospective and lagging current events. Real-time risk analysis enables a dynamic assessment of risk exposure as transactions occur and conditions change. This continuous surveillance allows organizations to detect anomalies, trends, and emerging risks the moment they arise, dramatically shortening the response window.

The backbone of real-time risk monitoring is a technology infrastructure that can support vast streams of live data. Modern FP&A leverages high-velocity data processing frameworks and in-memory computing to handle the torrent of real-time data. Cloud-based platforms and services afford scalability and accessibility, while the Internet of Things (IoT) extends monitoring capabilities to a multitude of sources and endpoints.

Visualization tools and interactive dashboards are instrumental in translating the complex mosaic of data into an intelligible format for swift decision-making. They provide a visual narrative of risk exposure that is both current and historically contextual, allowing for patterns and outliers to be readily discerned. Stakeholders can thus gauge the current risk status immediately, with the granularity to drill down into specific areas of concern.

Automated alert systems, powered by sophisticated algorithms, serve as sentinels that notify relevant parties of risk indicators surpassing predefined thresholds. They are customized to the organization's unique risk profile and tolerance levels, offering granular control over the triggers for escalation. These systems are crucial in mitigating risks before they magnify into crises, providing FP&A professionals the latitude to implement corrective actions proactively.

Predictive models, incorporating machine learning and statistical techniques, are integrated into the real-time environment to forecast potential risk scenarios. These models adapt and refine their predictive capabilities as new data is ingressed, ensuring that risk predictions remain relevant and accurate. Advanced simulations and stress tests can be conducted in real-time, offering insights into the resilience of financial strategies under various conditions.

Artificial Intelligence (AI) plays a pivotal role, capable of discerning complex risk patterns that elude traditional analysis. AI systems can process unstructured data, such as news feeds and social media, to capture the sentiment and emerging risks that may not yet be reflected in structured data. This capability enriches the risk monitoring process with a layer of external intelligence, offering a comprehensive view that spans beyond internal operational metrics.

With the increased reliance on real-time data flows, cybersecurity becomes an overarching concern. FP&A systems must incorporate advanced cybersecurity measures to ensure the integrity and confidentiality of risk data. This includes the deployment of encryption, intrusion detection systems, and access controls, as well as adherence to stringent data protection protocols.

Operationalizing real-time risk analysis and monitoring necessitates a cultural shift within FP&A, embracing agility and continuous learning. Teams must be equipped with the skills to interpret real-time data and empowered to act decisively. Processes must be adapted to support rapid response, and collaboration across departments should be streamlined to facilitate the flow of risk intelligence throughout the organization.

Real-time risk analysis and monitoring represent a paradigm shift in FP&A, embodying a proactive approach to risk management. By leveraging cutting-edge technology and fostering a culture attuned to immediate action, organizations can not only anticipate and mitigate risks in the present but also fortify their strategic planning for the future. This responsiveness and foresight are essential in an era where the financial landscape is perpetually in flux, and the margin for error continues to narrow.

Data Governance and Quality Issues

In the labyrinthine digital ecosystems of modern enterprises, data governance and quality issues take center stage as pivotal concerns for Financial Planning & Analysis (FP&A) professionals. The integrity of financial forecasts, strategic decisions, and risk assessments hinges upon the reliability of data. Hence, an intricate understanding of data governance and its role in ensuring data quality is a sine qua non for astute fiscal management.

Data governance is an overarching framework that defines who can act upon data, under what circumstances, and using what methods. It comprises the policies, procedures, standards, and metrics that ensure the effective and efficient use of information in enabling an organization to achieve its goals. The framework ensures that data is consistent, trustworthy, and not misused.

The dimensions of data quality are numerous—accuracy, completeness, consistency, reliability, and timeliness are among the key facets. FP&A units must establish and adhere to quality standards that address these dimensions, ensuring that the data used for analysis upholds the highest level of integrity. This is achieved through rigorous data cleansing, validation, and reconciliation processes.

Clear ownership and stewardship are vital elements of robust data governance. Data stewards are appointed to oversee data assets, ensuring compliance with governance policies and resolving quality issues as they arise. They play a critical role in maintaining the data dictionary, metadata management, and facilitating a shared understanding of data definitions across the organization.

Maintaining data quality is an ongoing challenge, exacerbated by the volume, velocity, and variety of data that organizations encounter. Disparate systems, legacy infrastructure, and siloed departments often result in fragmented data landscapes. Inconsistencies in data collection methods and a lack of standardization can further compound the challenges.

To address these issues, FP&A departments must implement data quality frameworks that include robust processes for continuous monitoring and improvement. Automated data quality tools can assist in detecting and rectifying errors in real-time. Regular audits and quality assessments help to maintain standards and reinforce the importance of data quality.

Technological advancements play a crucial role in data governance. Tools for data lineage tracking offer transparency in data's origin and transformation as it flows through the system. Blockchain technology can provide immutable audit trails for data transactions, enhancing trust and security. Machine learning algorithms can predict data quality issues based on historical patterns, facilitating preemptive corrections.

Financial regulatory compliance mandates rigorous data governance practices. Regulations such as GDPR, SOX, and Basel III impose strict rules on data handling, privacy, and reporting. FP&A departments must ensure that governance frameworks are aligned with these requirements to avoid legal and financial repercussions.

Beyond policies and tools, cultivating a culture that values data governance is essential. Training and education initiatives raise awareness about the importance of data quality. Incentives and performance metrics aligned with data stewardship encourage accountability and reward diligent management of data assets.

Data governance and quality issues are integral to the fabric of FP&A operations. By instituting rigorous governance frameworks, embracing technological enablers, and fostering a culture of data stewardship, organizations can safeguard the integrity of their financial data. This, in turn, empowers FP&A professionals to deliver analyses and insights that drive strategic decisions, manage risks adeptly, and maintain the financial health of the enterprise amidst the complexities of the global market.

Cybersecurity Risks Associated with Big Data

In an age where big data has become a cornerstone of competitive advantage, cybersecurity risks stand as formidable adversaries in the quest for data-driven decision-making within Financial Planning & Analysis (FP&A). The burgeoning volumes of data harvested from myriad sources present a veritable goldmine for insights yet simultaneously open the floodgates to a host of security vulnerabilities.

Cybersecurity, in the big data realm, pertains to the measures and mechanisms put in place to protect massive sets of data from unauthorized access, breaches, and other forms of malicious attack. As FP&A departments increasingly rely on big data for forecasting and strategic analysis, the specter of cyber threats looms large, threatening to undermine the confidentiality, integrity, and availability of critical financial information.

The inherent characteristics of big data—volume, velocity, and variety—amplify its susceptibility to cyber risks. The sheer volume of data strains traditional security infrastructures, while the velocity of data flow necessitates real-time security checks, which can be challenging to implement effectively. The variety of data, with structured and unstructured forms comingling, creates complex security scenarios that demand sophisticated handling.

Cyber threats targeting big data repositories are manifold. They include, but are not limited to, unauthorized data exfiltration, malware intrusions, Denial of Service (DoS) attacks, and Advanced Persistent Threats (APTs) that stealthily siphon data over extended periods. Social engineering tactics, such as phishing, exploit human vulnerabilities to gain access to sensitive data sets.

Robust encryption is the first line of defense, ensuring that data remains unintelligible to unauthorized parties. Access controls and authentication mechanisms must be stringent, with multi-factor authentication becoming a standard practice. Anomaly detection systems leveraging machine learning can spot irregular patterns that may indicate a breach or attempted infiltration.

FP&A departments can employ data masking and tokenization techniques to obfuscate sensitive information while maintaining data usability. These techniques replace identifiable data elements with non-sensitive equivalents, rendering them useless to attackers without the proper decryption keys or context.

Compliance with data security regulations and standards is non-negotiable. Regular security audits and compliance checks ensure adherence to frameworks such as the Payment Card Industry Data Security Standard (PCI DSS) and ISO/IEC 27001. These audits also serve as opportunities to identify potential weak spots and reinforce security postures.

Not all threats originate from outside the organization. Insider threats, whether malicious or inadvertent, pose significant risks to big data security. Rigorous training programs and a culture of security awareness are essential in mitigating these internal risks. Moreover, implementing the principle of least privilege ensures that individuals only have access to the data necessary for their roles.

Artificial intelligence and machine learning algorithms are increasingly deployed in cybersecurity solutions to predict, detect, and respond to threats in real time. These systems can process vast quantities of data, identifying subtle anomalies that may elude traditional security systems.

As the landscape of cyber threats continues to evolve, so too must the cybersecurity strategies of FP&A units. The integration of big data with emerging technologies such as the Internet of Things (IoT) and blockchain offers new avenues for securing data transactions and enhancing traceability.

Cybersecurity risks in the big data domain present a significant challenge to the sanctity of FP&A functions.

Vigilance, constant innovation in security practices, and a holistic approach encompassing technology, processes, and people are the key ingredients in fortifying big data against the ever-present cyber threats. In mastering these domains, FP&A professionals can ensure the integrity and resilience of their data-driven analytical capabilities, safeguarding the financial strategies that propel enterprises towards growth and success.

Blockchain for Risk Transparency and Mitigation

The introduction of blockchain technology has ushered in a new paradigm of transparency and risk mitigation in the realm of Financial Planning & Analysis (FP&A). This decentralized ledger technology offers unparalleled security features that are reshaping how financial data is recorded, stored, and shared.

At its core, blockchain consists of a distributed database that records transactions in a series of immutable blocks, each cryptographically linked to its predecessor. This creates an unalterable record of data transactions, offering transparency and traceability that is fundamental to risk assessment and mitigation in FP&A.

Blockchain's inherent transparency stems from its public ledger, where all transactions are visible to participants. In FP&A, this transparency allows for real-time tracking of financial assets, providing a clear audit trail and reducing the opacity that can lead to financial misreporting or fraud.

The decentralized nature of blockchain mitigates the risk of a single point of failure, which is a vulnerability in centralized systems. Each participant, or node, maintains a copy of the ledger, ensuring the system's integrity even if parts of the network are compromised.

One of the most transformative applications of blockchain in FP&A is the use of smart contracts—self-executing contracts with the terms directly written into code. These can automate compliance with financial regulations and contractual obligations, reducing the risk of human error and ensuring consistent execution of financial agreements.

Blockchain employs various consensus mechanisms, like Proof of Work or Proof of Stake, to validate transactions. These mechanisms require network participants to agree on the veracity of transactions before they are added to the blockchain, thereby reducing the risk of fraudulent activities.

In traditional finance, counterparty risk arises from the possibility that one party may default on a transaction. Blockchain minimizes this risk by ensuring that transactions are irreversible once confirmed, thus enhancing the trustworthiness of financial engagements.

For FP&A, the challenge often lies in integrating blockchain with existing financial systems. Interoperability platforms are being developed to facilitate communication between different blockchains and legacy systems, reducing the risks associated with data silos and inconsistent financial reporting.

Despite its potential, blockchain faces regulatory challenges that impact its adoption in FP&A. Regulatory clarity is essential for organizations to confidently leverage blockchain for risk management. Efforts are underway to standardize blockchain practices which will further enhance its utility in mitigating financial risks.

Practical applications of blockchain in FP&A include streamlining payments and settlements, enhancing the accuracy of financial forecasting through reliable data, and reducing the costs and risks associated with cross-border transactions. Additionally, blockchain can enhance the robustness of supply chain finance, providing transparency across the entire value chain.

Blockchain's future in risk management is promising, with ongoing advancements in scalability and privacy-enhancing technologies. As these developments unfold, FP&A functions can expect to leverage blockchain for more comprehensive and sophisticated risk management strategies.

Blockchain technology presents FP&A with a powerful tool for risk transparency and mitigation. By capitalizing on its decentralized nature, immutable record-keeping, and consensus-driven validation, FP&A professionals can navigate the complex financial landscape with greater confidence and security. As blockchain continues to mature, its role in reshaping risk management practices in the financial sector is set to expand, offering new opportunities for innovation and strategic advantage.

Use Cases in Smart Contracts and KYC

In the labyrinthine world of financial regulation, Know Your Customer (KYC) requirements stand out as a sentinel at the gates of the financial system, ensuring that entities are protected against fraud, corruption, and money laundering. Smart contracts, an innovative offshoot of blockchain technology, have emerged as a potent mechanism for reinforcing KYC protocols, thus fortifying the bastions of financial security.

Smart contracts transcend the traditional contract paradigm by codifying terms and conditions onto a blockchain. They self-execute and self-enforce contractual obligations without the need for intermediaries. Integrating KYC procedures into smart contracts provides a seamless and automated approach to compliance that aligns with the relentless demand for efficiency in the financial domain.

By embedding regulatory requirements into the code of smart contracts, financial institutions can automate the adherence to KYC norms. These contracts can be programmed to trigger only when a counterparty has been verified and all requisite KYC documentation is in place, thereby ensuring compliance by design.

Each transaction or interaction within a smart contract is recorded on the blockchain, creating an immutable audit trail. This permanence is instrumental in satisfying the stringent record-keeping requirements of regulatory bodies, as every action is traceable and time-stamped, providing irrefutable evidence of due diligence.

Onboarding customers is often a cumbersome and time-intensive process fraught with redundancy. Smart contracts streamline customer onboarding by automating identity verification and due diligence checks. Once a customer's information is validated and stored on the blockchain, it can be reused, reducing the onboarding time for subsequent services across the financial ecosystem.

Financial transactions often carry an inherent risk due to the opaqueness of counterparty activities. Smart contracts offer a transparent solution where all parties have access to the same information, significantly diminishing the risk of fraud and misrepresentation.

Smart contracts can facilitate the secure and confidential sharing of KYC data across different institutions. With the consent of the customer, verified KYC data can be accessed by other parties, eliminating repetitive processes and fostering a more interconnected and efficient financial system.

Use Cases in the Financial Sector:

1. Trade Finance:

   - Smart contracts automate and secure the flow of goods, payment, and credit in trade finance. Incorporating KYC ensures that all parties involved in a transaction are verified, which is critical in a sector that hinges on trust and the reliable exchange of commodities.

2. Securities Settlement:

   - In securities trading, the settlement cycle is greatly accelerated by smart contracts. They enforce the exchange of shares for payment only after all regulatory checks, including KYC, have been satisfied, streamlining the process and mitigating settlement risk.

3. Insurance Claims Processing:

- Insurance claims are often fraught with the potential for fraudulent claims. Smart contracts integrated with KYC can systematically verify the identity of claimants and the authenticity of claims, leading to faster payouts and less fraud.

4. Peer-to-Peer Lending:

- The P2P lending market benefits from the precision of smart contracts to enforce loan agreements and repayment terms. Embedding KYC into these contracts ensures that borrowers are thoroughly vetted, reducing the risk for lenders.

As with any emerging technology, the integration of KYC processes within smart contracts presents challenges. Privacy concerns, the varying nature of global KYC regulations, and the need for standardization must be addressed. Furthermore, the technology's nascent state means that broader acceptance and trust from regulators and institutions are still forthcoming.

The fusion of smart contracts with KYC procedures delineates a future of financial interactions that are more secure, efficient, and compliant. These use cases exemplify the transformative impact that such integration holds for the financial sector, promising a streamlined approach to regulatory adherence and risk management. As these technologies continue to develop, their adoption will likely become a hallmark of modern, forward-thinking financial institutions striving for excellence in compliance and customer service.

Disrupting Traditional Risk Management Models

In a milieu where change is the only constant, traditional risk management models often fall short of addressing the dynamic forces that define the modern financial landscape. Innovative approaches are not merely advantageous; they are imperative for survival and success. Blockchain technology, with its immutable ledger and decentralized nature, stands as a paradigm-shifting force, its tremors felt across the conventional frameworks of risk management.

Traditional risk management models typically hinge on centralized systems, which, while standardized, are vulnerable to systemic failures and centralized points of attack. Blockchain disrupts this centralization, providing a decentralized alternative where trust is built into the system through distributed consensus mechanisms, ensuring resilience and mitigating the risk of single points of failure.

With blockchain, risk ownership is democratized. Each participant in the network shares responsibility for the integrity of the entire system. This not only disperses risk but also incentivizes participants to adhere to best practices, as the consequences of negligence or malfeasance are shared among all.

The cryptographic underpinnings of blockchain ensure that data once entered the ledger remains unalterable and secure. For risk management, this translates into higher confidence in the data's integrity, which is foundational for accurate risk analysis and decision-making.

Smart contracts represent a quantum leap in automating and enforcing compliance and contractual obligations. By executing conditions only when pre-defined criteria are met, they reduce the risk of non-compliance and contractual disputes. Moreover, they provide automated mitigation strategies that activate in response to identified risks or events, ensuring real-time responsiveness.

Blockchain inherently offers unparalleled transparency and traceability of transactions. This feature allows for a more granular tracking of risk exposure across all transactions, enabling a proactive rather than reactive approach to risk management.

In the blockchain realm, the settlement of transactions can occur almost instantaneously, obviating the need for traditional clearinghouses. This real-time settlement minimizes counterparty risks, as the time window for a counterparty to default on its obligation is drastically shortened.

Use Cases in Risk Management:

1. Credit Risk Evaluation:

 - Blockchain enables more transparent and comprehensive credit risk assessments by providing access to a borrower's historical financial transactions and behavior, thus allowing for a more informed and data-driven decision.

2. Operational Risk Monitoring:

 - By leveraging the immutable record-keeping capabilities of blockchain, companies can track and monitor operational processes in real-time, swiftly identifying any deviations or anomalies that may signify operational risk.

3. Regulatory Compliance Tracking:

- Blockchain's transparent nature facilitates the continuous and automated tracking of compliance with regulations, easing the burden of regulatory reporting and ensuring that compliance is continually maintained.

4. Fraud Detection and Prevention:

- The indelible and transparent record of transactions maintained by blockchain makes fraudulent activities easier to detect and harder to perpetrate, thereby acting as a deterrent and a tool for fraud prevention.

The adoption of blockchain in the realm of risk management is not without challenges. The technology's novelty means there is a steep learning curve, and regulatory uncertainty persists. Moreover, interoperability with existing systems and the scalability of solutions remain significant hurdles.

However, the path forward is illuminated by the technology's potential. As understanding deepens and regulatory frameworks evolve to accommodate these new models, blockchain's role in risk management is poised to expand. Traditional models will gradually be supplanted by blockchain's more dynamic, secure, and efficient approach, heralding a new era of financial security and risk intelligence.

Potential in Fraud Reduction

The specter of fraud looms large over the financial landscape, presenting a perennial challenge to institutions and enterprises. Traditional risk management systems have waged a relentless but often reactive battle against fraudulent activities. The introduction of blockchain technology, however, heralds a transformative era in which the very architecture of financial transactions is re-engineered to not just combat but pre-emptively reduce the potential for fraud.

At the center of blockchain's fraud reduction potential is its ledger, immutable and indelible. It ensures that once a transaction is recorded, it cannot be altered retroactively without a consensus across the network. This characteristic not only fortifies the transaction against tampering but also acts as a formidable deterrent to would-be fraudsters.

Blockchain technology employs complex cryptographic protocols that validate and secure each transaction. These protocols necessitate the verification of transactions by multiple parties in the network, which serves to weed out fraudulent activities at the source and create a robust environment of mutual oversight.

Decentralization of Authority:

The decentralized nature of blockchain stands in stark contrast to traditional centralized databases. By distributing the data across a network of nodes, blockchain ensures that no single entity has control over the entirety of the information, thereby reducing the risk of fraudulent manipulation by insiders.

Real-Time Auditing:

Blockchain's inherent transparency allows for real-time auditing of transactions. The continuous validation process by the network of nodes means that each transaction is under constant scrutiny, reducing the time window within which fraudulent activities can occur undetected.

Smart Contracts and Automated Compliance:

Smart contracts embedded in blockchain networks are self-executing contracts with the terms of the agreement directly written into code. They can be programmed to enforce compliance automatically and execute transactions only when certain conditions are met, thus ensuring that regulatory and contractual standards are upheld, reducing the risk of fraud related to non-compliance.

Case Studies and Applications:

1. Supply Chain Transparency:

   - In supply chain finance, blockchain can be used to create a transparent and verifiable trail of goods from origin to delivery, making it significantly more challenging for fraudulent misrepresentation of product origin or quality.

2. Identity Verification and Security:

   - Blockchain facilitates secure identity management. By storing personal identification on the blockchain, individuals and organizations can verify identities with greater accuracy, mitigating the risk of identity theft and related fraud.

3. Insurance Claims Processing:

   - Implementing blockchain within the insurance sector can help eliminate fraudulent claims by providing an immutable record of transactions and policies, allowing for immediate cross-referencing and validation.

Despite its potential, blockchain's integration into risk management, particularly for fraud reduction, requires overcoming technical, operational, and regulatory challenges. These include ensuring the robustness of the technology, addressing privacy concerns, and fostering regulatory acceptance that keeps pace with technological advancements.

The adaptability of blockchain technology suggests a future where its mechanisms for fraud reduction are deeply integrated into the operational fabric of financial institutions. As the technology matures and regulatory frameworks adapt, blockchain is set to become a cornerstone of a proactive and preventative approach to fraud reduction, transforming the narrative from one of risk management to one of risk aversion.

In summary, blockchain technology represents a significant leap forward in the fight against fraud. Its capacity to ensure the authenticity of transactions, coupled with the ability to enforce compliance and facilitate transparency, positions it as a pivotal tool in redefining risk management strategies. The path ahead will be shaped by continued innovation, cross-sector collaboration, and a commitment to embracing these advancements for a more secure financial future.

Challenges in Adoption and Scaling

The advent of blockchain technology as a bulwark against fraud presents a compelling narrative of modernization in risk management. Yet, as organizations attempt to pivot from legacy systems to this new paradigm, they encounter a series of challenges that can impede the adoption and scaling of blockchain solutions. These challenges span technical, operational, regulatory, and cultural domains, each weaving an intricate layer in the mosaic of blockchain implementation.

Blockchain's innovative nature brings with it a complexity that can be daunting. The difficulty in understanding its intricacies not only affects the ease of adoption but also poses challenges for scaling up. Developing or procuring the requisite blockchain infrastructure requires specialized knowledge and skills, which are in high demand but limited supply. Moreover, integrating this technology with existing IT systems poses a significant hurdle for many organizations.

The seamless integration of blockchain into current business processes can be an onerous task. The operational shift from centralized to decentralized systems requires a fundamental change in how data is handled and transactions are processed. Businesses must re-evaluate their workflows, which often involves dismantling and redesigning legacy structures—a process fraught with resistance and potential disruption to ongoing operations.

The regulatory landscape surrounding blockchain is still

in flux, with many jurisdictions lacking clear guidelines or having disparate regulations that can hinder cross-border operations. The ambiguity and evolving nature of blockchain-related policies create a climate of uncertainty for organizations, making it challenging to commit significant resources to technology still under legislative scrutiny.

Adopting blockchain technology necessitates not just a technological shift but also a cultural one. It requires fostering an organizational mindset that values transparency, shared governance, and a collaborative approach to data management. This cultural transformation can be particularly challenging in hierarchically structured or siloed organizations unaccustomed to the decentralized ethos of blockchain systems.

Blockchain technology, particularly in its earlier forms, faces issues of scalability. The ability to process a high volume of transactions quickly and cost-effectively is a concern, with the current infrastructure of many blockchain platforms struggling to match the throughput of conventional financial systems. This limitation can deter large-scale adoption, particularly by organizations that deal with significant transaction volumes.

Different blockchain platforms often lack interoperability, making it challenging for various systems to communicate and transact with one another. In a financial ecosystem that increasingly relies on interconnectedness, the lack of standardized protocols can lead to fragmentation and inefficiencies, hindering widespread adoption.

While blockchain's transparency is one of its strengths, it also raises concerns about data privacy. Balancing the immutable nature of the blockchain with the need to protect sensitive information is a delicate act. Additionally, while blockchain itself is secure, the endpoints—such as user interfaces and wallets—can be vulnerable to attacks, necessitating robust security measures at all access points.

The initial investment for blockchain adoption can be substantial. The costs associated with technology acquisition, process re-engineering, staff training, and regulatory compliance can be prohibitive, particularly for smaller organizations. Additionally, the ongoing operational costs, primarily related to energy consumption for certain blockchain types, add another layer to the financial considerations.

To understand the practical aspects of these challenges, one might consider the example of a multinational corporation that embarked on a blockchain project to enhance its supply chain transparency. The organization faced initial setbacks due to the lack of in-house blockchain expertise, incompatible legacy systems, and hesitancy from stakeholders resistant to change. However, by adopting a phased implementation strategy, seeking regulatory guidance, and fostering a culture of innovation, the organization successfully integrated blockchain technology into its operations, setting a precedent for others in the industry.

As we gaze toward the horizon of financial innovation, these challenges represent the gatekeepers to a new era of risk management and fraud prevention. Navigating through them requires a confluence of strategic vision, technological acumen, and unwavering commitment to the transformative promise of blockchain technology. Only by addressing these multifaceted hurdles can organizations unlock the full potential of blockchain and scale it effectively, ensuring they remain at the forefront of this financial evolution.

CHAPTER 6: FINANCIAL INSTRUMENTS FOR RISK MANAGEMENT

In the vigilant pursuit of stability within the ever-shifting sands of the financial markets, a diverse arsenal of instruments has been devised to manage and mitigate risk. These tools, often complex and intricate in their construction, serve as the bulwark against uncertainties that can erode the financial foundations of an enterprise. Financial instruments for risk management are the lifeblood of a robust financial planning and analysis (FP&A) strategy, enabling organizations to navigate the turbulent seas of market volatility with greater assurance.

Derivatives stand as sentinels in the world of financial instruments. Futures, options, and swaps are the primary derivatives used in hedging strategies, providing organizations with mechanisms to lock in prices, hedge against potential adverse movements in market rates, and transfer specific risks to other parties. These instruments are like the finely tuned components of a mechanical timepiece, each serving a distinct purpose yet interrelated in maintaining the equilibrium of the financial ecosystem.

Futures contracts are standardized agreements to buy or sell an underlying asset at a predetermined price at a specified future date. They serve as a commitment between two parties, offering a haven from the capricious winds of price fluctuations. As a cornerstone of risk management, futures enable organizations to establish a fixed cost or revenue stream, ensuring that budgetary projections remain unscathed by market turbulence.

Options grant the holder the right, but not the obligation, to purchase or sell an asset at an agreed-upon price within a certain period. These instruments are akin to a strategic gambit in chess, providing the flexibility to capitalize on favorable market movements while limiting potential losses. Call options safeguard against rising prices, while put options protect against price declines, each offering a calculated form of insurance for the financial strategist.

Swaps are customized contracts that allow two parties to exchange cash flows or other financial variables. Interest rate swaps, currency swaps, and commodity swaps are the most prevalent, each designed to balance exposures to diverse types of market risks. In the intricate dance of financial risk management, swaps are the partners that enable a harmonious alignment of cash flow expectations with actual market conditions.

The utilization of derivatives is not without its complexities. Pricing and valuation of these instruments demand a deep understanding of the underlying assets and the factors that influence their market dynamics. Counterparty risk—the possibility that the other party in a derivative contract will default—adds a layer of strategic consideration that must be meticulously assessed and managed.

In the quest for financial stability, derivatives are potent yet double-edged swords. Their misuse can lead to magnified losses and unforeseen consequences, as history has shown in numerous financial debacles. Thus, their adoption within an FP&A framework must be accompanied by prudent policies, rigorous due diligence, and an unwavering focus on aligning these instruments with the strategic objectives of the organization.

The judicious selection and application of financial instruments for risk management are integral to the art and science of FP&A. Each organization must calibrate its approach to these tools, tuning them to the unique frequency of its risk profile and strategic goals. Whether it is through the measured use of futures to stabilize commodity costs or deploying options to harness the growth potential of an equity portfolio, the mastery of these instruments lies at the heart of sound financial stewardship.

Derivatives: Futures, Options, Swaps

The realm of derivatives is a complex constellation within the financial universe, where entities seek to predict and protect against the fickle moods of market forces. In the pursuit of managing risk, futures, options, and swaps emerge as the triptych of derivative instruments, each with its own distinct capabilities and applications within financial planning and analysis (FP&A).

Futures contracts stand as covenants between parties, offering a glimpse of certainty in an uncertain market.

A buyer and seller enter into an agreement where the former is obligated to purchase, and the latter to sell, a specific quantity of an asset at a pre-determined price, on a specified future date. These contracts are traded on regulated exchanges and are standardized in terms of quality, quantity, and delivery time, reducing the risk of default and ensuring a greater degree of liquidity.

In FP&A, futures are invaluable for entities requiring a predictable cash flow, such as agricultural producers who lock in prices for their crops to hedge against the risk of a fall in market prices. Conversely, an airline may use fuel futures to secure a steady price for jet fuel, insulating itself from the volatility in oil markets.

Options are contracts that provide the holder with the right, but not the obligation, to buy or sell the underlying asset at an agreed-upon price, known as the strike price, within a specified period. A call option allows the holder to purchase the asset, beneficial when prices rise above the strike price, while a put option permits the sale of the asset, advantageous when prices drop below the strike price.

The strategic acumen here lies in the right to choose. FP&A professionals leverage options to maintain flexibility, as markets evolve and new information emerges. As a form of risk management, options can be likened to an insurance policy, demanding an upfront premium for the potential future benefit, without the compulsion to act unless it aligns with financial strategy.

Swaps are bespoke agreements to exchange cash flows or other financial variables between two parties. These over-the-counter contracts are tailored to the needs of the parties involved and are not traded on standard exchanges, which introduces counterparty risk that needs to be carefully managed.

Interest rate swaps, where parties exchange fixed interest rate payments for floating rate payments, are a common tool for managing exposure to interest rate fluctuations. Corporations with fixed-rate liabilities may enter an interest rate swap to benefit from a declining interest rate environment, effectively converting their fixed rates to floating rates. Currency swaps and commodity swaps function similarly, allowing entities to manage foreign exchange and commodity price risks, respectively.

The valuation of derivatives like futures, options, and swaps is underpinned by complex models that consider numerous factors, including the current market price of the underlying asset, the strike price, the time to expiration, and the risk-free rate of return, among others. The Black-Scholes model for options pricing and the binomial model are examples of the theoretical frameworks that guide FP&A professionals in their valuation exercises.

Managing the associated risks, such as counterparty risk in swaps or the premium cost in options, requires a strategic blend of financial acumen and market insight. FP&A functions must establish rigorous risk assessment processes, employ due diligence in partner selection, and implement robust monitoring systems to ensure the derivatives strategies align with the organization's overall risk management objectives.

Derivatives are powerful instruments that, when used effectively, can protect and enhance the financial health of an organization. Futures provide a shield against price volatility, options offer strategic flexibility, and swaps enable the transfer of specific financial exposures. The successful integration of these instruments into the FP&A framework demands a meticulous and informed approach, ensuring they are employed not as speculative devices but as prudent safeguards and strategic enablers in the intricate dance of risk management.

Types and Uses in Hedging Strategies

In the grand chessboard of financial risk management, derivatives stand as strategic pieces, skilfully maneuvered in hedging strategies to safeguard an organization's financial health against market unpredictability. Hedging, in essence, is the practice of taking an offsetting position in a derivative in order to balance any potential losses gained from adverse movements in spot market prices. By delving into the several types of derivatives used and their specific applications within hedging strategies, one can appreciate the nuanced tactical play that underpins financial planning and analysis (FP&A).

The use of futures in hedging strategies is akin to placing a sentry at the gate, standing watch against price fluctuations. Commodity producers and consumers routinely engage in futures contracts to secure a future price for goods ranging from agricultural products to metals and energy sources. By locking in prices, these entities hedge against the price risk that could severely impact their financial results.

For example, a coffee manufacturer fearing a rise in bean

prices due to a potential poor harvest season might purchase futures contracts for coffee. Should prices indeed rise, the hedge provides a financial counterbalance, as the gains from the futures contract offset the higher costs faced when purchasing the actual beans at the elevated spot prices.

Options offer a different flavor of security: the ability to harness opportunity while limiting downside risk. Unlike futures, which carry a fulfillment obligation, options grant the right, but not the obligation, to execute the contract. This asymmetry makes options a preferred hedging tool when uncertainty is high, and flexibility is prized.

Consider a real estate investment trust (REIT) that seeks to hedge against interest rate hikes that would increase its borrowing costs on its variable-rate debt. The REIT might purchase interest rate cap options, which would pay out if interest rates rise above a certain level, thus compensating for the increased interest expenses.

Swaps are utilized in hedging to exchange one type of cash flow for another, thereby mitigating exposure to fluctuations in interest rates, currency exchange rates, or commodity prices. A classic hedging strategy using interest rate swaps might involve a corporation with floating-rate debt that expects interest rates to rise. By entering a swap to pay a fixed rate and receive a floating rate, the corporation effectively locks in the interest cost, shielding itself from future rate hikes.

Alternatively, a multinational corporation facing exposure to foreign exchange risk due to operations in multiple countries might employ currency swaps. By swapping cash flows in different currencies, it secures a more predictable expense and revenue stream in its home currency, mitigating the risk posed by currency fluctuations.

While derivatives are potent tools in the FP&A arsenal, their use in hedging is not without complication. The effectiveness of a hedging strategy depends upon a multitude of factors, including the correct selection of derivative type, the sizing of the hedge relative to the exposure, and the timing of execution. Moreover, constant vigilance is required to assess the hedge's performance and to make adjustments as market conditions evolve.

For practitioners of FP&A, hedging is both a science and an art—a careful balance of mathematical precision and market intuition. It demands a thorough understanding of the organization's risk profile, meticulous planning, and continuous monitoring. Derivatives, when wielded with skill and foresight, become not just protective measures, but strategic enablers that contribute to the financial stability and operational efficiency of the enterprise.

Pricing and Valuation Complexities

Financial derivatives—are a key instrument in the hedging strategies of modern finance—is marked by complex pricing and valuation challenges that demand a sophisticated blend of mathematical models, market insight, and risk consideration. The intricacies involved in the pricing and valuation of derivatives such as futures, options, and swaps are pivotal for their effective use in financial planning and analysis (FP&A).

At the heart of option pricing lies the renowned Black-Scholes model, a groundbreaking formula that transformed financial markets with its elegant solution to valuing European options. The model encapsulates critical factors including the current price of the underlying asset, the option's strike price, time until expiration, risk-free interest rates, and the asset's volatility. By synthesizing these variables, the Black-Scholes model provides a theoretical price for an option, serving as a foundational benchmark in option trading and risk management.

For FP&A professionals, the Black-Scholes model is not just a pricing tool but an essential litmus test for market prices. It informs whether an option is undervalued or overvalued in the market, guiding strategic decisions on option transactions. However, the model's assumptions—such as constant volatility and interest rates, along with the notion that the option can't be exercised before expiry—invite scrutiny and adaptation in practice.

Pricing futures contracts also serves up its distinct set of complexities, rooted in the convergence theory. This principle suggests that as a futures contract nears its delivery date, its price will converge with the spot price of the underlying asset. Factors like carrying costs (including storage and insurance) and the time value of money play pivotal roles in determining futures prices.

For commodities, seasonal and geopolitical factors may add layers of complexity to pricing. An FP&A specialist must possess a profound understanding of these dynamics to effectively incorporate futures into a hedging strategy. The concept of basis risk—the potential for slippage between the futures price and the spot price—must be rigorously managed to ensure the hedge remains effective.

The valuation of swaps, particularly interest rate swaps, is a multifaceted process involving the netting of expected future cash flows from fixed and floating rate payment streams. The challenge lies in accurately forecasting future rates and adjusting for the time value of money. The swap valuation aligns with the current market conditions through discount factors derived from the yield curve, representing the market's consensus on future interest rates.

In the context of currency swaps, additional layers of complexity emerge in the form of exchange rate projections and country-specific economic outlooks. For the FP&A professional, this necessitates an awareness of global economic indicators, monetary policies, and the political climate that could influence currency values.

A sophisticated approach to derivative pricing is the risk-neutral valuation, which posits that investors expect to receive, at a minimum, the risk-free rate of return. Under this framework, the expected returns of all assets are adjusted to reflect this baseline, simplifying the pricing of derivatives by focusing on the arbitrage opportunities rather than risk preferences. This technique is particularly useful in an FP&A setting for valuing complex derivatives and structuring hedging strategies that align with the organization's risk tolerance.

In practice, the FP&A function must navigate these pricing and valuation complexities with finesse. It is not enough to rely solely on theoretical models; market realities, institutional knowledge, and regulatory considerations must also be integrated into the decision-making process. The ability to apply, adapt, and challenge these models is a testament to the analytical acumen required in FP&A.

Counterparty Risk Considerations

In the intricate financial ballet of derivatives and other complex financial instruments, counterparty risk, also known as credit exposure, plays a vital role in the choreography. This risk arises when one party in a financial transaction may fail to fulfill its contractual obligations, potentially leading to financial loss for the other party. In the landscape of FP&A, a profound understanding and meticulous management of counterparty risk is paramount.

At the outset, FP&A professionals must assess the creditworthiness of potential counterparties. This process involves a deep dive into the counterparty's credit history, financial health, and overall reliability. Credit rating agencies offer a baseline for such assessments; however, they are not infallible. The due diligence extends to reviewing annual reports, market news, and financial statements to gauge the counterparty's ability to honor the terms of the contract.

Mitigation of counterparty risk in derivatives transactions often involves the use of collateral agreements, such as Credit Support Annexes (CSAs) under the framework of the International Swaps and Derivatives Association (ISDA). These agreements require the posting of collateral for positions that accrue significant exposure, thus providing a buffer against potential default. Dynamic hedging strategies also play their part, enabling FP&A experts to adjust their positions in response to changes in the counterparty's credit profile.

The post-2008 financial landscape has seen a crucial shift towards centralized clearing of standardized derivative contracts through clearinghouses. These intermediaries act as the counterparty to both sides of a transaction, significantly reducing the risk of default. They enforce margin requirements and perform daily mark-to-market valuations to ensure adequate collateral coverage. For FP&A professionals, this introduces an additional layer of security but also brings into play the clearinghouse's own credit risk and the associated costs of clearing.

Bilateral and multilateral netting arrangements further reduce counterparty risk by offsetting claims between parties to determine a single net payment obligation in the event of default. Such arrangements streamline settlements, reduce the quantum of required collateral, and lessen operational complexity. A proficient FP&A department must understand the legal enforceability of netting agreements across different jurisdictions, especially when dealing with global counterparties.

Quantifying counterparty risk requires sophisticated models that incorporate potential future exposure (PFE), credit valuation adjustment (CVA), and debt valuation adjustment (DVA). PFE estimates the extent of exposure at a specific confidence level over a certain time horizon. CVA adjusts the risk-free valuation of a derivative by the market value of counterparty credit risk, while DVA reflects the entity's own credit risk in its liabilities. These metrics necessitate advanced quantitative skills and a strong grasp of probabilistic modeling from FP&A professionals.

Contractual clauses such as covenants, representations, warranties, and termination events are all designed to clarify the actions and remedies available in the event of a breach. Legal recourse may include the right to demand additional collateral, suspend transactions, or terminate contracts. FP&A teams must work closely with legal advisors to ensure that contracts are robust and protective measures are actionable.

To dilute the concentration of counterparty risk, diversification strategies are crucial. This involves spreading derivative transactions across multiple counterparties, rather than being reliant on a single entity. The FP&A function should continuously monitor counterparty exposures against risk tolerance thresholds and adjust the distribution of transactions accordingly.

In an era of heightened regulatory scrutiny, compliance with anti-money laundering, know your customer (KYC), and other regulatory requirements is non-negotiable. Ethical considerations also compel FP&A professionals to avoid transactions with counterparties whose practices may pose reputational risk.

Counterparty risk considerations demand an intricate understanding of legal, financial, and ethical dimensions, along with the application of rigorous risk assessment and mitigation techniques. The following sections will further elaborate on the practical aspects of managing counterparty risk in the context of FP&A, ensuring that the reader is equipped with the necessary knowledge to navigate this nuanced and critical facet of financial risk management.

Accounting for Derivative Instruments

As we delve into the domain of derivative instruments within the FP&A framework, it is crucial to navigate the labyrinth of accounting standards that govern their recognition, measurement, and disclosure. Derivatives, with their inherent complexity and potential for significant budgetary impact, require meticulous accounting practices to reflect their true economic essence and manage the risks they pose to an organization's financial statements.

The journey through the thicket of derivative accounting begins with the recognition of these financial instruments on the balance sheet. Upon entering a derivative contract, an entity must recognize it as either an asset or a liability, measured initially at fair value. The fair value is the price that would be received to sell an asset or paid to transfer a liability in an orderly transaction between market participants at the measurement date, often determined by market prices or valuation models in the absence of observable market data.

Derivatives are frequently used for hedging purposes—to shield against fluctuations in exchange rates, interest rates, or commodity prices. Accounting for hedging activities necessitates a determination of the type of hedge: fair value, cash flow, or net investment. Each type has its own set of accounting rules under the relevant financial reporting frameworks, such as IFRS or US GAAP.

For a hedge to qualify for hedge accounting, it must satisfy several criteria, including formal documentation at inception, a high degree of effectiveness in achieving offsetting changes in fair value or cash flows, and reliable measurability of the hedging relationship. Failure to meet these criteria will preclude the use of hedge accounting, resulting in immediate recognition of gains or losses in the income statement, potentially leading to significant volatility.

After initial recognition, derivatives must be measured at fair value at each reporting date. Changes in fair value are accounted for depending on the purpose of the derivative and whether it qualifies for hedge accounting. For derivatives not designated as hedging instruments, fair value changes are recognized in profit or loss. For derivatives that are part of a hedging relationship, the accounting treatment of the fair value changes depends on the nature of the hedge.

Furthermore, impairment considerations may come into play if there are indications that a derivative's counterparty may fail to fulfill its obligations. FP&A professionals must be vigilant in reviewing credit exposures and the potential need to record impairment losses.

Derivative accounting also extends to comprehensive disclosure requirements, designed to provide transparency to financial statement users regarding an entity's risk management activities and the effect of derivatives on its financial position and performance. These disclosures include information about the fair values of derivatives, their accounting treatment, risk management objectives and strategies, and any credit risk related to derivative instruments.

Accounting for derivative instruments is a mosaic of intricate rules and practical challenges—a nexus where the theoretical principles of finance converge with the gritty realities of business operations. It demands a confluence of analytical expertise, regulatory knowledge, and strategic foresight. As we progress through the subsequent sections, we will unravel the layers of complexity associated with derivative instruments and their role in the broader landscape of financial risk management, all while maintaining fidelity to the overarching themes and stylistic nuances of this text.

Insurance and Alternative Risk Transfers (ART)

Navigating the tumultuous waters of financial risk, organizations often seek the shelter of insurance and alternative risk transfer mechanisms. These financial navigational tools not only serve as bulwarks against potential financial storms but also manifest as intricate components of a broader risk management strategy.

Insurance, the stalwart of risk mitigation, operates on the principle of risk pooling and transfer. By paying a premium, a company can transfer specified risks to an insurer, thereby reducing the volatility of its financial outcomes. The insurer, through the law of large numbers, predicts and quantifies losses within a pool of similar risk exposures, ensuring that the premiums collected are sufficient to cover the claims and still return a profit.

However, the utilization of insurance within FP&A is not a mere transaction—it requires an analytical approach to determine the optimal coverage levels, deductibles, and policy terms that align with the company's risk appetite and financial objectives. The intricacies of risk assessment, such as loss frequency and severity, are pivotal in sculpting an insurance strategy that underpins both financial stability and strategic agility.

For certain risks, traditional insurance products may not suffice or may prove cost-prohibitive. Herein enters the realm of Alternative Risk Transfers (ART), a suite of innovative solutions that offer customization and flexibility beyond conventional insurance offerings. ART mechanisms, including captives, risk retention groups, and securitization of risk through instruments like catastrophe bonds, empower organizations to tailor their risk financing strategies with greater precision.

Captives, for example, are insurance companies owned by a parent firm to insure the risks of its group. This internalization of risk allows for enhanced control over claims management, potential tax benefits, and the accrual of underwriting profits within the organization.

Securitization of risk involves the transformation of uncertain financial exposures into tradable securities. Through this financial alchemy, a company can distribute its risk across the capital markets, drawing upon a diverse pool of investors seeking uncorrelated returns. The coupling of insurance with capital market mechanisms in this manner not only broadens the avenues for risk distribution but also introduces novel dynamics to the organization's financial landscape.

Integrating insurance and ART within FP&A is akin to conducting a symphony where each instrument plays a vital role in harmony. The FP&A professional, therefore, must act as a maestro—orchestrating the interplay between risk identification, insurance procurement, ART structuring, and the organization's financial strategies. This involves continuous monitoring of the market, assessing the evolving nature of risks, and aligning risk transfer mechanisms with the company's financial planning cycles.

Inherent within this integration is the need for dynamic financial models that account for the costs and benefits of risk transfer decisions. The models must encapsulate the range of outcomes and their implications on financial metrics such as cash flow stability, earnings volatility, and capital adequacy.

Finally, the interweaving of insurance and ART with FP&A dictates a need for foresight and sophistication. It is an intellectual exercise that demands not only a grasp of the financial instruments at hand but also an understanding of their interdependencies and the broader economic environment in which they operate. As we progress within this tome, we shall further explore how these risk management conduits can be fine-tuned to fortify an organization's financial fortifications, ensuring that it remains robust in the face of the unpredictable tides of risk and uncertainty.

Role of Insurance in Risk Management

In the intricate lattice of risk management, insurance emerges as a pivotal mechanism, a bulwark against the unforeseen calamities that can buffet an organization. It is the proverbial safety net that captures the financial fallout from stochastic events, be they wrought by natural disasters, litigation, or the caprices of market dynamics. Herein, we dissect the role of insurance in risk management, distilling its essence through the prism of financial planning and analysis (FP&A).

The genesis of insurance lies in the mutualisation of risk—a concept as old as human enterprise itself. From the caravans of the Silk Road to the maritime adventurers of the Age of Discovery, the pooling of resources to defray individual losses has been a cornerstone of commerce. Modern risk management strategies have refined this concept into robust frameworks, integrating insurance into a comprehensive risk mitigation repertoire.

At its core, insurance serves to redistribute risk by transferring the fiscal impact of potential losses to an insurer in exchange for premium payments. This arrangement permits organizations to balance the scales of risk and capital preservation, ensuring that a single misfortune does not destabilize their financial foundations. The underlying principle is one of shared risk; the premiums of the many indemnify the losses of the few.

In the realm of FP&A, risk management is incomplete without the strategic deployment of insurance. Companies must meticulously evaluate their risk profiles, identifying assets and operations vulnerable to disruption. This assessment is twofold—quantitative in appraising the potential cost of risks, and qualitative in gauging their likelihood and impact on the business continuum.

Once risks are inventoried and appraised, the judicious selection of insurance products ensues. Property and casualty insurance guard against damage to physical assets, while liability insurance provides defence against claims of injury or damage inflicted by the organization's activities. Not to be overlooked are the specialized domains of cyber insurance and intellectual property coverage, increasingly relevant in today's digital and innovation-driven marketplace.

The alchemy of insurance in risk management lies not merely in its protective capacity but also in its ability to facilitate growth and entrepreneurial boldness. With the knowledge that certain risks are hedged, organizations can venture into new markets, launch innovative products, and engage in strategic alliances with a greater degree of confidence. Insurance, therefore, is not a mere expense but an investment in stability and opportunity.

The strategic role of a CFO transcends the actuarial aspects of insurance. As the architect of risk management strategy, the CFO must navigate the complex interplay of insurance coverage, costs, and corporate objectives. This involves crafting a risk management portfolio calibrated to the enterprise's risk appetite and financial thresholds. It is a meticulous balancing act, where the cost of premiums must be weighed against the potential for value erosion in the event of uncovered losses.

Furthermore, insurance is a dynamic instrument, responsive to the evolving landscape of risks. Regulatory shifts, technological advancements, and socio-economic trends all bear influence on the nature of risks and the corresponding insurance solutions. The prudent CFO stays abreast of these changes, ensuring that the organization's insurance coverage adapts in lockstep with its risk profile.

The role of insurance in risk management is fundamental and multifaceted. It mitigates financial exposure, empowers strategic ventures, and sustains the corporate edifice against the vicissitudes of fortune. For the finance professional, insurance is an indispensable tool in the orchestration of a resilient and forward-leaning enterprise. As we chart the course of FP&A, the astute integration of insurance within the broader risk management strategy remains a testament to financial prudence and visionary leadership.

Captive Insurance Companies

Captive insurance companies represent a strategic departure from traditional insurance markets. They permit their parent organizations to finance risks internally, circumventing the broader insurance sector and its attendant volatility in premiums and coverage terms. By establishing a captive, an entity secures a bespoke shield, one forged with the specificity of its risk landscape in mind.

A foundational element in understanding captives recognizes their classification. They range from pure captives, insuring only the risks of their parent company or companies, to group captives that insure risks of member companies typically within the same industry. There are also rent-a-captives, providing insurance to non-owner companies and acting as a stepping stone for organizations experimenting with captive insurance without the commitment of forming a separate entity.

The strategic implementation of a captive insurance

company involves an intricate calculus. Financial leaders must weigh the initial capital investment against the potential for reduced insurance costs over time. Actuarial expertise is paramount in this equation—accurate risk assessment and premium setting are the lifeblood of a successful captive. Furthermore, the tax implications of establishing a captive, while potentially favorable, require careful navigation to remain within regulatory bounds and to optimize financial outcomes.

Captive insurance companies also serve as a nexus for enhancing risk management practices. As self-contained entities, they incentivize robust risk control and loss prevention strategies. There is a direct correlation between effective risk management and financial performance for captives; better loss experiences translate into retained earnings and the potential for reduced premiums.

One of the more sophisticated applications of captive insurance is in accessing reinsurance markets. Captives can cede portions of their risk to reinsurers to secure additional capacity or to mitigate catastrophic exposures. This strategy enables parent companies to enjoy the dual benefits of tailored coverage and the risk spreading mechanisms of the broader reinsurance industry.

However, the path to establishing a captive is paved with complexity. Regulatory hurdles, capital requirements, and the need for ongoing management are significant considerations. Entities must decide on domicile—selecting a jurisdiction with favorable regulatory, tax, and operational conditions. This decision impacts governance structures, compliance obligations, and the strategic flexibility of the captive.

The role of the CFO and the FP&A unit in the oversight and integration of a captive insurance company is critical. They must ensure that the captive aligns with the organization's broader financial strategies, serves its risk management objectives, and complies with accounting standards. The FP&A function, with its analytical prowess, is integral to the ongoing assessment and recalibration of the captive's performance, ensuring its contributions to the organization's health remain positive.

In sum, captive insurance companies are a sophisticated financial tool within the arsenal of corporate risk management. Their purposeful creation represents an intentional stride towards financial self-reliance and proactive risk mitigation. They are emblematic of an organization's commitment to the meticulous stewardship of its risk profile—a commitment that, when executed with acumen and foresight, can lead to substantial strategic advantages.

Securitization of Risk through Alternative Risk Transfer

Nestled within the complex realm of financial risk management lies the concept of Alternative Risk Transfer (ART), a mechanism that stands as a testament to human ingenuity in crafting sophisticated instruments of risk mitigation. ART encompasses a range of strategies, but at the heart of this domain is the securitization of risk—a process that repackages portfolios of risk into tradable securities.

Securitization of risk through ART involves the

transformation of uncertain financial exposures into securities, such as bonds, that can be sold to investors. This transmutation introduces a new paradigm, wherein risks are not simply underwritten and retained but are dispersed across the capital markets. Such an approach can increase the capacity of organizations to manage large and complex risks that may be beyond the appetite of traditional insurers or captive insurance entities.

The anatomy of a typical risk securitization transaction begins with the identification of a pool of risks that are to be transferred. This pool could consist of various exposures, from credit risk to natural catastrophes. These risks are then transferred to a Special Purpose Vehicle (SPV), a legally separate entity created solely for the transaction. The SPV issues securities that are linked to the performance of the underlying risk pool—securities that investors can purchase, thereby providing the capital required to back the risks.

One of the most recognizable forms of risk securitization in ART is the Catastrophe Bond (Cat Bond). These securities are designed to provide liquidity to insurers in the aftermath of catastrophic events such as hurricanes or earthquakes. The yields on these bonds are typically higher to compensate investors for the risk of potentially losing their principal should a qualifying catastrophe occur.

For the issuer, the allure of securitization through ART is manifold. It offers an alternative form of risk financing that can be more cost-effective than traditional insurance. It also allows for the diversification of risk transfer mechanisms, reducing reliance on the insurance market and broadening the base of potential capital sources. Furthermore, these instruments can be structured in a manner that matches the specific risk profiles of issuers, offering a bespoke solution to risk financing that aligns with strategic financial planning.

However, securitization also carries its own set of complexities. It requires rigorous risk modeling and assessment to structure the securities in a way that is palatable to investors. Investors must be convinced of the robustness of the underlying risk data and the actuarial soundness of the securities' pricing. Additionally, regulatory considerations play a pivotal role, as the issuance of risk-linked securities must navigate the intricate waters of financial regulation.

The Financial Planning & Analysis (FP&A) leader plays a crucial role in the orchestration of an ART securitization strategy. They must ensure that the organization's risk management objectives are harmoniously integrated with its funding strategies, liquidity needs, and overall financial health. The FP&A team's analytical capabilities are leveraged to conduct scenario analyses and stress testing, informing the decision-making process and ensuring that the securitization aligns with the organization's risk tolerance and capital structure.

In essence, the securitization of risk through ART is a vibrant illustration of the financial alchemy that turns uncertainty into opportunity. It reflects the dynamic nature of risk management, where innovation in financial engineering enables organizations to engage with the capital markets in managing exposures that once might have been uninsurable. As part of a comprehensive risk management strategy, ART offers FP&A leaders a powerful tool to secure financial resilience and to navigate an ever-evolving landscape of risks.

Assessing Insurable Risks and Coverage Adequacy

The process of assessing insurable risks requires a meticulous analysis of the organization's exposure to potential losses. This assessment is far from a cursory glance; it is a deep examination of the company's operations, assets, and external factors that contribute to its risk profile. This risk profiling entails evaluating the likelihood of specific events and the magnitude of their potential impact on the organization's financial health.

The FP&A professional begins by cataloging the organization's tangible and intangible assets, considering factors such as property values, critical supply chains, intellectual property, and reputation. For each identified asset, potential risks are pinpointed—ranging from physical damage due to natural disasters to business interruption and cyber threats. Additionally, the organization must consider liability risks that may arise from its operations, products, or professional conduct.

Once risks are identified, the next step is to evaluate existing insurance policies to determine whether the coverage in place aligns with the organization's risk profile. This scrutiny involves dissecting policy terms, exclusions, and limits to identify gaps in coverage that could leave the organization vulnerable. The FP&A leader must question, debate, and confirm the sufficiency of coverage amounts, ensuring they are proportional to the value of insured assets and the scale of potential liabilities.

A poignant example of this exercise could involve a company with global operations. Such an entity may face diverse risks, from political unrest in one region affecting supply chains to regulatory changes in another impacting market access. An FP&A leader must ensure that the company's insurance coverage encapsulates these multinational facets, offering a safety net that is as broad and diverse as the risks themselves.

To aid in this complex task, FP&A leaders often utilize quantitative tools, including actuarial models that estimate loss frequencies and severities. They also employ qualitative assessments, including industry benchmarking and expert consultations. Furthermore, they must stay abreast of market trends and emerging risks that could necessitate adjustments to insurance coverages.

Effectively, the goal is to craft an insurance architecture that is not just a patchwork of policies, but a tailored suit of armor—flexible, yet robust, and capable of expanding or contracting in response to the business's evolving landscape. It's about striking a delicate balance between being over-insured, which unnecessarily ties up capital, and under-insured, which can lead to catastrophic financial exposure.

In tandem with assessing insurance coverages, the FP&A leader must also evaluate the organization's risk retention strategy. This involves determining the optimal level of risk to retain in-house versus transferring through insurance. Through a considered analysis of the organization's risk appetite and financial capacity, the leader sets deductibles and self-insured retentions that reflect the company's willingness and ability to absorb losses.

Assessing insurable risks and coverage adequacy, therefore, becomes an ongoing dialogue, not a once-off conversation. It requires constant vigilance and periodic review, for the risk landscape is as mutable as the market itself. It's a dialogue that demands FP&A leaders to be both historians, learning from past losses, and futurists, anticipating the impact of the next black swan event.

The assessment of insurable risks and the adequacy of coverage is a cornerstone of strategic risk management. It is an intricate dance between identifying potential perils and crafting a defense that is both cost-effective and comprehensive. For the FP&A leader, it is a critical endeavor that ensures the organization's resilience in the face of uncertainty, securing its assets, and safeguarding its future prosperity.

Credit Enhancements and Guarantees

Navigating the labyrinthine world of finance, FP&A professionals must wield the tools of credit enhancements and guarantees with the deftness of a master sculptor chiseling away risk to reveal the robust figure of financial stability beneath. In this detailed exegesis, we will dissect these financial instruments and their pivotal role in fortifying an organization's credit standing, thereby expanding its access to capital markets and securing more favorable borrowing terms.

Credit enhancements are financial strategies employed by debt issuers to improve the credit profile of a financial obligation, thus reducing the perceived risk for investors. These strategies serve as a bulwark, reinforcing the issuer's commitment to repaying its debt and, in doing so, lower the cost of borrowing. Guarantees, a subset of credit enhancements, represent a solemn vow by a third party —often a parent company, insurance firm, or government entity—to fulfill debt obligations should the issuer default, thereby imbuing the debt instrument with increased trustworthiness.

The landscape of credit enhancements is diverse, each type tailored to address specific facets of credit risk. Let's navigate the nuances of these instruments:

Letters of Credit: These are assurance documents issued by a bank on behalf of the debtor guaranteeing timely payment to the creditor. In the event of default, the bank undertakes to cover the outstanding debt, thereby providing a cushion that can bolster the borrower's creditworthiness.

Surety Bonds: Here, a surety company assures the timely and full performance of the debtor's obligations. This financial guarantee is often used in construction and government contracts, acting as a sentinel protecting the project's financial integrity.

Credit Insurance Products: These policies shield the lender from losses stemming from a debtor's failure to make payments. Credit insurance enhances the quality of the debt, rendering it more palatable to cautious investors.

Corporate Guarantees: In this arrangement, a parent company or affiliate provides a binding promise to assume the debt responsibilities of the borrower in the event of default. Such guarantees knit a safety net beneath the borrower, engendering confidence among investors regarding the debt's security.

These instruments share a common purpose: to assuage the trepidation of lenders and investors by providing additional layers of security. They are the financial equivalent of reinforced concrete in the architecture of debt issuance—unseen yet indispensable for structural integrity.

In the strategic realm of FP&A, credit enhancements are not summoned without deliberation. The decision to employ such instruments involves a nuanced analysis of their cost versus benefit. While they can reduce interest rates and broaden the pool of potential investors, they also come with a price tag—fees for letters of credit, premiums for insurance policies, and implications for the balance sheet in the case of corporate guarantees.

Moreover, FP&A professionals must tread with caution, ensuring that the pursuit of credit enhancements does not lead to an over-leveraged position that might imperil the organization's financial standing. The careful calibration of these instruments is paramount, requiring a harmonious balance between leveraging their benefits and maintaining prudent debt levels.

The thorough assessment of credit enhancements and guarantees is a testament to the FP&A leader's strategic foresight. It is a critical component of the overarching mission to secure the organization's financial future, a task that demands the precision of a laser and the wisdom of a sage.

As we continue to articulate organizational strategies for managing credit risk, it is imperative to recognize that credit enhancements and guarantees represent more than mere financial tools. They are the sinews and tendons that reinforce the muscle of credit transactions, enabling organizations to navigate the financial markets with agility and grace. They embody the strategic interplay between risk and opportunity that lies at the heart of FP&A—ensuring that the organization not only survives but thrives in the dynamic arena of global finance.

Letters of Credit and Surety Bonds

Letters of Credit and Surety Bonds play a quintessential role as financial guarantors, ensuring that contractual promises are not mere words etched on paper but are backstopped with tangible security. These instruments, while distinct in their mechanics and applications, share a common thread: they are vital cogs in the machinery that drives trade, construction, and various transactions requiring a seal of financial trust.

Letters of Credit: A Financial Keystone

Letters of Credit (LCs) are instruments of trust issued by banks that stand as a testament to the buyer's ability to pay the seller. An LC is a fulcrum upon which trade balances, particularly in international transactions where the distance and differing legal frameworks amplify risk. The LC assures the seller of payment, contingent upon the fulfillment of specified terms, such as the delivery of goods within a stipulated timeframe and the presentation of requisite documents.

There are several types of LCs, each serving different trade needs:

- The Commercial LC, or Documentary Credit, which is routinely used in international trade.

- The Standby LC, acting more as a safety net, is called upon only if the buyer fails to make direct payment.

- The Revolving LC accommodates multiple uses over a period, useful in ongoing trade relationships.

- The Transferable LC allows the original beneficiary to pass the credit onto others, often used in intermediary trade transactions.

The LC serves a dual purpose: it provides security to the seller that they will receive payment, even if the buyer defaults, while also assuring the buyer that no payment will be made until they receive confirmation that the terms of the transaction have been met. This duality maintains equilibrium in trade dynamics, facilitating a smoother flow of commerce across borders.

Surety Bonds: A Pledge of Performance

Surety Bonds are contractually-binding pledges wherein a third party, the surety, guarantees the performance or obligations of a principal to an obligee. Commonly used in construction, they serve as a financial guarantee that contractual obligations, such as the completion of a project or payment to subcontractors, will be fulfilled.

Critical types of Surety Bonds include:

- The Bid Bond ensures that a contractor can meet the terms of a bid if selected.

- The Performance Bond provides a guarantee that the project will be completed per the contract specifications.

- The Payment Bond assures that subcontractors and suppliers will be paid, thus mitigating the risk of liens against the project owner's property.

- The Maintenance Bond offers a warranty against defects in materials or workmanship after project completion.

These bonds are integral to the construction industry, providing a layer of security that strengthens the relationship between project owners, contractors, and subcontractors. They instill confidence and ensure that a project's financial risks are mitigated, protecting all parties involved from the cascading effects of a contractor's failure to perform.

Implementing LCs and Surety Bonds requires a meticulous approach, wherein the FP&A professional must understand the nuances of each instrument and the context of its application. It demands an evaluation of the financial standing of the parties involved, the specifics of the underlying contract, and the associated legal and regulatory requirements.

These financial instruments are not merely passive vehicles of guarantee; they are proactive agents of assurance in the world of FP&A. Through them, organizations can navigate the treacherous waters of financial risk, armed with the certainty that their voyage across the complex seas of commerce is secured by steadfast financial anchors.

Credit Insurance Products

Credit insurance products occupy a vital niche in risk management strategies, safeguarding businesses against the perils of customer non-payment due to insolvency or protracted default. As financial risk mitigation tools, these insurance products allow companies to extend credit to customers with greater confidence, secure in the knowledge that their cash flow and capital reserves are protected.

The Fabric of Credit Insurance

At its core, credit insurance is designed to cover the payment risk associated with the delivery of goods and services on credit terms. The policies are underwritten by insurers who assess the creditworthiness of the insured's customers and set coverage limits based on the risk profile. Coverage typically includes:

- Whole turnover policies, which cover a portfolio of buyers, offering a broad safety net across all receivables.

- Single buyer policies, where coverage is tailored to individual buyers or contracts, often used for high-value transactions or when trading with buyers that present a higher risk.

- Top account policies, focusing on the insured's largest and most significant customers, where their default could pose a critical financial threat.

Credit insurance serves a multidimensional purpose:

1. It enhances borrowing capacity, as insured receivables may be more readily accepted as collateral by financing institutions.

2. It empowers businesses to expand into new markets with less hesitation about the creditworthiness of new customers.

3. It provides a competitive edge, enabling companies to offer more attractive credit terms to buyers.

The underwriting process in credit insurance involves rigorous analysis of the financial health of the insured's customers, industry sector trends, and macroeconomic factors. Insurers leverage extensive databases, analytics tools, and credit scoring models to determine the likelihood of customer default and to set premium rates that reflect this risk.

A key aspect of credit insurance is the constant monitoring of buyers' credit status. Insurers may adjust coverage limits in response to changes in a buyer's financial situation or wider economic conditions. This dynamic approach allows businesses to respond swiftly to potential credit risks without constant direct oversight of their customers' financial stability.

In the event of a claim, the insurer will compensate the insured for the covered portion of the unpaid receivable, subject to the policy's terms and conditions. The insurer may also undertake the recovery process, employing specialists to pursue outstanding debts, thus alleviating the administrative burden from the insured.

For FP&A professionals, integrating credit insurance into a company's financial fabric requires thoughtful alignment with overall risk management objectives. It involves:

- Evaluating policy costs against the potential impact of customer defaults.

- Assessing the concentration of credit risk within the customer base and determining if credit insurance provides a cost-effective method for diversification.

- Considering the use of credit insurance in conjunction with other risk mitigation instruments, such as LCs and surety bonds, to create a comprehensive risk management portfolio.

In summary, credit insurance products are not just a financial safeguard; they are strategic enablers. They fortify a company's resilience against credit risks and facilitate proactive financial planning, supporting sustainable growth in an ever-evolving commercial landscape. As such, FP&A practitioners must adeptly navigate the nuances of credit insurance to amplify their organization's capacity to weather the uncertainties of trade receivables.

Corporate guarantees constitute a crucial instrument in the financial toolkit of companies, particularly when seeking to assert creditworthiness and secure financing. These guarantees act as a commitment from one entity, usually a parent company or a major stakeholder, to fulfill the financial obligations of another entity, typically a subsidiary or affiliate, in the case of default.

The fundamental purpose of a corporate guarantee is to enhance the credit profile of a borrowing entity. In the realm of corporate finance, these guarantees are pivotal in facilitating access to capital by providing lenders with an additional layer of security. The guarantor pledges to assume the debt responsibilities should the primary obligor fail to meet them.

Such financial commitments are common in scenarios where:

- Subsidiaries, which may lack a substantial credit history, require loans or lines of credit.

- Joint ventures or special-purpose entities engage in projects that necessitate external funding.

- Companies bid for large contracts and must assure project owners of their financial stability.

Risks and Considerations

While corporate guarantees can be potent in leveraging the financial strength of a related party, they must be issued judiciously. The guarantor assumes a contingent liability that could materialize as a direct obligation if the guaranteed party defaults. This potential liability must be factored into the guarantor's risk management and financial planning processes.

FP&A experts play a critical role in assessing the risks associated with issuing or receiving corporate guarantees:

- Examining the financial strength of the guarantor and the

likelihood of a guarantee being called upon.

- Analyzing the impact of potential guarantee-triggering events on cash flows and balance sheet strength.

- Ensuring adequate disclosure of contingent liabilities in financial reporting to preserve transparency for investors and creditors.

The structure of a corporate guarantee is tailored to the specific needs of the transaction and the risk appetite of involved parties. Guarantees can cover the entirety or a portion of the obligation and may include covenants that allow the guarantor to mitigate risks. For example, a guarantee may be secured by collateral or accompanied by rights to influence the management decisions of the debtor entity.

Corporate guarantees are often juxtaposed with other credit enhancement tools to achieve an optimal financing structure. They can be particularly effective when used in tandem with credit insurance products or when integrated into a broader strategy of asset-backed financing. The synergy created by such combinations can lead to improved loan terms and a reduction in the cost of capital.

The enforceability of a corporate guarantee is contingent upon the precise legal language that defines the obligations of the guarantor. Legal due diligence is paramount to ensure that the guarantee is binding and enforceable across jurisdictions, especially in international transactions.

FP&A professionals must anticipate the logistical requirements for executing a guarantee, including:

- Compliance with internal policies and governance frameworks related to guarantee issuance.

- Coordination with legal teams to draft and review the guarantee documentation.

- Maintenance of records and monitoring systems to track the status and conditions of all outstanding guarantees.

Corporate guarantees represent a powerful financial instrument that carries significant implications for corporate finance and risk management. They necessitate a strategic approach, combining rigorous financial analysis with careful legal consideration. For FP&A practitioners, mastery of the intricacies of corporate guarantees is essential to harness their potential benefits while mitigating associated risks, thereby contributing to the robustness and agility of an organization's financial architecture.

Enhancing Borrowing Capacity

To enhance borrowing capacity is to expand the financial horizons of a company, enabling it to secure the necessary capital for growth and investment opportunities. This section delves into the theoretical underpinnings and practical applications of augmenting an entity's ability to raise funds through various mechanisms and strategic financial maneuvers.

A fundamental concept within corporate finance is the judicious use of leverage to amplify the return on equity. By increasing debt, a company can potentially boost its earnings per share, provided the cost of debt remains below the return on investment. However, this strategy must be employed with an acute understanding of the company's debt capacity —the maximum level of debt that can be sustained without incurring undue risk.

FP&A analysts rigorously assess the debt capacity of a company by evaluating several factors:

- Historical and projected cash flows, to ascertain the firm's capacity to service additional debt.

- Asset base and collateral availability, which may be utilized to secure further borrowings.

- Debt covenants and existing financial obligations, which can impose constraints on additional leverage.

Capital Structure Optimization

Optimizing the capital structure is a dynamic and complex challenge that seeks to balance debt and equity in a manner that minimizes the cost of capital while maximizing firm value. Theoretical models such as the Modigliani-Miller theorem provide a foundation for understanding the implications of capital structure on company valuation, though they must be adapted to the practicalities of market imperfections and tax considerations.

FP&A professionals leverage these theoretical frameworks to guide strategic decision-making, taking into account:

- The trade-offs between tax benefits of debt and the costs of financial distress.

- The signaling effects of capital structure choices to investors and market analysts.

- The impact of market conditions and investor sentiment on the optimal debt-equity mix.

Credit Rating Enhancement

A company's credit rating is a critical determinant of its borrowing capacity, influencing both the availability and the cost of funds. By improving its credit rating, a firm can access broader financing options and negotiate more favorable terms.

FP&A teams focus on several credit-enhancing initiatives:

- Strengthening the balance sheet by improving liquidity ratios and managing debt maturities.
- Enhancing profitability and operational efficiency to signal financial stability to rating agencies.
- Developing comprehensive risk management strategies to mitigate the potential for default.

Alternative Financing Avenues

In the quest to enhance borrowing capacity, companies must explore a spectrum of financing sources beyond traditional bank loans and bond issuances. Alternative financing avenues include asset-based lending, mezzanine finance, and private placements. Each of these channels offers distinct advantages and fits within a broader capital-raising strategy.

FP&A experts analyze alternative financing options by:

- Assessing the cost and flexibility of alternative finance

relative to traditional debt.

- Considering the impact of alternative financing on the company's overall risk profile.

- Evaluating the strategic alignment of financing sources with long-term corporate objectives.

Synergies with Corporate Development

Enhancing borrowing capacity is not solely a financial exercise—it is inextricably linked with a company's strategic development. Through mergers, acquisitions, and organic growth initiatives, a company can scale its operations and diversify its revenue streams, thus improving its borrowing capacity by presenting a stronger financial and strategic outlook to lenders.

FP&A's role is pivotal in aligning financial strategy with corporate development:

- Conducting due diligence to ensure that strategic initiatives bolster financial strength.

- Integrating financial planning with business development to create coherent growth narratives.

- Collaborating with corporate development to forecast the fiscal impact of strategic moves.

Enhancing borrowing capacity is an endeavor that transcends traditional financial analysis, encompassing a broad spectrum of strategic, operational, and market considerations. It requires a concerted effort from FP&A practitioners to construct a robust financial framework that supports the company's strategic ambitions while preserving financial integrity and flexibility. The resulting augmentation in borrowing capacity empowers the company to pursue its vision with greater financial command and confidence.

Diversification and Risk Pooling

The act of diversification is a cornerstone of risk management, serving as a potent antidote to the idiosyncratic perils that individual investments may harbor. This section will explore the sophisticated theoretical framework and the empirical strategies that underpin diversification and risk pooling in finance.

At the heart of diversification theory lies the principle that a well-constructed portfolio can reduce unsystematic risk—the risk unique to individual assets—through the inclusion of non-correlated investments. The theory posits that as the number of assets in a portfolio increases, the cumulative effect of their individual volatilities diminishes, thus stabilizing the portfolio's overall returns.

Modern Portfolio Theory (MPT), pioneered by Harry Markowitz, quantitatively captures this notion through the concept of an 'efficient frontier'—a graphical representation of the most efficient portfolios that offer the highest expected return for a given level of risk. FP&A practitioners draw on MPT to construct portfolios that are attuned to a company's risk tolerance and financial objectives.

Risk pooling, akin to diversification, involves the aggregation of several types of risks to take advantage of the law of large numbers. This concept is particularly salient in the insurance industry, where risks spread across a large number of policies reduce the variability of the overall risk exposure.

In corporate finance, risk pooling can be observed in conglomerates or diversified firms that operate across different sectors or regions, effectively pooling diverse economic, operational, and geopolitical risks. By doing so, such firms can potentially reduce the impact of adverse events affecting a single line of business or geographic area.

The practical application of diversification is embodied in the meticulous process of portfolio construction, where asset allocation is a critical decision. FP&A professionals must consider various asset classes—stocks, bonds, real estate, commodities—and determine the appropriate mix that aligns with the company's strategic vision and financial goals.

Asset allocation strategies are influenced by factors such as:

- Expected return and risk profiles of different asset classes.
- Correlation coefficients between asset classes to ensure true diversification benefits.
- Market conditions and economic forecasts that may affect asset class performance.

Diversification Across Industries and Geography

An advanced diversification strategy involves spreading investments across various industries and geographic locations. This approach hedges against industry-specific downturns and region-specific disruptions, such as regulatory changes or political instability.

In executing such a strategy, FP&A analysts evaluate:

- The growth potential and risk factors inherent in different industries.
- Economic indicators and trends within various global markets.
- Exchange rate risk and the impact of currency fluctuations on international investments.

Dynamic Diversification and Continuous Monitoring

Diversification is not a 'set-and-forget' strategy; it demands ongoing scrutiny and adjustment in response to evolving market dynamics. FP&A teams must engage in continuous monitoring of portfolio performance, rebalancing assets as necessary to maintain the desired risk-return profile.

Key activities in this regard include:

- Periodic review of asset performance against benchmarks and re-evaluation of risk exposure.
- Tactical shifts in asset allocation in anticipation of macroeconomic changes.
- Utilizing financial derivatives and other instruments to manage and hedge portfolio risks.

Integrating Diversification with Corporate Strategy

Ultimately, the pursuit of diversification must be deeply integrated with a company's overarching corporate strategy. FP&A professionals play a vital role in ensuring that investment strategies not only mitigate risk but also contribute to the enterprise's strategic goals and value creation.

To achieve this synthesis, the FP&A function:

- Aligns investment plans with the company's vision and long-term objectives.
- Collaborates with business units to understand and incorporate sector-specific insights.
- Communicates the rationale and benefits of diversification strategies to stakeholders.

Diversification and risk pooling are powerful concepts that, when applied with precision and foresight, can greatly enhance a company's financial stability and capacity for sustained growth. By navigating the delicate balance between risk and return, FP&A experts can steer their organizations towards a future marked by resilience and strategic agility.

Portfolio Theory in Risk Management

Portfolio theory, a fundamental aspect of risk management, is predicated on the axiom that risk-averse investors can construct portfolios to optimize or maximize expected return based on a given level of market risk, emphasizing that risk is an inherent part of higher reward. Central to this theory is the notion of diversification, which posits that holding a variety of non-correlated assets can significantly reduce the unsystematic risk of a portfolio.

The origins of portfolio theory date back to the seminal work of Harry Markowitz in the 1950s. His model, known as Modern Portfolio Theory (MPT), introduced the concept of an 'efficient frontier,' a boundary in the risk-return space comprising portfolios that maximize expected return for a given level of risk. This model serves as a blueprint for financial analysts and portfolio managers in the construction of optimized portfolios.

The risk-return trade-off is a critical principle in portfolio theory. It is the balance that investors must determine between the desire for the lowest possible risk and the highest possible returns. Portfolio theory strives to mathematically capture this trade-off, allowing for the calculation of the efficient set of portfolios through optimization models.

One of the pillars of portfolio theory is the use of correlation coefficients to evaluate the degree to which two securities move in relation to each other. By incorporating assets with low or negative correlations into a portfolio, investors can theoretically reduce the volatility of the portfolio without necessarily sacrificing returns.

The Capital Asset Pricing Model (CAPM) extends the concepts of MPT to introduce the market portfolio, risk-free rate, and beta coefficient. The CAPM asserts that the expected return of a portfolio is equal to the rate on a risk-free asset plus a risk premium. The risk premium is derived by multiplying the market premium—the difference between the expected market return and the risk-free rate—by the portfolio's beta, or sensitivity to market movements.

Financial Planning & Analysis (FP&A) professionals

apply portfolio theory to optimize corporate investment portfolios. They use it to assess the risk of different projects or business units and to determine the appropriate discount rates for capital budgeting decisions. Portfolio theory also informs the hedging strategies that a company might use to insulate itself from various financial risks.

Despite its wide application, portfolio theory is not without its criticisms. Detractors argue that the assumption of a rational, risk-averse investor does not always hold true in practice. Moreover, the theory relies heavily on the past performance of assets to predict future risk and returns, which may not always be indicative of future market conditions.

Behavioral finance has emerged to challenge some of the core assumptions of portfolio theory, particularly the notion that investors always act rationally and are immune to psychological biases. FP&A practitioners must consider factors such as investor overconfidence, herd behavior, and loss aversion when applying portfolio theory to real-world scenarios.

Asset Allocation Strategies

Asset allocation stands as the cornerstone of robust financial planning and investment management, providing a scaffold upon which the edifice of long-term wealth generation is built. Strategic asset allocation involves a tailored blend of investments that aligns with an investor's risk profile, investment horizon, and financial objectives, underpinning the principle that different asset classes offer varying levels of return and risk over time.

Asset allocation is the process of distributing investments across various asset categories—such as stocks, bonds, real estate, and commodities—to balance risk and reward in accordance with an individual's goals, risk tolerance, and investment horizon. This strategic division is predicated on the idea that the performance of asset classes can diverge significantly over time and through different economic cycles.

Strategic asset allocation establishes a base policy mix—a proportional combination of assets based on expected rates of return for each asset class. This approach assumes a long-term investment strategy, remaining relatively constant regardless of short-term market fluctuations. In contrast, tactical asset allocation allows for short-term, flexible deviations from the base policy mix to capitalize on market inefficiencies or strong market sectors.

The investment time horizon—how long an investor plans to hold their portfolio before spending it—is a critical determinant in asset allocation. Long-term investors may prefer a heavier allocation to equities for potential growth, while short-term investors may opt for more liquid and less volatile assets like cash or short-term bonds to preserve capital.

Investors' risk tolerance—their willingness and ability to withstand losses in their investment portfolios—plays a pivotal role in determining asset allocation. Aggressive investors, comfortable with large market swings, might allocate a significant portion to volatile assets, while conservative investors might veer towards stable, income-generating investments.

Effective asset allocation is synonymous with diversification. By investing in a broad range of assets, investors aim to reduce the impact of any single investment's deficient performance on the overall portfolio. Diversification is not limited to asset types but extends to sectors, industries, geographic regions, and investment styles.

Portfolio rebalancing, the practice of realigning the weightings of a portfolio of assets, ensures that asset allocation remains aligned with an investor's risk profile and goals. Rebalancing involves buying or selling assets periodically to maintain the original or desired level of asset allocation and risk.

In the realm of FP&A, asset allocation strategies are not only applied to manage personal wealth but also to administer corporate investments and pensions. Such strategies guide treasurers and CFOs in the optimal distribution of corporate resources across various projects, subsidiaries, or asset classes to enhance the company's value while managing financial risks.

While asset allocation is a powerful tool, it is not infallible. Market dynamics and economic indicators must be monitored, as they can necessitate adjustments to the asset mix. Asset allocation models that incorporate predictive analytics and machine learning can offer more dynamic and responsive strategies.

Correlation and Risk Reduction

In the orchestration of a meticulously calibrated investment portfolio, the concept of correlation occupies a position of paramount importance. It is the statistical measure that captures the degree to which two assets move in relation to one another. By understanding and leveraging these interdependencies, financial professionals can adeptly mitigate risks and enhance the resiliency of an investment portfolio.

At its core, the correlation coefficient quantifies the relationship between two investment vehicles, ranging from -1 to +1. A coefficient near +1 signifies that the assets typically move in the same direction, while a figure close to -1 indicates an inverse relationship. A correlation of zero suggests no discernible pattern in the movement of the assets relative to each other.

The power of diversification is partly harnessed through the strategic pairing of assets with varying degrees of correlation. A diversified portfolio combines assets with low or negative correlations, ensuring that when one asset experiences a downturn, the other may hold steady or even appreciate, thereby smoothing out the volatility and mitigating overall risk.

The reliability of correlation can be enigmatic; it may change over time and can be influenced by alterations in market conditions. During periods of market stress or financial crises, correlations between asset classes can converge, often leading to a breakdown in diversification strategies. This phenomenon necessitates the continuous analysis and adaptation of correlation assumptions in portfolio management.

In FP&A, understanding and applying correlation is integral to crafting hedging strategies and managing portfolio risks. For instance, a CFO might employ correlation analysis to determine the extent of exposure to foreign exchange risk and implement currency hedges to protect the firm's international revenue streams.

The strategic weighting of assets within a portfolio needs to incorporate correlation insights to optimize risk-adjusted returns. For example, the inclusion of alternative investments like real estate or commodities, which typically exhibit lower correlations with traditional equity and fixed-income assets, can provide a buffer against market turbulence.

While the advantages of using correlation in risk management are clear, it is not without its challenges. Correlations can be unstable over time, influenced by economic cycles, geopolitical events, and policy changes. Therefore, it is crucial for financial professionals to utilize advanced analytical tools and to remain vigilant, adjusting their strategies in response to evolving correlation patterns.

The advent of sophisticated analytics software and AI-enhanced tools has augmented the capability to model and predict correlation dynamics more accurately. Such technology aids in stress testing portfolios against a variety of hypothetical scenarios, providing deeper insights into potential risk exposures.

Correlation serves as an indefatigable sentinel in the realm of risk management. By assiduously mapping the interconnections between diverse assets, finance professionals can construct portfolios that are not only resilient in the face of systemic shocks but also aligned with the strategic imperatives of value preservation and growth. In the ever-shifting landscape of financial planning, the judicious application of correlation analysis is indispensable in the pursuit of enduring stability and profitability.

Sector and Geographic Diversification

The canvas of global investment is vast, and for the astute financial planner or analyst, it offers a spectrum of opportunities—each with its inherent levels of risk and return. The construct of a robust investment portfolio is often underpinned by a strategic mix of sector and geographic diversification, a tactic designed to mitigate systemic risk and capitalize on growth across different industries and regions.

Sector diversification involves the allocation of investment capital across various economic sectors such as technology, healthcare, finance, or consumer goods. Each sector responds differently to economic cycles; while some may thrive, others may not perform as well. By spreading investments across multiple sectors, an investor can reduce the impact that any single sector's downturn might have on the overall portfolio performance.

Geographic diversification takes the principle of not putting all one's eggs in one basket and applies it to the global stage. By investing in markets across different countries and regions, investors can exploit the potential of emerging markets and offset the volatility inherent in any single market. Different economies may be at various stages of growth, offering a balance between risk and potential return in a global portfolio.

The intersection of sector and geographic diversification is where astute strategic allocation shines. For example, investing in the technology sector within a developed market like the United States may offer stability and innovation, whereas investing in consumer goods in an emerging market could tap into rapid urbanization and a growing middle class.

When deploying capital globally, one must navigate the labyrinth of regulatory environments and political climates. Changes in trade policies, taxation laws, and political stability can all influence the return on investment in each sector or geography. Thus, keeping abreast of international news and maintaining a network of global contacts is crucial.

An additional layer of complexity in geographic diversification is currency risk. Fluctuations in exchange rates can significantly affect the value of an investment. Hedging strategies, such as the use of currency forwards or options, can be employed to manage this risk, although they come with their own costs and considerations.

Staying informed about technological advancements and consumer trends can offer foresight into which sectors are poised for growth. For instance, the rise of renewable energy may signal a long-term growth trajectory for the clean tech sector, justifying a larger allocation within a diversified portfolio.

It's also vital to consider the liquidity of investments in

various sectors and geographies. Some emerging markets may offer high growth potential but could be hampered by low liquidity, making it difficult to enter or exit positions without impacting market prices.

Effective sector and geographic diversification requires a combination of quantitative analysis—such as evaluating historical returns, volatilities, and correlations—and qualitative judgment, such as assessing the quality of governance in a particular country or the innovation cycle within a sector.

A meticulously diversified portfolio, both in terms of sector and geography, stands as a bulwark against the torrents of market fluctuations. It enables investors and CFOs to nimbly navigate through the intricate web of global economic interdependencies while positioning their portfolios to capture the upside of diverse growth trajectories. The confluence of analytical rigor and experienced intuition is central to mastering the art of diversification, a critical element in the financial alchemy of risk management and value creation.

CHAPTER 7: REGULATORY COMPLIANCE AND RISK MANAGEMENT

In the complex labyrinth of modern financial systems, regulatory compliance emerges as the sine qua non of risk management—a bedrock principle that underpins the stability and integrity of financial planning and analysis (FP&A). This section delves into the multifaceted relationship between regulatory mandates and the strategic management of risk within organizations.

At its core, regulatory compliance involves adhering to laws, guidelines, and specifications relevant to business operations. For FP&A professionals, compliance is not merely about avoiding legal repercussions; it is about understanding and managing the risks that non-compliance poses to an organization's financial health and reputation.

FP&A professionals must proactively engage with the evolving landscape of regulations. This involves continuous monitoring for changes in legislation that could affect financial operations, such as tax laws, reporting standards, or capital requirements. By staying ahead of these changes, the FP&A team can mitigate risks associated with non-compliance and strategically advise leadership on necessary adjustments to business practices.

Effective integration of regulatory compliance into risk management necessitates a structured approach. This may involve mapping out all relevant regulations, assessing the risks of non-compliance for each, and developing mitigation strategies. Regular risk assessments, coupled with the implementation of internal controls, are vital to ensure that the organization remains within the bounds of regulatory frameworks while pursuing its financial objectives.

Advancements in technology have ushered in sophisticated tools that aid in compliance and risk management. Automated compliance management systems can track regulatory changes, manage documentation, and ensure timely reporting. They also play a crucial role in disseminating information across an organization, ensuring that all departments are aware of compliance requirements.

FP&A cannot operate in a silo when it comes to regulatory compliance. Cross-functional collaboration is essential, as compliance touches various aspects of a business. For instance, coordination with the legal department can provide clarity on the interpretation of regulations, while cooperation with IT is crucial for the protection of financial data and ensuring cybersecurity compliance.

Organizations must foster a culture where compliance is ingrained in the ethos of every employee. This is achieved through regular training programs, clear communication of policies, and the establishment of a compliance function within the FP&A team. A culture of compliance also involves encouraging ethical behavior and providing channels for employees to report suspected breaches without fear of retaliation.

For multinational corporations, compliance is further complicated by the need to navigate a patchwork of international laws and standards. In such cases, an in-depth understanding of the regulatory environment in each market is fundamental to risk management. Strategies need to be adaptable to accommodate diverse legal requirements while maintaining a coherent global compliance posture.

While the costs of compliance can be significant, so too can the costs of non-compliance, including fines, legal fees, and reputational damage. FP&A teams should therefore measure and report on the impact of compliance activities on financial performance, highlighting how proactive compliance management can contribute positively to the bottom line.

Regulatory compliance is an indispensable element of risk management within FP&A. It demands vigilance, foresight, and a strategic approach from those charged with the stewardship of an organization's financial future. By successfully navigating the complexities of regulatory compliance, FP&A teams can shield their organizations from the perils of non-compliance and bolster their competitive advantage in an ever-regulatory business environment.

Understanding Compliance Requirements

The mosaic of compliance requirements is inherently complex, reflecting the myriad legal, regulatory, and ethical standards that organizations must navigate. The onus of comprehension and adherence falls heavily upon the FP&A function, which serves as the nexus between financial data and strategic regulatory alignment. This section will dissect the elements of compliance requirements, focusing on their pertinence to FP&A activities and the overarching business strategy.

Compliance requirements are multi-dimensional, often varying by industry, jurisdiction, and the nature of financial transactions. For FP&A professionals, these requirements translate into a series of obligations that range from accurate financial reporting, adherence to tax laws, and observance of anti-money laundering (AML) protocols, to environmental, social, and governance (ESG) standards, among others.

Interpreting compliance requirements is a strategic exercise that transcends mere conformance. It involves deciphering the intent behind regulations and integrating this understanding into financial planning processes. FP&A teams play a pivotal role in this respect, utilizing their analytical acumen to forecast regulatory impacts and drive informed business decisions.

Far from being a hindrance, robust compliance mechanisms can be leveraged as strategic assets. They serve as proof points of organizational integrity and reliability, which can foster trust among investors, partners, and customers. This trust, in turn, can lead to favorable financing terms, preferred partnership status, and enhanced market reputation.

Compliance requirements are inextricably linked to risk management, as non-compliance poses significant financial and reputational risks. FP&A must, therefore, ensure that risk management frameworks incorporate compliance risks, with clear escalation paths and response strategies for potential breaches.

Understanding compliance requirements necessitates a holistic view of the compliance ecosystem. This includes recognition of the roles played by regulatory bodies, the influence of industry best practices, and the implications of emerging trends such as data privacy regulations and increasingly stringent anti-corruption laws.

For FP&A teams, a strategic compliance roadmap is indispensable. This involves setting clear compliance goals, identifying requisite resources, establishing timelines for implementation, and defining metrics for ongoing evaluation. This roadmap serves as a guide for maintaining alignment with compliance requirements while pursuing the organization's financial objectives.

In an era defined by technological innovation, FP&A teams must harness digital solutions to streamline compliance processes. From regulatory technology (RegTech) for real-time monitoring to artificial intelligence (AI) for predictive compliance analytics, technology can be a powerful ally in meeting complex compliance demands.

FP&A's efforts to understand and meet compliance requirements must be supported by cross-departmental collaboration. This includes working with legal counsel for regulatory interpretation, engaging with IT for data security compliance, and coordinating with Human Resources to ensure employee adherence to internal compliance policies.

In summation, understanding compliance requirements is

a critical component of risk management and strategic planning within FP&A. It demands a multifaceted approach, combining keen regulatory insight with strategic foresight and technological proficiency. By demystifying compliance requirements and integrating them into the fabric of financial operations, FP&A teams can safeguard their organizations against compliance-related risks while capitalizing on the strategic benefits of a strong compliance posture.

Sarbanes-Oxley (SOX) and Corporate Governance

In the wake of financial scandals that shook the corporate world at the turn of the millennium, the Sarbanes-Oxley Act (SOX) emerged as a legislative response to restore public trust in the financial reporting of publicly traded companies. SOX fundamentally reshaped the landscape of corporate governance and imposed stringent reforms on corporate financial practices. Within this framework, FP&A professionals are not mere executors of compliance tasks but are strategic participants in upholding the principles of SOX.

SOX, enacted in 2002, introduced major changes to financial regulation with the aim of protecting investors by improving the accuracy and reliability of corporate disclosures. The act contains several key provisions that impact FP&A directly, including enhanced financial disclosures, stricter penalties for fraudulent financial activity, and increased responsibilities for corporate management.

FP&A teams play a critical role in ensuring SOX compliance. This involves the generation of accurate financial reports, the implementation of effective internal controls over financial reporting, and the establishment of protocols for the appropriate treatment of non-compliance issues. Furthermore, FP&A must engage in rigorous financial analysis and projections that anticipate and mitigate the risks of misstatement in financial reports.

SOX compliance requires an organizational culture that values transparency, accountability, and ethical conduct. FP&A functions must champion these values by fostering a work environment that encourages ethical financial reporting and provides channels for voicing concerns about dishonest practices without fear of retaliation.

Central to SOX compliance is the establishment and maintenance of robust internal controls. This requires FP&A teams to evaluate and document the effectiveness of these controls regularly. It also entails collaboration with internal and external auditors to review and test the financial and operational procedures that contribute to the accuracy and completeness of financial statements.

Advancements in technology have provided FP&A with powerful tools to automate and enhance the compliance process. From software that aids in internal control documentation to platforms that streamline the reporting process, technology has become an indispensable ally in achieving and maintaining SOX compliance.

A critical aspect often overlooked is the continuous education of the workforce regarding the implications of SOX. FP&A professionals must understand the nuances of the act to guide their actions and decisions. Moreover, they must ensure that employees across the company are aware of

SOX requirements and the importance of internal controls.

The influence of FP&A on corporate governance extends beyond compliance. By providing strategic insights based on financial data and forecasts, FP&A can influence decision-making processes at the highest levels of corporate leadership, ensuring that the organization not only complies with SOX but thrives under its directives.

While navigating the challenges of SOX compliance, FP&A teams must remain adaptable and responsive to regulatory updates. Adopting best practices, such as maintaining rigorous documentation processes, conducting regular training, and leveraging technology, can transform the compliance burden into a strategic advantage.

The interplay between SOX and corporate governance requires FP&A to adopt a proactive stance, weaving compliance into the strategic fabric of financial planning. By integrating SOX principles into everyday financial operations, FP&A teams contribute to the fortification of corporate governance, ensuring the organization stands on a foundation of integrity and trust.

Dodd-Frank Act Implications

The Dodd-Frank Wall Street Reform and Consumer Protection Act, commonly referred to as the Dodd-Frank Act, represents a comprehensive overhaul of financial regulation in the United States. Passed in response to the 2008 financial crisis, it aims to decrease various risks in the financial system. For the FP&A professional, understanding the implications of the Dodd-Frank Act is critical not only for compliance but also for strategic financial planning.

The Dodd-Frank Act's numerous provisions aim to promote stability and transparency within financial markets. It established several new government agencies tasked with overseeing the implementation and enforcement of its various sections. Of note are the Financial Stability Oversight Council (FSOC), tasked with monitoring the stability of the financial system, and the Consumer Financial Protection Bureau (CFP, focused on consumer protection.

FP&A teams must navigate the complexities introduced by the Dodd-Frank Act, particularly in the areas of risk management and reporting requirements. The act increased the accountability and liability of senior executives and board members for the accuracy of reported financial information, thereby amplifying the importance of the FP&A function in ensuring data integrity.

Under the Dodd-Frank Act, financial institutions are required to perform stringent stress tests and report findings to regulators and the public. FP&A plays a vital role in these stress tests, conducting comprehensive risk assessments that project the company's financial position under various economic scenarios.

A significant aspect of the Dodd-Frank Act is the introduction of new regulations in the derivatives market, particularly for swap dealers and major swap participants. FP&A professionals must understand the implications of these reforms for their hedging strategies and ensure that all derivative transactions meet the new requirements.

The Volcker Rule, part of the Dodd-Frank Act, impacts FP&A by restricting banks from engaging in proprietary trading and from owning or sponsoring hedge funds or private equity funds. FP&A teams must work with legal and compliance departments to ascertain that their institution's investment and trading activities adhere to these rules.

The Dodd-Frank Act places increased emphasis on recordkeeping and transparency, mandating the retention of extensive records of financial transactions and the reporting of swap transactions to central repositories. FP&A professionals must ensure that systems and processes are adequate for maintaining such records and facilitating the necessary reports.

The Dodd-Frank Act introduced provisions to protect whistleblowers who report violations of financial regulations. FP&A teams should be cognizant of these protections, encouraging a culture of compliance and ethical conduct throughout the organization.

The Dodd-Frank Act requires financial institutions to maintain higher levels of capital and to have robust liquidity management practices. FP&A must develop and maintain financial models that account for these requirements and assist in strategic decision-making that aligns with capital adequacy and liquidity standards.

FP&A professionals must be vigilant in monitoring and responding to the ongoing developments and regulatory adjustments related to the Dodd-Frank Act. This vigilance positions FP&A not merely as a function of compliance but as a strategic adviser that helps navigate the regulatory landscape.

Global Regulations Affecting FP&A

In the labyrinthine domain of global finance, regulations such as the General Data Protection Regulation (GDPR) and the Markets in Financial Instruments Directive II (MiFID II) introduce complex layers of compliance for Financial Planning & Analysis (FP&A) professionals. These regulations, albeit domiciled in specific jurisdictions, have far-reaching implications for organizations operating on the world stage.

GDPR, a regulatory framework instituted by the European Union (EU), governs data protection and privacy, impacting organizations worldwide that process the data of EU citizens. For FP&A, GDPR necessitates a meticulous approach to handling personal data within financial forecasts, budgeting, and reporting. FP&A must ensure that all personal data used is processed lawfully, transparently, and for legitimate purposes.

FP&A teams must work closely with data protection officers to ensure adherence to GDPR's principles regarding data minimization, accuracy, storage limitation, and integrity. The responsibility extends to implementing data protection 'by design and by default' in all FP&A-related systems and processes.

For multinationals, GDPR complicates the transfer of personal data across borders. FP&A professionals must navigate the requirements for international data transfers, utilizing standard contractual clauses or adhering to frameworks such as the EU-US Privacy Shield where applicable.

MiFID II, which focuses on securities markets and

investment intermediaries, aims to increase transparency and strengthen investor protection within the EU. FP&A must comprehend how MiFID II affects the financial instruments they analyze and the implications of market structure changes for corporate financial strategies.

MiFID II mandates detailed reporting of transactions and real-time public disclosure of trade data. FP&A must work with compliance and IT departments to ensure systems are capable of handling increased data volumes and reporting requirements.

FP&A must factor in the costs associated with compliance to MiFID II, including investment in technology upgrades and potential changes in market liquidity and transaction costs. These costs have direct implications for financial forecasting and strategic investment planning.

Both GDPR and MiFID II underscore the need for a proactive regulatory strategy within FP&A. The team must not only ensure compliance but also advise on the strategic implications of these regulations for corporate finance activities.

As FP&A units operate within a global framework, they encounter diverse regulatory landscapes. This divergence requires a nimble approach to adapt financial models and risk assessments to different regulatory requirements, whether they stem from the EU's GDPR and MiFID II, the Asia-Pacific region's varied financial regulations, or the evolving standards in emerging markets.

To meet the challenges posed by GDPR, MiFID II, and other global regulations, FP&A should leverage technology. From advanced analytics to secure data management platforms, technology provides the tools to enhance compliance, improve reporting accuracy, and drive strategic decision-making.

For FP&A, global regulations like GDPR and MiFID II are not just compliance checkboxes but strategic imperatives that shape financial practices and influence the competitive positioning of the organization. By integrating a deep understanding of these regulations into FP&A activities, professionals can guide their organizations safely through the complex terrain of global finance, ensuring robust compliance and strategic alignment in an interconnected world.

Compliance Audits and Internal Controls

In the intricate mosaic of corporate fiscal management, compliance audits and internal controls form the warp and weft that reinforce the fabric of financial integrity and accountability. This section delves into the theoretical framework and practical nuances of conducting compliance audits and establishing robust internal controls within an organization's financial planning and analysis functions.

Compliance audits are systematic evaluations designed to ascertain whether an organization adheres to regulatory guidelines. The theoretical basis for these audits lies in the principles of transparency, accountability, and stewardship. Such audits not only safeguard against legal and financial repercussions but also serve as a barometer of the company's ethical compass.

The scope of a compliance audit in FP&A spans various

dimensions, from verifying the accuracy of financial reports to ensuring the integrity of forecasting methods. Audits scrutinize the alignment of FP&A practices with standards such as the International Financial Reporting Standards (IFRS) or Generally Accepted Accounting Principles (GAAP), alongside specific regulatory mandates.

Internal controls, an assortment of procedures and mechanisms, are designed to prevent and detect errors or irregularities in financial processes. The theoretical construct of internal controls rests on the concept of risk mitigation, acting as a preventative bulwark against operational, financial, and compliance risks.

Designing effective internal controls involves identifying the areas of highest risk within FP&A activities and tailoring control mechanisms to address these risks. Implementation requires a blend of automated systems—such as software that flags anomalies in transactional data—and manual checks, like managerial reviews of financial models.

Emerging technologies, such as artificial intelligence and data analytics, are revolutionizing the way organizations approach compliance audits and internal controls. These tools offer unprecedented precision in identifying risk patterns and ensuring compliance, thereby bolstering the overall reliability of FP&A processes.

Best practices for compliance audits include maintaining a clear audit trail, ensuring auditor independence, and conducting audits at regular intervals. Additionally, incorporating feedback mechanisms to address audit findings and refine processes is paramount to ensuring continuous improvement.

Despite the theoretical robustness of internal controls, practical challenges persist. These range from the complexity of global operations, which may dilute control efficacy, to the dynamic nature of regulations that demand constant adaptation of control frameworks.

FP&A professionals play a critical role in compliance and internal control by providing accurate financial data and analysis that inform audit processes. Their strategic input is vital for interpreting audit outcomes and implementing changes to financial strategies and models in response to audit findings.

Anti-Money Laundering (AML) and Fraud Prevention

An essential aspect of financial planning and analysis (FP&A) is the rigorous prevention of criminal financial activity, including money laundering and fraud. These nefarious actions not only tarnish a firm's reputation but can also lead to significant legal and financial penalties. This section explores the theoretical underpinnings and practical applications of anti-money laundering (AML) and fraud prevention measures in intricate theoretical detail.

At the core of AML and fraud prevention lies the theory of criminology, which studies the reasons why individuals commit financial crimes. By understanding these motivations, organizations can better implement strategies and controls to deter such actions. The principles of risk management also play a significant role, as they help identify areas within financial operations most susceptible to illicit activities.

The establishment of comprehensive AML frameworks is critical to protect the financial system against the risks posed by money laundering. These frameworks often include customer due diligence (CDD), which entails verifying the identity of clients and assessing their risk profiles. Other components of an AML framework include ongoing monitoring, suspicious activity reporting (SAR), and adherence to international AML standards set by bodies like the Financial Action Task Force (FATF).

Innovative technologies such as blockchain, machine learning, and artificial intelligence are increasingly instrumental in detecting fraudulent transactions and patterns indicative of money laundering. These technologies allow for real-time analysis of transactional data and can identify anomalies that human oversight might miss.

Fraud prevention encompasses a suite of strategies designed to detect and prevent unauthorized financial activities. These techniques include setting up alerts for unusual transactions, implementing multi-factor authentication for financial operations, and regular audits of financial records to detect irregularities.

FP&A professionals contribute significantly to AML and fraud prevention efforts by integrating financial insights into the design and operation of control systems. They work in tandem with compliance departments to ensure that financial projections and analyses consider the risk of fraud and money laundering.

Organizations must also focus on employee training and awareness programs as frontline defenses against financial crimes. Such programs keep personnel informed about the latest methods used by fraudsters and the internal procedures for reporting suspicious activities.

The dynamic nature of financial crime means that AML and fraud prevention measures must constantly evolve. FP&A professionals face the challenge of adapting processes and technologies to keep pace with emerging threats, including those posed by increasingly sophisticated cybercriminal activities.

Regulations play a pivotal role in AML and fraud prevention. Compliance with laws such as the Bank Secrecy Act (BSA) in the United States, the Proceeds of Crime Act (POCA) in the United Kingdom, and other global directives is mandatory. FP&A must ensure that financial planning and operational practices are aligned with these legal requirements, and that all mandatory reports are accurate and submitted in a timely fashion.

FP&A's role in AML and fraud prevention is multifaceted and integral to the financial health and legal compliance of an organization. By employing a combination of theoretical understanding, practical applications, and innovative technologies, FP&A can safeguard an organization's assets and reputation from the risks associated with money laundering and financial fraud.

AML Frameworks and Best Practices

In the labyrinthine world of finance, the spectre of money laundering presents a formidable challenge to the integrity of global economic systems. Financial Planning & Analysis (FP&A) professionals are at the vanguard of combating this illicit activity, employing robust Anti-Money Laundering (AML) frameworks and best practices that form the bulwark against the taint of criminal finances.

AML frameworks are the structured approaches that organizations adopt to comply with legal and regulatory standards aimed at preventing, detecting, and reporting money laundering activities. These frameworks are not static; they are dynamic, evolving with new legislative amendments and technological advancements.

The Cornerstones of AML Compliance

A foundational element of any AML framework is the establishment of a compliance program tailored to the risk profile of the institution. This program typically encompasses the following pillars:

1. Risk Assessment: Before establishing controls, an organization must first understand its exposure to money laundering risks. This understanding is gleaned through a comprehensive risk assessment that scrutinizes customer bases, product offerings, transaction volumes, and geographic locations.

2. Policies and Procedures: Institutionalizing policies and procedures that articulate the acceptable standards of conduct and the controls in place to mitigate identified risks is critical. These documents serve as references for staff and regulators alike, delineating the organization's stance on AML compliance.

3. Customer Due Diligence (CDD): This process involves verifying the identity of customers and understanding the nature of their business. Enhanced Due Diligence (EDD) is reserved for higher-risk customers, requiring more detailed scrutiny.

4. Continuous Monitoring: Transactions must be monitored continuously to detect unusual or suspicious patterns that may suggest money laundering. This process is bolstered by automated systems capable of flagging anomalies for further investigation.

5. Training: Employees must be trained to recognize signs of money laundering and understand their roles within the AML framework. Training must be ongoing to refresh knowledge and accommodate new threats and regulatory changes.

6. Independent Testing: External audits or independent reviews of the AML program help ensure its effectiveness and identify areas for improvement, maintaining the integrity of the framework.

Best practices in AML often transcend local legislation, drawing on global standards set by international bodies such as the Financial Action Task Force (FATF). The FATF's 40 Recommendations serve as a gold standard for AML efforts, advocating for international cooperation and the adoption of consistent AML measures by countries worldwide.

Technological advancements have equipped FP&A professionals with powerful tools to streamline AML processes. These include machine learning algorithms that enhance the detection of suspicious activities and blockchain technology that provides an immutable ledger for transaction verification.

Despite the robustness of AML frameworks, challenges persist. The agility of financial criminals, the complexity of financial products, and the rapid pace of technological change mean that AML frameworks must adapt continually. FP&A professionals must therefore remain vigilant and proactive, ensuring that their AML strategies are always one step ahead.

A crucial component of AML best practices is the timely reporting of suspicious activities to regulatory authorities. This ensures that a network of information is established, enhancing the collective efforts to deter and detect money laundering activities.

Ultimately, the most effective AML frameworks are those embedded within the culture of an organization. When compliance is seen not as a regulatory burden but as a core value, it becomes part of the daily operation, strengthening the organization's defenses against financial crime.

The intricate mosaic that is AML frameworks and best practices relies on a confluence of institutional commitment, regulatory compliance, technological innovation, and continuous education. FP&A plays a critical role in weaving these threads together, safeguarding the financial sector from the ever-present threat of money laundering and ensuring the ethical conduct of business operations.

Detecting and Preventing Fraud

An impervious defense against the malevolent specter of fraud is a non-negotiable imperative for organizations. Fraud detection and prevention are essential components of financial stewardship, representing the meticulous scrutiny and guardianship that FP&A professionals must exercise to shield their organizations from financial miscreants.

Fraud Detection: The Forensic Pursuit of Deception

Fraud detection involves the identification of fraudulent activities or irregularities within an organization's operations. It is a proactive and ongoing process powered by an array of techniques and analytics aimed at uncovering and addressing irregular transactions before they balloon into significant financial or reputational damage.

1. Data Analytics: The use of sophisticated data analytics tools enables financial experts to sift through vast quantities of transactional data to spot anomalies that may indicate fraudulent activities. Patterns, trends, and outliers that deviate from the norm are scrutinized and may trigger further investigation.

2. Automated Monitoring Systems: Continuous real-time monitoring systems are crucial in the early detection of fraud. These systems can be programmed with algorithms to detect unusual behavior, including transactions that are too large, too frequent, or inconsistent with a customer's usual activity pattern.

3. Internal Controls: A robust system of internal controls, including segregation of duties and access controls, serves as a deterrent against fraud. It reduces the opportunity

for fraudulent activities to occur by ensuring that no single individual has control over all aspects of a financial transaction.

4. Whistleblower Policies: Encouraging and protecting whistleblowers is vital. Employees who report unethical behavior can be an organization's best defense against internal fraud. A secure and anonymous reporting channel is critical for empowering employees to come forward without fear of retaliation.

Fraud Prevention: Building Impenetrable Ramparts

Fraud prevention requires a strategic and comprehensive approach that encompasses policy, culture, and technology to create a formidable barrier against fraudulent activities.

1. Fraud Risk Management Policy: An explicit fraud risk management policy establishes the organization's stance on fraud and lays out the responsibilities across the organization, from the boardroom to entry-level employees.

2. Employee Education and Awareness: Regular training and awareness programs educate employees about common fraud schemes, the importance of adhering to policies, and the procedures for reporting suspected fraud.

3. Due Diligence: Rigorous due diligence in hiring and ongoing relationships with vendors and partners can help mitigate the risk of fraudulent activities. Background checks and monitoring ensure that those with a history of fraudulent behavior or red flags are identified early.

4. Cybersecurity Measures: Cybersecurity is an integral part of fraud prevention. Measures such as firewalls, intrusion detection systems, and regular security assessments protect against external threats that could lead to data breaches and subsequent fraud.

Technological Vanguard: The Role of AI and ML

Artificial Intelligence (AI) and Machine Learning (ML) are revolutionizing fraud detection and prevention. These technologies can process large datasets to identify complex patterns that are indicative of fraudulent behavior. They also learn and adapt over time, improving the accuracy of fraud detection mechanisms.

Fraud prevention is not solely a technical challenge; it is also a cultural one. An organizational culture that emphasizes ethical behavior, transparency, and accountability is critical in mitigating fraud risks. When integrity is woven into the corporate fabric, the likelihood of fraud taking root diminishes.

Detecting and preventing fraud is a multifaceted endeavor that requires a symbiotic relationship between humans and technology. By leveraging cutting-edge analytics, fostering an ethical culture, and implementing stringent controls, FP&A professionals ensure the financial sanctity of their organizations. This fortitude not only serves to protect assets but also to uphold the organization's reputation as a paragon of integrity in a landscape fraught with potential fiscal malfeasance.

Using Technology for AML Compliance

Anti-Money Laundering (AML) compliance stands as a bulwark against the insidious flow of illicit funds. Technology's role in fortifying this bulwark is becoming increasingly pivotal as financial institutions grapple with ever-evolving threats.

Innovative Tech at the Forefront of AML Efforts

Technological advances have reshaped the terrain of AML compliance, offering powerful tools that enhance the ability of financial institutions to detect and prevent money laundering activities.

1. Integration of Compliance Software: Modern AML compliance software seamlessly integrates with banking systems to monitor transactions in real-time. This integration permits the swift flagging of suspicious activities, ensuring rapid response to potential threats.

2. Machine Learning Algorithms: ML algorithms are adept at discerning patterns in data that would elude human analysts. These algorithms can be trained to recognize the hallmarks of money laundering, such as structuring deposits to evade detection thresholds or rapid movement of funds across accounts.

3. Natural Language Processing (NLP): NLP is employed to analyze vast quantities of textual data, such as customer communications, to identify risk factors associated with money laundering. This includes the detection of coded language or communication patterns that are atypical or suspicious.

4. Blockchain Technology: Blockchain provides an immutable ledger of transactions, offering a transparent and secure means of tracing the flow of funds. Its use in AML compliance helps ensure the authenticity of transactional data and the integrity of financial records.

Enhancing Due Diligence through Technology

Technological solutions significantly bolster the due diligence process, enabling institutions to conduct more thorough background checks with greater efficiency.

1. Digital Identity Verification: Advanced digital identity verification systems use biometrics and document authentication to swiftly and accurately establish customer identities, reducing the risk of identity fraud.

2. Risk Assessment Tools: Automated risk assessment tools evaluate customer profiles and transactional behaviors against known risk parameters. These tools generate risk scores that aid in the prioritization of compliance efforts.

3. Global Watchlist Screening: Real-time screening against global watchlists and sanctions lists ensures that institutions do not inadvertently facilitate transactions for individuals or entities associated with money laundering or terrorist financing.

Compliance as a Dynamic Process

The dynamic nature of financial crime necessitates that AML compliance be an adaptive process. Technology enables ongoing learning and adjustment to compliance strategies, vital for staying ahead of sophisticated money launderers.

1. Feedback Loops: Implementing feedback loops from detection systems back into the risk modeling process allows for the continual refinement of detection parameters and the improvement of false positive rates.

2. Adaptive Analytics: An adaptive analytical framework can incorporate new data sources and typologies as they emerge, keeping the institution's AML measures aligned with current trends and tactics used by criminals.

Regulatory Technology (RegTech): A Synergy of Compliance and Innovation

RegTech solutions are designed to ease the burden of regulatory compliance through innovation. These solutions offer compliance automation, reporting efficiency, and a reduction in the operational costs associated with AML efforts.

Collaboration between institutions and technology providers is crucial for AML compliance. By sharing information and insights, the financial sector can create a united front against money laundering, leveraging technology as the shared sword and shield in this critical battle.

Leveraging technology for AML compliance is not a mere option; it is an imperative for financial institutions determined to stem the tide of money laundering. Through the integration of sophisticated compliance software, machine learning, NLP, and blockchain technology, institutions enhance their AML defenses, ensuring both regulatory adherence and the protection of the global financial system from abuse. The future of AML compliance rests in the hands of those who skillfully harness these technologies, weaving them into the very fabric of their financial operations.

Case Studies of Compliance Failures

Peering into the annals of financial history, one finds a treasure trove of cautionary tales—narratives fraught with the scars of compliance failures. These tales not only serve as stark reminders of the consequences of oversight but also as invaluable learning resources for those seeking to understand the complex fabric of regulatory adherence.

In an era where compliance is king, the downfall of a renowned banking institution due to AML oversights stands as a sobering testament to the perils of non-compliance. This case involved the bank's failure to implement adequate transaction monitoring systems, resulting in the unchecked flow of illicit funds through its corridors for years.

A detailed analysis of the breakdown reveals a series of missteps—ineffective risk assessment procedures that underestimated exposure, insufficient staff training that left employees ill-equipped to identify red flags, and a pervasive culture of complacency that undermined the seriousness of AML obligations.

Another harrowing account chronicles a financial service provider whose reliance on outdated technology precipitated a compliance debacle. Despite embracing digital innovation in customer-facing operations, the firm's AML systems remained antiquated, lacking the robust analytical capabilities required to parse through complex layers of modern financial crime.

The case study underscores the dire consequences of technological stagnation, where the absence of machine learning and adaptive analytics rendered the firm's AML procedures obsolete. The result was a cascade of undetected fraudulent transactions that culminated in punitive regulatory sanctions and a tarnished industry reputation.

A different case study illustrates the pitfalls of superficial customer screening processes. An investment company, lured by the promise of high-net-worth clients, skirted the depths of due diligence. The initial verification checks were cursory at best, bypassing the rigorous vetting required to uncover the intricate web of shell corporations and offshore entities used by money launderers.

In this instance, the company's failure to employ digital identity verification tools and comprehensive background investigations led to the inadvertent facilitation of money laundering, drawing the ire of regulatory bodies and resulting in hefty fines.

Each case study serves as a stark illustration of the various facets where AML compliance can falter. From internal culture and training deficiencies to the misapplication of technology and due diligence shortcuts, the narratives converge on a central theme—the necessity of a holistic and dynamic approach to AML compliance.

The lessons derived from these compliance failures are manifold. They echo the critical need for continuous investment in state-of-the-art AML technologies, the cultivation of a risk-aware corporate ethos, and the unyielding pursuit of thorough due diligence. For financial institutions, these case studies are not merely tales of yore but pivotal guides for navigating the treacherous waters of financial regulation, ensuring that history's missteps are not repeated in their own legacies.

Tax Risk Management

Tax legislation presents a formidable challenge to any financial institution, demanding a blend of precision, foresight, and agility. Tax risk management, therefore, emerges as a critical discipline within financial planning and analysis, one that requires a nuanced understanding of both domestic and international tax landscapes.

Central to effective tax risk management is the development of a strategy that anticipates the potential fault lines in tax compliance. This includes staying abreast of the ever-shifting tax regulations that vary not only by country but also by state and local jurisdictions. A robust strategy must factor in the intricacies of transfer pricing, the complexities of cross-border transactions, and the evolving nature of digital taxation.

Transfer pricing stands as one of the pillars of tax risk management, representing the method by which prices are set for goods, services, and intangible assets transferred between entities within a multinational enterprise. Ensuring that these transactions meet the arm's length principle—reflective of fair market value—is paramount to avoiding the scrutiny of tax authorities that could lead to punitive adjustments and severe financial penalties.

In the digital age, the application of advanced analytics to tax management can provide a competitive edge. Predictive modeling tools allow for the simulation of various tax scenarios, enabling finance professionals to optimize tax planning and mitigate risk. By adopting AI-driven tax software, companies can enhance their compliance processes, reduce human error, and streamline the reporting required by tax authorities.

A cornerstone of tax risk management is the preparation for and navigation of tax audits. This entails maintaining meticulous documentation, ensuring the clarity of tax positions taken, and preparing a cogent defense of tax filings. Proactive engagement with tax auditors and the use of collaborative technology platforms can facilitate a more efficient audit process and reduce the risk of adverse findings.

As businesses expand across borders, they encounter a patchwork of tax regimes that necessitate sophisticated risk management approaches. Strategies must be tailored to address issues like the implications of the Base Erosion and Profit Shifting (BEPS) initiative, the complexities of withholding taxes on international payments, and the risks associated with tax havens and controlled foreign corporations (CFC) rules.

Tax risk management is a dynamic field that requires ongoing vigilance and strategic adaptation. It is a critical aspect of FP&A, where the implications of tax decisions reverberate through financial statements and impact the bottom line. In this light, the section has dissected the multi-faceted challenges of tax risk management and underscored the importance of remaining agile and informed in an environment characterized by constant change and complexity.

Transfer Pricing and International Taxation Risks

Within the domain of international business, transfer pricing is not merely a transactional affair but a strategic enigma entwined with the threads of global fiscal policy. It encompasses the meticulous calibration of prices for transactions between associated enterprises across different tax jurisdictions, each with its distinct demands and nuances.

The key tenet of transfer pricing is adherence to the arms-length principle—a concept mandating that the prices charged in inter-company dealings mirror those that would have been charged between independent entities under similar circumstances. This principle is the bulwark against tax evasion and avoidance strategies that can erode a nation's tax base, making compliance a top priority for multinational enterprises.

Transfer pricing becomes a hazardous landscape fraught with the perils of double taxation and non-compliance penalties when crossing international frontiers. Tax authorities globally have sharpened their focus on transfer pricing practices, spurred by initiatives like the OECD's BEPS actions, which aim to prevent profit shifting and ensure fair tax competition.

To navigate this treacherous terrain, corporations must rigorously document their transfer pricing policies, justifying their methods with comprehensive benchmarking analyses. These documents serve as both a shield and a compass, guiding companies through audits and offering protection in disputes—yet the task is arduous and demands constant attention to the evolving international tax landscape.

As financial landscapes grow increasingly complex, technology emerges as a valuable ally. Automated transfer pricing solutions offer real-time compliance tracking, reducing the burden of manual calculations and documentation. They also enable scenario planning, allowing corporations to anticipate the tax impact of strategic decisions in different jurisdictions.

The risks of international taxation are not confined to transfer pricing alone. With global expansion, companies must confront varying tax rates, anti-avoidance rules, and the constant flux of tax legislation. Tax teams must be alert to the risks of permanent establishment, which can unwittingly subject companies to additional tax liabilities, and mindful of the subtleties of tax treaties that can either mitigate or exacerbate tax exposures.

Complicating the picture further is the intersection of transfer pricing with customs valuations—the valuation of goods for import and export duties. Inconsistencies between transfer pricing and customs valuations can trigger audits and financial penalties, necessitating a harmonized approach to valuation that satisfies both tax and customs authorities.

A harmonious alliance between meticulous documentation, astute use of technology, and keen awareness of legislative currents form the bedrock of successful transfer pricing and international tax risk management. As we progress, we will delve into the specific strategies that fortify this alliance, equipping leaders with the insights to turn the potential peril of taxation into strategic advantage.

Tax Optimization Strategies

Tax optimization—arguably one of the most scrutinized arenas of corporate finance—revolves around the legal framework of maximizing tax efficiency. It involves a strategic approach to financial planning that aims to align business operations with tax systems across multiple jurisdictions to minimize tax liability and maximize after-tax income.

Understanding the pillars of tax optimization is essential. These include deferral, where companies delay tax obligations to future periods; reduction, which involves employing tax credits, deductions, and exemptions to decrease taxable income; and elimination, the process of removing tax liabilities through various planning instruments.

Deferral tactics involve structuring transactions to capitalize on differences in tax rates across periods. Retirement plans and pension contributions serve as prime examples, where contributions reduce current taxable income and taxes are deferred until funds are withdrawn. However, such strategies are not without risks, as they rely on assumptions about future tax rates and financial needs.

Reduction strategies harness the potential of tax credits and incentives. Research and development credits, renewable energy incentives, and investment tax breaks are tools that can lead to significant savings if applied judiciously.

However, these incentives often come with complex qualification criteria. Companies must meticulously document their activities and expenditures to substantiate their claims and avoid the pitfalls of non-compliance.

Elimination efforts, such as engaging in cross-border structuring, involve establishing entities in low-tax jurisdictions for specific purposes, such as holding intellectual property or financing operations. Double tax treaties play a pivotal role here, potentially offering relief from dual tax burdens. However, these arrangements are under increasing scrutiny, and companies must navigate the fine line between tax planning and aggressive tax avoidance, which could result in reputational damage and legal penalties.

As explored in the previous section, transfer pricing directly impacts tax optimization strategies. Firms must ensure that their transfer pricing policies align with their overall tax strategy, particularly when it involves shifting profits to lower-tax jurisdictions. Vigilance and compliance with the arms-length principle are non-negotiable to withstand the scrutiny of tax authorities.

Tax optimization strategies require an intricate balancing act between global operational goals and local compliance demands. For instance, a multinational utilizing a cost-sharing arrangement for its R&D activities must consider the tax implications in each jurisdiction where the R&D benefits will be realized, ensuring that each contributes an appropriate share of costs in accordance with local tax laws.

Proactive tax planning involves continuous scenario analysis —a forward-looking approach that evaluates the tax consequences of potential business decisions such as mergers, acquisitions, or divestitures. Scenario analysis becomes a key decision-making tool, aiding CFOs and tax directors in understanding the tax impacts and aligning their decisions with overall business strategies.

In the following segments, we will delve deeper into the specific instruments and methodologies that underpin tax optimization, unraveling the complexities and presenting actionable insights for FP&A professionals seeking to refine their tax strategies.

Managing Tax Audits and Disputes

In the labyrinthine world of corporate finance, tax audits and disputes form a complex subset that demands not only an in-depth understanding of tax laws but also a strategic approach to navigate the potential repercussions on an enterprise's financial landscape. This section dissects the nuances of managing tax audits and disputes, emphasizing the pre-emptive strategies and responsive maneuvers that can mitigate risks and fortify an organization's fiscal fortifications.

When a siren call from the tax authorities arrives, it signals the onset of an audit—a critical examination of an organization's tax returns to verify their accuracy and compliance with tax laws. The encounter with tax audits can be a daunting saga, fraught with intricacies and potential pitfalls. Companies must be prepared with meticulous record-keeping, an articulate understanding of the tax positions taken, and the readiness to substantiate them with unwavering evidence.

The opening gambit in this chess game of fiscal scrutiny is the pre-audit phase. Companies poised for success approach this phase with a proactive stance, by conducting internal reviews and reconciliations that mirror the rigor of external examinations. A thorough pre-audit can unearth discrepancies and areas of vulnerability, allowing the enterprise to address these issues before they blossom into full-fledged disputes.

When the tax authorities delve into the company's financial records, the curtain rises on the actual audit phase. Here, the focus sharpens on the provision of documentation and the elucidation of complex transactions. The enterprise must navigate this phase with precision and diplomacy, fostering an environment of cooperation and transparency, while also safeguarding its interests.

The plot thickens should disagreements arise, catapulting the company into the realm of tax disputes. In this landscape, the power of negotiation comes to the fore. Armed with robust documentation and a well-founded rationale for their tax positions, finance leaders embark on the delicate dance of dispute resolution. This might involve presenting compelling arguments to the tax authorities or, in cases where common ground proves elusive, escalating the matter to a formal appeal or even litigation.

The art of managing tax audits and disputes is a refined blend of proactive measures and reactive strategies. It requires an agility to adapt to the ever-evolving tax regulations and an acute awareness of the implications each decision may have on the organization's financial narrative.

As we chart the course through this section, we will dissect case studies from diverse industries, examining the successful tactics employed and the lessons etched into the corporate memory. We will scrutinize the role of tax advisors and legal counsel, the importance of cross-departmental collaboration, and the strategic application of technology to manage and streamline the audit and dispute resolution process.

In the theater of tax audits and disputes, the CFO acts not only as a director but also as a strategist, ensuring that every move on the board aligns with the company's overarching financial goals. It is imperative that the CFO maintains a pulse on regulatory changes and leverages insights from past audits to fortify the company's defense against future scrutiny.

Emerging Tax Considerations (Digital Services Tax)

As the global economy strides into the digital era, tax systems face the formidable challenge of keeping pace with the rapid evolution of technology and the novel forms of value creation it engenders. This section delves into the burgeoning domain of emerging tax considerations, with a particular focus on digital services taxes (DST) that have been stirring up waves across international borders.

A digital services tax represents a jurisdiction's attempt to capture revenue from digital operations that often skirt traditional tax paradigms. As digital platforms transcend physical boundaries, they render obsolete the conventional nexus-based taxation rules. The DST is thus a response to the need for a tax structure that can effectively target the profits generated by digital giants from activities within a country, even in the absence of a physical presence.

The theoretical underpinnings of the DST revolve around the principle of value creation. Where is value created in the digital world, and how can it be quantified and taxed? The DST posits that user participation and the generation of user data are pivotal to value creation for digital companies, and these activities can be tethered to specific locales, forming the basis for taxation.

The implementation of a DST, however, is not without its complexities. The first layer of intricacy arises in defining the scope of taxable services—determining which digital activities should be taxed and at what thresholds. Will the tax apply to online marketplaces, streaming services, data monetization, or cloud computing? And what revenue benchmarks will trigger the tax liability?

Furthermore, the DST raises questions regarding international tax equity and the potential for double taxation. With each country potentially devising its own DST regulations, multinational digital enterprises might find themselves navigating a labyrinth of disparate tax rules, complicating compliance and raising the specter of being taxed multiple times on the same income.

CHAPTER 8: HUMAN FACTORS AND RISK CULTURE

When dissecting the anatomy of risk culture within an organization, we must shine the spotlight on the myriad human factors that influence behaviors and attitudes towards risk. The theoretical underpinning of risk culture is an amalgamation of psychological theories, organizational behavior, and human resource practices. This section meticulously unpacks these concepts and examines their interplay in shaping the risk culture of financial planning and analysis (FP&A).

Recognizing and mitigating cognitive biases is tantamount to steering a vessel through the Sirens' treacherous waters; a single misstep in judgment can lead to dire consequences. This section meticulously examines the insidious influence of cognitive biases on risk assessments, which, if left unchecked, can distort the FP&A professional's perception and decision-making abilities, ultimately jeopardizing the fiscal health of an organization.

The essence of risk assessment lies in the ability to evaluate potential future events with clarity and precision, a task that is often marred by the inherent biases of the human mind.

Cognitive biases are psychological patterns that consistently deviate from rationality or good judgment, and they can significantly affect the risk assessment process in FP&A.

One must first understand the taxonomy of biases that an FP&A professional might encounter. Confirmation bias, for instance, leads individuals to favor information that confirms their pre-existing beliefs or hypotheses, neglecting data that contradicts them. In risk assessments, this bias can result in underestimating potential threats that do not align with one's initial analysis, potentially leaving the organization vulnerable to unforeseen risks.

The availability heuristic, another prevalent bias, influences individuals to overestimate the likelihood of events based on their recency or memorability rather than on objective data. For example, if an FP&A leader has recently experienced a particular risk event, they may give undue weight to its occurrence in future assessments, potentially skewing the risk landscape.

Representativeness bias causes decision-makers to draw inferences about the probability of an event based on how closely it resembles other instances or a broader category, disregarding statistical information. In FP&A, this can lead to miscalculations of risk probabilities when an event appears like typical cases, even if data suggests otherwise.

Risk assessment in FP&A also involves making judgments under conditions of uncertainty. The bias known as ambiguity aversion describes the tendency to prefer known risks over unknowns, even when the latter may offer better outcomes. This predisposition can prevent FP&A departments from capitalizing on potentially lucrative opportunities that are accompanied by uncertain risks.

Risk assessments can also be compromised by hindsight bias, where individuals view past events as having been more predictable than they were, leading to overconfidence in their predictive abilities. FP&A professionals must be vigilant to avoid 'predicting the past' with an illusory lens of inevitability, as this can skew future risk assessments and the development of mitigation strategies.

To counteract these cognitive biases, FP&A teams can employ various debiasing techniques. Ensuring diverse perspectives in risk assessment discussions can challenge confirmation and representativeness biases by introducing alternative viewpoints. Structured analytical methods, such as decision trees and probabilistic modeling, can help mitigate the availability heuristic and ambiguity aversion by providing a more objective basis for risk estimation.

Promoting a culture of critical thinking and encouraging skepticism towards initial assumptions can further safeguard against cognitive biases. Additionally, leveraging advancements in AI and ML can assist in identifying patterns that may elude human analysis, providing a complementary tool to the FP&A professional's expertise.

Understanding and mitigating cognitive biases is not a mere academic exercise but a practical necessity for FP&A professionals. By integrating an awareness of these biases into their risk assessment processes, financial leaders can enhance the accuracy of their evaluations and fortify their organizations against the capricious nature of risk. The true mastery of risk assessment, therefore, lies not only in the quantitative proficiencies but equally in the qualitative wisdom to transcend the limitations of human cognition.

Overconfidence and Risk-Taking Behaviors

Overconfidence stands as a formidable sentinel, influencing FP&A practitioners with seductive whispers of certainty where uncertainty reigns. This section delves into the intricate dynamics between overconfidence and risk-taking behaviors, unraveling their theoretical underpinnings and the consequential impact on the sanctity of financial assessments.

Overconfidence, in the context of FP&A, can be conceptualized as an overestimation of one's predictive capabilities, a belief in the precision of one's knowledge, and an inflated view of one's ability to control events. It is a psychological construct that can lead to an unwarranted escalation of commitment to one's initial forecasts or strategies, even in the face of contrary evidence.

In the mosaic of financial decision-making, overconfidence can skew the risk assessment process by fostering a propensity for excessive risk-taking. It is a bias that insidiously encourages financial leaders to assume positions of greater risk under the guise of opportunity, often neglecting the probabilistic nature of outcomes and the volatility of markets.

Theoretical insights suggest that overconfidence can emerge from various sources. One such source is the illusion of control, where individuals believe they can influence outcomes that are, in fact, determined by chance. In FP&A, this may manifest in the overvaluation of projects or investments, predicated on the belief that personal expertise can mitigate inherent risks.

Another fountainhead of overconfidence is self-attribution bias, where individuals attribute successful outcomes to their skills and abilities while attributing failures to external factors. In the financial domain, this can lead to an underappreciation of the role of luck or market forces in the success of investment decisions, setting the stage for riskier positions based on a flawed understanding of past performance.

Overconfidence also intertwines with confirmation bias, as financial analysts may selectively seek information that supports their confident predictions, disregarding data that may signal the need for caution. The resulting feedback loop fortifies the overconfidence, leading to an increased likelihood of undertaking disproportionate risks.

The practical implications of overconfidence are multifold. It can lead to the underestimation of project costs, the overestimation of future revenues, and a diminished sensitivity to warning signs that suggest a revision of the risk landscape. The human proclivity for overconfidence implies that FP&A departments must vigilantly calibrate their risk-taking behaviors to align with a more realistic assessment of capabilities and uncertainties.

Mitigating overconfidence requires structural and cultural interventions within FP&A teams. Implementing systematic review processes, fostering an environment that values humility in forecasting, and encouraging the consideration of worst-case scenarios are strategies that can temper overconfident assertions. Scenario planning and sensitivity analysis can serve as quantitative counterbalances to overconfidence, compelling analysts to confront the full spectrum of potential outcomes.

Moreover, cultivating a culture that embraces intellectual humility and recognizes the fallibility inherent in financial forecasting can act as a bulwark against overconfidence. Encouraging FP&A professionals to consider alternative viewpoints and dissenting opinions can reduce the risk of groupthink and promote a more balanced approach to risk-taking.

Overconfidence is a cognitive bias with the power to shape the risk profile of an organization significantly. By dissecting its theoretical dimensions and implementing strategies to dampen its effects, FP&A leaders can ensure that risk-taking behaviors are not the byproducts of misplaced confidence but rather the result of thorough, critical, and informed analysis. The finesse in risk management, thus, lies not only in the numbers but in navigating the nuanced psychological terrain that influences every financial decision.

Anchoring and Adjustment in Forecasting

Anchoring in the realm of financial forecasting operates as a cognitive tether, where initial estimates exert a gravitational pull on subsequent assessments and decisions. It's the invisible hand that subtly guides FP&A professionals as they navigate through the tempestuous seas of market predictions and financial projections. This subsection excavates the theoretical bedrock of the anchoring heuristic and its implications for adjustment processes within the forecasting discipline.

Anchoring is the psychological tendency to rely heavily on

the first piece of information encountered—the "anchor"—when making decisions. In forecasting, this often translates to an undue influence of initial estimates or data points on final analytical outcomes, regardless of their relevance. The anchor sets the stage for all following deliberations, often leading to biased adjustments that do not stray far from the initial value.

Theoretical exploration into this bias reveals its pervasiveness and potency. Anchoring can stem from explicit numerical information, such as past financial performance or initial budget figures, but it can also emanate from subtler cues, including suggestive questions or strategically framed financial scenarios. Even when analysts are aware of the potential for bias, the anchor's tenacity can be remarkably resistant to full cognitive dislodgment.

Adjustment from the anchor is typically insufficient; as forecasts are revised, they tend to hover close to the original number, a phenomenon exacerbated by uncertainty and complexity. The pernicious effect of this cognitive shortcut is that it can lead to underreaction to added information, particularly when that information requires a substantial shift from the established anchor.

In FP&A, the anchoring and adjustment heuristic can manifest in budgeting processes, where last year's figures might unduly influence the current year's budget, regardless of market changes or internal shifts in strategy. It can similarly affect projections of sales growth, cost estimates, and risk assessments, implicitly skewing analyses toward historical anchors.

To combat the influence of anchoring, FP&A professionals

can deploy several strategies. One such approach is to foster a culture of critical questioning, which encourages analysts to challenge initial estimates and consider a wider range of data. Engaging in pre-mortem analysis, where teams envisage possible failures and then work backward to understand what could lead to such outcomes, helps in recalibrating thought processes away from established anchors.

Another effective remedy is the use of multiple models or scenarios that do not share common anchors, thus providing a spectrum of independent perspectives that can be synthesized for a more balanced forecast. This practice not only enriches the analytical process but also dilutes the cognitive grip of any single anchoring figure.

The implementation of structured analytic techniques, such as Delphi methods, where expert opinions are aggregated and refined through iterative rounds, can also mitigate anchoring. This technique leverages collective wisdom while minimizing the influence of any singular initial judgment.

The anchoring and adjustment heuristic is deeply embedded in the fabric of financial forecasting, with theoretical and practical ramifications that extend into various dimensions of FP&A. By recognizing and addressing the subtle yet profound sway of anchoring, financial professionals can refine their forecasting methodologies to be both more reflective of reality and less susceptible to cognitive inertia. It is through such diligent and deliberate cognitive recalibration that FP&A can aspire to transcend the bounds of bias and achieve a more enlightened state of financial prescience.

Mitigating Biases through Structured Decision-Making Processes

Structured decision-making is a disciplined framework that seeks to systematically deconstruct decision-making into smaller, more manageable components. By applying a formalized process, FP&A experts can dissect complex financial problems into their fundamental elements, scrutinizing each piece through a lens unclouded by personal predispositions or psychological biases.

The essence of this approach lies in its methodical nature, which serves as a bulwark against the insidious ingress of cognitive distortions. It introduces rigor into the decision-making paradigm, demanding evidence over instinct and analysis over assumption. The intention is to create a replicable pathway that can be followed consistently, irrespective of the financial conundrum at hand.

One pivotal element of this structure is the establishment of clear, objective criteria against which options can be evaluated. This may involve the use of scoring systems or decision matrices that quantitatively weigh the pros and cons of different financial strategies. By quantifying preferences and aligning evaluations with strategic objectives, decision-makers can navigate away from the reefs of bias.

In this vein, the structured decision-making process also enshrines the principle of accountability. This is realized through documentation at each step of the process, from the initial framing of the problem to the final selection of the preferred solution. Such meticulous recording not only serves as a historical ledger for future review but also enforces a discipline of thought and rationale that counteracts the whims of intuition.

Scenario planning, another key tactic in the structured decision-making arsenal, plays a vital role in mitigating biases. By envisioning a variety of potential futures and rigorously testing plans against these diverse backdrops, FP&A professionals can extend their perspective beyond the present—or the preferred—and into the realm of the possible. It is a process that tempers the optimism of the forecasting heart with the skepticism of the analytical mind.

Furthermore, structured decision-making processes often incorporate stages of iteration and feedback. This iterative cycle, which may include simulations or stress tests, allows for the refinement of decisions through successive rounds of critical evaluation. The feedback loop is not only internal but also external, drawing upon diverse stakeholders to ensure that the decision-making process is insulated from the echo chamber of groupthink.

The use of technology, particularly decision-support systems that leverage artificial intelligence and machine learning, can also be instrumental. These tools assist in processing vast amounts of data, revealing patterns and insights that may elude the human cognitive process. When integrated into a structured decision-making framework, they augment human intuition with empirical grounding.

Ultimately, the judicious application of structured decision-making processes is akin to navigating by the stars in an age of digital maps. It offers a timeless compass by which to steer the complex decisions intrinsic to FP&A, enabling financial leaders to not only identify and understand their inherent biases but also to effectively circumvent them. Through such disciplined intellectual navigation, the financial professional can aspire to reach the zenith of objective analysis and sound strategic judgment.

Talent Management and Skills Development

Within the dynamic domain of financial planning and analysis, the cultivation of a robust talent pool is indispensable. Talent management and skills development represent the strategic sinews that empower an organization to flex its analytical capabilities and generate incisive insights. The fostering of such talent necessitates a multifaceted strategy, one that aligns with the organization's overarching objectives while adapting to the ever-evolving financial landscape.

The conceptual framework for talent management in FP&A must be rooted in a profound understanding of the competencies required to excel in this field. It is a terrain where analytical acumen, prowess in predictive modeling, and an agility in adapting to technological innovations are not merely desirable but essential. As such, the organization must undertake a thorough skills gap analysis, assessing the current competencies of its workforce against the future needs dictated by strategic goals and market forces.

Skills development, then, becomes a targeted endeavor, focusing on elevating the proficiency of the FP&A team in areas that offer the greatest leverage for performance improvement. This might manifest in specialized training programs designed to enhance expertise in complex data analysis, financial modeling, or regulatory compliance. Such programs should not be static but must be continuously re-evaluated and updated to ensure alignment with the latest financial methodologies and tools.

This commitment to ongoing education forms the bedrock of a learning culture that must permeate the organization. A learning culture encourages not just formal training but also a spirit of intellectual curiosity and critical inquiry. It is a culture that values the lessons gleaned from both successes and failures, recognizing each as a stepping stone for growth. Encouraging team members to engage with professional associations, webinars, and industry conferences further enriches this culture, infusing it with external perspectives and innovative knowledge.

In parallel, talent management in FP&A must embrace the richness of diversity—diversity of thought, background, and approach. By assembling teams that reflect a broad spectrum of experiences and viewpoints, the organization safeguards against the myopia of homogeneity. Such diversity fosters innovative problem-solving and a robustness of strategy formulation that can withstand the multifarious challenges encountered in financial stewardship.

A pivotal component of talent management is the identification and nurturing of high-potential individuals who can ascend to leadership roles. This process involves not just recognizing talent but actively developing it through mentorship programs, leadership training, and opportunities for cross-functional collaboration. It is an investment in the human capital that will bear fruit in the form of a visionary leadership pipeline, prepared to steer the financial helm in the turbulent seas of global markets.

Moreover, talent management must be attuned to the psychological and motivational underpinnings that drive performance. Incentive structures that reward not just results but also the innovative processes that yield those results can galvanize a workforce towards excellence. Recognition programs that spotlight exceptional contributions reinforce a culture of achievement and encourage the sharing of best practices across the organization.

Talent management and skills development in FP&A is an intricate mosaic woven from strands of strategic planning, continuous learning, and motivational psychology. It demands a proactive stance, one that anticipates the needs of the future while fortifying the skills of the present. By embracing this comprehensive approach, financial leaders can forge an FP&A team that is not merely competent but exceptional—a team that is the embodiment of the organization's commitment to financial excellence and strategic foresight.

Staff Competencies for Effective Risk Management

The architecture of a robust risk management system is inextricably linked to the competencies of the staff tasked with its operation. In the realm of FP&A, where risk is both an adversary and an informant, the proficiency of personnel forms the bedrock upon which risk strategies are both construed and executed.

Effective risk management is underpinned by a set of core competencies that transcend the basic knowledge of financial principles. These competencies are the amalgamation of technical prowess, strategic thinking, and a nuanced understanding of the organization's industry and its position within the larger economic ecosystem. They are the catalysts for discerning the subtle interplays between diverse risk factors and the enterprise's aspirations.

At the heart of these competencies lies analytical acuity —a skill that empowers staff to dissect complex datasets and extract salient insights. Analytical thinkers are adept at identifying trends, patterns, and anomalies within data, interpreting their potential implications for the organization. Their capacity for critical analysis is further augmented by an understanding of statistical methods and predictive analytics, which allows for a more sophisticated approach to risk evaluation.

Strategic risk management also demands a keen grasp of financial modeling. Personnel must be agile in constructing and manipulating models that can simulate a range of scenarios. Their ability to engage in what-if analysis is crucial for anticipating potential outcomes and devising strategies to either capitalize on opportunities or mitigate threats. This competency hinges not only on technical skill but also on the ability to conceptualize the multifarious ways in which variables can interact over time.

Communication, both articulate and succinct, is an essential competency in risk management. The nuances of risk must be conveyed to stakeholders with varying degrees of financial literacy, necessitating clarity and the ability to translate complex concepts into actionable intelligence. Whether communicating upward to executives or laterally across departments, the effectiveness of risk management practices is in part dependent on the clarity with which information is presented and decisions are rationalized.

Further, staff involved in risk management must exhibit a profound ethical compass and a commitment to integrity. As custodians of sensitive information and influential analyses, they must navigate the moral landscapes of disclosure and discretion with unwavering principle. Their decisions and recommendations may significantly impact the organization's trajectory, making a staunch adherence to ethical standards a non-negotiable competency.

Adaptability in an ever-shifting risk environment is another key competency. The financial landscape is in a state of perpetual flux, colored by regulatory changes, technological advancements, and global economic shifts. Risk management professionals must therefore be lifelong learners, continuously updating their arsenal of skills and knowledge to remain at the forefront of industry practices. Their readiness to embrace new tools and methodologies is what will keep the organization's risk management strategies both current and effective.

The competencies required for effective risk management in FP&A are a composite of hard skills—like analysis and financial modeling—and soft skills, such as communication and adaptability. It is this combination that equips staff with the ability to navigate the complexities of risk and contribute to the organization's sustained resilience and success. By investing in the cultivation of these competencies, an enterprise lays a solid foundation for its risk management initiatives, ensuring that its guardians are well-armed to protect and propel its financial ambitions.

Upskilling and Reskilling for the Digital Age

In an age where digital innovation reshapes landscapes with relentless momentum, the need for upskilling and reskilling emerges as a pivotal strategy in the arsenal of risk management. This section delves into the intricacies of cultivating a workforce adept at navigating the digital terrain, a crucial determinant of an organization's agility in the face of risk.

The digital age heralds a plethora of advanced tools and platforms, each with the potential to revolutionize risk management practices. However, the efficacy of these technological advancements is contingent upon the proficiency with which staff can wield them. Upskilling —enhancing current skills to meet the evolving demands of one's role—is a critical initiative. It ensures that employees stay competent and confident in leveraging new technologies and methodologies.

Reskilling, on the other hand, involves training employees to take on entirely separate roles within the organization. This process is often necessitated by the automation of certain tasks, rendering some skill sets obsolete. Through reskilling, an enterprise can retain valuable institutional knowledge and employee engagement, while also redirecting resources to areas that promise greater strategic benefit.

The digital transformation mandates a shift in the organization's learning culture. Risk management, once considered a domain strictly for specialists, now requires a broader base of digital literacy across the workforce. Employees must not only comprehend the implications of digital risks but also be proficient in using analytics software, cybersecurity protocols, and other tools that fortify the organization's defenses against digital threats.

To this end, comprehensive training programs must be designed with an emphasis on hands-on experience and practical application. Simulations and real-world case studies can provide employees with a sandbox in which to hone their digital skills without endangering actual operations. Through iterative learning, mistakes become valuable lessons, and confidence is built upon the scaffold of experience.

Leadership plays a crucial role in driving the upskilling and reskilling agenda. They must not only advocate for the importance of digital competencies but also lead by example. By actively engaging in their own professional development, leaders send a clear message about the organization's commitment to continuous learning.

Moreover, fostering a culture that encourages experimentation and innovation is vital. Employees should feel empowered to explore latest ideas and approaches within the realm of risk management, without the fear of reprisal for failure. Such a culture not only nurtures skill development but also stimulates creative solutions to complex risk-related challenges.

The strategic integration of upskilling and reskilling initiatives into talent management frameworks is also imperative. Clear pathways for career progression and skill advancement must be established, providing employees with a vision of their future within a digitally mature enterprise. This approach not only aligns individual aspirations with organizational goals but also reduces the talent attrition that often accompanies the introduction of new technologies.

The intricate theoretical landscape of upskilling and reskilling for the digital age is one marked by continuous evolution and adaptability. It is a multifaceted process that underpins the resilience of an organization's risk management framework, ensuring that its human capital remains its greatest asset in the ceaseless march of progress. Through dedicated efforts to enhance the digital competencies of its workforce, an enterprise cements its position at the vanguard of innovation, poised to meet the challenges of risk management head-on in a perpetually transforming world.

Attracting and Retaining Top Talent in FP&A

At the confluence of financial prowess and industry foresight, the ability to attract and retain top talent in the field of Financial Planning & Analysis (FP&A) is tantamount to harnessing the winds that propel an organization forward. This expansive domain of expertise, where analytical rigor meets strategic forecasting, demands a talent pool that is not only adept at navigating the complexities of finance but also visionary in leveraging data for future growth.

The ongoing challenge for businesses lies in identifying individuals who embody a rare blend of quantitative acuity and qualitative insight—professionals who can decipher the story behind the numbers and craft narratives that guide executive decisions. The quest for such talent calls for a nuanced understanding of the multifarious motivations that drive high-caliber professionals towards or away from an organization.

Attracting such talent begins with the cultivation of an employer brand that resonates with the values and career aspirations of sought-after FP&A professionals. It is essential to articulate a clear and compelling vision of the company's future, one that delineates opportunities for impact and innovation. The promise of engaging in work that is both intellectually stimulating and has a tangible effect on the company's trajectory can be a powerful lure for top performers.

The recruitment process itself must be reflective of the strategic nature of FP&A roles. Prospective employees should be evaluated not only on their technical expertise but also on their strategic acumen and ability to think holistically about business challenges. Interactive case studies and scenario-based interviews can serve as effective tools in discerning a candidate's problem-solving capabilities and cultural fit.

However, attracting talent is but one facet of the equation. Retention is where the true challenge lies, as it requires the creation and maintenance of an environment where top talent can thrive. Professional development opportunities are paramount, offering pathways for continuous learning and advancement. Tailored training programs, mentorship initiatives, and access to industry conferences can foster a culture of growth and prevent intellectual stagnation.

Financial incentives, while important, are often not the sole motivators for FP&A professionals who seek a deeper sense of fulfillment from their work. Organizations must also focus on providing a collaborative culture that values and rewards creativity, initiative, and strategic input. Transparent communication about company performance and strategic direction can fortify a sense of belonging and purpose.

Flexibility in work arrangements has also emerged as a critical factor in an era where work-life balance has taken center stage. A degree of autonomy, allowing for remote work or flexible hours, can contribute significantly to an employee's satisfaction and loyalty. This flexibility signals trust and respect for the employee's ability to manage their productivity and time effectively.

Furthermore, in the realm of FP&A, the impact of one's work on decision-making is a strong driver of job satisfaction. Ensuring that FP&A professionals are included in strategic discussions and their insights are valued at the executive level reinforces the significance of their role within the company. This level of involvement empowers professionals and cements their commitment to the organization's mission.

The intricate task of attracting and retaining top talent in FP&A necessitates an approach that extends beyond mere financial recompense. It demands a holistic strategy that encompasses the promise of impactful work, opportunities for personal and professional development, flexible work cultures, and a seat at the table where the consequential decisions are made. By cultivating such an environment, an organization positions itself as a desirable destination for the brightest minds in FP&A, thereby securing a competitive advantage in an increasingly complex and dynamic business world.

Succession Planning and Knowledge Transfer

The continuity of leadership and the seamless transfer of specialized knowledge stand as critical pillars for enduring corporate success. Succession planning and knowledge transfer are not merely administrative tasks; they are strategic initiatives that safeguard the organization's future by ensuring that the intellectual capital, honed over years of experience, is preserved and passed on.

Succession planning within FP&A is a foresighted process, one that anticipates the inevitable changes in leadership and preempts potential vacuums in expertise. It involves a systematic approach to identifying and grooming potential leaders who possess not only the requisite technical skills but also the strategic mindset to steer the organization through future financial landscapes.

The theoretical underpinnings of this process are rooted in the recognition that knowledge is a perishable asset if left unmanaged. The departure of a seasoned professional can lead to a significant erosion of institutional memory, thereby impacting the organization's ability to make informed decisions. A robust succession plan, therefore, entails a proactive identification of key roles and the competencies required to fulfill them, followed by an alignment of these roles with individuals who exhibit the potential to grow into these critical positions.

Knowledge transfer, on the other hand, is the tactical counterpart to succession planning. It is the mechanism through which an organization's proprietary methodologies, analytical techniques, and strategic insights are codified and communicated across generations of FP&A professionals. This process goes beyond the mere dissemination of information; it is about instilling a deep-seated understanding of the reasoning and intuition that underlie financial analyses and projections.

Effective knowledge transfer begins with the creation of a knowledge repository—a centralized database that captures the wealth of information generated by FP&A activities. This repository serves as a living library, cataloging best practices, lessons learned, and decision-making frameworks that are readily accessible to the entire FP&A team.

Complementing this repository are structured mentorship programs, which pair seasoned professionals with emerging talents. Through one-on-one mentorship, the tacit knowledge that resides in the minds of experienced analysts and managers is articulated and imparted. This personalized transfer of insight is often the most potent form of learning, as it allows for the nuanced subtleties of FP&A to be explored and understood in context.

Another critical aspect of knowledge transfer is the ongoing documentation of FP&A processes and decision-making rationales. Standard operating procedures, analytical models, and strategic reports should be annotated with insights into their development and application. This documentation serves not only as a reference for incoming talent but also as a tool for revisiting and refining strategies as the organization evolves.

As FP&A operates in a dynamic environment, characterized by regulatory changes, market shifts, and technological advancements, succession planning and knowledge transfer must be agile and continuous. Workshops, simulations, and cross-training initiatives are essential to keeping the knowledge transfer mechanisms vibrant and relevant.

In setting the stage for future chapters, it is imperative to recognize that succession planning and knowledge transfer are indispensable strategic endeavors. They are how an organization ensures that the collective wisdom of its FP&A team is not transient but rather a sustainable asset that fuels its competitive advantage and informs its strategic direction for years to come.

By embracing these processes with the meticulous care and thoughtful consideration they demand, organizations can create an enduring legacy of financial intelligence and strategic acumen, positioning themselves for enduring success in the uncertain seas of the global economy.

Organizational Dynamics and Change Management

Change, a constant within the financial sector, demands a harmonized response from every stratum of an organization. FP&A, as the nexus of financial insight, must not only adapt to change but often act as the harbinger, guiding the organization through the ebbs and flows of economic and regulatory shifts. The theoretical frameworks that underpin this process draw from a broad spectrum of disciplines, including psychology, sociology, and business management.

At its core, organizational dynamics refers to the patterns and behaviors that emerge from the interactions among an organization's members. These dynamics are influenced by a myriad of factors such as corporate culture, leadership styles, communication patterns, and power structures. Understanding these factors is paramount for FP&A leaders who must engender a culture that embraces change rather than resists it.

Change management, then, is the systematic approach taken to transition individuals, teams, and organizations from their current state to a desired future state. It is a multi-faceted endeavor that encompasses both the tactical execution of change initiatives and the more subtle art of managing the human response to change.

FP&A professionals must be astute in applying change management theories such as Lewin's three-stage model, which conceptualizes change as a process of unfreezing, changing, and refreezing. This model posits that for change to be effectively implemented, the organization must first be brought out of stasis (unfreezing), then transition through the process of adopting new behaviors or practices (changing), and finally establish a new equilibrium (refreezing).

A pivotal component of managing change is communication. Clear, transparent, and timely communication can alleviate uncertainty and build trust among stakeholders. FP&A leaders must utilize a variety of channels to convey the vision, the rationale behind changes, and the expected outcomes to all levels of the organization.

Leadership, too, is critical in change management. Leaders must not only champion change but also demonstrate their commitment through actions. They must be able to articulate a compelling narrative that aligns with the organization's strategic objectives and resonates with the team's values and goals.

Resistance to change is an inherent part of the change

process. FP&A leaders should anticipate and identify potential sources of resistance, whether rooted in fear, misunderstanding, or a perceived threat to status quo. Addressing these concerns through empathy, engagement, and involvement can facilitate a smoother transition and foster a more conducive environment for change.

In terms of organizational structure, FP&A must ensure that it can flex and pivot in response to changing circumstances without compromising the integrity of the financial planning process. This may involve re-evaluating roles and responsibilities, streamlining processes, or integrating recent technologies that enhance analytical capabilities and reporting accuracy.

The process of change is not a singular event but rather a continuous journey. It requires ongoing reassessment and adaptation as new information and feedback are obtained. It is about cultivating a culture where learning, iteration, and evolution are ingrained in the organization's DNA.

As we delve deeper into the subsequent chapters, we will examine the tools and techniques that FP&A can employ to effectively manage change while maintaining alignment with the organization's strategic vision. We will explore how structured decision-making frameworks, coupled with a nuanced understanding of organizational behavior, can drive successful outcomes in the ever-changing landscape of finance.

Change management within FP&A is not just about navigating the present; it is about proactively shaping the future. It is about orchestrating a coordinated response to external pressures while fostering internal agility, thus ensuring the organization remains robust and responsive in the face of unceasing change.

Navigating Corporate Politics and Silos

In the nuanced theatre of corporate operations, the FP&A specialist must be adroit in navigating the intricate maze of corporate politics and organizational silos that can emerge within any company. This subsection delves into the theoretical and practical elements associated with bridging departmental divides and fostering collaborative synergy.

Corporate politics often manifest as a byproduct of the inherent power structures and individual ambitions found within an organization. These dynamics can either be a subtle undercurrent or a prominent force that influences decision-making processes and resource allocation. An adept FP&A leader must be able to identify and understand these political landscapes to navigate them effectively and leverage influence wisely.

Understanding the motivations and interests of key stakeholders is crucial. FP&A professionals must develop the acumen to discern the overt and covert objectives of various factions. They must employ emotional intelligence to build networks and alliances across different organizational strata, advocating for transparent communication and alignment with the organization's overarching goals.

Silos, both structural and cultural, represent another challenge for FP&A. These are created when departments or teams within an organization operate in isolation from others, often due to a focus on individual targets or a lack of overarching vision. Silos can lead to duplicated efforts, inefficiencies, and a myopic understanding of the business's financial health.

To dismantle these barriers, FP&A leaders should promote a culture of cross-functional collaboration. They can achieve this by championing initiatives that require interdepartmental cooperation, such as integrated planning sessions, cross-training programs, and shared performance metrics that encourage a holistic view of the organization's success.

The theoretical framework of systems thinking is a valuable tool in addressing silos; it encourages an appreciation of the organization as an interconnected whole rather than a collection of independent parts. This approach facilitates a broader perspective that values the interdependencies and feedback loops within the corporate ecosystem.

Moreover, FP&A can drive change by instituting regular communication forums where insights and challenges can be shared across departments. These platforms serve as a conduit for transparency and a catalyst for breaking down informational silos that can stifle innovation and agility.

In strategizing for organizational cohesion, the FP&A function must also consider the impact of its own operations. It should strive to be the exemplar of cross-functional integration, modeling the behavior it seeks to instill in others. By providing clear, comprehensive financial analyses that reflect the entirety of the business, FP&A can illuminate the interconnectedness of various functions and the implications of siloed behaviors.

Another key factor in mitigating the negative effects

of corporate politics and silos is the promotion of a shared vision. When individuals and departments are coalesced around a common purpose, the propensity for political maneuvering and compartmentalized thinking is diminished. The FP&A leader plays a pivotal role in articulating and reinforcing this vision, ensuring that it resonates with all stakeholders and serves as a guiding beacon for collective action.

As we progress through the chapters, we will explore specific methodologies and case studies that highlight successful navigation of corporate politics and the dismantling of silos. The insights garnered will equip FP&A professionals with the dexterity to foster an environment where finance is not only a number-crunching domain but also a strategic partner in driving organizational unity and efficacy.

In the realm of FP&A, understanding and influencing the complex interplay of corporate politics and silos is not an optional skill—it is an imperative. It is about harnessing the dynamism of human behavior to facilitate a cohesive and agile organization, ready to adapt and thrive in the perpetually shifting sands of the business landscape.

Leading Change in Control Environments

Embarking on change within a control environment is akin to steering a vessel through treacherous waters— precision, foresight, and a keen understanding of the currents and winds are critical to a successful journey. For the FP&A leader, change in control environments entails not just regulatory compliance and adherence to established protocols, but also the strategic calibration of these elements to facilitate improvement and innovation.

Control environments are the foundation of an organization's corporate governance, providing the framework within which its financial integrity, operational effectiveness, and compliance obligations are upheld. A robust control environment is characterized by a well-defined organizational structure, clear lines of authority, comprehensive policies and procedures, and a culture that emphasizes the importance of controls.

Leading change in such a setting requires an intricate understanding of both the theoretical underpinnings of control mechanisms and the practical implications of altering them. Change must be managed with a delicate balance, ensuring that the core principles of risk management and internal controls are preserved while enabling the organization to adapt and evolve.

One theoretical approach to leading change is through the lens of the systems theory, which posits that organizations are complex, adaptive systems. Changes in one part of the system inevitably have repercussions throughout the organization, necessitating a holistic and integrated approach to change management.

FP&A leaders can leverage the systems theory by first mapping out the existing control environment, identifying all the interrelated components that make up the system. This includes understanding how information flows between departments, how decision-making processes are structured, and how different control measures are interconnected.

Once the current state is clearly understood, the FP&A

leader can begin to introduce changes that align with the organization's strategic objectives. This might involve redesigning processes to enhance efficiency, implementing innovative technologies to improve data accuracy, or developing training programs to ensure all employees understand new regulations or control mechanisms.

Change in control environments is often met with resistance, as employees may be accustomed to long-standing procedures and wary of the unknown. To overcome this, the leader must demonstrate strong change management skills, employing both empathy and assertiveness. This involves clearly communicating the reasons for change, the benefits it will bring, and the potential risks of complacency.

Kurt Lewin's change management model—unfreeze, change, refreeze—can be instructively applied here. First, the FP&A leader must unfreeze the existing state by challenging the status quo and encouraging employees to let go of old habits. In the change phase, new procedures and controls are introduced and implemented. Finally, the refreeze stage solidifies the new state as the standard operating environment.

A practical aspect of leading change in control environments is the use of pilot programs. Before a full-scale rollout, testing changes in a controlled setting can provide invaluable insights and allow for adjustments without risking the integrity of the wider control environment. This approach also serves as a proof of concept, which can help to garner support from skeptical stakeholders.

Moreover, change should be incremental where possible,

allowing for gradual adaptation and minimizing disruption. Incremental change also facilitates continuous feedback, which is essential for fine-tuning controls and processes to ensure they remain effective and aligned with the organization's dynamic needs.

Throughout the process, the FP&A leader must maintain a delicate balance between enforcing necessary controls and fostering an environment that encourages innovation and flexibility. This often requires a reevaluation of risk appetite, as a too stringent control environment can stifle creativity and slow down decision-making.

In summary, leading change in control environments is an endeavor that requires both theoretical knowledge and practical wisdom. FP&A leaders must navigate these waters with a strategic mindset, employing change management techniques that ensure control integrity while advancing the organization's ability to adapt and excel in an ever-changing business landscape.

Communication Strategies for Risk Management Initiatives

Conveying the essence and importance of risk management initiatives within an organization is an artful blend of clarity, persuasion, and timing. For the financial leader charged with this task, the communication strategy is a fulcrum upon which the success of these initiatives often hinges. It is through the lens of strategic communication that such initiatives transition from mere concepts to active and embraced components of a company's risk culture.

An effective communication strategy for risk management

begins with the comprehension of the audience's psyche. A diverse array of stakeholders, from board members to front-line employees, must be considered, each requiring a tailored approach to engagement. The theoretical framework of audience analysis provides a foundation for understanding the various needs, concerns, and levels of understanding that distinct groups within the organization may possess.

At the heart of this communication strategy lies the principle of transparency. The goal is to demystify the complexities of risk management and to elucidate the direct impact that these initiatives may have on each stakeholder's role. To achieve this, financial leaders often employ the use of plain language and vivid analogies to distill intricate concepts into digestible, relatable content.

One must also consider the channels of communication employed. In an era where digital platforms have transformed the way information is disseminated, a savvy leader must leverage the right mix of mediums—from traditional memos and town hall meetings to webinars, intranet posts, and social media. The decision on channels should reflect not only the message's nature but also the cultural norms and technological comfort levels of the intended audience.

Engagement is another critical component of the communication strategy. Active engagement involves creating opportunities for dialogue, where stakeholders can ask questions, express concerns, and provide feedback. This two-way communication not only bolsters understanding but also fosters a sense of ownership among stakeholders, as they begin to see themselves as active participants in the organization's risk management narrative.

Timing and consistency are also pivotal in communication strategies. Information regarding risk management should be conveyed with enough lead time to allow stakeholders to fully grasp and adapt to the changes. Moreover, consistent messaging helps in reinforcing the importance and maintaining the momentum of risk management initiatives.

Additionally, storytelling can be a powerful tool in the communicator's arsenal. A compelling narrative that illustrates the real-world consequences of ignoring risks— or the benefits of proactive risk management—can resonate more deeply than abstract concepts. By sharing success stories or lessons learned from past experiences, financial leaders can provide concrete examples that underscore the value of risk management practices.

The communication strategy must also account for the measurement of its effectiveness. Through surveys, feedback forms, and other metrics, the organization can gauge how well the risk management message has been received and understood. This feedback loop is vital in refining the communication approach and ensuring that the message resonates as intended.

In crafting these communication strategies, the FP&A leader must keep in mind the cultural nuances of the organization. The tone and approach should align with the company's values and the existing communication climate. A mismatch here can lead to dissonance and reduce the efficacy of the risk management message.

In summary, communication strategies for risk management initiatives should be thoughtfully designed, with attention to the audience, content, channels, engagement, timing, and measurement. By applying these principles, the FP&A leader can ensure that risk management initiatives are not only heard but also understood, valued, and integrated into the organization's fabric, contributing to a robust and resilient risk-aware culture.

Building Resilience and Adaptability in Teams

In the volatile tableau of modern finance, resilience and adaptability are not merely advantageous traits but essential ones for teams within any forward-looking organization. To construct teams robust enough to weather market vicissitudes and agile enough to pivot with alacrity requires a deliberate and strategic approach, assimilating both psychological fortitude and operational flexibility into their very sinews.

Building resilience in a team is akin to tempering steel; it is a process of strengthening under stress, learning from challenges, and emerging tougher without becoming brittle. This begins with fostering a mindset that views failures and setbacks not as insurmountable obstacles but as invaluable learning experiences. The theoretical underpinning of this approach leans heavily on Carol Dweck's concept of the 'growth mindset,' which encourages continuous personal development and a focus on effort and improvement rather than innate talent or intelligence.

In parallel, adaptability is about cultivating a team's capacity to scan the horizon for emerging trends, to anticipate shifts, and to respond swiftly to changing circumstances. It requires a culture where innovation is not just tolerated but celebrated, where unconventional thinking is not suppressed but sought. Teams should be encouraged to engage in scenario planning, exploring a range of future possibilities and developing contingency plans that can be rapidly deployed as needed.

Investing in team members' skills and competencies is a cornerstone in this construction. Training programs and professional development opportunities can provide the technical and soft skills necessary to navigate the complexities of risk management. This also involves cross-training members to ensure a broad understanding of various roles and functions, thereby increasing the team's versatility and collective knowledge.

Resilient and adaptable teams are also marked by diversity, not just in demographics but in thought and experience. A team composed of members who bring different perspectives is more likely to identify potential risks and opportunities that might otherwise be overlooked. By valuing cognitive diversity, the organization is better equipped to deal with unpredictable challenges and to innovate beyond the conventional wisdom.

Communication within such teams must be open and constant. Leaders should establish and maintain clear channels of communication that foster transparency and trust. This includes regular check-ins to discuss both the team's performance and the well-being of its members. In doing so, team leaders encourage a sense of community and mutual support, which are critical to resilience.

Furthermore, teams must be empowered with the appropriate tools and authority to make decisions. This empowerment, underpinned by a well-defined governance framework, allows teams to respond dynamically to risks and opportunities as they arise, without being stymied by bureaucratic inertia.

An organizational environment that supports experimentation and learning from mistakes is crucial in fostering resilience and adaptability. Such an environment nurtures a team's ability to innovate and to recover quickly from mishaps. It is a culture that understands that the occasional failure is the price of innovation and that such failures, when effectively managed, are the stepping stones to success.

In implementing strategies to build resilience and adaptability, leaders must be acutely aware of the individual needs and stress thresholds of their team members. Personalized support mechanisms, such as mentorship programs or resilience workshops, can provide team members with the individual coping strategies necessary to thrive in a high-pressure, dynamic environment.

Ultimately, the measure of a team's resilience and adaptability is not found in its performance during times of calm but in its ability to maintain functionality and coherence under stress. To this end, regular team assessments and reflections on past responses to adverse events can help identify areas for improvement and recalibrate strategies as necessary.

PART 3: IMPLEMENTING AND SUSTAINING EFFECTIVE RISK MANAGEMENT PRACTICES

Chapter 9: Risk Management Frameworks and Methodologies

The cornerstone of robust risk management is a structured framework, a cohesive blueprint that guides the identification, assessment, and response to risks. One such paradigm is the Committee of Sponsoring Organizations of the Treadway Commission's (COSO) Enterprise Risk Management (ERM) Framework. This framework is revered for its comprehensive approach, encompassing internal environment setting, objective establishment, event identification, risk assessment, risk response, control activities, information and communication, and monitoring. Each component is meticulously designed to fortify an organization's resilience against a multitude of risks.

Another touchstone in risk management is the ISO 31000 standard, which provides a universally recognized benchmark for risk management. Its principles, framework, and process guidelines offer a systematic approach to managing risk across various organizational contexts. ISO 31000 emphasizes a continuous, iterative process to improve decision-making through effective risk management.

The Basel Accords, a series of banking supervision accords, also play a pivotal role in the financial sector by setting out robust risk management practices and capital requirements. These accords underscore the importance of maintaining sufficient capital to absorb unexpected losses and thus, promote financial stability.

Advancing beyond these traditional frameworks, the risk landscape now sees the emergence of dynamic methodologies that leverage technology for a more granular analysis of risks. Advanced analytics and predictive modeling have become integral to contemporary risk management practices, offering deeper insights and foresight into potential risks.

Financial institutions have adopted hybrid frameworks that integrate regulatory requirements with advanced risk assessment tools to tailor their risk management processes to their unique operational contexts. This bespoke approach allows for a more agile and responsive risk management strategy that aligns with the specific risk profile and appetite of the organization.

The implementation of Key Risk Indicators (KRIs) serves as a navigational beacon for organizations, providing timely alerts to potential risks and enabling proactive risk management. Crafting effective KRIs involves a deep understanding of the business, its processes, and the external environment. Real-time monitoring through dashboards has become an indispensable tool, allowing organizations to visualize and respond to risk data with agility.

The methodologies and technologies at our disposal are continually evolving, and so must our approaches to risk management. The frameworks mentioned provide a foundational structure, yet they require customization and continual adaptation to remain effective in an ever-changing risk landscape.

This section of the book delves into these frameworks and methodologies with the precision of a master horologist disassembling a timepiece—each component examined for its function and contribution to the holistic risk management strategy. Through this intricate exploration, readers will gain a comprehensive understanding of how to construct a robust risk management edifice that stands resilient in the face of both known and unforeseen challenges.

COSO ERM Framework

The COSO Enterprise Risk Management Framework, a beacon for organizations navigating the complex seas of enterprise risks, stands as a testament to structured and strategic risk management. Developed by the Committee of Sponsoring Organizations of the Treadway Commission, it presents a comprehensive model that integrates risk management into the very core of an organization's operational fabric.

This framework is not a static construct but a living organism within the corporate body, adaptable and responsive to the changing dynamics of the business environment. It operates on a set of interrelated components and principles that, when combined, provide a robust mechanism for identifying, assessing, managing, and monitoring risks across the enterprise.

At the heart of the COSO ERM Framework lies the alignment of risk appetite and strategy, ensuring that an organization's mission, vision, and core values are not only protected but also propelled by its approach to risk management. It encourages entities to view risk not just as a threat, but as a potential strategic advantage that can be harnessed to achieve competitive leverage.

The framework embodies a set of eight interrelated components:

1. Internal Environment: This encompasses the organization's culture, setting the tone for the importance of risk management and the expected integrity and ethical values.

2. Objective Setting: Objectives must be aligned with the organization's risk appetite and its capacity to manage risk.

3. Event Identification: Internal and external events affecting the achievement of an organization's objectives must be identified, distinguishing between risks and opportunities.

4. Risk Assessment: Risks are analyzed to determine their potential impact and likelihood, forming the basis for determining how they should be managed.

5. Risk Response: Organizations determine how to 'respond' to risk, balancing the costs and benefits of potential risk responses.

6. Control Activities: These are the policies and procedures that help ensure risk responses are effectively carried out.

7. Information and Communication: Relevant information is identified, captured, and communicated in a form and timeframe that enable staff to carry out their duties.

8. Monitoring: The entire ERM process is monitored, and modifications are made as necessary.

These components are underpinned by a set of principles that guide organizations in designing and implementing an effective ERM framework. Each principle correlates with one of the components, ensuring that the framework operates cohesively and comprehensively.

To illustrate, the COSO ERM Framework is akin to the architectural plan for a fortified structure, where each component serves a distinct purpose in the integrity of the overall building. The internal environment acts as the foundation, setting standards and expectations. Objectives are the design plans, outlining the desired outcome. Event identification and risk assessment form the structural analysis, determining where strengths and weaknesses lie. Risk response is the construction phase, where plans are put into action. Control activities represent the quality assurance checks, information and communication are the electrical wiring enabling everything to work together, and monitoring is the ongoing maintenance ensuring the structure remains solid and functional.

The implementation of the COSO framework into an organization's risk management practices requires meticulous planning, execution, and continuous improvement. It demands a top-down approach, starting from the highest levels of management, to instill a culture that understands and respects the complexities and necessities of comprehensive risk management.

Core Components and Principles

The COSO Enterprise Risk Management (ERM) Framework's robust architecture is constructed upon a set of core components and principles which serve as the underpinnings of an effective risk management strategy. These components, interwoven with guiding principles, shape the risk management philosophy of an organization, influencing decision-making at all levels. They provide a blueprint for embedding a risk-conscious culture within every thread of an organization's operations.

Let us dissect these core components and the corresponding principles that anchor them:

1. Governance and Culture:

   - Demonstrates commitment to integrity and ethical values.

   - Ensures board independence and oversees the development of the ERM framework.

   - Establishes authority, responsibility, and appropriate organizational structures.

   - Demonstrates a commitment to attracting, developing, and retaining competent individuals.

- Fosters an accountable enterprise-wide risk management culture.

2. Strategy and Objective-Setting:

- Analyzes business context to align strategy with the mission and vision.

- Evaluates alternative strategies through the lens of risk.

- Formulates risk appetite as a guidepost for strategy.

- Ensures that business objectives integrate risk considerations and align with the risk appetite.

- Implements risk-informed performance targets and measures progress.

3. Performance:

- Identifies risk that may impact the achievement of strategic goals.

- Prioritizes risks for assessment and response.

- Implements risk responses based on identified risk strategies.

- Develops portfolio views to provide a holistic perspective on risk.

- Reports on risk, culture, and performance to enable continuous improvement.

4. Review and Revision:

- Assesses the suitability of the ERM framework for evolving business contexts.

- Reviews risk management practices and revises them considering new information or changes.

- Considers the need for revisions based on performance

variances, weaknesses, or changes in risk appetite.

- Ensures that revisions are made to maintain the relevance and effectiveness of the ERM process.

5. Information, Communication, and Reporting:

- Leverages information systems to capture, aggregate, and disseminate risk information.

- Communicates risk information across the organization, from top management to operational levels.

- Reports on risk in multiple formats to meet the diverse information needs of stakeholders.

- Uses ongoing dialogue to continually improve risk identification, assessment, and response.

These components and principles are not isolated islands but are interconnected, each influencing and enhancing the other. The ERM framework, when implemented effectively, acts as a dynamic and flexible process that guides organizations through the complex and often turbulent business landscape.

The governance and culture component ensures the alignment of risk appetite and strategy. This alignment is crucial for setting objectives that are both ambitious and within the organization's capacity to manage risk. Performance components emphasize the importance of identifying and responding to risk in a way that supports the achievement of strategic goals, while review and revision ensure that the ERM framework remains relevant and responsive to changes in the external and internal environment.

Finally, information, communication, and reporting act as

the nervous system of the ERM framework, ensuring the free flow of information that is essential for informed decision-making and effective risk management.

Implementing the COSO Framework

The implementation of the COSO Enterprise Risk Management (ERM) Framework within an organization is a deliberate and methodical process that requires meticulous planning, stakeholder engagement, and continuous refinement. To operationalize the COSO ERM Framework effectively, organizations must embark on a journey that transcends mere compliance, aiming instead for a cultural transformation where risk awareness permeates every stratum of the enterprise.

The initiation of this transformative journey begins with a comprehensive evaluation of the organization's current risk management capabilities against the COSO ERM components and principles. This diagnostic phase involves a thorough gap analysis to identify areas of strength and potential vulnerabilities within the existing risk management structures.

Following this assessment, the organization must develop a tailored implementation plan that addresses these gaps and aligns with the organization's unique risk profile, culture, and business objectives. This plan should outline:

- A clear vision for risk management that resonates with the organizational mission and strategic goals.

- Defined roles and responsibilities for risk management activities throughout the organization.

- A detailed roadmap with milestones that guide the transition from current practices to a fully integrated ERM framework.

- Education and communication strategies to foster a risk-aware culture and ensure buy-in from all organizational levels.

With the plan in place, the organization must then engage in the process of operationalizing the COSO ERM Framework. This involves:

- Establishing a governance structure that provides oversight and accountability for risk management, typically spearheaded by a Chief Risk Officer or equivalent.

- Integrating risk management into business processes, ensuring that risk considerations are embedded into decision-making, from strategic planning to day-to-day operations.

- Developing risk management policies and procedures that are clear, actionable, and aligned with the organization's risk appetite.

- Implementing risk assessment tools and techniques that provide a consistent approach to identifying, analyzing, and responding to risks.

- Leveraging technology to support the capture, analysis, and reporting of risk information, facilitating transparency and informed decision-making.

A critical element of successful implementation is the ongoing education and training of personnel at all levels. Such initiatives ensure that staff are not only aware of the risk management framework and their individual responsibilities within it but are also equipped with the skills and knowledge needed to identify and manage risks effectively.

Once the framework is operational, it is vital to maintain momentum through regular review cycles. These reviews assess the effectiveness of the ERM processes and seek opportunities for improvement. They may involve:

- Monitoring the outcomes of risk responses and the effectiveness of controls.
- Evaluating the impact of new risks or changes in the external environment on the ERM framework.
- Soliciting feedback from stakeholders to fine-tune risk management practices.

Successfully implementing the COSO ERM Framework is not a destination but a continuous journey. It demands perseverance, agility, and a commitment to excellence. The fruits of this labor are manifold: enhanced strategic decision-making, improved operational efficiency, and ultimately, a fortified position to capitalize on opportunities that risk presents.

The COSO ERM Framework is not merely about managing risk; it is about enabling the organization to achieve its fullest potential by turning risk into a strategic asset. Through diligent implementation, organizations can not only weather the storms of uncertainty but also sail the winds of change to reach new horizons of success and sustainability.

Case Studies of COSO in Action

Delving into the nuanced application of the COSO ERM Framework, we examine a series of case studies that illuminate the transformative impact of this paradigm on organizations across various industries. Each case study underscores the practicalities of embedding risk management into the corporate fabric, illustrating the diverse pathways through which the COSO principles materialize in real-world settings.

The first case study features a multinational corporation in the energy sector, grappling with the complexities of regulatory compliance and environmental stewardship. The implementation of the COSO ERM Framework enabled the organization to systematically identify and evaluate risks associated with legislative changes, geopolitical dynamics, and advancements in sustainable technology. Through the establishment of a robust governance structure, the corporation aligned its risk management initiatives with its long-term strategic goals, fostering a proactive approach to environmental risk that not only safeguarded its operations but also bolstered its reputation as an industry leader in sustainability.

Another case study highlights a financial institution that faced the perils of cyber threats and technological disruptions. The COSO ERM Framework played a pivotal role in overhauling the institution's cybersecurity posture. By integrating risk management into their information technology systems and cultivating a culture of cybersecurity awareness, the institution was able to anticipate and mitigate potential threats effectively. The COSO-driven approach empowered the organization to not only protect sensitive financial data but also maintain customer trust in an increasingly digitalized banking landscape.

A healthcare provider serves as an additional case in point, where patient safety and data privacy are paramount. Implementing the COSO ERM Framework helped the provider to navigate the intricacies of healthcare regulations and the inherent risks of medical procedures. Through continuous risk assessments and an emphasis on a risk-aware culture, the organization was able to enhance patient outcomes and secure personal health information, thereby delivering high-quality care while upholding its commitment to safeguarding patient rights.

In the realm of retail, we observe a case study of a global retailer that utilized the COSO ERM Framework to manage the risks associated with its supply chain and consumer trends. By embedding risk considerations into procurement and inventory management processes, the retailer was able to respond with agility to disruptions such as supplier instability or shifts in consumer behavior. This strategic integration of risk management enabled the retailer to ensure product availability, optimize stock levels, and maintain competitive edge in a fast-paced industry.

Each of these case studies presents a narrative that resonates with the challenges and opportunities inherent to implementing the COSO ERM Framework. From enhancing regulatory compliance and environmental responsibility to fortifying cybersecurity and patient privacy, the real-world applications demonstrate the framework's versatility and efficacy. By learning from these examples, organizations can glean insights into the practical aspects of operationalizing the COSO principles and leverage these lessons to craft a bespoke risk management strategy tailored to their unique context.

In synthesizing the knowledge gained from these case studies, the overarching theme is clear: the COSO ERM Framework is not merely a theoretical construct but a dynamic and adaptable tool that, when wielded with skill and foresight, can drive organizations toward resilience, operational excellence, and strategic success.

Challenges and Solutions in Adoption

The journey toward institutionalizing the COSO ERM Framework is fraught with a plethora of challenges, ranging from cultural inertia to resource constraints. This section delves into the intricacies of these challenges and proffers pragmatic solutions to facilitate the seamless adoption of the framework within organizations.

A primary challenge that organizations encounter is resistance to change. Employees and management alike may exhibit apprehension towards the overhaul of established procedures and the introduction of new risk management practices. To surmount this obstacle, it is crucial for organizations to embark on comprehensive change management initiatives. This involves transparent communication about the benefits of the COSO ERM Framework, engaging stakeholders through participatory workshops, and providing clear demonstrations of how the new system enhances decision-making and safeguards the organization's assets.

Resource allocation presents another significant hurdle. Implementing the COSO ERM Framework necessitates both financial and human capital investments. Smaller organizations might struggle with dedicating the required resources without impacting their operational budgets. A solution to this constraint lies in phased implementation, starting with the most critical areas of risk management and progressively extending the framework across the organization. Additionally, employing cost-effective training modules and leveraging technology to automate certain aspects of the ERM process can optimize resource utilization.

The complexity of integrating the COSO ERM Framework into existing systems and processes is also a substantial challenge. Organizations often have ingrained procedures that may not align with the framework's principles. To address this, organizations should conduct a thorough gap analysis to identify discrepancies between current practices and COSO recommendations. This analysis enables the creation of a tailored action plan that incrementally aligns existing processes with the framework, thereby minimizing disruption and enhancing compliance.

Another challenge is the measurement of the effectiveness of the ERM program. Organizations might struggle to quantify the benefits of risk management initiatives, which can undermine the perceived value of the COSO ERM Framework. To tackle this, organizations should establish key risk indicators (KRIs) and performance metrics that are aligned with strategic objectives. Regular reporting on these metrics can provide tangible evidence of the framework's impact, facilitating continuous improvement and justifying the investment in ERM initiatives.

Lastly, the dynamic nature of the risk landscape means that the COSO ERM Framework must be adaptable to evolving threats and opportunities. Organizations may face challenges in maintaining the relevance of their risk management practices. To ensure the ERM framework remains current, organizations should foster a culture of continuous learning, encourage regular updates to risk assessments, and stay abreast of emerging trends that could affect their risk profile.

The adoption of the COSO ERM Framework is not without its challenges; however, with a strategic approach to change management, resource optimization, process integration, performance measurement, and adaptability, organizations can effectively navigate these obstacles. By addressing these challenges head-on with targeted solutions, organizations can harness the COSO ERM Framework to bolster their resilience and achieve strategic objectives with confidence and clarity.

ISO 31000 Risk Management Guidelines

Navigating the seas of uncertainty, organizations globally are increasingly anchoring their risk management practices to the ISO 31000 Risk Management Guidelines. This section meticulously explores the theoretical foundations and practical implications of these guidelines within the corporate risk management sphere.

ISO 31000 provides a universally recognized paradigm for managing risk that transcends industry boundaries. The guidelines are predicated on a set of principles that advocate a systematic, transparent, and credible approach to risk management. These principles are designed to be tailored to the unique contours of each organization, enabling a flexible yet robust risk management strategy.

At the core of ISO 31000 lies a framework that delineates a structured process for managing risk. The process begins with the establishment of the context—both internal and external—within which the organization operates. This encompasses understanding the strategic objectives, governance structures, legal requirements, and the risk appetite that defines the organization's threshold for uncertainty.

Following context establishment, the next phase involves risk identification. This is a critical step that requires organizations to be astutely observant of the potential risks that could impair their objectives. These risks may be operational, strategic, financial, or compliance related. The identification process benefits from a cross-functional approach, ensuring a comprehensive risk landscape is captured.

The intricacies of risk analysis and evaluation are then addressed. ISO 31000 advocates for a nuanced analysis that considers both the likelihood and the impact of identified risks. This dual lens enables organizations to prioritize their risk mitigation efforts effectively. Evaluating risks in relation to the organization's risk appetite ensures that resources are allocated to manage risks in alignment with corporate strategies.

Risk treatment, another fundamental element of the ISO 31000 guidelines, involves devising strategies to mitigate, transfer, accept, or avoid risks. This step demands an innovative mindset as organizations design bespoke responses to their prioritized risks. The selection of risk treatment options should be guided by cost-benefit analyses, ensuring that the chosen approaches are not only effective but also economically viable.

Monitoring and review is an ongoing process that ensures the risk management framework remains dynamic and responsive to any changes in the organization's internal or external environment. ISO 31000 emphasizes the importance of continuous improvement, advocating for regular reviews of the risk management process and its outcomes.

Communication and consultation are woven throughout the ISO 31000 process. Stakeholder engagement is paramount, as it enriches the risk management process with diverse perspectives and fosters a culture of shared responsibility for managing risk.

The theoretical underpinnings of ISO 31000 are complemented by practical guidance on implementation. For organizations embarking on this journey, the guidelines serve as a blueprint for developing a risk management strategy that is both systematic and adaptable. The iterative nature of the framework encourages organizations to evolve their risk management practices as they learn from experience and as the external environment shifts.

ISO 31000 Risk Management Guidelines offer a scaffold upon which organizations can construct a resilient and strategic risk management edifice. By internalizing the guidelines' principles, embracing its process, and fostering a culture of risk awareness and continuous improvement, organizations can navigate the complexities of risk with confidence and agility. The adoption of ISO 31000 is not merely about compliance; it is about embedding a forward-thinking, proactive approach to managing risk that underpins the organization's pursuit of its objectives.

Understanding ISO 31000 Principles

ISO 31000 principles form the bedrock upon which the edifice of risk management is constructed, providing a compass by which organizations can navigate the murky waters of risk in a structured and principled manner. This section delves into the granular detail of these foundational principles, illuminating their role in the orchestration of an effective risk management strategy.

The first principle espouses the value of risk management as an integral part of all organizational processes. It asserts that risk management is not a separate, siloed activity but a lens through which all decisions should be viewed. This principle posits that a proactive risk-aware culture, cultivated across all echelons of the organization, fundamentally strengthens decision-making and strategic planning.

The second principle emphasizes a tailored approach. It acknowledges the unique mosaic of every organization—its culture, context, and risk appetite—and advocates for a bespoke risk management framework that is aligned with the organization's specific objectives and resources. This bespoke approach ensures that risk management strategies are not only relevant but also resonate with the operational realities of the organization.

Thirdly, ISO 31000 champions the principle of inclusivity. A broad spectrum of stakeholders should be involved in the risk management process. This principle values diversity of thought and perspective, recognizing that engaging with a wide range of stakeholders enriches the risk assessment with varied insights and fosters collective ownership of risk management outcomes.

The fourth principle insists on the dynamic nature of risk management. It acknowledges that both the internal and external environments are in constant flux and that risk management strategies must be agile enough to adapt. This dynamic approach requires continuous monitoring of the risk landscape and the flexibility to pivot or escalate responses as needed.

Structured and comprehensive in approach, the fifth principle dictates that an effective risk management framework should be systematic and methodologically robust. This principle underscores the importance of a well-organized process that leaves no stone unturned, ensuring that every aspect of risk is identified, analyzed, and managed with rigorous attention to detail.

The sixth principle underscores the importance of best available information. Decision-making in risk management should be based on the best information available at the time, including historical data, expert judgment, and stakeholder insights. This principle emphasizes the need for information to be timely, clear, and accessible to all participants in the risk management process.

The seventh principle concerns human and cultural factors, recognizing that the behaviours and perceptions of people within and outside the organization can greatly influence risk management. This principle calls for the consideration of human factors in all aspects of the risk management process, from risk assessment to the design of risk treatment strategies.

Integrated into decision-making, the eighth principle asserts that risk management is an integral part of organizational governance and must be embedded in the institution's decision-making processes. This integration ensures that risk is considered in all business decisions, from strategic initiatives to day-to-day operations.

Finally, the ninth principle of continual improvement stresses that risk management is a journey, not a destination. Organizations should learn from their experiences and strive for improvement in their risk management practices. This principle advocates for a cycle of reviewing and enhancing risk management frameworks to respond effectively to evolving risk profiles and to foster an environment of sustained learning and adaptation.

Understanding and applying these principles is a testament to an organization's commitment to embedding a robust and proactive risk management culture. It ensures a strategic alignment with the overarching goals of the organization while equipping it to face uncertainties with resilience. The principles of ISO 31000, thus, serve as guiding stars for organizations seeking to enhance their risk management capabilities and secure their strategic objectives against the backdrop of an ever-changing risk environment.

Aligning with International Standards

Embracing international standards, such as ISO 31000, is akin to adhering to a global dialect of risk management— a language that transcends borders and harmonizes diverse corporate practices. The alignment with these standards is not only beneficial but imperative for organizations seeking to fortify their reputation and operational efficacy on the world stage.

Alignment with international standards offers myriad advantages, the foremost being the enhancement of credibility and trust among stakeholders. By adopting a universally recognized framework, organizations signal their commitment to a high calibre of risk management. This acts as a powerful differentiator in the marketplace, instilling confidence in investors, customers, and partners.

Moreover, the convergence with international standards facilitates smoother interactions with foreign entities, be they regulatory bodies, potential collaborators, or cross-border clientele. A shared understanding of risk management processes reduces friction and the need for extensive due diligence, enabling swifter and more efficient business dealings.

From a strategic standpoint, alignment with standards like ISO 31000 provides a blueprint for constructing a risk management architecture that is both resilient and responsive. It ensures that an organization's risk management practices are not insular but are informed by a wealth of global expertise and best practices—a collective wisdom that has been distilled into a coherent and comprehensive framework.

This global alignment also eases the navigation of the complex web of international regulations and guidelines. As organizations expand their operations across borders, they encounter a patchwork of regional compliance requirements. International standards serve as a keystone, providing a consistent basis upon which organizations can build to meet varied regulatory demands without losing sight of their holistic risk management strategy.

In the operational realm, aligning with international standards can streamline processes and systems, allowing for greater interoperability and efficiency. It can lead to a reduction in redundancy, as standardized procedures are more easily replicated and scaled across different departments and geographies. This not only optimizes resources but also ensures a uniformity in the quality and effectiveness of risk management practices throughout the organization.

Furthermore, the standardization of risk management practices enables benchmarking against global peers. Organizations can gauge their risk management maturity and identify areas for enhancement by comparing their practices to those of counterparts around the world. This benchmarking can foster a culture of continuous improvement, driving innovation and progress in risk management techniques.

The pursuit of alignment with international standards should be a deliberate and strategic endeavor. It requires a careful assessment of existing practices, a thorough understanding of the chosen standards, and a concerted effort to bridge gaps. This may involve training personnel, revising policies, implementing modern technologies, or re-engineering processes—all with the goal of achieving a harmonious integration of global best practices into the organizational fabric.

Aligning with international risk management standards

is not merely a compliance exercise; it is a strategic imperative that positions organizations to operate with greater confidence and competence on the global stage. It is an investment in establishing a common language of risk that resonates with stakeholders, facilitates international collaboration, and upholds the integrity and sustainability of business practices in a world of ever-increasing interconnectedness and complexity.

Benefits of Certification

Certification in internationally recognized risk management standards, such as those offered by ISO 31000, is more than a mere attestation of compliance; it is a testament to an organization's unwavering commitment to the pinnacle of risk management excellence. This commitment is not merely symbolic; it carries with it tangible benefits that ripple across the entirety of the organization, reinforcing its structural integrity and market stature.

The certification process itself fosters a meticulous examination of existing risk management protocols, compelling organizations to scrutinize and refine their practices. This introspective journey ensures that every facet of the risk management framework is aligned with the rigorous requirements of the standard, thereby elevating the organization's risk management capabilities.

One of the cardinal advantages of certification is the assurance of consistency in risk management practices across the organization. Through certification, a uniform set of procedures and principles is established, providing a clear roadmap for employees at all levels. This consistency ensures that risk is assessed, managed, and mitigated in a standardized manner, which is particularly crucial for multi-national corporations that must navigate a myriad of risk landscapes.

Certification also acts as a catalyst for fostering stakeholder confidence. Stakeholders, including investors, clients, and regulators, are assured that the organization adheres to a framework that is proactive and comprehensive in managing risk. This assurance can be instrumental in securing business deals, attracting investment, and maintaining a competitive edge in the marketplace.

Furthermore, the process of achieving certification can serve as a driver for organizational improvement. It often uncovers inefficiencies and areas that require enhancement, prompting the development of innovative solutions and the adoption of innovative technologies. The continuous improvement ethos embedded in the certification process ensures that an organization does not become complacent but is always striving for better risk management methodologies.

From a strategic perspective, certification aids in decision-making by providing a robust foundation for evaluating risk in relation to organizational objectives. The insights gained through a certified risk management process enable leaders to make informed decisions that balance risk and reward optimally. This strategic advantage is vital in today's fast-paced and uncertain business environment, where the ability to make swift, yet sound decisions can be the difference between success and failure.

In addition to bolstering reputation and strategic decision-making, certification can also yield financial benefits. It can lead to lower insurance premiums, as insurers recognize the reduced risk profile of certified organizations. Moreover, it can mitigate the costs associated with risk events, due to the proactive measures and controls that are part and parcel of a certified risk management system.

The pursuit of certification also demonstrates compliance with legal and regulatory requirements, potentially averting financial penalties and legal entanglements. It showcases an organization's dedication to adhering to the highest standards of risk management, which can be particularly persuasive in industries that are heavily regulated.

In essence, certification in international risk management standards is an investment in the organization's future. It is a strategic choice that reaps dividends in the form of enhanced operational efficiency, heightened credibility, and improved financial outcomes. The journey towards certification may be demanding, but it is a path that leads to a bastion of resilience and strategic acuity in the domain of risk management.

Continuous Improvement and Review Processes

The ceaseless quest for operational refinement through continuous improvement and review processes stands at the vanguard of effective risk management. This dynamic, iterative approach ensures that an organization does not stagnate amidst the rapidly evolving landscape of global business risks but instead thrives through perpetual evolution and adaptation.

In the context of risk management, continuous improvement is the lifeblood of an organization's strategic defense mechanisms. It hinges on the principle of Kaizen, a concept borrowed from Japanese business philosophy, which posits that small, ongoing positive changes can reap significant improvements. The application of this principle within the framework of risk management necessitates a culture where feedback is not only encouraged but acted upon with alacrity.

The review process is integral to this culture of continuous improvement. It involves regular assessments of the risk management system, scrutinizing its effectiveness in identifying, assessing, and mitigating risks. This review is not a superficial glance but a deep dive into the qualitative and quantitative metrics that inform the health of the system. It involves examining the alignment of risk strategies with business objectives, the responsiveness of risk mitigation actions, and the relevance of the risk management framework in light of emerging threats.

By institutionalizing these review processes, an organization ensures that its risk management strategies remain reflective of the current risk environment. It is akin to the regular maintenance of a complex machine; without it, the system would inevitably degrade, potentially leading to catastrophic failure when faced with unanticipated stressors.

The review process also plays a crucial role in identifying areas for improvement. It highlights inefficiencies, bottlenecks, and gaps in the existing risk framework, providing a clear directive for enhancement. This feedback loop is essential for fostering a state of continuous learning and growth, where each iteration of the risk management process is more refined than the last.

One of the key methodologies employed in the continuous improvement and review process is the PDCA cycle—Plan, Do, Check, Act. Organizations begin by planning changes based on identified risks and inefficiencies. They then implement these changes (Do), monitor their impact (Check), and adjust their actions accordingly (Act). This cyclical process ensures that risk management is not a one-time project but an ongoing endeavor.

In addition to internal reviews, organizations may also engage in benchmarking against industry standards or competitors. This external perspective provides a broader context for how an organization's risk management practices measure up to others, inspiring a drive towards best-in-class performance.

Moreover, the review processes are often augmented by technology, such as data analytics tools and risk management software, which can provide real-time insights and predictive analytics. These tools enable organizations to proactively identify trends and patterns that may signal the need for adjustments in the risk management approach.

The benefits of continuous improvement and review processes extend beyond the confines of risk management. They instill a culture of excellence and accountability throughout the organization, where every employee is attuned to the importance of risk awareness and is empowered to contribute to the risk management dialogue.

Continuous improvement and review processes are not

merely a component of a robust risk management strategy; they are the very mechanisms by which risk management evolves from a reactive protocol to a proactive, strategic asset. Through diligent application and unwavering commitment to excellence, organizations can fortify their defenses against the multifaceted risks of the modern world, positioning themselves for sustainable success and resilience.

Other Risk Management Approaches

In the mosaic of risk management, a multitude of approaches beyond the conventional frameworks exist, each tailored to address the unique contours of an organization's risk landscape. These other risk management approaches, while less ubiquitous than models like COSO or ISO 31000, offer alternative perspectives and solutions that can be pivotal in managing risks in specific sectors or under certain conditions.

One such approach is the Three Lines Model, which delineates clear roles and responsibilities across the organization to ensure effective risk management and control. The first line consists of operational managers who own and manage risks, the second line comprises risk management and compliance functions that oversee risks, and the third line is the internal audit, which provides independent assurance. This model promotes clarity and encourages a collaborative approach to risk management, with each line playing a distinct yet complementary role.

The Basel Accords, specifically targeting the banking sector, present another specialized risk management approach. Developed by the Basel Committee on Banking

Supervision, these international regulatory frameworks aim to strengthen the regulation, supervision, and risk management within the banking industry. They set forth rigorous standards on capital adequacy, stress testing, and market liquidity risk, fundamentally shaping the risk management strategies of financial institutions worldwide.

Industry-specific methodologies also come into play, where the risk profiles are markedly different from those found in mainstream business environments. For instance, the healthcare sector might employ risk management approaches that emphasize patient safety and data security, while the energy sector might focus on environmental risks and regulatory compliance. These specialized methodologies consider the sector's unique risk factors, regulatory landscapes, and stakeholder expectations.

Hybrid frameworks are also emerging, combining elements from established risk management standards with custom-tailored features that align more closely with an organization's specific operational context. These hybrid models allow for a more flexible and nuanced approach to risk management, acknowledging that one size does not fit all when it comes to managing an organization's diverse and complex risk profile.

For organizations operating in highly volatile or innovative markets, agile risk management approaches are gaining traction. These approaches emphasize flexibility, speed of response, and the ability to pivot quickly in the face of rapidly changing risk scenarios. They draw from agile methodologies in software development, focusing on iterative progress, collaboration, and adaptability.

In the quest for a holistic risk management strategy, some organizations may also adopt an integrated approach, where risk management is embedded within all business processes and decision-making frameworks. This integration ensures that risk considerations are not an afterthought but a fundamental component of strategic planning and operational execution.

Another emerging trend in risk management approaches is the concept of resilience, which goes beyond risk mitigation and focuses on building an organization's capacity to absorb shocks and recover from adverse events. This approach involves understanding the interconnectedness of different risk types and preparing for the unexpected by fostering adaptability and learning within the organization.

Other risk management approaches offer a rich mosaic of methodologies that can be woven into the fabric of an organization's risk management strategy. By exploring and integrating these alternative models, organizations can develop a more nuanced and effective risk management program that is both responsive to their specific circumstances and resilient in the face of uncertainty. Each approach adds a strand of sophistication to the overall risk management framework, creating a resilient and adaptive system capable of withstanding the tests of a tumultuous business environment.

The Three Lines Model

The Three Lines Model, celebrated for its streamlined clarity, operates on the maxim of structured governance, delineating responsibility and fortifying the edifice of organizational risk management. This model is predicated on a tripartite structure, each 'line' representing distinct echelons of accountability and operational execution within the company's risk management and control landscape.

At the vanguard, the First Line encompasses the operational managers. These individuals are the custodians of their respective domains, tasked with the direct management of risks intrinsic to their operational activities. They are the sentinels on the ground, equipped with the insight and authority to implement risk controls and engage in frontline decision-making. Their role is to embed risk considerations into the daily rhythm of business operations, ensuring that the pursuit of the organization's objectives is not derailed by unforeseen contingencies.

The Second Line is the domain of the specialized risk management and compliance units. This line functions as an oversight body, providing guidance, frameworks, and methodologies to ensure the First Line's risk management practices are robust and in alignment with the company's overarching risk appetite. The architects of this line are responsible for the development of risk policies, the establishment of compliance procedures, and the provision of an objective lens through which the organization's risk profile is continually assessed and refined.

Ascendant to the Second Line is the Third Line—the realm of the internal audit. Internal auditors operate with a mandate for independence and objectivity, dispassionately evaluating the effectiveness of risk management and control processes established by the First and Second Lines. They provide the board and executive management with assurances that the risk management framework is functioning as intended and that the reporting of risk exposures is both accurate and transparent.

The Three Lines Model encourages a harmonious interplay between the lines, fostering a collaborative environment where communication channels are robust and information flows freely. This ensures that risks are identified promptly, assessed accurately, and managed effectively across the organization. Moreover, the model supports a culture of shared responsibility for risk management, where accountability is clearly defined, and every individual understands their role in the collective safeguarding of the company's assets and reputation.

In an era where agility is paramount, the Three Lines Model also provides flexibility. Organizations can adapt the roles and interactions of the lines to fit their size, complexity, and specific risk context. By encouraging adaptability, the model proves itself to be not just a static prescription but a dynamic framework capable of evolving alongside the organization it serves.

In implementing the Three Lines Model, it is imperative that organizations consider the nuances of their operational landscape. They must tailor the model to their unique environment, ensuring that risk management is not just a compliance exercise but a strategic enabler that contributes to the achievement of business objectives.

Basel Accords' Impact on Financial Institutions

The Basel Accords stand as a testament to the collective resolve of global financial regulators to fortify the banking sector against the shocks and stresses that have historically beset the industry. These international regulatory frameworks, initiated by the Basel Committee on Banking Supervision (BCBS), represent a series of iterative reforms designed to enhance the stability and soundness of banks worldwide.

The Basel I Accord, introduced in 1988, marked the inception of standardized minimum capital requirements, primarily focused on credit risk. Its cornerstone was the establishment of a risk-weighted assets (RWA) framework, which mandated that banks hold capital equivalent to at least 8% of their RWAs. This initiative sought to create a level playing field for international banks, mitigating the risk of competitive disparities in capital standards.

The turn of the millennium witnessed the evolution of the accords with the advent of Basel II. This iteration brought forth a more nuanced approach to risk management, expanding beyond mere credit risk to include operational and market risks. Basel II promulgated the "three pillars" concept: minimum capital requirements, supervisory review, and market discipline. These pillars sought to refine the regulatory framework, encouraging banks to develop and use better risk management techniques in monitoring and managing their exposures.

The financial crisis of 2007-2008 served as a crucible, revealing vulnerabilities within the Basel II framework that necessitated further reform. Thus, Basel III emerged, ushering in a raft of enhancements to improve the quality and quantity of bank capital. Notable advancements included the introduction of capital conservation buffers, countercyclical buffers, and the leverage ratio—a non-risk-based measure to supplement the RWA framework. Basel III also introduced liquidity measures, such as the Liquidity Coverage Ratio (LCR) and the Net Stable Funding Ratio

(NSFR), to ensure that banks maintain a stable funding profile in the face of potential liquidity disruptions.

The impact of the Basel Accords on financial institutions is manifold. At the forefront, these regulations have compelled banks to bolster their capital structures, thus enhancing their ability to absorb losses and reducing the likelihood of insolvency. By emphasizing the importance of high-quality capital, such as common equity, the accords have improved the resiliency of the banking system.

Furthermore, the accords have catalyzed a cultural shift within financial institutions, embedding risk management into their organizational DNA. Banks have been incentivized to develop sophisticated risk assessment models and robust internal controls, fostering a proactive stance toward risk identification and mitigation.

The implementation of the accords has also had profound implications for the strategic operations of banks. Financial institutions have been prompted to reassess their business models, product offerings, and market activities considering the risk-based capital requirements. The resultant strategic recalibration has, in many instances, led to a divestiture of riskier assets and a more cautious approach to balance sheet management.

However, the Basel Accords have not been without their critics and challenges. The complexity and cost of compliance have been points of contention, particularly for smaller banks that may lack the resources to implement the elaborate regulatory reporting and risk management systems mandated by the accords. Moreover, the standardized nature of the regulations has raised concerns about their suitability across diverse banking environments and their potential to stifle innovation.

In this section, we will dissect the specific ways in which the Basel Accords have influenced the operational paradigms of financial institutions. We will explore case studies that exemplify the strategic reprioritization undertaken by banks in response to these regulations, analyze the efficacy of the frameworks in mitigating systemic risk, and debate the balance between regulatory prudence and the need for financial institutions to remain dynamic and competitive.

Navigating the intricate web of Basel regulations, readers will gain a comprehensive understanding of the pervasive influence these accords exert on the global financial landscape. We will journey through the corridors of risk management strategy, illuminated by the guiding principles of the Basel Accords, as we chart the course of banking stability in the contemporary financial epoch.

Industry-Specific Methodologies

Bearing in mind the intricate mosaic of risk that various industries face, industry-specific methodologies for risk management have been tailored to address the unique challenges and regulatory landscapes particular to each sector. These specialized methodologies are not mere derivatives of general risk management principles; instead, they are bespoke frameworks crafted through the infusion of industry insights, practical experience, and regulatory mandates.

The financial sector, for instance, is governed by a litany of industry-specific guidelines, such as the Basel Accords tailored for banking institutions. Similarly, the insurance industry adheres to the Solvency II directive in the European Union, which sets out robust standards for capital adequacy, risk management, and disclosure, ensuring that insurers maintain sufficient reserves to meet their future obligations.

In the pharmaceutical realm, risk management methodologies must contend with a unique spectrum of risks, from drug development and clinical trials to regulatory compliance and patent cliffs. The Pharmaceutical Risk Management Plan (RMP), for example, is a comprehensive document that outlines the strategies for identifying, quantifying, and mitigating the risks associated with medicinal products. It encompasses both the safety profile of the drug and the plans for post-marketing surveillance.

The energy sector, grappling with risks ranging from volatile commodity prices to geopolitical tensions, leans on methodologies such as the Enterprise Risk Management (ERM) approach, which aligns risk management with the company's overall strategic objectives. A nuanced aspect of risk management in the energy industry is the assessment of environmental and sustainability risks, which often necessitates the integration of advanced predictive analytics and scenario modeling to forecast the potential impact of environmental regulations and shifts in energy policy.

Technological innovation has also given rise to sector-specific methodologies in industries like cyber security. The NIST Cybersecurity Framework provides a policy framework of computer security guidance for how private sector organizations in the United States can assess and improve their ability to prevent, detect, and respond to cyber attacks. It encompasses aspects such as asset management, access controls, and incident response planning.

In the realm of manufacturing, risk management takes on a more tangible form with methodologies focusing on supply chain resilience, quality control, and safety management. Tools like Failure Mode and Effects Analysis (FMEA) enable manufacturers to anticipate potential points of failure in their production processes and devise mitigative actions to reduce the likelihood of defects or downtime.

The adoption of industry-specific methodologies equips organizations with a tactical advantage—the ability to foresee and navigate the challenges that define their operational environments. It also enables them to meet the expectations of industry regulators and maintain the confidence of stakeholders. By embracing these tailored methodologies, companies can transform risk management from a defensive tactic into a strategic asset that underpins their competitive positioning.

Hybrid and Custom Frameworks

In an ecosystem where one-size-fits-all solutions are often inadequate, hybrid and custom frameworks for risk management have emerged as bespoke solutions for organizations seeking to navigate the complex interplay of industry-specific and idiosyncratic risks. These frameworks, carefully architected to fit the unique contours of an organization, represent the confluence of standardized best practices and inventive, tailor-made strategies.

Hybrid frameworks typically graft elements from established methodologies such as COSO's Internal Control

—Integrated Framework or the ISO 31000 risk management guidelines with specialized modules that address peculiar risks or operational nuances. This integrative approach allows companies to maintain alignment with universally recognized risk management principles while also catering to their specific operational realities.

Custom frameworks, on the other hand, are developed from the ground up, often in response to the absence of suitable industry-specific guidelines or when traditional risk management practices fall short. These are the avant-garde constructs of the risk management spectrum, born out of necessity and innovation, and sculpted through a deep understanding of an organization's risk appetite, culture, and strategic objectives.

For example, a tech company that is venturing into uncharted territories of digital innovation may find that existing risk management frameworks are insufficient for their pioneering business model. A custom framework in this scenario would draw from the company's repertoire of past experiences, stakeholder expectations, and the agile nature of its industry to construct a living system that evolves in tandem with its technological advancements and market dynamics.

Likewise, in the realm of non-profit organizations, where the traditional metrics of financial performance and shareholder value are supplanted by social impact and donor accountability, custom frameworks are indispensable. These frameworks often emphasize ethical fundraising practices, program efficacy, and transparency, tailoring risk management to the ethos and mission of the organization.

Creating a hybrid or custom framework is a meticulous process that demands a thorough risk assessment, stakeholder engagement, and a commitment to continuous improvement. It involves identifying unique risk drivers, mapping out potential impact scenarios, and designing controls that are both effective and adaptable. Moreover, it requires a governance structure that ensures the ongoing relevance of the risk framework to the organization's changing landscape.

In crafting these frameworks, multidisciplinary expertise is leveraged, drawing from fields such as finance, operations, compliance, and IT. This collective intelligence is pivotal in constructing a framework that is not only robust and comprehensive but also reflective of the organization's collective wisdom and learning agility.

Monitoring and Key Risk Indicators (KRIs)

The vigilant monitoring of risks is an indispensable part of an organization's risk management strategy. It is akin to a navigational system on a vessel braving the open seas, where constant adjustments are made to ensure a safe and efficient passage. To steer this course, organizations rely on Key Risk Indicators (KRIs), which serve as the beacons illuminating the potential hazards on the horizon.

KRIs are carefully selected metrics that provide an early warning of increasing risk exposure, allowing organizations to take preemptive action. These indicators are typically quantitative but can also be qualitative in nature, providing a snapshot of risk that is tied to the organization's strategic objectives and risk appetite.

Developing effective KRIs requires a clear understanding of the business environment, the specific risks faced, and the ways in which these risks can impact the organization's operational and strategic goals. This involves a granular analysis of past incidents, a thorough examination of the risk landscape, and a forward-looking approach to identifying emerging threats.

Efficient KRIs are characterized by their relevance, measurability, comparability, and timeliness. They must align with the organization's risk profile, be capable of being measured consistently over time, allow for comparison across different areas of the business or time periods, and be available promptly to enable swift decision-making.

For instance, a financial institution may monitor KRIs related to credit risk, such as the ratio of non-performing loans to total loan portfolio, or operational risk indicators like the frequency of failed transactions or breaches in cybersecurity. In contrast, a manufacturing entity might focus on KRIs pertaining to supply chain disruptions, such as supplier delivery times or the rate of product defects.

Once KRIs are established, they need to be integrated into the organization's broader risk management framework. This involves setting thresholds that, when breached, trigger a response. The thresholds should be calibrated to provide enough lead time for action before the risk materializes into a significant issue.

An effective monitoring system also includes reporting mechanisms, ensuring that KRIs are communicated to relevant stakeholders in a clear and actionable manner. Dashboards, for instance, can provide a dynamic view of KRIs, highlighting trends and deviations that warrant attention. The reporting process should foster a proactive risk management culture, where information is not just reported but acted upon.

In an era where data is abundant, the challenge often lies not in the availability of metrics but in distilling them into meaningful KRIs. It requires sifting through noise to identify signals that truly matter. Organizations, therefore, need to employ data analytics and expert judgment to refine their KRI selections continuously.

Designing Effective KRIs

The process of designing KRIs begins with the identification of specific risks that are critical to the organization's objectives and operations. This identification is rooted in a comprehensive risk assessment, where risks are mapped to their potential impact and likelihood of occurrence. The aim is to pinpoint areas where the occurrence of a risk could lead to significant strategic, operational, or financial setbacks.

Adept risk managers understand that KRIs should be incisive and actionable. To achieve this, the indicators must be relevant to the core activities of the business and sensitive to the changes in risk levels. They must offer a clear indication of when a risk is escalating and provide actionable intelligence to decision-makers.

Relevance is determined by aligning KRIs with the

company's strategic goals, risk appetite, and tolerance levels. This alignment ensures that KRIs serve as true indicators of potential deviations from the set path, signaling when recalibration or course correction is necessary. For instance, in a financial institution, a rise in the loan default rate beyond the established risk tolerance level would be a vital KRI that necessitates immediate attention.

The sensitivity of KRIs hinges on their ability to reflect the real-time status of risk exposure. They must be capable of detecting minute changes in risk levels, thereby allowing for a timely response. Such sensitivity can be enhanced by leveraging advanced analytics and employing predictive models that take into account various risk factors and their interdependencies.

In constructing KRIs, one must also consider their measurability and quantifiability. This involves establishing clear definitions and units of measurement, ensuring that KRIs can be consistently tracked over time. Quantitative indicators, such as financial ratios or transaction volumes, are often preferred for their objectivity and ease of interpretation.

However, qualitative KRIs also play a critical role, particularly in areas where quantitative measures are insufficient or unavailable. These may include assessments of risk culture, employee morale, or the strength of internal controls. Qualitative KRIs require a structured approach to measurement, often involving scales, surveys, or expert evaluations to translate subjective assessments into actionable data.

The thresholds set for each KRI are as crucial as the

indicators themselves. These thresholds act as the triggers for risk responses and are set based on historical data, industry benchmarks, and risk modeling. They must be calibrated to provide alerts that are neither too sensitive—resulting in false positives—nor too dull, which would delay necessary actions.

An effective KRI system is dynamic, allowing for periodic review and adjustment. As the business environment and organizational priorities evolve, so too should the KRIs. This iterative process involves reassessing risks, reevaluating existing KRIs for their continued relevance, and developing new indicators to capture emerging risks.

Designing effective KRIs is not a static exercise but a continuous journey of refinement and adaptation. It requires a blend of empirical analysis and strategic foresight, ensuring that KRIs serve as potent tools in the risk manager's arsenal, enabling organizations to glide through uncertainty with confidence and control.

Dashboards and Real-Time Monitoring

The advent of dashboards and real-time monitoring in risk management represents a significant leap forward in the quest for operational vigilance and strategic agility. These powerful tools serve as the nexus between data and decision-making, offering a panoramic view of an organization's risk landscape with unparalleled immediacy.

At the core of these dashboards is the integration of real-time data feeds, which provide a continuous stream of information crucial for the proactive management of risks. These feeds are meticulously curated to include key risk indicators (KRIs) and other relevant metrics, ensuring that stakeholders are apprised of current conditions immediately. The ability to monitor these metrics in real-time is a cornerstone of modern risk management, as it facilitates rapid response to potential threats and opportunities alike.

The design of these dashboards strikes a delicate balance between comprehensiveness and clarity. While they must encapsulate a wide array of data points to furnish a holistic risk profile, they also need to be intuitively structured to allow for ease of interpretation. This is achieved through judicious selection of visual elements such as charts, gauges, and heat maps, which translate complex data into digestible, actionable insights.

Customization is paramount in dashboard design, as the needs of risk managers and stakeholders can vary widely across different sectors and even within different departments of the same organization. The ability to tailor the dashboard to reflect specific risk appetites and thresholds allows for a personalized risk monitoring experience. This customization extends to the granularity of data presented, with some users requiring high-level overviews while others may need to drill down into the minutiae of specific risk factors.

The utility of dashboards is further enhanced by their interactivity. Users can dynamically filter, sort, and explore data to uncover underlying patterns or to investigate the root causes of risk indicators breaching predefined thresholds. This interactivity fosters an exploratory approach to risk management, where hypotheses can be tested and insights can be gleaned through direct manipulation of the data presented.

Real-time monitoring, facilitated by these dashboards, also plays a crucial role in crisis management. In instances where risks materialize into actual events, the dashboard acts as a command center from which rapid assessments can be made and response protocols can be activated. The immediacy of data refresh and alerting mechanisms ensures that no critical development goes unnoticed, and that the time to respond is minimized.

To contextualize the application of dashboards and real-time monitoring, we delve into case studies where these tools have been instrumental in averting financial crises, safeguarding against operational disruptions, and securing competitive advantage. We see how, in the realm of cybersecurity, dashboards have enabled real-time threat detection and response, while in the financial sector, they have provided traders with instantaneous market analysis to inform their strategies.

Furthermore, the integration of advanced analytics into these dashboards promises an even more revolutionary future for risk management. Predictive analytics and machine learning algorithms can process vast amounts of historical and real-time data to forecast potential risk events, offering pre-emptive alerts and recommendations for mitigative actions.

Dashboards and real-time monitoring represent a quantum leap in risk management capabilities. They not only encapsulate the present state of risks but also empower organizations to anticipate and navigate the future with confidence. The continual evolution of these tools, fueled by technological advancements, will undoubtedly forge new frontiers in the domain of risk anticipation and strategic foresight.

Linking KRIs to Performance Metrics

The interconnection between Key Risk Indicators (KRIs) and performance metrics constitutes a vital component of an organization's strategic management. This integration enables a company to align its risk management objectives with its performance goals, ensuring that the pursuit of business targets does not compromise its risk posture.

KRIs are carefully selected metrics that serve as barometers for potential adverse events, providing early warning signals of possible threats to organizational objectives. Performance metrics, on the other hand, are quantifiable measures that gauge the effectiveness and efficiency of various processes and outcomes against defined targets. Linking these two sets of metrics creates a synergy that facilitates a more nuanced understanding of the organization's operational environment.

The process of establishing this link begins with the identification of KRIs that have a direct or indirect impact on critical performance indicators. For example, a financial institution might track the KRI of loan default rates as it can significantly affect the performance metric of profit margins. By monitoring these metrics in tandem, the institution can better understand the interplay between credit risk and financial performance.

To effectively link KRIs to performance metrics, organizations must undertake a thorough analysis to determine the correlation between risk exposure and performance outcomes. This involves the meticulous mapping of risks to business processes and identifying how these risks could influence the achievement of key performance objectives. Advanced statistical methods and risk modeling techniques can be employed to quantify the degree of impact and to establish threshold levels that trigger risk responses.

The articulation of this relationship is often visualized through integrated dashboards that juxtapose KRIs with performance metrics, allowing decision-makers to observe trends and correlations in real-time. These dashboards are not static; they are dynamic tools that facilitate scenario analysis, enabling organizations to simulate the effects of risk events on performance outcomes and to test the robustness of their risk mitigation strategies.

For instance, consider the case of a retail company that links its inventory turnover ratio—a performance metric—with the KRI of supplier delivery delays. By understanding how delays can affect inventory levels and sales, the company can proactively adjust its supply chain processes to minimize the risk's impact on its ability to meet customer demand.

Effective linkage of KRIs to performance metrics also requires the establishment of a feedback loop where actual performance can be reviewed against risk-adjusted expectations. This feedback loop is essential for continuous improvement, as it provides actionable insights that inform risk management practices and performance optimization efforts.

The strategic integration of KRIs with performance metrics thus serves as a dual-purpose tool. It not only enhances the organization's ability to manage risks proactively but also ensures that the pursuit of performance excellence is grounded in risk-aware decision-making. This holistic approach is particularly crucial in an era where businesses operate in an increasingly complex and interconnected global landscape.

The fusion of KRIs with performance metrics is a sophisticated exercise that encapsulates the essence of strategic risk management. It necessitates a deep understanding of the organization's operational processes, a rigorous analysis of risk-performance interdependencies, and the implementation of advanced data visualization and analytics tools. Organizations that master this integration are well-positioned to navigate the ever-evolving risk terrain, steering towards their performance objectives with clarity and confidence.

Responding to KRI Warnings and Thresholds

The strategic impetus of Key Risk Indicators (KRIs) is to forewarn an organization of potential risk exposures that could threaten its operational integrity or strategic objectives. Responding effectively to KRI warnings and thresholds is an exercise in precision, requiring a blend of proactive measures and rapid response mechanisms to mitigate potential risks.

KRIs are designed to be predictive, offering foresight into risk trends and emerging threats. They are set against predefined thresholds which, when breached, necessitate immediate attention and action. The response to these warnings is a multi-tiered process, often encapsulated within an organization's risk management framework.

Upon a KRI crossing its threshold, the initial response is typically an alert mechanism. This alert, which can be automated through risk management information systems, is communicated to relevant stakeholders tasked with risk oversight. The immediacy and clarity of this communication are critical, as it sets the stage for subsequent actions.

The stakeholders responsible for managing the risk associated with a particular KRI must then convene to assess the situation. This risk assessment phase is crucial, as it evaluates the severity of the breach, its potential impact on the organization, and the urgency required in the response.

Following the assessment, the organization must decide upon a course of action. This decision-making process is informed by a set of predetermined response strategies developed during the risk planning stages. These strategies range from risk acceptance, where the risk is deemed within the organization's tolerance levels, to risk transfer, where the risk is shifted to another party, such as through insurance.

In cases where the risk requires mitigation, the organization must deploy its response plans. These plans often involve cross-departmental efforts, where coordination and collaboration are key. For example, a KRI warning related to cybersecurity might trigger a sequence of IT protocols designed to tighten network security and mitigate the threat of a data breach.

As the response unfolds, continuous monitoring is integral to ensure the effectiveness of the actions taken. Adjustments and escalations may be necessary if the situation evolves or if the initial response proves inadequate. It is here that the robustness of an organization's risk management processes is truly tested.

One illustrative example is the financial sector's response to market liquidity risks. Should a KRI indicate a liquidity threshold has been crossed, banks may respond by adjusting their asset portfolios, increasing their holdings of liquid assets, or taking measures to secure additional funding sources. These responses are often governed by regulatory requirements and internal risk management policies.

It is also important to conduct a post-event analysis once the immediate threat has passed. This analysis delves into the cause of the threshold breach, the efficacy of the response, and the lessons learned. It is an opportunity to refine KRI thresholds and response strategies, enhancing the organization's resilience.

The effective response to KRI warnings and thresholds is underpinned by a culture of risk awareness and a structured approach to risk management. It demands agility, clear communication channels, and an unwavering commitment to preserving the organization's strategic interests. By honing these capabilities, organizations can navigate the uncertainties of their operational landscapes with greater confidence and control.

CHAPTER 10: RISK MANAGEMENT PROCESSES AND CONTROLS

Risk management processes and controls constitute the architecture through which organizations identify, assess, and manage risks. Within the domain of FP&A, these processes are not merely routine protocols but are integral to ensuring financial stability and driving strategic initiatives. The schematics of these processes are methodologically structured and are reinforced by a suite of controls designed to safeguard the organization against a multitude of risk exposures.

The genesis of risk management processes begins with risk identification. This is a systematic exercise that traverses across all organizational strata to catalogue potential risks that could impede financial objectives. Utilizing both top-down and bottom-up approaches ensures a comprehensive risk inventory. This phase involves the collaboration of cross-functional teams, leveraging their domain expertise to elucidate risks that may not be immediately apparent.

Once risks are identified, the next procedural waypoint is

risk assessment. This involves evaluating the likelihood of risk occurrence and its potential impact on the organization. FP&A teams employ a variety of quantitative and qualitative tools to gauge risk magnitude, from financial modeling and scenario analysis to expert judgment and historical data examination. The outcome of this assessment is a risk profile that categorizes risks by severity and guides prioritization.

The prioritization of risks leads to the development of response strategies. These strategies align with the organization's risk appetite and are designed to address risks in order of precedence. Risk responses can take various forms, including risk avoidance, reduction, sharing, or acceptance, each with its own set of tactical implementations. For instance, a company may decide to avoid risk by exiting a volatile market or reduce risk by implementing stricter credit controls.

Critical to the risk management process is the establishment of controls. These are the mechanisms put in place to prevent or detect the occurrence of risks. Controls range from policies and procedures that restrict unauthorized activities to physical and logical access controls that protect sensitive information. In FP&A, financial controls are vital, encompassing budget approvals, expenditure monitoring, and segregation of duties to prevent fraud.

The effectiveness of these controls is reliant on their integration into the organizational fabric. This integration is facilitated through a control environment that enshrines risk management in the operational ethos. It supports a culture where risk awareness permeates every decision and action.

To ensure that risk management processes and controls remain relevant and effective, ongoing monitoring is paramount. This involves regular reviews of control performance and the risk environment to identify any changes that necessitate adjustments in risk processes. Continuous monitoring enhances the organization's ability to respond dynamically to new or evolving risks.

An example of such dynamism can be seen in the approach to credit risk management. Considering shifting market conditions, an FP&A team may regularly review and adjust credit policies, monitor debtor portfolios for signs of distress, and implement responsive controls to mitigate credit exposure.

The risk management cycle concludes with reporting and communication. This ensures transparency and informed decision-making. Reports on risks, control effectiveness, and incidents are disseminated to stakeholders, including management and the board, who require clear and concise information to fulfill their oversight responsibilities.

Risk management processes and controls are not static constructs; they are living systems that evolve with the organization's strategic direction and the external environment. They are the bulwarks against uncertainty, enabling financial planning and analysis to proceed with foresight and precision, underpinned by a robust framework that anticipates and navigates the multifarious nature of risk.

Risk Appetite Statement and Policy Development

The development of a risk appetite statement and related policies is an essential strategic exercise that defines the contours within which an organization is prepared to accept risk in pursuit of its objectives. It is a foundational component of a sound risk management framework, setting the tone for how risk is approached and managed across the enterprise.

A risk appetite statement articulates the level and types of risk that an organization is willing to undertake. It encapsulates the collective mindset of the board and senior management, converging on a strategic vision that balances aggressive growth ambitions with prudent risk-taking. The statement serves as a guiding beacon for decision-makers, ensuring that the risks they choose to engage with are congruent with the organization's capacity to absorb potential losses.

Developing a risk appetite statement demands an intricate blend of introspection and foresight. The process begins with an examination of the organization's strategic goals, financial health, operational capabilities, and market position. Stakeholders engage in robust discussions to align on the core values and mission of the organization, which will inherently shape the risk landscape they are prepared to navigate.

The crafting of this statement is both an art and a science, integrating empirical data with the collective judgment of the organization's leadership. It requires a granular understanding of the business environment, competitor behavior, regulatory constraints, and the volatility of financial markets. For example, a financial services firm may establish a risk appetite that tolerates higher credit risk in exchange for greater market share, provided that the potential returns justify the exposure.

The risk appetite statement then cascades into the formulation of risk policies. These policies are the tangible instruments that operationalize the risk appetite in day-to-day activities. They delineate procedures, assign responsibilities, and specify limits and thresholds for various risk categories.

Policy development is an iterative process that involves stakeholders from across the organization. It is crucial to ensure that policies are not only comprehensive and enforceable but also adaptable to evolving risk scenarios. Policies typically cover areas such as investment decisions, credit exposure, market engagement, operational procedures, and compliance requirements.

Take, for instance, the development of a credit risk policy. This policy would outline the criteria for customer credit evaluations, set credit limits based on risk classifications, and establish monitoring protocols to track credit portfolio performance. It would also prescribe actions to be taken in the event of credit breaches, providing clear guidelines to manage and mitigate risk.

Risk policies must be communicated effectively throughout the organization to ensure widespread understanding and compliance. Training sessions, policy manuals, and intranet resources are common methods to disseminate policy information. A well-informed workforce is a critical defense line in the risk management architecture.

Lastly, the implementation of the risk appetite statement and policies is not a one-off event but a dynamic process. Regular reviews and updates are necessary to account for changes in the internal and external environment. This might involve adjusting risk thresholds in response to economic downturns or tightening investment criteria due to shifts in regulatory landscapes.

The development of a risk appetite statement and risk policies is a meticulous process that requires deep theoretical and practical insights into the nature of the organization and the ecosystems in which it operates. It is a discipline that fuses strategic intent with risk intelligence, ensuring that the pursuit of organizational aspirations is underpinned by a calibrated and conscious approach to risk-taking.

Formulating a Clear Risk Appetite Statement

In the realm of financial planning and analysis, formulating a clear risk appetite statement is a pivotal step in delineating an organization's boundaries for risk-taking. This statement is an explicit declaration that guides not only the risk management team but all operational levels of the organization, ensuring that every stakeholder understands the risks that are acceptable in pursuit of strategic objectives.

To craft a clear risk appetite statement, organizations must first undertake a comprehensive analysis of their strategic objectives, which serve as the north star for risk-taking activities. The process entails a thorough assessment of the internal and external environments in which the organization operates, as well as the potential risks and opportunities that these environments present.

The statement should be concise, articulate, and aligned with the organization's long-term vision and short-term goals. Clarity is paramount; the statement must leave no room for ambiguity, as it will influence decision-making across all departments. For instance, an organization may articulate a risk appetite statement as follows: "We aim to achieve sustainable growth by engaging with market risks to a moderate extent, while maintaining a conservative approach towards operational and reputational risks."

In translating the organization's risk capacity into a well-defined statement, several key factors are considered:

1. Risk Capacity: This is the maximum level of risk the organization can sustain, which is determined by its financial robustness and ability to absorb losses without jeopardizing its survival.

2. Risk Tolerance: This defines the levels of risk that the organization is willing to accept in pursuit of its goals, and is often expressed in quantitative terms, such as earnings volatility, capital adequacy ratios, or credit exposure limits.

3. Risk Appetite: Distinct from risk tolerance, risk appetite reflects the organization's desire to take on risk in anticipation of a reward. It is the active choice of which risks to pursue and which to avoid, and it is influenced by the organization's culture, leadership, and external pressures.

The process of formulating the risk appetite statement is an iterative one, involving input from stakeholders across the organization. The board of directors, in consultation with senior management, plays a critical role in this process, as they bring a broad perspective on risk relative to the strategic direction of the company.

Once the risk appetite statement is articulated, it must be operationalized into specific guidelines and limits that can be measured and monitored. For example, a financial institution may state that its risk appetite includes expanding into emerging markets, but with exposures not exceeding 20% of its total portfolio value.

Moreover, the risk appetite statement is not static; it requires regular review and recalibration considering organizational performance, changes in the external business environment, and strategic shifts. Such a review might occur annually or in response to significant events such as mergers, acquisitions, or market disruptions.

In essence, the risk appetite statement is a powerful tool that encapsulates the essence of an organization's approach to risk. It is the foundation upon which risk policies and procedures are built and is crucial for maintaining the delicate balance between risk and reward. Crafting a clear, actionable, and adaptable risk appetite statement is both a strategic imperative and a reflection of the organization's commitment to prudent and purposeful risk management.

Creating and Updating Risk Policies

The formulation of a clear risk appetite statement is complemented by the creation and continual refinement of risk policies—dynamic instruments that operationalize the organization's approach to risk management into actionable protocols.

Creating robust risk policies begins with a granular understanding of the organization's risk landscape. This involves identifying and categorizing the various risks that can affect the entity, such as market volatility, credit defaults, cyber threats, or regulatory changes. Each category of risk demands a tailored policy that outlines how the organization plans to manage, mitigate, or capitalize on these risks in alignment with its stated risk appetite.

Risk policies must be comprehensive and prescriptive, providing clear guidance on the procedures for risk identification, assessment, and response. They should delineate roles and responsibilities across the organization, ensuring that risk management is not siloed but integrated across departments and functions. For instance, a policy might specify the process for reporting a potential risk, the criteria for its evaluation, and the steps for escalating concerns to the appropriate decision-makers.

An effective risk policy also establishes the metrics and thresholds for risk measurement. These benchmarks help to quantify the level of risk exposure and serve as triggers for pre-defined responses. For example, a policy may stipulate that crossing a certain threshold of credit exposure necessitates a review of lending practices or the initiation of risk mitigation strategies, such as diversification or the procurement of credit insurance.

In addition to clear guidelines, risk policies should encourage a proactive risk management culture within the organization. This involves not only adherence to compliance requirements but also the promotion of open communication about risk and the encouragement of forward-thinking strategies to anticipate and address potential issues.

Updating risk policies is as critical as their creation. The dynamic nature of both the business world and the broader socio-economic context necessitates that risk policies be living documents—subject to regular review and amendment. Changes in technology, consumer behavior, market conditions, or legislation can all impact the risk profile of an organization, prompting a need for policy revisions.

The process of updating risk policies should be systematic and include a mechanism for capturing lessons learned from risk events, both internal and external to the organization. Incorporating insights from actual incidents enhances the relevance and efficacy of risk policies. For example, after experiencing a cybersecurity breach, an organization may revise its risk policy to incorporate stricter access controls and more rigorous monitoring systems.

Engagement with stakeholders is fundamental during both creation and updating of risk policies. Employees at all levels, particularly those who deal directly with risk, should be involved in the development process to ensure policies are practical and grounded in the reality of day-to-day operations. Likewise, the board and senior management should endorse the policies, signifying their commitment to risk management as a critical component of corporate governance.

The goal of creating and updating risk policies is to craft a framework that not only protects the organization from adverse outcomes but also positions it to capitalize on opportunities that risks may present. Such policies are the bedrock upon which a risk-aware, resilient, and agile organization can be built, with the capacity to navigate the uncertainties of the business landscape with confidence and strategic acumen.

Communicating Policies to Internal and External Stakeholders

The dissemination of risk policies constitutes a pivotal step in the broader risk management framework. Effective communication ensures that all internal and external stakeholders are aware of the organization's risk stance and the procedures in place to manage risk.

Internally, the communication strategy should be multifaceted, utilizing various channels to reach employees at all levels. This may include formal training sessions, intranet postings, newsletters, and regular meetings. The objective is to ensure that risk policies are not only accessible but also understood by everyone, from the board members to the front-line staff. For instance, a department may hold a workshop to walk through the risk policies relevant to its function, encouraging questions and discussions to facilitate a deeper understanding.

For external stakeholders, such as investors, regulators, customers, and suppliers, the communication of risk policies must be clear, consistent, and transparent. These communications can take the form of annual reports, press releases, corporate governance statements, and even dedicated sections on the company website. The goal is to build trust by openly sharing how the organization identifies, evaluates, and responds to risks.

A crucial component of communicating risk policies is the articulation of how these policies align with the organization's overall strategy and values. By doing so, stakeholders can appreciate the congruence between risk management practices and the company's long-term objectives and ethical standards.

It is imperative to tailor the communication to the audience's needs and level of expertise. For example, while employees may require detailed procedural guidance, investors might be more focused on understanding how risk management contributes to financial stability and growth potential.

Feedback mechanisms should be integrated into the communication strategy, allowing stakeholders to share their insights and concerns regarding risk policies. Such feedback not only aids in evaluating the effectiveness of the communication but also surfaces opportunities for improving the risk management framework.

External communication must also consider the legal and regulatory requirements governing the disclosure of risk information. This includes compliance with the relevant financial reporting standards and providing the necessary documentation to regulatory bodies. It is essential that the organization's risk policies and their communication comply with these requirements to avoid legal repercussions and maintain regulatory goodwill.

Furthermore, in times of crisis or when significant risk events occur, having established communication channels and protocols is invaluable. These channels enable the organization to quickly disseminate information about the event, the anticipated impact, and the steps being taken to address it. This rapid response capability can mitigate the negative fallout from such events and reassure stakeholders that the organization is in control and taking appropriate action.

In summary, communicating risk policies to internal and external stakeholders is a critical function of risk management. It reinforces the organization's commitment to risk awareness and promotes a culture of transparency and accountability. When executed effectively, it not only informs but also engages stakeholders, fostering a collaborative approach to managing the uncertainties inherent in the business world.

Aligning Risk Policies with Business Strategies

In the quest to safeguard an organization's assets and ensure its strategic viability, the alignment of risk policies with business strategies emerges as a cornerstone of sound financial planning and analysis. This nexus between risk management and strategic objectives is where the true art of corporate governance is painted in broad yet precise strokes.

Strategically-aligned risk policies act as both shield and compass, protecting against threats while guiding the enterprise toward its aspirations. The formulation of these policies demands a nuanced understanding of the organization's goals, market dynamics, and the risk landscape. A dynamic process, it requires a continuous recalibration in response to evolving business strategies and external pressures.

To begin this intricate alignment, one must delve into the organization's strategic plan, distilling its core objectives and initiatives. Risk policies should be designed to support these ambitions, enabling the pursuit of opportunities while mitigating potential setbacks. For instance, a firm aiming to expand into emerging markets might develop risk policies that emphasize due diligence, cross-cultural competence, and geopolitical analysis, thus fostering a secure and informed international growth.

The interplay between risk policies and business strategies extends to the operational level, where tactical decisions are made. Here, risk policies must be embedded within decision-making processes, ensuring that risk considerations are integral to the operational strategies. For example, a company's supply chain strategy might include risk policies that prescribe diversification of suppliers and the adoption of flexible contracts to buffer against disruptions.

Another key aspect of alignment is the risk appetite of the organization, which should reflect its strategic priorities. Defining the acceptable level of risk in pursuit of specific goals ensures that risk-taking is deliberate and controlled. A technology startup, for example, may have a higher risk appetite when it comes to investment in research and development, accepting greater uncertainty in exchange for the potential of a groundbreaking innovation.

Risk policies must also be synchronized with the financial strategies of the organization. This includes ensuring that capital allocation, investment decisions, and financial controls are all congruent with the defined risk appetite and strategic objectives. For example, a company with an aggressive growth strategy may set policies that allow for higher leverage ratios, while a company focused on stability may prioritize conservative financial management and strong liquidity reserves.

The harmonization of risk policies and business strategies is not a one-time event but a cyclical process of review and adaptation. As the business environment changes and the organization's strategies evolve, the risk policies must be reassessed and tweaked. This iterative process calls for robust feedback mechanisms and a culture of open communication to capture insights from across the organization and external stakeholders.

Furthermore, aligning risk policies with business strategies involves educating all levels of the organization about the strategic implications of risk management. It is essential for employees to understand how their day-to-day activities relate to the broader strategic goals and the role they play in managing risk.

Finally, the alignment of risk policies with business strategies should be evident in the reporting and monitoring systems. Key risk indicators (KRIs) and performance metrics should be designed to provide insights into both the effectiveness of risk management and the progress toward strategic objectives. This ensures that the board of directors and senior management have the information they need to make informed decisions and adjust course as necessary.

In conclusion, the detailed craftsmanship of aligning risk

policies with business strategies is a critical endeavor that requires foresight, adaptability, and a deep understanding of the organization's vision. It is a strategic synthesis that, when executed with precision, can steer the organization towards its desired future, navigating the ever-present uncertainties with confidence and clarity.

Control Environment and Risk Mitigation

Risk mitigation, the strategic bulwark against potential losses, is inextricably linked to the control environment— the foundation upon which an organization constructs its risk management edifice. It is within this framework that policies and procedures are meticulously crafted, not merely to deter or minimize risks, but to instill a robust culture of accountability and control.

At the heart of this environment lies a comprehensive constellation of internal controls, designed with the precision of a master watchmaker. These controls are the gears and springs that ensure the organization ticks with integrity and precision, safeguarding assets and ensuring the reliability of financial reporting.

The control environment is built upon several pillars, each critical to the fortress of risk mitigation. The first of these is the organizational structure, meticulously architected to delineate clear lines of authority and responsibility. This structural clarity is paramount, as it dictates the flow of information and decision-making authority within the company. Positioning risk management roles within this structure ensures that risk considerations are not siloed but are integrated seamlessly into all business activities.

Another pillar is the set of written policies and procedures that guide employees in their day-to-day operations. These documents are not mere formalities but are living scripts for a disciplined approach to business. They outline the accepted methods for reporting financial transactions, managing conflicts of interest, and ensuring compliance with laws and regulations. They also encompass the control activities —checks and balances—that validate the integrity of the organization's operations and the veracity of its financial statements.

A paramount component of the control environment is the ethos that permeates the organization's culture—the shared values and attitudes toward risk and control. This intangible yet potent force shapes behavior and sets the tone from the top, influencing how policies and procedures are enacted in practice. Leadership's commitment to a strong control environment is communicated through their actions, reinforcing the importance of risk management and internal controls at every level of the organization.

Risk mitigation strategies are only as effective as the information systems that support them. These systems must be engineered to provide timely, relevant, and accurate data that serve as the lifeblood of decision-making. In this digital age, the technological underpinnings of these systems are key to detecting and responding to risks with agility. Automated alerts, exception reporting, and continuous monitoring are hallmarks of a sophisticated risk information system.

Within this control environment, risk assessments are conducted with surgical precision, identifying and analyzing risks across the organization's landscape. These assessments inform the development of risk responses—policies and procedures tailored to mitigate identified risks. Such responses may include risk avoidance, reduction, sharing, or acceptance, each chosen based on a careful evaluation of the risk's likelihood and impact.

The implementation of mitigation strategies is a dance of coordination, requiring the orchestration of various departments and functions. It calls for training and communication to ensure that all employees are aware of their roles in the risk mitigation process. This includes understanding how to identify emerging risks, how to respond to incidents, and how to communicate issues up the chain of command.

An organization's commitment to risk mitigation is also reflected in its investment in employee development and training. By equipping employees with the knowledge and tools to manage risks effectively, the organization demonstrates its dedication to a proactive and resilient control environment.

Lastly, the control environment must be subjected to regular review and testing to ensure its effectiveness. Internal audits play a crucial role in this evaluation, offering an independent assessment of the control environment and risk mitigation measures. These audits provide assurance to management and the board that the controls are functioning as intended and that the organization's risk management objectives are being achieved.

The control environment is the sum total of an organization's attitudes, actions, and systems regarding risk management and control. By weaving together the threads of structure, authority, information, and communication, an organization solidifies its stance against the specters of risk, poised to respond with agility and informed judgment to the ever-changing mosaic of the business world.

Internal Control Frameworks (e.g., COBIT, ITIL)

Internal control frameworks stand as the bedrock of integrity, efficiency, and compliance. These frameworks are the architectural blueprints that dictate the construction of a company's control environment, laying the foundation for sound governance and risk management. Two prominent structures in the vast landscape of internal control frameworks are COBIT and ITIL—each with its distinctive features and focal points.

COBIT, which stands for Control Objectives for Information and Related Technologies, is a framework designed to develop, implement, manage, and improve IT governance and management practices. In a world where digitalization is ubiquitous, COBIT serves as a compass that guides enterprises in aligning IT processes with business objectives, while providing the tools necessary to navigate the complex terrain of regulatory compliance, risk management, and value delivery. As we delve into COBIT's structure, we witness its encompassing nature, focusing on business alignment, value delivery, risk management, resource optimization, and performance measurement—a holistic approach to IT governance.

ITIL, or Information Technology Infrastructure Library, is another pivotal framework that emphasizes best practices in IT service management (ITSM). Unlike COBIT, which has a broader governance scope, ITIL zeroes in on the lifecycles of IT services, from their inception and design through to their delivery and continuous improvement. ITIL assists organizations in managing risk, strengthening customer relations, establishing cost-effective practices, and building stable IT environments that allow for growth, scale, and change.

As we explore the intricacies of these frameworks, one can appreciate their theoretical underpinnings. COBIT's principles are rooted in the convergence of IT and business strategies, where governance is a shared responsibility among executives and IT leaders. It's a narrative that underscores the importance of alignment and harmony in corporate symphonies. ITIL, conversely, orchestrates the flow of IT services, ensuring that each note— each interaction—is harmonized to support the enterprise's operations and service delivery.

In the context of FP&A, these frameworks are not just theoretical constructs, but practical tools. Through COBIT, financial leaders can ensure that IT-related decisions are made with a clear line of sight to financial objectives. The framework's ability to dissect and streamline IT processes translates into enhanced reliability and quality of financial data—cornerstones of sound financial planning and analysis.

ITIL offers a complementary perspective, particularly in its approach to service delivery and management. For the FP&A function that increasingly relies on IT services—be they data analytics platforms, forecasting tools, or automated reporting systems—ITIL provides a methodology to ensure these services are reliable, efficient, and responsive to the needs of the business.

To encapsulate, the intricate theoretical detail of internal control frameworks such as COBIT and ITIL extends far beyond the mere provision of a set of rules and guidelines. They represent the convergence of governance, technology, and strategic business objectives. A sophisticated understanding of these frameworks is indispensable for financial leaders who must ensure that their organizations not only survive but thrive in the tumultuous seas of the modern business landscape. As we continue to navigate through the chapters of this guide, the role of these frameworks in enacting effective risk management practices will become even more pronounced, illustrating their indispensability in the FP&A domain.

Segregation of Duties and Checks and Balances

The ethos of a robust financial control system is encapsulated in the segregation of duties—a principle that acts as the bulwark against financial misstatements and malfeasance. Within this fortress of fiduciary soundness, checks and balances operate as the sentinels, maintaining vigilance over the accuracy and integrity of financial records.

Segregation of duties is essential in the intricate machine of financial operations, where the division of responsibilities is critical to prevent errors and fraud. By allocating specific tasks within a transaction cycle to different individuals, an organization ensures that no single individual wields enough control to both perpetrate and conceal inappropriate actions. This division of labor is not merely a tactical maneuver but a strategic design that fortifies the organization's defenses against risks.

Intricately woven into this mosaic is the concept of checks and balances. This system ensures that various departments or roles have the authority to verify each other's actions, creating a dynamic interplay where each function acts as both the creator and the critic of financial data. It is a dance of precision, where every step is measured, every move is observed, and every turn is validated.

The theoretical underpinnings of segregation of duties and checks and balances are rooted in the concept of dual control. In this construct, critical tasks require the cooperation of at least two individuals or systems, reducing the likelihood of unilateral error or intentional subversion of processes. By dissecting the responsibilities associated with authorizing, processing, recording, and reviewing financial transactions, an organization instills a culture of mutual oversight and accountability.

For the FP&A professional, implementing a system of segregation of duties is not merely about compliance with regulatory standards but is an exercise in strategic risk management. It is about designing a system where the inherent risks in financial reporting are distributed across various checkpoints, each serving as a fail-safe that guards against inaccuracies and improprieties.

Checks and balances also extend to the broader organizational structure. They include mechanisms such as managerial oversight, internal audits, and board governance, ensuring that financial planning and reporting are subject to scrutiny at various levels. These controls are particularly pertinent when it comes to complex financial modeling, budgeting, and forecasting activities that underpin strategic decision-making.

In the contemporary FP&A landscape, technology plays a pivotal role in reinforcing segregation of duties, checks, and balances. Automated systems can enforce permissions and approval hierarchies, log activities for audit trails, and generate alerts for exceptions. The integration of such systems into the FP&A framework enhances the ability to monitor and control financial processes, delivering a higher level of assurance to stakeholders.

The detailed theoretical fabric of segregation of duties and checks and balances is integral to the financial stewardship within an organization. It is a meticulous arrangement that requires careful planning, unwavering vigilance, and a commitment to maintaining the integrity of the financial reporting process. As we traverse the evolving narrative of risk management in FP&A, the significance of these principles will continually surface, emphasizing their role as cornerstones of an effective internal control system.

Mitigation Strategies for Identified Risks

Once risks have been identified and assessed, the next critical step in the risk management process is the development and implementation of mitigation strategies. These strategies are targeted actions designed to either reduce the likelihood of a risk event occurring or to lessen its impact should it materialize.

In FP&A, risk mitigation is a nuanced art, a blend of predictive foresight and responsive adaptability. It requires a deep understanding of the organization's risk appetite and a strategic approach that aligns with long-term objectives. The formulation of these strategies emanates from a thorough analysis of each identified risk, considering its unique characteristics and the context within which it exists.

The theoretical foundation of risk mitigation strategies is grounded in four primary tactics: avoidance, reduction, transfer, and acceptance. Avoidance involves altering organizational plans to circumvent the risk entirely, an approach that can be prudent but might also lead to missed opportunities. Reduction strategies are designed to decrease either the likelihood or the impact of the risk, often through process improvements or control implementations.

Transfer strategies shift the risk to a third party, typically through insurance or contractual agreements, which can include hedging financial exposures using derivatives. Acceptance is a conscious decision to retain the risk, either because it is deemed insignificant or because the cost of mitigation exceeds the potential benefit.

In FP&A, the intricacies of these mitigation strategies become particularly relevant when dealing with financial risks such as market volatility, credit exposure, and liquidity constraints. For instance, in addressing market risks, an organization may utilize financial instruments such as options and futures to hedge against adverse price movements. Credit risks may be mitigated through stringent credit assessments and the establishment of credit limits for customers, while liquidity risks may be managed by maintaining adequate cash reserves and arranging for lines of credit.

The development of mitigation strategies should involve a

cross-functional approach, drawing insights from across the organization. These strategies benefit from the inclusion of diverse perspectives, encompassing not only finance experts but also operational leaders, human resources, and information technology specialists. Such collaboration fosters a comprehensive understanding of risks and the formulation of holistic strategies that address the root causes.

Technology plays a transformative role in risk mitigation by providing sophisticated tools for monitoring risks and executing strategies. Advanced analytics, for instance, can anticipate risk scenarios and model the effectiveness of different mitigation approaches. Artificial Intelligence (AI) and Machine Learning (ML) enhance the organization's capacity to predict and respond to risks in real-time, crafting a proactive risk management posture.

In implementing mitigation strategies, it is vital to establish clear accountability and to communicate the strategies effectively across the organization. This ensures that all relevant stakeholders are aware of their roles in mitigating risks and that there is cohesion in the approach taken.

Monitoring and reviewing the effectiveness of risk mitigation strategies is an ongoing process. It requires a dynamic system that is responsive to changes in the internal and external environment. Performance indicators and metrics should be established to measure the effectiveness of mitigation efforts, with regular reviews to refine and adjust strategies as necessary.

Risk mitigation in FP&A is a strategic endeavor that demands a confluence of theoretical knowledge, practical experience, and continuous innovation. It is through meticulous planning, collaborative effort, and the leverage of technological advancements that an organization can adeptly navigate the uncertainties of the financial landscape, securing its assets and ensuring its longevity.

Crisis Management and Business Continuity Planning (BCP)

Crisis management and Business Continuity Planning (BCP) are critical facets of an organization's resilience framework, essential for navigating through disruptions and ensuring sustained operations. In the domain of FP&A, the theoretical underpinnings of crisis management and BCP revolve around the identification of potential crises, the development of strategies to mitigate their impacts, and the creation of plans to ensure the continuity of critical business functions.

Crisis management within FP&A begins with a preemptive assessment—identifying areas where financial stability could be jeopardized by unforeseen events. These events range from economic downturns to natural disasters, each with the capability to profoundly affect financial operations. Theoretical models, such as the crisis lifecycle, offer a structured approach to understanding the stages of a crisis, from its potential inception through to resolution, enabling finance leaders to formulate targeted responses at each phase.

The strategic core of crisis management lies in developing a comprehensive response plan. This plan delineates the protocols for rapid decision-making, communication channels to disseminate crucial information, and the roles of cross-functional crisis response teams. The plan stands on a foundation of robust governance structures and clear leadership directives, ensuring that, when a crisis strikes, the organization can respond with agility and coordination.

Business Continuity Planning (BCP) takes a complementary approach, focusing on maintaining business functions in the face of disruptions. BCP is grounded in theoretical constructs, such as the Business Impact Analysis (BIA), which helps to prioritize critical functions based on their financial and operational significance. By identifying essential processes, resources, and personnel, FP&A professionals can develop strategies to maintain or quickly resume operations.

The intricacies of BCP involve not only the preservation of operational integrity but also the protection of financial data and the systems that manage it. Backup facilities, data redundancy, and recovery protocols form the technical backbone of a robust BCP. Scenario planning and simulation exercises play pivotal roles in testing the plan's effectiveness and uncovering areas for refinement.

FP&A's role in BCP extends to financial forecasting and modeling under crisis scenarios, providing a quantitative understanding of potential impacts. This allows for the formulation of contingency budgets and the allocation of resources to areas most at risk. Through stress testing and sensitivity analysis, FP&A can evaluate the organization's financial resilience against a range of crisis scenarios.

The integration of technology in crisis management and

BCP is imperative. Modern software solutions enable real-time monitoring of critical indicators, automated alerts, and streamlined communication during a crisis. The adoption of cloud-based platforms ensures that financial data and applications are accessible, even when primary business locations are compromised.

Communication is a linchpin in the successful execution of both crisis management and BCP. It must be clear, timely, and effective, with predefined channels to reach internal and external stakeholders. During a crisis, transparent communication can mitigate the impact on stakeholder trust and maintain confidence in the organization's ability to manage the situation.

In implementing crisis management and BCP, training and simulations are invaluable in preparing personnel for their roles. Regular drills that mimic crisis conditions help to build familiarity with response procedures and can highlight areas where plans may need to be adjusted.

Ultimately, the theoretical and practical implementation of crisis management and BCP in FP&A serves to insulate the organization from the volatility of the external environment. It is through diligent planning, proactive risk assessment, and responsive strategy execution that financial leaders can safeguard their organizations against crises, ensuring their capability to thrive in the face of adversity.

Risk Assessment and Response Planning

Risk assessment and response planning constitute a pivotal element in the strategic fabric of FP&A, emblematic of a rigorous analytical mindset bent on safeguarding the organization's financial health against potential adversities. It is within this context that we dissect the theoretical and applied nuances of this indispensable process.

At the heart of risk assessment lies the imperative to systematically identify, analyze, and evaluate the risks that may beset an organization. The process begins with a comprehensive inventory of potential risks, which entails delving into the vast array of uncertainties that businesses face—financial, operational, strategic, and beyond. The assessment hones in on the vulnerabilities and threats that could derail the organization's objectives, with a discerning eye on both internal and external factors.

The theoretical framework of risk assessment in FP&A is grounded in both qualitative and quantitative analysis. Qualitative methods provide a narrative lens through which risks can be understood in terms of their nature and potential impact. Quantitative approaches, conversely, deploy statistical and financial modeling techniques to estimate the probability and fiscal implications of these risks. Tools such as the risk heat map and the value at risk (VaR) model serve as the quantitative bedrock, enabling finance professionals to project the potential financial impacts in monetary terms.

Risk response planning, the subsequent phase, is where the theoretical analysis of risks translates into actionable strategies. This facet is characterized by the formulation of a risk response matrix that aligns each identified risk with a specific strategy—avoidance, mitigation, transfer, or acceptance. Within this matrix, each strategy is substantiated with detailed action plans that delineate the steps necessary to manage the risks effectively.

Avoidance strategies may involve altering business plans to circumvent high-risk activities, whereas mitigation strategies focus on reducing the likelihood or impact of risks through controls and safeguards. Risk transfer often emerges in the form of insurance or contractual agreements that shift the financial burden to a third party. Lastly, acceptance is reserved for those risks deemed tolerable within the organization's risk appetite.

FP&A's role in response planning is not only to provide the financial rationale for each strategy but also to ensure that the cost of implementing these strategies does not outweigh the benefits. This entails a scrupulous cost-benefit analysis, often utilizing techniques such as the net present value (NPV) to ascertain the long-term economic viability of the proposed responses.

In translating theory into practice, risk assessment and response planning require the FP&A function to operate in a cross-collaborative manner. Engaging with diverse organizational units enables a holistic view of risks and the pooling of expertise that enriches the response strategies. Additionally, the establishment of communication protocols ensures that risk information is disseminated effectively across the organization and that stakeholders are aligned in their understanding and commitment to the response plans.

The dynamic nature of risk necessitates that these assessments and plans are not static but rather living documents subject to regular review and revision. As the business environment evolves, so too must the risk profiles and response strategies. This adaptability underscores the importance of keeping abreast with market trends, regulatory changes, and emerging risks that could necessitate a recalibration of the organization's risk management approach.

In fostering a culture of continuous improvement, FP&A professionals must solicit feedback, conduct debriefs following risk events, and integrate lessons learned into future planning. This iterative process embeds risk awareness into the organizational DNA and fortifies the strategic decision-making prowess of those who hold the reins of financial governance.

Thus, risk assessment and response planning emerge as more than mere procedural obligations; they are a testament to the strategic foresight and analytical acumen that underpin robust FP&A functions. It is a disciplined endeavor, steeped in theoretical rigor and executed with an unwavering commitment to the financial fortitude of the organization.

Comprehensive Risk Assessments

The mosaic of comprehensive risk assessments is a multi-faceted narrative, each thread representing a systematic process designed to illuminate the potential dangers that could undermine a company's objectives and operations. This analytical expedition mandates a meticulous scrutiny of every conceivable risk, no matter how obscure, that could pose a threat to the organization's solvency or success.

Embarking on this rigorous journey, one must dissect the process of a comprehensive risk assessment, an endeavor that interweaves various methodologies to form an all-encompassing review of potential adversities. The methodology begins with the identification phase, where risks are unearthed and catalogued with an astute awareness of their origins and characteristics. This phase extends beyond mere enumeration, delving into the very fabric of each risk, unraveling its DNA to comprehend its genesis and potential pathways through the business landscape.

Following identification, the assessment phase engages in a critical examination of the risks, assigning them a measurable form. This quantification is pivotal, as it allows for the juxtaposition of diverse risks on a comparable scale, facilitating prioritization. The probabilistic models, such as fault tree analysis or Bayesian networks, are employed to anticipate the likelihood of each risk eventuating, while impact analyses attempt to forecast the potential damage, should these risks come to fruition.

To thoroughly explore the theoretical constructs underlying this phase, one must delve into the intricacies of risk matrices and scoring systems. These tools are instrumental in providing a visual and numerical representation of the risks, enabling stakeholders to assimilate the assessment's outcomes with clarity and precision. The matrix plots risks along axes of likelihood and impact, rendering a strategic overview that guides decision-making.

The subsequent phase, evaluation, is where the theoretical collides with the operational. Here, the assessed risks are weighed against the organization's risk tolerance and appetite, guiding the strategic response. This evaluation isn't merely an academic exercise; it's rooted deeply in the business context, reflective of the organization's unique landscape, resources, and objectives.

This critical evaluation phase is underpinned by a set of

rigorous, intellectually robust theories such as risk utility theory and expected utility theory, which examine the organization's disposition towards risk in terms of expected outcomes. Through this theoretical lens, organizations can rationalize their choices, balancing the potential for gain against the aversion to loss.

In the context of FP&A, the comprehensive risk assessment process must be endowed with the flexibility to adapt to the ever-shifting economic sands and the agility to pivot as new risks emerge or existing ones morph. This necessitates a robust methodology that incorporates continuous monitoring and reassessment, ensuring that the risk landscape is an accurate reflection of the current environment.

Moreover, this process must not occur in isolation but rather in concert with the broader organizational strategies and objectives. It demands cross-functional collaboration, bringing together expertise from various domains to ensure that no stone is left unturned in the quest to shield the enterprise from the specters of risk.

The outcome of a comprehensive risk assessment is a detailed dossier of the identified risks, their assessed magnitudes, and the potential strategies for managing them. It is a living document, iteratively refined as new data comes to light and as the organization traverses the unpredictable terrain of the business world.

As we forge ahead, the comprehensive risk assessments stand as a bulwark against the caprice of chance, a beacon for those who navigate the treacherous waters of financial planning and analysis. Through a blend of theoretical depth and applied acumen, it provides a platform for FP&A professionals to exercise their stewardship with confidence, equipped with the knowledge to not only confront but also curate the risks that shape the fabric of their enterprises.

Action Plans for High-Priority Risks

Crafting action plans for high-priority risks is akin to charting a course through tumultuous seas; it requires not only an understanding of where the shoals lie but also the navigational acumen to steer clear of them. This intricate theoretical detail is not merely about contingency; it is about strategic foresight and the deployment of resources to mitigate risks that pose the most significant threat to an organization's continuity and prosperity.

To contextualize the importance of action plans, consider the financial landscape as a dynamic ecosystem, where risks evolve and intersect with complex patterns much like the unpredictable weather systems of the Pacific Northwest. These plans are the embodiment of a proactive stance, crafted to not only react to the present risks but also to anticipate future ones, ensuring organizational resilience amidst financial uncertainties.

In practice, the development of action plans for high-priority risks follows a structured process grounded in the principles of risk management. Once risks are identified and prioritized, organizations must embark on the meticulous task of formulating response strategies tailored to each specific risk. This exercise extends beyond a prescriptive approach; it is an intellectual pursuit that hinges on the nuanced understanding of each risk's idiosyncrasies.

The quintessential step in this process is the delineation of the risk's attributes—its triggers, potential impacts, and the velocity with which it can affect the organization. This understanding shapes the framework for action, guiding the tactical maneuvers that will be employed to counteract the risk. It involves a blend of financial acumen and strategic agility, the ability to allocate capital and operational capabilities where they will be most effective.

At the core of these action plans is the concept of risk treatment—options that range from avoidance to reduction, sharing to acceptance. In the case of high-priority risks, where the stakes are particularly high, avoidance or reduction is often preferred. These strategies may manifest as diversification to spread the risk, hedging to protect against market fluctuations, or investing in cutting-edge cybersecurity to combat digital threats.

An integral component of these plans is the establishment of clear roles and responsibilities, ensuring that when a risk event occurs, there is no ambiguity regarding who must take action and what that action should entail. This clarity is essential for rapid response, a trait that can mean the difference between a contained incident and a full-blown crisis.

Action plans must also be infused with adaptability, allowing for iterative refinement as new information surfaces or as the risk landscape transforms. This flexibility is particularly crucial in the realm of FP&A, where financial projections and market conditions are in constant flux, demanding that action plans are regularly revisited and revised accordingly.

The theoretical underpinning of these plans draws from decision theory and game theory, where strategies are evaluated not in isolation but in the context of an interconnected world where competitors, regulators, and economic forces are constantly in play. This perspective is crucial for understanding not only the direct consequences of risks but also their second- and third-order effects.

A robust action plan for high-priority risks is, therefore, not a static protocol but a living, breathing strategy that evolves in tandem with an enterprise's strategic objectives and the external environment. It is a definitive guide, a compass by which an organization can orient itself when the inevitable storms of uncertainty rage.

In summary, when navigating the choppy waters of high-stakes financial planning, the preparation of action plans for high-priority risks is a crucial endeavor, shaping the organization's trajectory towards stability and success. With theoretical acuity and practical precision, these plans serve as an organization's bulwark against the forces that threaten its mission and objectives, embodying the very spirit of strategic risk management in FP&A.

Cost-Benefit Analysis of Risk Responses

In the disciplined pursuit of risk management within financial planning and analysis, the cost-benefit analysis (CBA) stands as a cornerstone, enforcing a balance between the fiscal prudence and the audacity to pursue growth. It is a quantitative evaluation that scrutinizes the trade-offs between the costs incurred and the benefits derived from implementing risk responses.

Delving into the granularities of CBA, one must recognize that this analytical tool is not merely a ledger of debits and credits; it is an intellectual examination—a fusion of economic theory and pragmatic decision-making. This financial calculus serves to distill complex risk scenarios into discernable, quantifiable juxtapositions, facilitating decisions that align with the organization's overarching strategic intents.

In theory, the CBA constitutes a series of methodical steps, each designed to elucidate the ramifications of potential risk responses. The initial phase involves an exhaustive inventory of potential costs, which may encompass direct financial outlays, opportunity costs, and intangible expenses such as reputational harm or strategic misalignment. The specificity and comprehensiveness of this appraisal are imperative, for omissions here can skew the analysis and lead to suboptimal decision-making.

Parallel to cost appraisal, the benefits of each risk response are meticulously quantified. In FP&A, this often translates into valuations of avoided losses, enhanced efficiencies, or competitive advantages accrued. The temporal aspect is a critical consideration, as benefits may not materialize contemporaneously with costs but may unfold over an extended horizon, warranting the application of techniques such as net present value (NPV) to properly account for the time value of money.

An astute cost-benefit analysis navigates beyond the immediate quantifiable impacts and encompasses broader strategic benefits. These may include the preservation of organizational agility, the fortification of stakeholder confidence, or the bolstering of market position. This acknowledgment of strategic premiums is where the theoretical sophistication of CBA intersects with the practical wisdom of seasoned finance professionals.

Conducting a CBA is not devoid of challenges, particularly when confronted with the inherent uncertainties of risk. The construction of probabilistic models and the leveraging of Monte Carlo simulations can offer deeper insights into the possible outcomes and their associated probabilities, transforming a static analysis into a dynamic exploration of potential futures. This approach enables decision-makers to weigh scenarios not only on expected values but also on the distribution of possible results, providing a nuanced understanding of risks and rewards.

Yet, the utilitarian beauty of CBA within risk management lies in its capacity for iteration and refinement. As new data surfaces, as market dynamics shift, or as organizational priorities evolve, the CBA can be recalibrated to reflect these changes, ensuring that the rationale for risk responses remains aligned with current circumstances. It is a feedback loop that promotes continuous learning and informed decision-making.

In operationalizing CBA, transparency and stakeholder engagement are critical. The assumptions underpinning the analysis must be communicated clearly, and the rationale for decisions must be articulated with cogency. This practice not only enriches the decision-making process with diverse perspectives but also fosters a culture of accountability and trust.

In summary, the cost-benefit analysis of risk responses is a rigorous exercise in valuation and strategic judgment. It demands a confluence of analytical prowess and strategic insight, guiding the navigation through the complexities of risk management in FP&A. It is through the meticulous execution of CBA that organizations can confidently chart their course, minimizing perils while maximizing opportunities in their journey towards sustainable success.

Incident Management and Escalation Procedures

The labyrinthine nature of financial risk management is such that, despite the most robust predictive models and preemptive measures, incidents—unforeseen events with potential adverse effects on an organization—will occur. The true test of an organization's resilience lies not in its ability to avoid all risks, but in its adeptness at responding to incidents with alacrity and precision. Herein, we delve into the theoretical underpinnings and structured methodology of incident management and escalation procedures within financial planning and analysis (FP&A).

At the foundation of incident management lies the Incident Response Plan (IRP), a premeditated blueprint that delineates systematic processes for detecting, reporting, and responding to financial incidents. The theoretical framework of an IRP is derived from risk assessments that identify potential incidents and outcome scenarios, thus serving as a prophylactic measure against possible disruptions.

The initial phase of an effective IRP is the detection and assessment stage. Financial anomalies, compliance deviations, and irregular transactions must be swiftly identified through ongoing monitoring systems. The use of advanced detection tools, such as anomaly detection algorithms and real-time auditing software, plays an instrumental role in this phase, ensuring that even subtle indicators of incidents are not overlooked.

Upon detection, incidents are immediately reported through a pre-established communication channel, typically to a designated incident response team. This team, often cross-functional, is charged with the first level of incident assessment and response. Ensuring that team members are well-versed in the nuances of financial risk and have clear guidelines on their roles and responsibilities is paramount for a swift and effective response.

As an incident evolves, so too must the response—this is where escalation procedures come into play. Escalation is not a mere elevation in awareness but a strategic decision that considers the severity and potential impact of the incident. The theoretical construct of escalation procedures advocates for a decision matrix, where incidents are categorized based on predefined criteria such as financial impact, likelihood of occurrence, and speed of onset. Each category corresponds to a specific escalation tier, dictating the urgency of the response and the level of management involvement required.

In complex FP&A environments, escalation often necessitates the convening of a higher echelon of decision-makers, potentially involving executive management or the board of directors. At this level, strategic decisions are made, such as the mobilization of additional resources, engagement with external stakeholders, or invocation of business continuity plans.

Throughout the incident response and escalation process,

documentation is a critical yet often understated component. A meticulous record not only provides a detailed chronology of the event and response measures but also serves as a learning tool for post-incident review and analysis. This documentation feeds back into the organization's risk management framework, enhancing future risk modeling and response strategies.

Theoretical models for incident management and escalation procedures are adept at outlining ideal responses, but the application of these models in practice is nuanced by organizational culture, the specificity of incidents, and the dynamic nature of financial markets. A successful IRP is, therefore, one that is both grounded in theory and adaptable to the malleable contours of real-world challenges.

In the final analysis, the robustness of an FP&A department's incident management and escalation procedures is a testament to its preparedness and strategic foresight. It is through the careful design and execution of these protocols that financial stability can be maintained, and the organization can navigate the unpredictable seas of risk with confidence and resolve.

Audit, Assurance, and Risk Reporting

Amid the evolving mosaic of financial regulation and oversight, Audit, Assurance, and Risk Reporting form the trinity of accountability and transparency in an organization's risk management stratagem. This section ventures into the theoretical and practical aspects of these pivotal functions within the complex mechanism of financial planning and analysis (FP&A).

Audit, in its essence, serves as the critical evaluative process through which an organization's financial records and operational conduct are scrutinized for accuracy, legality, and adherence to established standards and protocols. The audit process is underpinned by a set of theoretical principles which ensure the integrity, objectivity, and professional skepticism. Internal audits, conducted by an organization's own audit specialists, provide ongoing oversight and are an integral component of a proactive risk management framework. They offer a vantage point for early detection of potential risks and inefficiencies, thereby enabling timely corrective action.

External audits, performed by independent entities, bring an additional layer of scrutiny. They bolster stakeholders' confidence by affirming the veracity of financial statements and compliance with regulatory frameworks. The theoretical approach to external audits is governed by numerous standards, such as the International Standards on Auditing (ISA), which mandate the nature, timing, and extent of audit procedures.

Assurance goes hand in hand with audit, providing a formal attestation to the reliability of information presented by the organization. While audit is primarily focused on historical financial data, assurance extends to non-financial data and forward-looking information. It encompasses a variety of reports, including but not limited to, performance reviews, compliance with non-financial covenants, and sustainability reporting. The theoretical foundation of assurance lies in enhancing the degree of confidence that intended users can place on the subject matter, as informed by frameworks such as ISAE 3000.

Risk reporting, the third pillar, is the communication conduit through which insights gleaned from audits and assurance activities are disseminated. Effective risk reporting is not a mere chronicle of numerical data; it encapsulates strategic analysis, risk assessment outcomes, and recommendations. It is through these reports that an organization's risk profile is articulated, enabling stakeholders to make informed decisions. The theoretical underpinnings of risk reporting advocate for clarity, relevance, timeliness, and comparability—guiding principles that optimize the utility of the reports.

In the realm of FP&A, the confluence of audit, assurance, and risk reporting is particularly pronounced. They serve as a feedback loop, informing the strategic planning processes and contributing to the dynamic recalibration of risk models and forecasts. The granularity of risk reports, for instance, can influence investment decisions, guide risk mitigation strategies, and underpin negotiations with insurers for risk transfer mechanisms.

Furthermore, the ever-growing intricacies of financial instruments, the advent of new risk vectors such as cybersecurity threats, and the complexities of global supply chains necessitate a sophisticated approach to audit, assurance, and risk reporting. It calls for a blend of traditional techniques and innovative methods—leveraging advancements in data analytics, artificial intelligence, and continuous auditing—to navigate the intricate landscapes of modern FP&A.

In synthesizing these components into the FP&A framework, organizations must not only consider the theoretical dimensions of each function but also their interplay and collective impact on the broader risk management ecosystem. The integration of audit findings, assurance outcomes, and risk reports into the strategic decision-making process is critical to fostering resilience and driving sustainable growth.

As we conclude this section, Audit, Assurance, and Risk Reporting are not static functions but dynamic processes that evolve in tandem with the business environment. They are indispensable tools in the FP&A arsenal, providing the insights and oversight that undergird sound financial governance and strategic agility.

Internal Audit's Role in Risk Management

The internal audit function is an indispensable ally in the quest to govern an organization's risk landscape efficiently. It plays a critical role in risk management, standing as a sentinel to oversee the effectiveness of risk mitigation strategies and the integrity of financial reporting. This subsection delves into the theoretical frameworks and practical applications of internal audit within the risk management domain.

The internal audit's role in risk management is underpinned by a theoretical framework that emphasizes independence, objectivity, and a systematic, disciplined approach. The Institute of Internal Auditors (IIA) provides standards and guidance which delineate the scope and responsibilities of internal auditors in assessing and improving an organization's governance, risk management, and control processes.

An internal auditor's role extends beyond traditional financial audits to include operational, compliance, and strategic audits. Each of these audit types serves to uncover potential risks that could thwart an organization's objectives. Operational audits focus on the efficiency and effectiveness of operations, compliance audits assess adherence to laws and regulations, while strategic audits examine whether organizational strategies align with the mission and are likely to meet goals.

In practice, the internal audit function aids in risk management by:

1. Identifying and Assessing Risks: Internal auditors use risk assessment tools to identify and evaluate risks that could impact the organization. These risks are then prioritized based on their potential severity and likelihood of occurrence.

2. Testing Controls: Internal auditors test the design and effectiveness of internal controls put in place to manage risks. They assess whether these controls are functioning as intended and provide recommendations for improvement.

3. Monitoring and Reporting: Through continuous monitoring activities, internal auditors track risk exposures and the success of control measures over time. They report their findings to management and the board, enabling informed decision-making.

4. Advising on Risk Management Practices: Internal auditors provide insights into best practices in risk management, acting as advisors to management on how to better

align risk management policies and procedures with the organization's risk appetite and tolerance.

5. Fostering a Risk-Conscious Culture: By emphasizing the importance of risk management throughout their work, internal auditors help promote a culture where risk considerations are an integral part of decision-making processes.

The evolving nature of risks faced by organizations, driven by factors such as technological innovation, market volatility, and regulatory changes, demands that internal audit functions are agile and adaptive. They must continually update their knowledge and skills to provide assurance on new and emerging risks.

Leveraging technologies like data analytics and implementing continuous auditing techniques can enhance the internal audit's capacity to identify patterns and anomalies that signal risk. Predictive analytics, for example, can forecast risk scenarios and allow organizations to prepare or adjust their risk management strategies proactively.

Through a blend of rigorous methodology and innovative practices, the internal audit function fortifies an organization's risk management framework. It ensures that not only are risks identified, assessed, and managed but also that the process of risk management itself is subject to continuous improvement. The internal audit, therefore, is not just a guardian of compliance but a catalyst for organizational resilience and strategic foresight.

Third-Party Assurance Services

In the intricate web of modern business operations, third-party assurance services stand as a pivotal component in the ecosystem of risk management. These independent services offer a critical external perspective on an organization's risk profile, control environment, and compliance status.

By engaging in third-party assurance services, organizations procure an unbiased evaluation that not only corroborates their internal assessments but also instills confidence among stakeholders. There are several forms of third-party assurance services, each providing a targeted lens through which risk is examined and reported.

One of the primary assurance services is the external audit, which focuses on the accuracy and fairness of financial statements. Performed by certified public accountants (CPAs) or audit firms, this service ensures that an organization's financial reporting adheres to the applicable accounting standards and provides a true reflection of its fiscal well-being.

Beyond financial audits, third-party assurance services extend to:

1. Service Organization Control (SOC) Reports: These reports are crucial for organizations that handle or process information on behalf of other entities. SOC reports, specifically SOC 1 and SOC 2, provide assurance regarding the controls over financial reporting and the security,

availability, processing integrity, confidentiality, and privacy of data.

2. Compliance Audits: With the complexity of regulatory environments across industries, compliance audits are essential in verifying adherence to laws, regulations, and industry standards. These audits help organizations navigate the regulatory landscape, avoiding potential fines, penalties, or reputational damage.

3. IT and Cybersecurity Assessments: Given the escalating threats in the digital realm, third-party assessments of an organization's cybersecurity posture are indispensable. These services evaluate the effectiveness of information security policies, controls, and incident response mechanisms.

4. Sustainability and ESG Audits: As environmental, social, and governance (ESG) criteria become increasingly relevant, third-party audits in this area assess an organization's sustainability practices, social impact, and governance structures, providing a gauge of its long-term viability and ethical conduct.

5. Quality Assurance Reviews: These reviews are tailored to industries where quality control is paramount, such as manufacturing or pharmaceuticals. They ensure that products and services meet established quality standards and customer expectations.

When engaging third-party assurance providers, organizations must consider the provider's credentials, expertise, and the rigor of their methodologies. The selection process should ensure that the provider has a reputation for thoroughness and integrity, offering assurance services that align with the organization's specific needs and risk profile.

Moreover, the relationship between an organization and its third-party assurers should be grounded in transparency and open communication. This enables the assurers to gain a comprehensive understanding of the organization's operations, control environment, and risk management practices, leading to more accurate and insightful assessment outcomes.

The value of third-party assurance services is multifaceted. Not only do they validate the organization's risk management efforts, but they also provide insights that can drive improvements in internal controls and risk mitigation strategies. Additionally, the external validation these services offer enhances credibility with investors, regulators, and other key stakeholders.

Incorporating third-party assurance services into the broader risk management strategy empowers organizations to confront their risk landscapes with a greater sense of certainty and preparedness. It represents an acknowledgement that in an ever-evolving business environment, external expertise can augment internal vigilance, bolstering the organization's resilience and reputation in the face of risk.

Creating Meaningful Risk Reports for Various Audiences

Crafting meaningful risk reports is an art that balances technical precision with the narrative clarity, designed to convey complex risk information to a diverse array of audiences. Such reports must be meticulously structured to resonate with the unique perspectives and interests of each stakeholder group, from board members to operational teams, and from regulators to investors.

For board members and executive leadership, risk reports serve as the linchpin in strategic decision-making. The report should distill down the complexity of risk data into executive summaries that highlight key risk indicators (KRIs), emerging threats, and strategic risk exposures. It must articulate how these risks align with the organization's risk appetite and the potential impact on long-term objectives. The use of dashboards or heat maps can provide a high-level overview, enabling quick comprehension of the risk landscape and facilitating informed governance decisions.

Operational teams, on the other hand, require risk reports that delve deeper into the operational implications of various risks. These reports should provide actionable insights and detailed analysis of risk drivers, linking them to specific business processes. By doing so, operational managers can understand the risk context in relation to their day-to-day activities and can prioritize risk mitigation efforts effectively.

Regulators represent another critical audience for risk reports. Regulatory risk reports need to demonstrate compliance with the relevant laws and standards, providing evidence of the organization's commitment to regulatory requirements. These reports should be comprehensive, well-documented, and precise, often following prescribed formats or templates dictated by the regulatory bodies. The ability to trace the lineage of data and decisions within the report is paramount to satisfy regulatory scrutiny.

Investors and shareholders seek assurance that the organization is managing risks in a manner that protects and enhances value. Risk reports aimed at this audience should focus on the financial implications of risk exposures, how these are being managed, and the organization's risk-adjusted performance metrics. Clear communication of risk governance structures and the integration of risk management into business strategy can bolster investor confidence and potentially influence investment decisions.

In crafting these varied reports, several principles must be adhered to, ensuring that each report is:

1. Relevant: Tailoring the content to address the specific concerns and information needs of each audience.

2. Accurate: Presenting risk information that is verified and based on the most current data.

3. Timely: Delivering reports within a timeframe that allows for meaningful action or intervention in response to the identified risks.

4. Understandable: Using clear, non-technical language where possible, and explaining technical terms when necessary.

5. Actionable: Providing clear recommendations or options for risk response, enabling stakeholders to take decisive action.

To achieve these principles, risk reporting should be supported by a robust risk information system that aggregates data from various sources, ensuring consistency and reliability. It should also provide the flexibility to present information in various formats, including text, tables, charts, and graphics, to cater to different preferences and levels of risk literacy among stakeholders.

Furthermore, the process of creating risk reports should be iterative, with feedback mechanisms that allow for continuous improvement. Stakeholders should have the opportunity to provide input on the usefulness and clarity of the reports, so that subsequent iterations can be refined to better meet their needs.

Creating meaningful risk reports is a multifaceted task that requires a deep understanding of both the substance of risk management and the nuances of stakeholder communication. It's an endeavor that demands a rigorous approach to data and analysis, as well as a nuanced touch in crafting a compelling narrative around risk, tailored to the lenses through which various audiences view and process information.

Transparency and Disclosure in External Reporting

Transparency and disclosure in external reporting are not just regulatory requirements but strategic tools that can fortify stakeholder trust and provide a competitive edge. As the global financial landscape becomes increasingly interconnected and scrutinized, companies must navigate the delicate balance between information transparency and strategic discretion.

The principle of transparency in external reporting is grounded in the provision of clear, comprehensive, and timely information to stakeholders. This transparency is paramount for investors, who depend on accurate data to make informed decisions. For regulators, it ensures compliance and aids in maintaining the integrity of financial markets. Customers and the public also benefit from transparent reporting, as it provides insight into the company's operations and commitment to ethical practices.

Disclosure, the act of making this information available to the public, must be managed with precision and foresight. Reports must cover the full spectrum of financial performance, including earnings, revenue streams, and significant risks, as well as management's analysis of financial conditions and operational results. Furthermore, disclosures include forward-looking statements that shed light on the company's expectations and strategies for future performance, subject to legal and competitive constraints.

A key aspect of achieving transparency is the adherence to recognized reporting standards such as the International Financial Reporting Standards (IFRS) or Generally Accepted Accounting Principles (GAAP), depending on the jurisdiction. These standards provide a framework for consistent reporting, allowing stakeholders to compare and analyze financial information across different entities and time periods.

The external reporting process involves several critical components:

1. Financial Statements: These are the bedrock of external reporting, providing a historical record of the company's financial performance and position. They include the income statement, balance sheet, and cash flow statement.

2. Management Discussion and Analysis (MD&A): This section offers management's perspective on the financial

results, explaining the underlying reasons for changes and trends. It also discusses risks, uncertainties, and expectations going forward.

3. Notes to the Financial Statements: These notes furnish additional details that are crucial for understanding the context and methodologies behind the financial figures presented in the statements.

4. Supplementary Information: Often, companies will include additional data, such as segment reports or market analysis, that can provide stakeholders with a deeper understanding of the company's strategic position.

Transparency and disclosure also extend to the way companies communicate about non-financial performance indicators, especially those related to environmental, social, and governance (ESG) factors. The growing importance of sustainability and corporate responsibility means that companies must report on their ESG initiatives and their impact on long-term value creation.

To enhance the quality of external reports, companies should consider the following practices:

- Engaging with stakeholders to understand their information needs and expectations.

- Utilizing technology and data analytics to improve the accuracy and granularity of reported information.

- Implementing robust internal controls and governance practices to ensure the reliability of reported data.

- Regularly reviewing and updating disclosure policies to reflect changes in regulations, market conditions, and the company's operations.

The drafting of external reports should be viewed as an integral part of a company's communication strategy, a narrative crafted not just to satisfy compliance but to offer a window into the corporate soul. This narrative must be woven with the threads of candor and clarity, presenting a story that aligns financial data with the company's vision, operational strategies, and risk management ethos.

To this end, FP&A professionals must exercise a keen editorial eye, ensuring that each report is not only a ledger of past performance but also a forward-looking document that articulates the company's trajectory and potential. In doing so, they position themselves not just as scribes of what has been but as architects of what could be—a future built on the bedrock of transparency and the clear disclosure of both opportunities and challenges lying ahead.

CHAPTER 11: ONGOING RISK MANAGEMENT EDUCATION AND TRAINING

In the ceaseless pursuit of organizational resilience and adaptability, ongoing education and training in risk management emerge as pivotal elements. They are the sinew and spine of an enterprise's ability to not just withstand but also to capitalize on the ever-shifting tides of market dynamics. This section delves into the intricacies of constructing a robust risk management education and training program that continuously evolves to meet the demands of an unpredictable financial landscape.

Education and training in risk management must transcend the traditional transfer of knowledge. It should ignite a transformation in how employees perceive, analyze, and respond to risks. The program aims to engrain a profound understanding of risk in the company's DNA, fostering a culture where every decision is made with a clear-eyed assessment of its potential impact.

Structured learning paths should be delineated for various roles within the organization, recognizing that the granularity and complexity of risk management concepts vary across different levels of responsibility. For entry-level professionals, the focus might be on grasping the basics of risk identification and mitigation. Mid-level managers would delve deeper into risk assessment methodologies and decision-making processes, while senior leaders would explore strategic implications and enterprise-wide risk integration.

Curriculum development for these training programs must be meticulous in its approach—an amalgamation of theoretical knowledge and practical application. Core topics could include, but are not limited to:

- Fundamentals of Risk Management: Covering the basic principles, terminologies, and frameworks.

- Advanced Risk Analysis Techniques: Instructing on qualitative and quantitative methods, including scenario planning, Monte Carlo simulations, and stress testing.

- Regulatory Compliance: Providing updates on the latest legal standards and how they impact organizational policies and practices.

- Strategic Risk Decision-Making: Teaching how to incorporate risk considerations into strategic planning and business development.

- Technological Tools: Training on the use of software and analytics platforms that support risk management functions.

Interactive modalities such as workshops, simulations, and

case studies are crucial, as they bridge theory with the real-world challenges that practitioners face. These methods allow participants to experiment with decision-making in a controlled environment, where they can see the consequences of their actions without real-world repercussions.

Beyond structured training programs, fostering a continual learning environment is fundamental. This involves encouraging the workforce to remain abreast of emerging risks, industry trends, and innovative risk management practices. Organizations might facilitate this through the establishment of a knowledge-sharing platform, scheduling regular forums for discussion, or incentivizing self-paced learning through access to online courses and certifications.

Professional development opportunities, such as supporting employees in obtaining certifications from recognized risk management bodies (e.g., FRM, CRM), not only enhance the individual's skill set but also contribute to the organization's risk management acumen. Moreover, these certifications often require ongoing education, which reinforces the culture of continuous learning.

In the digital age, e-learning and virtual training tools have become indispensable. They offer flexibility, allowing employees to learn at their own pace and revisit complex topics as needed. These tools can also provide analytics to track progress and identify areas where additional focus may be required.

Measuring the effectiveness of these educational endeavors is as vital as their implementation. This can be achieved through assessments, feedback surveys, and by monitoring risk management performance metrics post-training. The goal is not merely to impart knowledge but to effectuate a palpable enhancement in how risks are handled across the organization.

In essence, ongoing risk management education and training are not just about knowledge dissemination; they are about shaping a corporate ethos where risk-awareness permeates every business process and decision. It is about creating a cadre of professionals who are not only versed in the art and science of risk management but who are also equipped to lead their organizations confidently through the complexities and uncertainties of the financial world.

Developing Risk Management Training Programs

The design and execution of risk management training programs are crucial facets in the armory of any forward-thinking organization. Such programs serve not merely as an edifice for knowledge but as a crucible for the synthesis of theory, practice, and strategic foresight. The development of these programs is a meticulous process, reflecting the nuances of the organizational ethos and the multifaceted nature of risk itself.

To commence, a needs assessment is imperative, a collaborative exercise involving key stakeholders to discern the specific risk training requirements that align with both individual role functions and broader organizational objectives. This assessment must consider the diverse proficiencies present within the workforce and the varying degrees of risk exposure inherent in each department.

The curriculum for a risk management training program

should be an embodiment of the organization's risk philosophy and strategic vision. It needs to encompass a broad spectrum of content, ranging from foundational concepts of risk management to specialized areas such as cyber risk, financial compliance, and environmental, social, and governance (ESG) factors. The curriculum should be dynamic, regularly updated to incorporate the latest regulatory changes, market conditions, and advanced analytical techniques.

A key component in developing these training programs is the selection of appropriate delivery methods. Traditional classroom settings may be augmented with online modules and interactive webinars to cater to a geographically dispersed workforce. Blended learning approaches, which combine face-to-face instruction with digital media, can be highly effective in engaging participants and reinforcing learning outcomes.

Simulated exercises and gamification can add a layer of practicality to theoretical constructs. Through simulation exercises, employees can engage in "what-if" scenarios, allowing them to experience firsthand the repercussions of risk-related decisions in a controlled environment. Gamification, the application of game-design elements in non-game contexts, can make learning about risk management more engaging and could potentially improve retention of complex concepts.

The application of advanced pedagogical tools, such as artificial intelligence (AI) and machine learning (ML), can tailor the learning experience to individual needs. AI-driven platforms can assess an individual's understanding in real-time and adapt the training content to address gaps in knowledge or comprehension. This personalization ensures that each employee's training experience is optimized for their learning curve and professional development path.

To ensure the efficacy of training programs, the establishment of clear benchmarks and performance metrics is essential. These should be crafted not only to evaluate the learners' comprehension and application of risk management principles but also to measure the program's impact on organizational risk posture. Feedback mechanisms should be instituted to gather participant input and refine the program iteratively.

Another aspect to consider in program development is the integration of external expertise. Inviting industry experts, regulators, or academic thought leaders to contribute can provide valuable insights and lend credibility to the training initiatives. Partnerships with professional bodies can also offer access to a wealth of resources and may lead to accreditation opportunities for the participants.

Continuous improvement and adaptation are the hallmarks of a successful training program. As the risk landscape evolves, so too must the educational content and methodologies. A regular review cycle, informed by participant feedback, emerging trends, and organizational needs, will ensure the program remains at the forefront of risk management training.

In forging a comprehensive risk management training program, one crafts more than a series of learning modules; one engenders a paradigm where risk intelligence is ingrained in the corporate consciousness. It is a sustained effort that moves beyond risk aversion to embrace risk optimization—a strategic enabler that empowers individuals and the organization to navigate the complexities of the contemporary business world with acumen and agility.

Customized Training for Different Organizational Levels

In risk management, the axiom 'one size fits all' is a misplaced notion. Customization is the keystone of any adequate training regimen to address the diverse spectrum of proficiency and responsibility across the organizational hierarchy. This chapter delves into the intricacies of tailoring risk management education to fit the unique needs of various levels within an institution.

At the foundational tier of the organizational pyramid, the training is oriented towards imparting a basic comprehension of risk principles among the wider workforce. Employees at this level engage with risk management tangentially, necessitating a focus on general awareness and the importance of adherence to risk policies. Interactive e-learning platforms and microlearning sessions —a pedagogical approach that delivers content in small, specific bursts—can provide these employees with a firm grasp of risk concepts without overburdening them with complexity.

As we ascend to the managerial echelons, the training becomes more nuanced, entailing a deeper dive into risk analytics and decision-making processes. Managers are at the crossroads of strategic planning and operational execution; therefore, their training must equip them with tools to identify and assess risks within their departments. Case studies, simulations, and role-playing exercises are valuable in this context, enabling managers to bridge theory with practical application.

For senior leaders, such as department heads and executives, the training shifts towards a strategic perspective, emphasizing the alignment of risk management with business goals and the regulatory landscape. This segment of the training program should foster a sophisticated understanding of how to balance risk and reward, and how to incorporate risk considerations into long-term planning. Workshops facilitated by seasoned experts, peer learning forums, and strategic war-gaming scenarios are conducive to honing the advanced acumen required at this level.

At the pinnacle, the board of directors and C-suite executives require a bespoke curriculum that encompasses governance, enterprise risk management, and crisis leadership. This high-level training must underscore the symbiotic relationship between risk and strategy, preparing these top-tier leaders for their role in setting the tone for risk culture and oversight. Executive education offerings from top-tier business schools and bespoke sessions with global risk management consultants may provide the necessary caliber of training for this echelon.

Effectual training at each level necessitates a granularity of design, taking into account the specific risk exposures of roles and the decision-making latitude afforded to each tier. Therefore, the training content for a financial controller will differ markedly from that of an IT manager, despite both being managerial roles, owing to the disparate nature of risks they encounter.

The development of these level-specific training modules must also be informed by insights gleaned from performance data and risk incident reports. Such data-driven customization enables the organization to create targeted educational experiences that not only address identified gaps but also preempt potential areas of risk vulnerability.

Moreover, the deployment of training is not a static process; it requires a continuous feedback loop. Post-training assessments, performance monitoring, and open forums for discussion help in refining and updating the training content to keep pace with the evolving risk landscape. The incorporation of adaptive learning technologies can further enhance this process by dynamically adjusting the training path based on the learner's progress and comprehension.

In the ultimate analysis, a stratified approach to risk management training is not merely an exercise in knowledge dissemination; it is about fostering an organizational milieu where each member, regardless of their rung on the corporate ladder, is a custodian of risk intelligence—cognizant of their role in the grander scheme of enterprise risk management.

Utilizing E-Learning and Virtual Training Tools

The digital age has ushered in an era where the traditional classroom is no longer the sole venue for education. E-learning and virtual training tools have emerged as pivotal in crafting a dynamic and flexible learning environment, particularly in the sphere of risk management training within organizations.

E-learning, with its myriad forms—from webinars and online courses to interactive simulations and gamified learning experiences—provides an accessible platform for employees to augment their understanding of risk concepts at their own pace and convenience. The key advantage lies in its adaptability; content can be tailored to different learning styles and comprehension levels, ensuring that everyone's educational needs are met effectively.

Virtual training tools go a step further by creating an immersive learning environment, often using virtual reality (VR) or augmented reality (AR). These technologies can simulate real-world risk scenarios, allowing learners to navigate complex situations in a controlled, yet realistic setting. For instance, VR can place financial analysts within a virtual market environment where they can observe the impacts of various risks on market dynamics and test their response strategies without real-world consequences.

Another significant aspect of virtual training is the capacity for real-time feedback and analytics. These systems can track progress, identify areas where learners struggle, and provide immediate corrective guidance. Such feedback is invaluable in risk management training, where understanding the nuances of risk assessment and mitigation strategies is crucial for effective application.

The flexibility of e-learning also facilitates continuous education, a must in the ever-evolving field of risk management. With regulations changing and new risks emerging, e-learning platforms can swiftly update or add modules to reflect the latest developments, ensuring that the organization's workforce remains at the frontline of risk management knowledge.

Moreover, e-learning and virtual training tools can

democratize learning across geographical divides. For global organizations, this means being able to deliver consistent training to employees worldwide, ensuring a unified approach to risk management across all locales. This global reach is essential in instilling a cohesive risk culture throughout the organization, irrespective of physical borders.

Virtual training environments are conducive to fostering collaboration as well. Online discussion forums, virtual classrooms, and collaborative projects enable employees from different departments and regions to exchange insights and approaches to risk management, enriching the learning experience through diverse perspectives.

However, the success of e-learning and virtual training hinges on thoughtful implementation. It begins with a robust technological infrastructure that supports uninterrupted access to training materials and interactive features. The content must be engaging, employing multimedia elements such as videos, infographics, and interactive quizzes to maintain learner engagement. Furthermore, the design of e-learning modules must align with clear learning objectives that directly relate to the risk management competencies the organization seeks to develop.

In the larger schema of risk management education, e-learning and virtual training tools represent an integral component of a comprehensive training strategy. When combined with traditional training methods and continuous professional development initiatives, they form a multifaceted educational framework capable of elevating the organization's risk management acumen to new heights.

The integration of these digital tools into the training program is not an end but a means to foster a more informed, agile, and risk-aware workforce. As such, the investment in e-learning and virtual training is an investment in the organization's resilience and strategic future.

Case Study and Simulation-Based Learning

Case study and simulation-based learning stand as two pillars that transform theoretical knowledge into practical skill. This section delves into the application of these methodologies within the framework of FP&A training programs, elucidating their potential to hone the decision-making and analytical prowess of financial professionals.

Case studies are narratives that present real-world business dilemmas or historical events, challenging learners to dissect the intricacies of each scenario. They are carefully selected to reflect the multifaceted nature of risk management, encompassing issues like market volatility, regulatory compliance, and strategic decision-making under uncertainty. Through case studies, trainees are invited to step into the shoes of CFOs and risk analysts, grappling with the same data and constraints these professionals encountered. This immersive approach encourages a deep engagement with the material, fostering a nuanced understanding of risk dynamics.

A well-crafted case study serves multiple functions. It not only illustrates the application of theoretical concepts in a tangible context but also stimulates critical thinking by requiring learners to evaluate the effectiveness of the decisions made. Additionally, case studies often serve as a springboard for group discussions, where diverse perspectives coalesce to enrich the collective learning experience. Such discussions are instrumental in revealing the multiplicity of approaches that can be taken in response to a single set of circumstances, underscoring the importance of judgment and creativity in risk management.

Simulation-based learning complements case studies by offering an interactive experience that mirrors the complexity of the financial world. Simulations create hypothetical environments where learners can experiment with different strategies and witness the consequences of their decisions without bearing real-world risks. These virtual models can range from simple spreadsheet-based scenarios to sophisticated, multi-user platforms that replicate the dynamism of financial markets or the operational challenges of business projects.

Simulations are invaluable for their ability to provide experiential learning—a form of education that cements knowledge through doing rather than observing. For instance, a simulation might task trainees with navigating a company through an economic downturn, adjusting investment portfolios in response to geopolitical events, or implementing risk mitigation strategies to safeguard against operational losses. Through repeated iterations, learners can test hypotheses, refine their tactics, and internalize key risk management principles.

The pedagogical potency of simulations is further amplified when coupled with debriefing sessions. These reflective discussions post-simulation are vital for unpacking the decisions made during the exercise, offering insights into alternative strategies, and cementing the takeaways from the experience. Debriefing transforms the act of 'playing the game' into a profound learning opportunity, ensuring that the lessons gleaned are carried forward into the learners' professional conduct.

For FP&A professionals, simulation-based learning is particularly relevant as it mirrors the predictive nature of their roles. By engaging with simulations that require forecasting and modeling under various scenarios, they sharpen their ability to anticipate risks and devise contingencies that can be readily applied in their day-to-day responsibilities.

Both case studies and simulations are conduits for bridging the gap between academic theory and practical application. They are the vehicles through which risk management principles are not merely learned but lived. In the development of an FP&A professional's competencies, these learning modalities are not luxuries but necessities, forming the bedrock upon which sound judgment and strategic acumen are built.

As we continue to explore the avenues of effective risk management practices, case study and simulation-based learning are indispensable tools. They endow financial practitioners with the experience and wisdom to navigate the uncertain waters of financial planning and analysis, equipping them to uphold the financial integrity and advance the strategic objectives of their organizations.

Measuring Training Effectiveness and Impact

To ascertain the value of training initiatives within the domain of risk management, it is imperative to establish robust mechanisms for measuring the effectiveness and impact of such programs. This section will illuminate the methodologies and metrics that are instrumental in evaluating whether training activities have achieved their intended objectives and the degree to which they have influenced organizational performance in financial planning and analysis (FP&A).

The evaluation of training effectiveness traditionally follows the Kirkpatrick Model, which consists of four hierarchical levels: Reaction, Learning, Behavior, and Results. In the context of FP&A risk management training, each level provides a critical lens for assessing the program's success from different vantage points. Let us examine these levels in greater depth.

At the first level, Reaction, the immediate responses of the participants are surveyed. Feedback is solicited regarding the training's relevance, engagement, and perceived value. For FP&A professionals, this might involve gauging their initial impressions on how well the training content aligns with their roles and the challenges they face in risk management. Reaction assessments are usually captured through questionnaires or interviews conducted shortly after the training session's conclusion.

Ascending to the second level, Learning, the focus shifts to measuring the knowledge or skills gained as a direct result of the training. In the case of risk management, this could entail pre- and post-training assessments designed to quantify the enhancement in the participants' understanding of risk assessment tools, financial modeling techniques, or regulatory compliance standards. Learning metrics often employ tests, simulations, or practical exercises that provide objective data on the participants' cognitive gains.

The third level, Behavior, examines the transfer of learned skills into the workplace. This level is pivotal for FP&A training, as it directly correlates the theoretical and simulation-based learning components to real-world application. Metrics at this juncture might include the observation of participants' performance over time, the frequency and effectiveness with which newly acquired risk management strategies are applied, or changes in decision-making patterns. Surveys and interviews with both the trainees and their supervisors can yield valuable insights into behavioural changes post-training.

Finally, the fourth level, Results, encompasses the broader impact of the training on organizational outcomes. This level seeks to link the training to quantifiable business metrics such as improved financial performance, reduced risk exposure, or enhanced compliance with regulatory standards. For FP&A training, this could translate into metrics like the accuracy of financial forecasts, the success rate of risk mitigation initiatives, or the reduction in audit findings. The analysis of key performance indicators (KPIs) pre- and post-training provides tangible evidence of the training's return on investment (ROI).

Beyond the Kirkpatrick Model, newer approaches such as the Kaufman Model of Learning Evaluation and the Anderson Model of Learning Evaluation introduce additional layers, including societal impact and contribution to the organization's mission. These models acknowledge that the true test of training effectiveness in risk management extends beyond individual or organizational boundaries, considering the broader ripple effects on stakeholders and the financial industry at large.

To measure the effectiveness and impact of FP&A risk management training comprehensively, a multi-faceted approach is warranted—one that synthesizes qualitative and quantitative data and accounts for the dynamic nature of the risk landscape. This approach ensures that training programs are not static entities but evolve continually to meet the ever-changing demands of the financial world.

In sum, the quest for measuring training effectiveness and impact in FP&A risk management is a continuous process of refinement, requiring a commitment to rigorous evaluation and a willingness to adapt based on the findings. Through meticulous measurement and dedicated follow-through, organizations can ensure that their training investments yield the highest dividends in competency development, risk preparedness, and strategic financial management.

Promoting a Continual Learning Environment

The cultivation of a continual learning environment within an organization is an indispensable element in the realm of financial planning and analysis (FP&A). This environment encourages the perpetual acquisition of knowledge and the refinement of skills, which is particularly crucial in the dynamic field of risk management. This section delves into the strategies and practices that engender a culture of continuous learning and improvement, thereby enhancing an organization's capacity to manage risks effectively.

One foundational strategy for promoting continual learning is to create an organizational culture that values curiosity and intellectual growth. This can be achieved by leadership demonstrating a commitment to their own professional development, thus setting a precedent for all team members to follow. In FP&A, where new risks and regulatory changes frequently emerge, fostering an atmosphere where staying abreast of the latest industry developments is the norm can be vital to maintaining a competitive edge.

Another key aspect is the implementation of knowledge-sharing platforms. These can range from internal wikis and forums to regular learning sessions where team members present insights from recent projects or external trainings they have attended. Such platforms not only disseminate valuable information but also encourage collaboration and cross-pollination of ideas across departments, which is especially beneficial when tackling complex risk management challenges.

Moreover, organizations can encourage continual learning by providing access to a variety of educational resources. This might include subscriptions to industry journals, sponsorship of attendance at relevant conferences, or the provision of online courses catering to the multifaceted aspects of risk management. Organizations that invest in a broad spectrum of learning opportunities signal to employees that they are valued assets whose growth is integral to the company's success.

In addition to structured learning opportunities, cultivating a continual learning environment in FP&A also involves informal learning and mentorship. The pairing of less experienced staff with seasoned professionals can facilitate on-the-job learning and tacit knowledge transfer. Mentorship can be especially effective in conveying the nuances of risk assessment and mitigation, which are often not captured in formal education but are gleaned through years of hands-on experience.

A comprehensive learning environment also embraces the practice of reflection and feedback. Providing platforms for employees to reflect on their experiences, successes, and mistakes, and to receive constructive feedback, enables a culture where learning from every outcome is ingrained. This reflective practice can be particularly instructive following the conclusion of major risk management initiatives, allowing teams to identify lessons learned and areas for improvement.

It is also crucial to recognize and reward employees who actively engage in learning activities and apply new knowledge in innovative ways. Incentives could include public acknowledgment, career advancement opportunities, or bonuses tied to personal development goals. Such rewards not only motivate individual learners but also reinforce the value that the organization places on continual learning.

Finally, to truly embed a continual learning ethos, organizations must be agile and responsive to the evolving educational needs of their workforce. This may require regular assessments of training programs' effectiveness, as outlined in the previous section, and the willingness to adapt learning strategies in response to feedback and changing market conditions.

In essence, the promotion of a continual learning environment is both a strategic imperative and a practical necessity for FP&A functions. It is a commitment to never-ending improvement, with the dual aims of enhancing individual competencies and ensuring organizational resilience amid the shifting tides of financial risks.

Encouraging Curiosity and Critical Thinking

In the grander mosaic of risk management within FP&A, the thread that stands out as both delicate and robust is the human mind—curious, agile, and primed for critical thought. It is within this cognitive framework that we explore the significance of fostering curiosity and critical thinking as integral components of an organization's risk management strategy. This section elucidates the methodologies and cultural paradigms that engender a workforce equipped with analytical acumen and an inquisitive ethos, essential for navigating the complexities of contemporary financial landscapes.

At its core, curiosity is the driving force behind innovation and discovery, and its role in FP&A cannot be overstated. An organization that nurtures a sense of wonder among its personnel lays the cornerstone for breakthroughs in risk identification, assessment, and mitigation. To kindle this curiosity, companies must create environments where questioning is not only tolerated but encouraged. This could be manifested in a multitude of ways, such as 'innovation labs,' where team members are invited to brainstorm and devise novel approaches to entrenched risk management problems.

Critical thinking, on the other hand, is the analytical yin to curiosity's exploratory yang. It is a disciplined process of actively conceptualizing, applying, and evaluating information gathered from observation, experience, or communication. In FP&A, critical thinking is the lens through which financial data is scrutinized, ensuring that decision-making is grounded in a meticulous analysis rather than intuition alone. To cultivate this mindset, organizations can offer training sessions focused on logical reasoning, problem-solving, and the dissection of complex financial constructs.

Integrating simulations and scenario-based exercises into the training regimen can prove particularly effective in honing critical thinking skills. By placing team members in simulated high-stakes situations, they are compelled to navigate through intricate risk scenarios, making swift yet informed decisions. Such experiential learning not only embeds critical faculties in the participants but also imbues them with confidence to tackle actual financial challenges that may arise.

The promotion of interdepartmental dialogues is another vital strategy for fostering curiosity and critical thinking. Bringing together diverse perspectives from across the organization can lead to an enriched understanding of risks and their interconnections. Weekly cross-functional meetings, where members from various departments discuss emerging risks and share insights, can serve as a fertile ground for collective critical thought and innovative problem-solving.

It is also imperative to acknowledge and address the cognitive biases that can impede curiosity and critical thinking. Training initiatives should include components that help recognize and mitigate common biases such as confirmation bias, anchoring, or overconfidence. By making team members aware of these mental traps, an organization can enhance the objectivity and depth of the risk management process.

A continual feedback loop, where employees are encouraged to provide and receive feedback on their risk analysis and decision-making processes, amplifies the learning experience. This feedback, when delivered constructively and regularly, can reinforce a culture of curiosity and sharpen critical thinking skills by showcasing real-world applications of theoretical concepts.

Cultivating curiosity and critical thinking within FP&A is not a static endeavor but a dynamic, ongoing process. It requires commitment from all levels of the organization —from executives who champion these values to team members who practice them daily. Through dedicated efforts to foster these cognitive capabilities, organizations can build a formidable defense against the ever-evolving risks that pervade the financial sector, ensuring robust and resilient financial planning and analysis functions.

Learning from Near-Misses and Loss Events

The lessons gleaned from near-misses and loss events are invaluable. They function as canaries in the coal mine, signaling potential hazards before they can inflict significant damage. This section delves into the mechanisms by which organizations can transform these near-misses and loss events into a rich repository of knowledge, thereby enhancing their risk management framework and reinforcing their strategic defenses.

To begin with, it is imperative to establish a systematic process for capturing and analyzing near-misses and loss events. An organization must ensure that it has a robust incident reporting system that is both accessible and non-punitive, encouraging employees to share information about any risks that were narrowly averted or any financial losses incurred. Each reported incident should trigger a thorough investigation to dissect the event, identify causative factors, and extract actionable insights.

A multidisciplinary approach to the investigation can yield a comprehensive understanding of the underlying issues. By involving teams from different departments, especially those with risk oversight, an organization can foster a holistic view of the incident, considering various angles—be it operational, strategic, or compliance-related.

Once the investigation is complete, the next step is to distill the findings into a format that can be easily communicated across the organization. Case studies, for instance, can be a compelling way to present near-misses and loss events, outlining the context, the risks involved, the actions taken, and the lessons learned. These narratives not only serve as educational tools but also help in embedding the knowledge deeply within the organizational culture.

Learning from these events also entails revisiting and, if necessary, overhauling the existing risk controls and mitigation strategies. The insights obtained from the analysis should inform the reassessment of the risk landscape, the recalibration of risk models, and the reinforcement of risk response plans. This proactive adjustment of risk management practices ensures that the organization remains agile and responsive to evolving financial threats.

An essential aspect of learning from near-misses and loss events is the creation of a feedback loop into the training programs and risk management protocols. Regular workshops and refresher courses that incorporate recent case studies can elevate the risk awareness of the workforce and sharpen their ability to identify and respond to potential risks.

Embedding the practice of learning from near-misses and loss events into the performance measurement framework can also reinforce its importance. By including risk management metrics and incident learning outcomes into performance appraisals, organizations can underline the value they place on risk intelligence and continual improvement.

Moreover, it is crucial to recognize and reward employees who contribute to the organization's understanding of risk by reporting near-misses and loss events. Positive reinforcement can cultivate an environment that values vigilance and transparency, key components for a robust risk management culture.

Near-misses and loss events are more than just historical data points; they are the empirical bedrock upon which an organization can build a more resilient and informed risk management strategy. By instituting a culture of learning and adapting from these occurrences, financial leaders can fortify their FP&A operations against the unpredictable ebbs and flows of the financial world, turning potential calamities into opportunities for growth and refinement.

Sharing Best Practices and Lessons Learned

In the dynamic realm of financial planning and analysis (FP&A), the dissemination of best practices and the lessons drawn from past experiences are critical to the collective advancement of the field. This section will explore the methodologies through which organizations can effectively identify, document, and communicate the best practices and lessons learned, thereby fostering a culture of continuous improvement and collective knowledge.

The first step in this knowledge-sharing journey is the meticulous documentation of successful strategies and processes. Organizations must establish a methodical approach to capturing best practices, whether it be through detailed process mapping, comprehensive documentation, or insightful case studies. These records should be curated within a centralized knowledge management system, making them readily accessible to all employees.

To ensure that these best practices are not merely theoretical but are grounded in real-world application, it is crucial to gather and present empirical evidence of their efficacy. This evidence may come in the form of performance metrics, feedback from stakeholders, or comparative analyses that demonstrate the tangible benefits of the practices in question.

A key to effective knowledge-sharing is to create platforms for dialogue and exchange, where professionals across the organization can convene to discuss these practices. Regularly scheduled forums, workshops, and symposia provide avenues for employees to present their successes, discuss challenges, and solicit feedback from their peers. Such interactions can spark innovation and inspire others to adopt and adapt these practices to their unique contexts.

In addition to internal dissemination, organizations should

also consider contributing to the broader FP&A community. Publishing findings in industry journals, presenting at conferences, and participating in professional networks can elevate the organization's profile as a thought leader while also benefiting the industry as a whole.

When discussing the lessons learned, it is essential to approach them with candor and humility. It means acknowledging mistakes and missteps as opportunities for learning and growth. This honesty fosters trust and encourages others to share their experiences, contributing to a rich database of knowledge that can prevent future misjudgments.

An effective strategy for embedding best practices into the organizational fabric is through mentorship and coaching programs. Experienced professionals can guide emerging talent, providing hands-on learning experiences that reinforce the application of best practices. These mentor-mentee relationships create a lineage of expertise that can perpetuate a cycle of learning and mastery.

To complement these efforts, the development of user-friendly tools and resources, such as checklists, templates, and guidelines based on these best practices, can aid employees in their day-to-day activities. These tools act as practical applications of the knowledge banked from previous successes and lessons learned.

Finally, organizational leadership must advocate for and reinforce the value of sharing best practices and learning from experience. Leaders can demonstrate their commitment by integrating these elements into strategic objectives, performance evaluations, and reward systems. By doing so, they signal the vital role that knowledge-sharing plays in driving excellence and innovation in FP&A.

The sharing of best practices and lessons learned is not a passive exercise but an active endeavor that requires thoughtful planning, committed participation, and an infrastructure that supports the free flow of knowledge. It is through these collaborative efforts that an organization can harness the collective intelligence of its workforce, galvanize its operations, and maintain a competitive edge in the ever-evolving landscape of financial management.

Societal and Industry Trends Impacting Risk

As the world evolves at an ever-accelerating pace, societal and industry trends significantly influence the risk landscape in financial planning and analysis (FP&A). This section will dissect these trends, considering their multifaceted impact on risk assessment, management, and mitigation strategies within FP&A.

One of the most pervasive societal trends is the rapid advancement of technology, which has reshaped the way businesses operate and interact with their customers. The emergence of fintech, digital currencies, and blockchain technologies has introduced both opportunities and risks. These innovations offer streamlined processes and new revenue streams but also bring challenges such as heightened cybersecurity threats and regulatory uncertainties.

Another societal factor altering the risk paradigm is the shifting demographic landscape. Aging populations in certain regions contrast with the burgeoning youth demographics in others, influencing market dynamics and consumer behaviors. FP&A professionals must adjust their forecasts and models to account for these demographic shifts, ensuring that their risk assessments align with potential changes in demand patterns and workforce availability.

The movement towards sustainability and corporate social responsibility (CSR) is another trend that demands attention. Consumers and investors increasingly expect companies to demonstrate ethical practices and environmental stewardship. This societal push has translated into a growing emphasis on Environmental, Social, and Governance (ESG) criteria in investment decisions. Consequently, companies must evaluate their exposure to ESG-related risks and develop strategies to address them as part of their comprehensive risk management framework.

In parallel, industry trends such as globalization and the intricate interdependencies between markets have amplified the transmission of economic shocks and financial contagions. FP&A professionals must consider the cascading effects of geopolitical events, trade disputes, and policy shifts on their risk calculations. This global interconnectedness necessitates a broader view of risk that transcends geographical boundaries and industry sectors.

The rapid pace of innovation itself is a trend with its inherent risks. The disruption caused by new business models and emerging competitors can quickly render existing strategies obsolete. FP&A must maintain a forward-looking approach, incorporating scenario planning and stress testing to evaluate the potential impacts of disruptive technologies and market entrants.

Furthermore, the regulatory environment continues to evolve, with new laws and standards being implemented in response to technological changes and societal pressures. Keeping abreast of regulatory changes is imperative for FP&A units to ensure compliance and to anticipate the associated costs or operational constraints that may arise.

Lastly, the trend of an increasingly data-driven society impacts risk management in FP&A. The abundance of data provides an opportunity for more granular and sophisticated risk analysis. However, it also introduces the risk of information overload and the potential for analysis paralysis. The challenge lies in harnessing big data effectively, utilizing advanced analytics and artificial intelligence to derive actionable insights while maintaining data integrity and security.

Certification and Professional Development

In an environment where global financial systems are becoming increasingly complex and interconnected, the need for rigorous certification and professional development in the field of financial planning and analysis (FP&A) has never been more pronounced. This section explores the critical role that structured learning programs, certifications, and continual professional development play in equipping FP&A professionals with the skills and knowledge necessary to adeptly manage risk in a dynamic corporate landscape.

Certification programs such as the Certified Financial Planner (CFP), Chartered Financial Analyst (CFA), and Certified Treasury Professional (CTP) represent hallmarks of proficiency within the finance sector. Attainment of these certifications signifies a comprehensive understanding of financial concepts, ethical standards, and the commitment to upholding the integrity of the financial profession. For FP&A practitioners, these credentials can be pivotal in fostering trust with stakeholders and instilling confidence in the strategic decisions made by the organization.

Professional development in FP&A often extends beyond traditional certifications. Indeed, it includes a spectrum of continuous learning opportunities—seminars, workshops, and advanced degrees—that keep professionals abreast of the latest industry developments, regulatory changes, and emerging technologies. FP&A professionals must remain lifelong learners, habitually engaging with new educational resources to refine their risk management strategies and ensure that they are aligned with contemporary best practices.

The importance of leadership and management development programs cannot be overstated. These initiatives help seasoned FP&A professionals transition from individual contributors to visionary leaders capable of steering their organizations through tumultuous financial climates. Such programs often address advanced topics, including strategic leadership, change management, and organizational dynamics, all of which are integral to maintaining a robust risk management framework.

Furthermore, professional associations play a vital role in the development of FP&A talent. Organizations such as the Association for Financial Professionals (AFP) and the Global Association of Risk Professionals (GARP) offer platforms for networking, collaboration, and knowledge exchange. They also provide resources for staying current on industry standards and practices—a necessity in a field where outdated knowledge can result in suboptimal risk management and potentially deleterious financial outcomes.

Networking, whether through professional associations or informal connections, serves as a conduit for sharing insights and experiences. It is through these interactions that FP&A professionals can learn from the successes and missteps of their peers, broadening their understanding of risk in different contexts and sectors.

Finally, the digital transformation of finance necessitates that FP&A professionals develop a proficiency in data analytics and the use of advanced software tools. Mastery in these areas allows for the construction of sophisticated financial models capable of simulating a range of scenarios and outcomes. This computational acumen is essential for performing predictive analyses that inform risk management decisions.

Options for Risk Management Certifications (e.g., FRM, CRM)

Nestled within the broader scope of professional development is the niche yet crucial domain of risk management certifications. These qualifications represent the pinnacle of specialized knowledge in identifying, assessing, and mitigating financial risks. Two of the most esteemed credentials in this arena are the Financial Risk Manager (FRM) certification and the Certified Risk Manager (CRM) designation.

The FRM certification is awarded by the Global Association

of Risk Professionals (GARP) and is globally recognized as the premier certification for financial risk professionals. To earn the FRM credential, candidates must pass two rigorous exams that cover a wide range of topics from quantitative analysis, market risk, credit risk, operational and integrated risk management, to risk management in investments. FRM holders are widely respected for their technical acumen and their ability to apply risk management tools and approaches in practical, real-world situations.

Pursuing the FRM certification is a journey that involves both self-study and structured learning. Participants are expected to dedicate significant time to mastering the complex bodies of knowledge underlying modern risk management. This certification is often pursued by professionals who aim to specialize in risk within banks, corporate treasuries, asset management firms, or regulatory agencies. The FRM credential serves as a testament to an individual's expertise and is often a differentiator in the job market, enabling career advancement and enhancing professional credibility.

On the other hand, the CRM designation focuses on a broader approach to risk management, encompassing all aspects of risks that organizations may face, including but not limited to financial risks. Offered by the National Alliance for Insurance Education & Research, the CRM program consists of five courses that cover all facets of risk management: principles of risk management, analysis of risk, control of risk, financing of risk, and the practice of risk management. The CRM is designed to provide a comprehensive understanding of the risk management process, from identification and analysis to control and financing. This certification benefits professionals seeking to implement robust risk management frameworks across various industries, not limited to finance.

Professionals who attain the CRM are recognized for their capacity to understand and manage risks in a holistic manner, contributing to the strategic planning and decision-making processes within their organizations. They are equipped to advise on risk management policies, design and implement risk mitigation strategies, and communicate effectively with stakeholders about potential risks and protective measures.

Both the FRM and CRM certifications require a commitment to ongoing education, with certified individuals expected to engage in continuous learning and adhere to professional standards. This commitment ensures that certified risk management professionals remain at the forefront of industry developments, regulatory changes, and emerging best practices.

The decision to pursue a risk management certification should be guided by one's career objectives, the specific industry in which one operates, and the types of risks that are most pertinent to their professional responsibilities. Whether choosing the FRM for its financial risk focus or the CRM for its broad-based risk approach, these certifications are invaluable assets in the toolkit of any serious risk management professional.

In conclusion, risk management certifications like the FRM and CRM are essential for those dedicated to the discipline of managing uncertainty in the financial world. They not only validate expertise but also open doors to advanced career opportunities, enhance professional stature, and contribute significantly to the robustness and resilience of the organizations that risk management professionals serve.

Continuing Education Requirements

In an environment that continually evolves with the advent of new regulations, technologies, and financial instruments, the mandate for continuous education in risk management cannot be overstated. Stalwarts in the field must engage in perpetual learning to maintain the validity of their certifications and, more importantly, to ensure their expertise remains relevant and actionable. The currency of knowledge serves not just as a professional requirement but as the lifeblood of effective risk management practices.

The continuing education requirements for risk management professionals are structured with the intent to enforce a regimen of learning that is both robust and responsive to market dynamics. For instance, the Global Association of Risk Professionals (GARP), governing the FRM certification, stipulates that certified professionals must earn 40 Continuing Professional Development (CPD) credits every two years to maintain their designation. These credits can be accrued through various activities, including attending industry conferences, participating in training workshops, or contributing to research and publications in the field of risk management.

Such structured educational pursuits ensure that FRM certificate holders remain conversant with the latest quantitative models, regulatory landscapes, and strategic risk management approaches. The knowledge gained through these activities ensures that financial risk professionals can navigate the complexities of market volatility, leverage emerging analytics technologies, and implement advanced risk assessment methodologies in their organizations.

Similarly, the CRM designation entails a commitment to lifelong learning, albeit with a more tailored approach to the broader spectrum of risk management. The CRM program encourages professionals to stay informed about the latest advancements in risk management strategies, insurance products, workplace safety protocols, and other areas pertinent to a comprehensive risk management approach. Certified Risk Managers are expected to undertake a minimum number of educational hours in approved programs to keep their certification current.

Continuing education for risk managers is not limited to formal settings or structured courses. It also encompasses on-the-job learning experiences such as cross-functional project participation, leadership in risk management initiatives, and mentorship roles that foster knowledge sharing within organizations. The synthesis of formal education and practical experiences shapes a more holistic and nuanced understanding of risk that transcends theoretical knowledge.

As risk managers forge ahead in their careers, the requirement for continuous education becomes an integral part of their professional development. These educational activities are not merely a compliance checklist but a strategic investment in their intellectual capital—an investment that pays dividends in the form of enhanced decision-making capabilities, improved risk mitigation outcomes, and a fortified reputation as leaders in the field of risk management.

Consequently, the continuous education of risk management professionals is a testament to their commitment to excellence and their foresight in preparing for the uncertain tides of the future. It is a professional imperative that ensures they retain their strategic edge, safeguard their organizations from unforeseen perils, and contribute meaningfully to the stability and prosperity of the financial systems they serve.

Leadership and Management Development Programs

In the crucible of modern corporate governance, the cultivation of astute leaders and managers stands paramount. The development programs designed for this purpose are not mere retreats or perfunctory training exercises but are the forges where the mettle of future leaders is tempered and tested.

These programs often commence with an introspective quest—the potential leaders must understand their own strengths and limitations. A well-structured leadership program, therefore, typically begins with a battery of assessments: psychological profiling, 360-degree feedback, and simulations that challenge their problem-solving, decision-making, and interpersonal skills.

An essential component of these programs is the focus on strategic acumen. Aspiring leaders are initiated into the art of seeing beyond the horizon, anticipating the ebb and flow of market forces, and gauging the subtle intricacies of global economic dynamics. They are taught to navigate through the labyrinth of competitive landscapes, discerning opportunities hidden within threats, and threats lurking within opportunities.

Management development programs are meticulously designed to build upon foundational leadership skills, often emphasizing specialized training for the digital age. Here, participants grapple with the latest technological tools and platforms that drive data analytics and business intelligence. They are encouraged to adopt a mindset of continuous innovation, exploring disruptive technologies such as blockchain, artificial intelligence, and internet of things (IoT) that are reshaping the industry paradigms.

The crucible of these programs is not confined to the theoretical; it extends into the realm of practical application. Case studies of triumphant turnarounds and cautionary tales of strategic missteps are dissected, with lessons meticulously drawn and assimilated. Through this methodical examination, participants cultivate the sagacity to discern the undercurrents of organizational dynamics and the foresight to steer clear of the pitfalls that have ensnared unwary businesses.

Integration of ethical decision-making is paramount, as leaders and managers are the moral compasses of their organizations. The programs delve into the philosophical as much as the fiscal, embedding principles of corporate social responsibility and ethical stewardship into the very fabric of decision-making processes. Participants are encouraged to reflect upon the wider impact of their choices, ensuring that profitability and sustainability are pursued in tandem.

To foster a culture of continuous learning, these programs often include action learning projects. Participants are tasked with addressing real-world challenges within their organizations, applying the insights gained from the program to drive tangible improvements. This hands-on approach ensures the transference of theory into practice, cementing the knowledge and skills imparted.

Upon conclusion, leadership and management development programs do not merely graduate candidates with a richer skill set; they engender a cadre of visionaries imbued with the acuity to lead, the agility to adapt, and the integrity to inspire. It is within these crucibles that the alchemy of leadership transforms the promise of potential into the gold standard of excellence.

Networking and Professional Associations

The intricate mosaic of the financial world is interwoven with a myriad of connections, each a potential conduit for knowledge exchange, opportunity, and influential partnerships. Networking in this context is an indispensable tool, a strategic endeavor that allows professionals to weave their own narratives within the broader financial industry.

Professional associations serve as the nexus for this networking, offering platforms for like-minded individuals to converge. These associations, ranging from the global to the local, operate as beacons that attract professionals from various tiers and sectors of finance, eager to engage with peers, thought leaders, and innovators.

Membership within professional associations can be likened to holding a key to a vast repository of collective wisdom. These organizations frequently facilitate a suite of events — conferences, seminars, and webinars — tailored to dissect the most pressing issues and emerging trends within financial planning and analysis. They provide a stage where theoretical knowledge meets practical insight, and where professionals can engage with the architects of financial policy, regulatory change, and technological disruption.

The value derived from networking within these associations is multifaceted. Firstly, there is the enrichment of knowledge. Professionals are afforded a front-row seat to cutting-edge research, case studies, and regulatory updates, which are crucial for maintaining the sharpness of one's expertise in a constantly evolving domain.

Secondly, the associations offer a powerful conduit for career advancement. They are fertile ground for talent scouting, where the demonstration of one's acumen can attract the attention of industry headhunters and lead to career-defining opportunities. Moreover, they often house job boards and career resources that are exclusively available to members.

Another key feature of such associations is their mentoring programs. Seasoned veterans of finance take under their wings the aspirants seeking to ascend the professional ladder. These mentor-mentee relationships are not transactional but transformational, with the transfer of tacit knowledge and the grooming of professionalism taking precedence.

Professional associations are also instrumental in advocacy and influence. They become the collective voice that represents the interests of financial professionals, engaging with policy-makers and regulatory bodies. This ensures that the practitioners' perspectives are heard and considered in the legislation that shapes the financial landscape.

Furthermore, these associations often maintain a repository

of publications — journals, newsletters, and research papers that serve as an intellectual reservoir. Staying abreast of such publications allows professionals to maintain a keen awareness of new theories, empirical studies, and analytical techniques that are propelling the industry forward.

In the realm of professional development, the associations frequently provide a suite of certifications and continuing education programs. These credentials are not just mere accolades but are emblems of one's commitment to excellence and professional growth.

The symbiotic relationship between networking and professional associations is thus clear. Being active in these communities can catalyze one's professional journey, providing avenues for growth, learning, and influence that are far greater than what could be achieved in isolation.

Role of Ethics in Risk Management

In an era where businesses are increasingly scrutinized for their ethical conduct, the role of ethics in risk management has ascended to a critical component of corporate governance. Ethical risk management is not just a defensive measure against reputational damage; it is a proactive strategy to cultivate trust and ensure long-term sustainability.

Ethical considerations in risk management extend beyond mere compliance with laws and regulations. They reflect the moral compass of an organization, guiding decision-making processes and the behavior of individuals at all levels. In this light, the development of an ethical framework within risk management is akin to creating a blueprint for organizational integrity.

The foundation of ethical risk management lies in the establishment of a code of conduct. This document serves as the cornerstone, outlining the principles and values that shape the corporate ethos. It sets the standard for acceptable behavior and provides a clear reference point for employees when encountering ethical dilemmas.

This code must be underpinned by policies that address specific areas of risk, such as conflicts of interest, bribery and corruption, data privacy, and fair dealing. Each policy needs to be crafted with precision, considering the nuances of the business and the myriad of challenges it may face in the operational landscape.

The efficacy of an ethical risk management strategy is heavily reliant on a top-down approach. Leadership must exemplify the values espoused in the code of conduct, setting a tone of ethical excellence that permeates the corporate hierarchy. This is not solely the purview of the CEO; board members, executives, and managers all play a pivotal role as ethical stewards.

Whistleblowing mechanisms are a critical facet of ethical risk management. They empower employees to report unethical behaviors safely and anonymously. Such mechanisms must be paired with a culture that encourages open communication and views whistleblowing as a protective measure for the company's health, rather than a betrayal of corporate loyalty.

Training and education are essential in cementing ethical practices within an organization. Regular sessions that review ethical scenarios, reinforce the code of conduct, and update employees on changes to policies are critical. They ensure a shared understanding and readiness to act ethically, regardless of the business circumstances.

Monitoring and auditing systems are the sensors that detect ethical lapses and areas of potential risk. They are instrumental in the early identification of issues, allowing for swift corrective action. Furthermore, they serve as a deterrent, as the knowledge of stringent oversight influences behavior and decision-making.

The role of ethics in risk management also extends to third-party relationships. Due diligence in selecting suppliers, partners, and clients must include an assessment of their ethical practices. Aligning with entities that share similar values amplifies the ethical stance of the organization and mitigates the risk of association with unethical practices.

In the broader context of risk management in FP&A, ethical considerations intersect with financial integrity. Accurate reporting, transparent financial practices, and prudent investment decisions are all reflective of an organization's ethical fabric. They inspire confidence among stakeholders — investors, customers, and employees alike — that the organization is not just financially sound, but morally robust.

In synthesizing the role of ethics within risk management, it becomes evident that ethics act as both a shield and a beacon — protecting the organization from internal and external threats while guiding it towards a future where ethical integrity is synonymous with corporate success. The subsequent sections will continue to unravel the intricate interplay between ethics and risk, reinforcing the narrative that ethical risk management is not a subsidiary task but a central pillar of contemporary corporate strategy.

Ethical Considerations in Risk Decisions

Navigating the complex landscape of risk decisions requires a compass that points beyond profit margins and shareholder returns—it demands an unwavering commitment to ethical principles. These principles act as a bulwark against the myopia of short-term gains, ensuring that each decision made is not only financially prudent but also morally defensible.

Within the realm of FP&A, risk decisions are multifaceted, requiring astute judgement and foresight. Ethical considerations in this domain take on a profound significance, as they have the capacity to influence not only the immediate financial outcomes but also the long-term reputation and viability of the organization.

The ethical dimensions of risk decisions manifest in various forms. One primary consideration is the transparency of reporting. The integrity of financial statements and communications with stakeholders is paramount. To obscure or manipulate data for the sake of presenting a more favorable outlook is not only unethical but also potentially damaging in the long run. Transparency engenders trust and solidifies the organization's credibility in the eyes of its stakeholders.

Another ethical consideration is the equitability of the outcomes resulting from risk decisions. This pertains to the distribution of benefits and detriments amongst stakeholders, including employees, customers, suppliers, and the community at large. Decisions that disproportionately benefit one group at the expense of another, or that unfairly distribute risk, can erode the moral fabric of an organization.

In the pursuit of growth and profitability, organizations might be tempted to engage in aggressive strategies that entail high levels of risk. Herein lies an ethical conundrum: how much risk is reasonable, and at what point does the pursuit of financial gain cross the line into recklessness? Ethically sound risk decisions should be balanced, informed by a thorough analysis of potential consequences, and aligned with the organization's core values and risk appetite.

The consideration of environmental and social impacts also represents a crucial ethical dimension in risk decision-making. FP&A professionals must weigh the potential environmental ramifications of their strategies and consider how their decisions might affect the community and society at large. It is a recognition that the organization's operations and choices are interconnected with a broader ecosystem, and there is an ethical imperative to uphold sustainable and socially responsible practices.

Furthermore, ethical considerations in risk decisions extend to the realm of compliance. While adherence to laws and regulations is foundational, ethical decision-making transcends legal compliance. It involves a proactive approach to risk management, anticipating changes in the regulatory landscape, and embedding ethical considerations into the decision-making framework before they become legal imperatives.

An organization's approach to risk is also reflective of its ethical stance. For instance, the deployment of sophisticated financial instruments such as derivatives must be undertaken with a clear understanding of their complexity and the ethical implications of their use. The misuse of such instruments can lead to significant ethical breaches, as history has shown.

Ethical risk decisions are ultimately a reflection of the leadership's values and the culture they instill. It is therefore incumbent upon leaders to foster an environment where ethical considerations are integral to the decision-making process. This can be achieved through clear communication of ethical standards, the provision of training and resources to support ethical decision-making, and the establishment of accountability mechanisms to ensure these standards are upheld.

In the intricate mosaic of risk management, ethical considerations act as the threads that add both strength and texture—fortifying decisions against the pressures of expediency and contributing to a mosaic that is both resilient and respected. As we thread our way through the succeeding sections, we shall continue to delve deeper into the practical applications of ethics in risk management, solidifying the understanding that ethical conduct is not merely an adjunct to business strategy, but an integral part of achieving sustainable success.

Creating an Ethical Code of Conduct

In the intricate web of financial decisions and risk management, an ethical code of conduct serves as the guiding star for navigating the often murky waters of corporate governance. Crafting such a code is not merely an exercise in compliance; it is the embodiment of an organization's commitment to integrity, accountability, and sustainability.

The process of creating an ethical code of conduct commences with defining the core values that underpin the organization's mission and vision. These values might include honesty, respect, fairness, and responsibility. Each value must then be translated into actionable principles that provide clear direction for behavior and decision-making across all levels of the organization.

An effective ethical code of conduct is both aspirational and practical. It articulates a vision for the highest standards of ethical behavior while also providing concrete guidelines for handling specific situations. This might encompass conflict of interest policies, guidelines for confidentiality, and protocols for transparent financial reporting.

In the sphere of risk management within FP&A, an ethical code of conduct must address the nuances of financial risk-taking. It should delineate acceptable levels and types of risk, ensuring that they align with both the organization's strategic objectives and its ethical principles. In doing so, the code becomes a crucial tool for maintaining the delicate balance between innovation and prudence.

Developing an ethical code of conduct is only the beginning —it must be embedded into the fabric of the organization to be effective. This requires a multifaceted approach, beginning with the endorsement and active support from top leadership. Leadership sets the tone for ethical behavior and must be seen to not only endorse the code but also adhere to it in their actions.

To disseminate the code throughout the organization, a comprehensive communication strategy is essential. This can include training programs, workshops, and regular discussions that reinforce the importance of ethics and the practical application of the code. These initiatives should aim to move beyond mere understanding to fostering a culture where employees feel empowered to make ethical decisions autonomously.

Moreover, the ethical code of conduct must be a living document, one that evolves with the changing tides of the business landscape, regulatory changes, and societal expectations. Regular reviews and updates ensure the code remains relevant and continues to reflect the highest ethical standards.

Accountability mechanisms are crucial for upholding the code of conduct. This includes establishing clear reporting channels for unethical behavior, protective measures for whistleblowers, and fair processes for investigating and addressing ethical breaches. Such systems must be transparent and impartial to maintain trust and credibility.

In the context of FP&A, an ethical code of conduct also emphasizes the role of accurate and ethical financial modeling, risk assessment, and forecasting. It guides professionals in maintaining the highest levels of integrity in their analyses and projections, avoiding the manipulation of data that could lead to erroneous or unethical risk-taking behaviors.

Creating an ethical code of conduct is more than a procedural necessity; it is the cornerstone of ethical corporate culture. When effectively implemented, it not only guides individuals in making ethical decisions but also shapes the collective conscience of the organization, fostering a legacy of integrity that transcends financial statements and profit margins. As we continue to navigate the subtleties of risk management in subsequent sections, the pervading influence of a well-crafted ethical code will become manifestly apparent—demonstrating its critical role in shaping decisions that are both ethically sound and strategically astute.

Dealing with Ethical Dilemmas

In an ever-shifting landscape of financial planning and analysis, ethical dilemmas are not only inevitable but are also critical tests of an organization's moral compass. Dealing with these dilemmas requires more than just a cursory nod to established norms; it necessitates a nuanced understanding of ethics in the context of complex financial environments.

Ethical dilemmas in FP&A often arise at the intersection of conflicting interests, where the right course of action may not be immediately apparent. They challenge professionals to weigh the consequences of decisions that can affect stakeholders, the organization, and the broader economic ecosystem. To navigate these quandaries effectively, a structured approach is pivotal.

Initially, it is essential to identify and articulate the dilemma clearly. FP&A professionals must ask themselves what values are in conflict and why this situation qualifies as an ethical dilemma. This clarity lays the groundwork for a systematic evaluation of options.

Once the dilemma is outlined, the next step is to assess the potential courses of action. This involves a rigorous analysis of the financial implications, the impact on stakeholder relationships, and the alignment with the organization's ethical code of conduct. Options must be evaluated not only for their immediate outcomes but also for their long-term repercussions.

Engaging in stakeholder consultation can provide diverse perspectives that may not be evident from a purely financial viewpoint. It can also foster a sense of inclusivity and transparency in the decision-making process. FP&A professionals should consider the views of investors, employees, customers, and other relevant parties who could be affected by the decision.

In dealing with ethical dilemmas, it is crucial to apply ethical theories and principles such as utilitarianism, deontology, and virtue ethics to frame potential solutions. These theories can offer a philosophical lens through which to view the dilemma, aiding in the discernment of the most ethically sound option.

FP&A professionals must navigate through this complexity with a forward-looking gaze. They should anticipate the potential narrative that will unfold from their decisions and consider the precedents they set. This includes being mindful of how decisions will be perceived externally, as public perception can significantly impact an organization's reputation and trustworthiness.

Documentation and rationale are vital components when dealing with ethical dilemmas. Decisions should be recorded with comprehensive justification, illustrating the thought process behind them. This not only provides a reference for future dilemmas but also serves as a safeguard against ethical drift, ensuring accountability and consistency in ethical decision-making.

At times, despite best efforts, ethical dilemmas may lead to situations with no clear resolution. In such cases, FP&A professionals must possess the resilience to make difficult choices, sometimes under considerable pressure. The decision-making process should remain transparent and be communicated effectively to all parties involved.

Ultimately, dealing with ethical dilemmas is a testament to an organization's integrity. It is a diligent exercise in balancing financial acuity with moral judgment. As we delve deeper into the various facets of risk management, the importance of a solid ethical foundation in dealing with such dilemmas becomes increasingly evident. It is through these challenging decisions that the true ethical character of an organization is both tested and fortified, underscoring the importance of ethics in sustaining a robust and principled approach to FP&A.

The Importance of Whistleblowing Mechanisms

Whistleblowing mechanisms serve as an organization's early warning system, a means by which potential threats to integrity and compliance can be identified and addressed before they escalate into full-blown crises. Within the domain of financial planning and analysis (FP&A), the establishment of robust whistleblowing protocols is not just a legal safeguard; it's a strategic imperative that underpins the ethical standing and resilience of the financial function.

To dissect the theoretical underpinnings of whistleblowing, one must first appreciate its role as a corrective force within the corporate structure. It's a process designed to encourage and protect those who have the courage to speak out against unethical or illegal activities. In doing so, it upholds the principles of transparency and accountability that are foundational to trust and good governance.

The design of effective whistleblowing mechanisms must be guided by the principles of confidentiality, impartiality, and protection. Confidentiality ensures that the identity of the whistleblower is shielded, reducing the risk of retaliation and fostering a culture where individuals feel secure in reporting malfeasance. Impartiality is achieved through the establishment of independent channels and committees responsible for investigating reported concerns, which helps to mitigate bias and conflicts of interest. Protection extends beyond keeping the whistleblower's identity secret; it also involves safeguarding them from any form of reprisal or discrimination because of their actions.

FP&A professionals must be adept at integrating these whistleblowing mechanisms into the broader risk management framework. They need to ensure that such systems are not only in place but are also well-communicated, accessible, and trusted by all members of the organization. Training and education play a crucial role in this regard, equipping employees with the knowledge to recognize ethical breaches and understand the procedures for reporting them.

The theoretical rationale for these mechanisms is underpinned by several bodies of research, including agency theory, which posits that whistleblowing can serve as a check on agents who might otherwise act contrary to the best interests of their principals (the shareholders). From a utilitarian perspective, whistleblowing can be seen to promote the greatest good by preventing harm to the organization and its stakeholders.

While the conceptual framework for whistleblowing is well established, its application in FP&A requires careful consideration of the unique financial risks and ethical challenges inherent in this field. These include complex accounting practices, financial reporting, regulatory compliance, and the potential for conflicts of interest. The FP&A function, therefore, must ensure that whistleblowing mechanisms are not only attuned to these specific risks but also integrated into financial training and reporting systems.

In practice, whistleblowing mechanisms should feature a clear, stepwise reporting process, from the initial disclosure to the final resolution. This involves setting up dedicated communication channels such as hotlines, web-based platforms, or secure messaging systems. Upon receiving a report, the responsible committee must act swiftly to assess the credibility of the information and determine the appropriate response, whether it be an internal investigation or referral to external authorities.

The rigorous documentation of the whistleblowing process is crucial, providing a detailed audit trail that can be critical in the event of regulatory scrutiny or legal proceedings. It also serves to refine the mechanism itself, offering insights that can be used to enhance the system over time.

In conclusion, whistleblowing mechanisms are indispensable in safeguarding the financial health and ethical integrity of an organization. They enable FP&A professionals to act proactively in detecting and addressing risks that could undermine the organization's financial standing and reputation. As part of a comprehensive risk management strategy, whistleblowing mechanisms play a pivotal role in fostering an ethical culture, ensuring that the practice of FP&A remains not only strategically sound but also steadfastly principled.

CHAPTER 12: FUTURE TRENDS AND INNOVATIONS IN RISK MANAGEMENT FOR FP&A

In the constantly evolving terrain of financial planning and analysis, the future portends a landscape where risk management not only reacts to change but anticipates it with precision. As we peer into the horizon of FP&A, several emerging trends and innovations are set to redefine the efficacy and scope of risk management.

At the forefront of these advancements is the maturation of data analytics and its integration with machine learning and artificial intelligence. The predictive capabilities afforded by these technologies are poised to transform risk assessment from a historically reactive task to a proactive strategy. Algorithms trained on vast datasets can identify subtle patterns and correlations that elude traditional analysis, flagging potential risks before they crystallize into tangible threats.

Another significant innovation on the rise is the application of blockchain technology in risk management. Blockchain's distributed ledger system offers a new paradigm for transparency and security, making it easier to trace transactions and validate the authenticity of financial records. This can significantly diminish the risk of fraud and errors in financial reporting, and it introduces a new level of confidence in the veracity of financial data.

Furthermore, the interconnectedness of global markets and the acceleration of digital transformation have given rise to cyber risk as a central concern for FP&A professionals. As financial operations rely increasingly on digital infrastructure, the potential impact of cyber incidents grows commensurately. This trend underscores the need for robust cybersecurity measures, including real-time monitoring and response protocols, to safeguard against data breaches and system intrusions that can have severe financial repercussions.

The integration of environmental, social, and governance (ESG) factors into risk management reflects a broader shift in corporate philosophy. FP&A professionals are beginning to recognize that risks related to climate change, social responsibility, and corporate governance can significantly affect an organization's financial performance and investor relations. Accordingly, risk management strategies are expanding to include ESG metrics and sustainability assessments, ensuring that FP&A practices remain aligned with evolving stakeholder values and regulatory landscapes.

Advances in risk management are also expected to benefit from the adoption of more sophisticated financial instruments. Tools such as stress testing, scenario analysis, and Value at Risk (VaR) models are becoming more refined, allowing FP&A teams to simulate a wide range of adverse conditions and their potential impacts on financial outcomes. These instruments help organizations prepare for volatility and adverse market conditions, ensuring they remain resilient in the face of uncertainty.

The future of risk management in FP&A also points to a more integrated approach to strategic planning. Risk considerations are being woven into the fabric of strategic decision-making processes, enabling organizations to balance risk and opportunity more effectively. This trend is supported by the development of risk-adjusted performance metrics that provide a more nuanced view of the organization's risk profile and its alignment with long-term strategic goals.

Lastly, the role of the Chief Financial Officer (CFO) is set to expand significantly, with risk management becoming an integral part of the CFO's remit. The CFO of the future will not only be tasked with safeguarding the organization's financial health but also with predicting and navigating the complex interplay of financial, strategic, and operational risks. This positions the CFO as a key architect of the organization's future, embedding a culture of risk awareness across all levels of the enterprise.

In sum, the future of risk management in FP&A is shaping up to be a dynamic confluence of technological innovation, strategic integration, and advanced financial instrumentation. These trends and innovations promise to enhance the foresight and agility of FP&A professionals, equipping them to steer their organizations through the uncertain waters of the future with confidence and acumen.

Emerging Risks and Global Trends

As the sentinel of an organization's financial future, the financial planning and analysis (FP&A) function must remain vigilant to the drumbeat of change that reverberates through the global economic and technological landscapes. Emerging risks and global trends present both formidable challenges and unprecedented opportunities for FP&A professionals, demanding a reimagined risk management playbook attuned to the subtleties of an increasingly complex world.

One of the most salient emerging risks is the rise of geopolitical instability. Across continents, shifting political alliances, trade disputes, and regulatory upheavals have the potential to unsettle markets and disrupt supply chains. FP&A teams must sharpen their geopolitical acumen, incorporating geopolitical risk assessments into their financial models and strategic forecasts to mitigate the adverse effects of instability on their organization's operations and investments.

The specter of economic volatility looms large as central banks around the world grapple with the dual challenges of inflation and economic growth. Currency fluctuations, interest rate risks, and the specter of recession require FP&A functions to adopt agile financial strategies that can pivot in response to monetary policy shifts and economic indicators. Scenario analysis becomes a vital tool, allowing FP&A professionals to explore the financial implications of diverse economic trajectories and to devise contingency plans for each potential outcome.

Technological disruptions, particularly those propelled by advancements such as the Internet of Things (IoT), 5G connectivity, and the proliferation of artificial intelligence, reshape the risk landscape with their dual-edged sword. While they offer remarkable opportunities for efficiency gains and data-driven insights, they also introduce new vulnerabilities, including cybersecurity threats and the risk of rapid obsolescence. FP&A units must monitor these technology trends, evaluating their impact on the organization's business model and incorporating them into both risk management frameworks and capital investment decisions.

In concert with these technological shifts, demographic changes and labor market transformations are altering consumption patterns and talent pipelines. Aging populations in developed economies and the rise of the millennial and Gen Z workforce are shifting the dynamics of consumer markets and employee expectations. FP&A must adjust its risk assessments and financial projections to account for these demographic shifts and to ensure that the organization can attract and retain the necessary talent to drive future growth.

Systemic risks, such as the threat of pandemics, have also emerged as a core concern, as evidenced by the global impact of COVID-19. The ripple effects of such health crises on economic activity, consumer behavior, and supply chains have highlighted the need for robust business continuity planning and the integration of health risk assessments into the FP&A function. This necessitates a multidisciplinary approach, drawing on insights from public health data and macroeconomic trends to fortify the organization against the financial fallout from future systemic risks.

In embracing these emerging risks and global trends, FP&A professionals are called to exercise a blend of foresight, adaptability, and strategic acumen. This requires a holistic view of the risk landscape, one that synthesizes diverse data streams and deploys advanced analytical tools to anticipate and mitigate risks. The future of FP&A lies in its ability to navigate these complexities, transforming challenges into strategic advantages and securing the organization's place within the ever-shifting mosaic of the global economy.

Geopolitical Instability and Economic Volatility

In the realm of FP&A, the capacity to foresee and navigate the treacherous waters of geopolitical instability and economic volatility stands paramount. These twin harbingers of uncertainty can precipitate rapid and often unpredictable changes in the financial landscapes, necessitating a profound theoretical and practical understanding of their undercurrents.

Geopolitical instability, a mosaic of international tensions, conflicts, and alliances, directly impacts global trade patterns, resource availability, and investment climates. For the FP&A professional, this translates into a need for vigilance and the development of a nimble financial strategy. Companies must continually assess the political climate in regions of operation or influence, keenly observing elections, policy shifts, and international relations to preempt and prepare for potential disruptions.

Economic volatility, on the other hand, presents a fluctuating panorama of market conditions influenced by a myriad of factors, including but not limited to shifts in consumer sentiment, labor market dynamics, commodity prices, and macroeconomic policies. The agile FP&A function employs econometric modeling and real-time data analytics to parse these variables, crafting financial strategies that weather the storms of market turbulence.

To mitigate the impact of geopolitical shifts, FP&A experts delve into the art of scenario planning—developing a suite of financial projections that reflect a range of possible future states. This involves creating and continuously updating detailed financial models that simulate the effects of various geopolitical events, from trade embargoes and sanctions to shifts in foreign policy and regional conflicts.

Furthermore, sensitivity analysis becomes an indispensable technique in gauging the resilience of a company's financial position to sudden shocks. By systematically varying key inputs and assumptions, FP&A practitioners can identify and quantify the potential impact on revenue streams, cost structures, and ultimately, the bottom line.

Understanding economic volatility requires a comprehensive approach, combining macroeconomic forecasting with microeconomic insights. FP&A teams must integrate data on business cycles, interest rate movements, inflation trends, and currency exchange rates into their financial modeling exercises. The use of sophisticated tools such as vector autoregressive models allows for the inclusion of multiple interdependent time-series variables, enhancing the accuracy of economic forecasts.

The FP&A function also benefits from harnessing the predictive power of leading indicators—economic metrics that signal future changes in the economic cycle. These indicators offer an early warning system, enabling proactive adjustments to financial plans and investment strategies. FP&A professionals must maintain a curated set of leading indicators, tailored to the specific sectors and geographies relevant to their company's operations.

In this environment of heightened uncertainty, risk management takes on an elevated role within FP&A. The function must not only identify and assess potential risks but also develop robust risk mitigation strategies. This includes diversifying investments, securing flexible supply chains, and implementing hedging strategies to insulate against currency and commodity price fluctuations.

The interplay between geopolitical instability and economic volatility requires FP&A professionals to adopt a holistic view, one that factors in the complex web of interdependencies that characterize the global economy. It is through this intricate understanding and strategic application of financial theories and tools that FP&A can guide organizations to thrive amidst the unpredictability of the global market landscape.

Technology-driven Disruptions (e.g., IoT, 5G, AI)

The crescendo of technological innovation resonates through every facet of global business, bringing with it a symphony of disruption that FP&A must not only harmonize with but also anticipate and harness. The advent of the Internet of Things (IoT), the rollout of 5G networks, and advancements in Artificial Intelligence (AI) represent a triad of technological forces poised to reshape the financial landscape.

IoT stands as a paradigm-shifting force in data collection and operational efficiency. An interconnected web of devices and sensors provides FP&A professionals with real-time, granular data previously unattainable. This influx of information feeds into predictive models, refining demand forecasting, optimizing inventory levels, and reducing operational costs. IoT's ability to provide instantaneous feedback loops allows for more dynamic and responsive budgeting processes, where financial plans can adapt to the operational realities of production cycles and consumer behavior.

The proliferation of 5G technology accelerates this data-driven transformation, offering unprecedented communication speeds and reliability. With lower latency and greater bandwidth, 5G expands the capabilities of mobile networks to support the vast data requirements of modern FP&A functions. Financial Analysts can leverage 5G to facilitate faster and more secure financial transactions, enable real-time analytics, and support the deployment of AI at the edge of corporate networks. This enhanced connectivity empowers FP&A teams to engage in more sophisticated and complex financial simulations and stress testing, ensuring that strategic decisions are informed by the most current and comprehensive data sets.

AI's role in driving financial innovation cannot be overstated. Advanced AI algorithms, through machine learning and deep learning, are revolutionizing FP&A by enabling predictive insights that transcend traditional analysis. AI can detect patterns and correlations within vast data sets that human analysts might overlook, offering a competitive edge in risk management and decision-making. FP&A teams can employ AI to enhance the accuracy of financial forecasts, personalize customer experiences, and automate routine tasks, freeing human capital to focus on strategic initiatives.

When considering the impact of AI, one must delve into the realm of cognitive automation—AI systems that can perform complex tasks which typically require human intuition. These systems can analyze market trends, regulatory changes, and competitive dynamics, providing FP&A professionals with actionable insights. The integration of AI into financial models also introduces dynamic learning capabilities; models can adjust their parameters in real time as they assimilate new data, leading to continuously improving forecasts and risk assessments.

The synthesis of IoT, 5G, and AI heralds a new era for FP&A, where the financial planning cycle is no longer static but an ever-evolving narrative shaped by real-time information and cutting-edge analysis. The FP&A function must embrace these technological disruptions, investing in the infrastructure, talent, and analytical tools necessary to capitalize on their potential. This entails fostering a culture of innovation within the finance team, where experimentation and adoption of new technologies are encouraged and supported.

Moreover, as these technologies become more pervasive, FP&A professionals must remain vigilant of the potential risks they introduce, such as cybersecurity threats and data privacy concerns. The function needs to work closely with IT departments to ensure robust security protocols are in place and to navigate the complex regulatory landscape that governs the use of such technologies.

Ultimately, the intersection of IoT, 5G, and AI with FP&A represents a frontier of unparalleled opportunity—a chance to redefine the parameters of financial analysis and elevate the strategic value of the function. By embracing these technological disruptions, FP&A can serve as a pivotal agent of transformation, steering organizations toward a future of informed decision-making and sustained financial health.

Demographic Shifts and Labor Market Changes

In this ever-evolving mosaic of global financial landscapes, demographic shifts and labor market changes stand as pivotal variables in the calculus of FP&A. They are silent, yet profound, currents reshaping the substratum of how organizations plan, forecast, and strategize. The demographic transformations sweep across nations, altering consumer bases, workforce composition, and ultimately, the financial fabric that FP&A professionals must navigate.

Graying populations in developed economies present a dual-edged sword. On one side, there's an expanding market for products and services tailored to older individuals—a demographic with significant purchasing power. On the other, this shift heralds a contracting workforce, straining pension systems, healthcare provisions, and leading to a reassessment of long-term financial obligations by organizations. FP&A must, therefore, incorporate these changing consumer and labor dynamics into their forecasts and strategic plans, ensuring that product portfolios and investment strategies align with these societal trends.

Emerging markets, conversely, experience a youth bulge, characterized by a growing number of young consumers entering the job market. This demographic shift opens new avenues for business expansion and workforce development. However, it equally imposes a responsibility on FP&A to forecast and manage the implications of such growth —investing in talent acquisition and development, and catering to the changing consumption patterns of this younger demographic. Companies positioned to capitalize on this burgeoning consumer segment can reap the benefits of scale and growth, provided their financial plans remain agile and responsive to the rapid pace of change.

Technological advancements and the gig economy are reshaping labor market structures, ushering in an era marked by flexibility and fluidity. The rise of remote work and freelance opportunities disrupts traditional employment models, prompting FP&A teams to recalibrate assumptions about staffing, overheads, and operational costs. With a growing segment of the workforce eschewing conventional employment for the autonomy of gig work, companies must adjust their labor cost models and consider the implications for employee engagement, loyalty, and intellectual capital retention.

Another facet of this changing landscape is the intensifying war for talent, particularly in sectors buoyed by technological innovation. As skills shortages become more pronounced, FP&A must take a proactive role in forecasting the costs associated with attracting and retaining top-tier talent. This includes mapping out competitive salary structures, benefits packages, and professional development opportunities. Moreover, FP&A professionals must work in concert with human resources to quantify the financial impact of training programs and the return on investment for upskilling initiatives.

The confluence of demographic shifts and labor market changes necessitates a forward-looking and adaptable approach to FP&A. Financial planning no longer merely extrapolates from historical data but must now embrace sophisticated modeling that accounts for the probabilistic nature of these trends. This involves leveraging predictive analytics and scenario-based planning to evaluate a range of outcomes and their respective financial implications.

FP&A functions must also cultivate a close relationship with data scientists and economists to harness demographic data and labor market analysis. By integrating this external expertise, financial models can more accurately reflect the potential impact of societal changes on business operations and financial performance.

The flux of demographics and labor markets invites FP&A to not just observe but also participate in steering the strategic direction of organizations. It commands a holistic view, where financial planning integrates cross-disciplinary insights, aligns with shifts in the global workforce, and anticipates the needs of a transforming consumer base. Through this lens, FP&A can bolster an organization's adaptability and resilience, ensuring its financial strategies are robust enough to thrive amidst the undulating contours of demographic and labor market evolution.

Pandemics and Other Systemic Risks

The stark reality of systemic risks, particularly pandemics, has imprinted itself indelibly on the consciousness of FP&A professionals. The financial upheavals triggered by such global events underscore the necessity for financial planning that is not only robust but also resilient to shocks that reverberate across industries and borders. These systemic risks demand a re-envisioning of risk management protocols and a more intricate theoretical approach to financial analysis.

Pandemics, as we've seen with the recent COVID-19 crisis, can precipitate a cascade of economic disruptions—halted production, fractured supply chains, volatile markets, and seismic shifts in consumer behavior. The resultant financial turbulence compels FP&A professionals to extend their horizons beyond conventional risk assessment models. It calls for a nuanced understanding of how interconnected and interdependent global systems can spawn financial uncertainties that ripple through time, sectors, and geographies.

The theoretical framework for addressing pandemics within FP&A pivots on several key considerations. Firstly, there's the need for dynamic financial models that can rapidly assimilate new data and provide real-time insights into the fiscal impact of unfolding health crises. These models must factor in government interventions, such as lockdowns and fiscal stimulus, as well as shifts in consumer sentiment and behavior, all of which have profound implications for revenue projections and cash flow analyses.

Secondly, scenario analysis emerges as a critical tool in the FP&A arsenal. The unpredictability of pandemics necessitates a range of scenarios that consider varying degrees of outbreak severity, durations, and policy responses. These scenarios must be stress-tested for their financial impact, enabling organizations to craft contingency plans that address potential liquidity crunches, solvency concerns, and the need for emergency funding.

Another theoretical facet is the examination of supply chain vulnerabilities. Pandemics can expose the fragility of globally dispersed supply networks, prompting a reevaluation of just-in-time inventory practices and the financial advantages of nearshoring or diversification of supply sources. FP&A must, therefore, integrate supply chain risk assessments into financial forecasts, modeling the cost implications of supply disruptions, and the potential benefits of alternative sourcing strategies.

The broader category of systemic risks extends beyond pandemics to encompass financial market crashes, geopolitical conflicts, and environmental disasters—each presenting unique challenges to FP&A. Financial planners must therefore consider cross-risk synergies and the potential for risk contagion. For instance, a market downturn can exacerbate the economic impact of a pandemic by restricting access to capital or increasing the cost of borrowing.

Addressing systemic risks also involves a keen focus on resilience planning. FP&A must champion the financial viability of diversified revenue streams, the preservation of capital reserves, and the assessment of insurance coverages that mitigate financial loss during large-scale disruptions. This requires a strategic alignment with risk management functions to ensure that financial planning is informed by a comprehensive appraisal of systemic risk exposures and mitigation strategies.

Furthermore, considering systemic risks, FP&A needs to advocate for organizational agility—the capacity to pivot operations and financial strategies swiftly in response to crises. This agility is underpinned by investments in technology that enable remote work, digital transformation initiatives that safeguard against operational paralysis, and financial policies that allow for rapid resource reallocation in times of need.

In synthesizing the theoretical and practical aspects of systemic risk management, FP&A can transcend traditional financial paradigacy. It becomes a proactive, predictive function, one that harnesses advanced analytics and scenario planning to navigate the volatile waters of global crises. By embedding systemic risk considerations into financial planning, FP&A fortifies an organization's financial health, ensuring its robustness and readiness to withstand and rebound from the shocks of pandemics and other systemic challenges.

The Evolving Role of the CFO in Risk Management

In the tempest of contemporary business, where risks are as variegated as they are volatile, the role of the Chief Financial Officer (CFO) has undergone a profound metamorphosis. Traditionally seen as the corporate sentinel of budgets and balance sheets, the modern CFO has transcended this archetype to become an integral architect of risk management strategy. This transformation is not only a response to the changing landscape of global business but also a proactive embrace of the potential that strategic risk management holds for value creation.

The evolving role of the CFO in risk management is characterized by a shift from a focus on financial stewardship to a broader mandate that encompasses strategic leadership and enterprise risk oversight. The CFO's purview now extends to identifying, assessing, and mitigating risks that could impede the organization's strategic objectives. This expanded role necessitates a deeper collaboration with other C-suite executives, ensuring that risk management is infused into every facet of organizational strategy and decision-making.

One of the catalysts for this evolution is the increased complexity and interconnectivity of risks. In an environment where financial markets are inextricably linked to geopolitical events and where technological advancements rapidly alter competitive landscapes, the CFO's ability to anticipate and navigate these risks becomes paramount. This requires a comprehensive understanding of both the external and internal risk environments and the development of sophisticated financial models that can simulate the impacts of various risk scenarios on the organization's financial health.

Incorporating risk management into strategic planning involves a more nuanced approach to risk appetite. The CFO must guide the board and executive team in defining the level of risk the organization is willing to accept in pursuit of its goals. This involves not only quantifying potential losses but also considering the potential for missed opportunities due to overly conservative risk postures. The CFO must balance prudence with boldness, leveraging risk management as a tool for strategic differentiation and competitive advantage.

The CFO's role also encompasses the championing of risk-adjusted performance measures, such as Risk-Adjusted Return on Capital (RAROC) and Economic Value Added (EVA). These measures help align risk exposure with financial performance, providing a clearer picture of how effectively the organization is managing risk in relation to its capital allocation decisions. Such metrics are instrumental in fostering a culture where risk considerations are ingrained in the decision-making processes at all levels of the organization.

Communication is another cornerstone of the CFO's expanded role. In the past, risk management discussions may have been relegated to specialist silos or confined to technical committees. Today, the CFO must ensure that risk management is a transparent and continuous dialogue across the organization. This includes educating the board on complex risk exposures, engaging with stakeholders to articulate the organization's risk posture, and reporting on risk management outcomes in a manner that is both accessible and actionable.

Moreover, the CFO must stay abreast of regulatory changes and ensure that the organization's risk management practices are compliant with evolving standards. This vigilance safeguards the organization against regulatory penalties and reputational damage, while also presenting opportunities to leverage regulatory frameworks as strategic enablers rather than mere compliance obligations.

In the digital era, the CFO's role in risk management is interwoven with technology. From the deployment of advanced data analytics for predictive risk intelligence to the integration of cybersecurity measures into financial processes, technology empowers the CFO to identify and mitigate risks with greater speed and precision. This technological adeptness must be matched with a commitment to ethical considerations, particularly as artificial intelligence and machine learning play increasingly significant roles in financial decision-making.

The future of risk management in FP&A is one where the CFO is not just a guardian of assets but a visionary strategist, a catalyst for innovation, and a communicator par excellence. By championing a holistic approach to enterprise risk management, CFOs can harness risk as a strategic asset, steering their organizations through the uncertainties of the business landscape while securing their trajectory towards sustained profitability and growth.

From Financial Overseer to Strategic Adviser

Gone are the days when the Chief Financial Officer (CFO) was confined to the back office, engrossed in ledgers and financial statements, emerging only to report on past performances. The CFO of the 21st century has ascended from the role of financial overseer to that of a strategic adviser, a profound shift catalyzed by the dynamism and complexity of modern business landscapes. This section delves into the transformative journey of the CFO, exploring the nuanced facets of their strategic advisory role and the impact on the broader enterprise.

In the matrix of today's corporate governance, the CFO emerges as a polymath, wielding a deep understanding of financial mechanics while also grasping the subtleties of cross-functional domains. The CFO's role has evolved beyond the traditional guardianship of financial integrity to encompass strategic inputs that shape the company's future. This metamorphosis involves a blend of foresight, agility, and strategic acumen, positioning the CFO as a key player in steering the organizational helm towards uncharted territories.

One significant aspect of the CFO's transfigured role is the emphasis on forward-looking insights. Rather than solely reporting historical financial data, the modern CFO interprets this data to forecast future financial scenarios. They employ predictive analytics and scenario planning to illuminate potential pathways, identifying risks and opportunities that lie ahead. This proactive approach empowers leaders to make informed decisions that align with long-term strategic goals.

The CFO's strategic advisory capacity extends to capital structure optimization, where they must skillfully balance debt and equity to fund growth initiatives while maintaining financial stability. In this capacity, they scrutinize investment proposals, ensuring that capital allocations are aligned with the organization's risk appetite and growth prospects. They also play a critical role in mergers and acquisitions, conducting due diligence and integrating financial systems to drive synergies and unlock value.

Moreover, as a strategic adviser, the CFO is pivotal in shaping corporate strategy. They provide insights that influence the company's direction, engaging in strategic planning sessions and contributing to the development of business models that are resilient in the face of volatility. Their analyses underpin strategic pivots, whether it's entering new markets, launching innovative products, or restructuring operations to enhance efficiency.

In guiding the organization's strategic financial planning, the CFO also becomes an advocate for sustainable practices, ensuring that environmental, social, and governance (ESG) principles are embedded within the financial planning process. This approach not only mitigates risks associated with sustainability concerns but also positions the company favorably in the eyes of investors, customers, and regulators who are increasingly prioritizing ESG performance.

The CFO's advisory role is not limited to the executive suite; it extends to the boardroom, where they are instrumental in articulating financial strategies and their implications. They facilitate board discussions on financial matters, translating complex financial concepts into strategic discussions that inform governance decisions. This requires the CFO to possess exceptional communication skills, enabling them to bridge the gap between financial intricacies and strategic imperatives.

In the era of digital transformation, the CFO's strategic advice is intimately tied to technological investments. They evaluate and endorse technological initiatives that drive operational efficiencies and unlock data-driven insights. The CFO's advocacy for digital tools, such as Enterprise Resource Planning (ERP) systems or advanced analytics platforms, is vital for maintaining a competitive edge and fostering a culture of innovation.

As a strategic adviser, the CFO also mentors emerging leaders within the finance function, nurturing the next generation of financial strategists. They champion professional development programs that equip their team with the necessary skills to navigate the evolving demands of the financial landscape. By investing in talent, the CFO ensures the sustainability of the finance function's strategic contribution to the organization.

The transformation from financial overseer to strategic adviser is not a mere change in title but a redefinition of the CFO's identity within the corporate fabric. It necessitates a harmonious blend of financial expertise, strategic insight, and leadership prowess. The modern CFO is a linchpin in the organization's strategic initiatives, wielding financial data as a strategic asset to inform decisions, drive change, and propel the organization towards its envisioned future.

The CFO has ascended to a role of strategic significance, no longer merely stewards of financial reports but visionaries who craft narratives of fiscal foresight and strategic sagacity. They are the oracles of economic potential, guiding their organizations through the ever-shifting tides of commerce with an unwavering commitment to both fiscal prudence and strategic boldness.

Engaging with Other C-suite Executives on Risk Issues

In an environment replete with uncertainties, the CFO's role as the principal financial guardian propels them into critical risk-centric dialogues with fellow C-suite executives. This section examines the intricate dynamics of how the CFO engages with the C-suite to navigate and mitigate risk, thereby safeguarding the organization's strategic ambitions.

Within the executive ensemble, the CFO's voice carries the weight of financial consequence, resonating through the discussions around risk management. They are essential in espousing a risk-aware culture that transcends silos, advocating for a unified approach where risk considerations are woven into every strategic thread. This collaborative stance is not about fostering consensus but about ensuring that risk is not an afterthought but a cornerstone of strategic decision-making.

The CFO's collaboration with the CTO or CIO is pivotal in addressing technological risks such as cybersecurity threats and data breaches. Together, they ascertain the organization's digital vulnerabilities and champion risk mitigation strategies that align with the technological roadmap. They work in tandem to balance innovation with risk, ensuring new tech deployments advance the organization's objectives without exposing it to undue peril.

When coordinating with the COO, the CFO brings financial acumen to operational risks. They dissect the cost-benefit analyses of operational strategies, illuminating the financial implications of production decisions, supply chain disruptions, and process optimizations. The synergy between the CFO and COO is crucial in crafting operational models that are not only efficient but also resilient in the face of potential disruptions.

The Chief Risk Officer (CRO), if the position exists, is a natural ally for the CFO in the realm of risk. Their interaction is a confluence of strategic financial planning and risk management expertise. While the CRO identifies and assesses risks, the CFO incorporates these insights into financial projections and strategic funding allocations. This partnership is crucial for developing a coherent risk appetite framework that informs business decisions at all levels.

In the dynamic landscape of market fluctuations and regulatory changes, the CFO's engagement with the Chief Legal Officer (CLO) or General Counsel is of paramount importance. The CLO provides legal perspective on risk, especially concerning compliance, litigation, and contractual obligations. The CFO relies on this legal insight to anticipate the financial impacts of regulatory shifts and to prepare for contingencies that may arise from legal challenges.

The Chief Marketing Officer (CMO) and the CFO's interaction are centered around market risk and brand reputation. The CFO evaluates the financial aspects of marketing campaigns and customer acquisition strategies, ensuring that investments in branding and market expansion are judiciously made and aligned with the company's risk-adjusted return objectives.

In matters of human capital and cultural risks, the CFO's dialogue with the Chief Human Resources Officer (CHRO) is instrumental. They scrutinize the financial aspects of talent management strategies, from workforce planning to compensation models, ensuring these initiatives are viable and contribute to a risk-conscious culture. Their collaboration is key to developing retention strategies that mitigate the risk of talent attrition, which can have significant financial repercussions.

The CFO's interaction with the C-suite culminates in the Executive Committee, where they articulate the financial narrative of risks and opportunities. Here, the CFO utilizes their unique position to foster a strategic alignment among the leadership, embedding financial risk considerations into organizational decision-making processes.

This engagement across the C-suite is not serendipitous; it is a deliberate act of leadership by the CFO, who must be adept at communicating complex financial risks in the language of each executive's domain. They must exhibit a blend of diplomatic acuity and analytical rigor to champion integrated risk management practices within the executive ranks.

The CFO's role in engaging with other C-suite executives on risk issues is thus a blend of interpreter, diplomat, and strategist. They are the nexus of financial insight and strategic risk management, ensuring the organization's leadership is cohesive, informed, and proactive in facing the multifaceted risks of today's business world.

Through these engagements, the CFO elevates the discourse on risk, transcending departmental boundaries to instill a collective sense of responsibility for the organization's financial well-being. By fostering a comprehensive, C-suite-wide perspective on risk, the CFO ensures that the company can not only withstand the storms of uncertainty but also navigate through them with strategic finesse.

The CFO's Role in Sustainability and Social Responsibility

As enterprises increasingly recognize the imperative of sustainable practices, the Chief Financial Officer (CFO) assumes a pivotal role in steering the organization towards a future that balances profitability with social responsibility. This section delves into the intricate layers of the CFO's involvement in integrating sustainability into the core financial strategy, ensuring that the organization not only thrives economically but also contributes positively to society and the environment.

The CFO's journey into the domain of sustainability begins with the acknowledgment that long-term financial health is inextricably linked to environmental stewardship and social well-being. To this end, the CFO becomes a champion of the "triple bottom line," a framework that measures the company's success not just by the traditional financial bottom line, but also by its social and environmental impact. This holistic approach necessitates a recalibration of financial strategies to include sustainability-driven investments and initiatives.

In fostering a sustainable business model, the CFO scrutinizes the financial implications of environmental risks, such as climate change and resource scarcity. They must assess and articulate the potential costs of environmental compliance, as well as the opportunities presented by sustainable technologies and practices. The CFO plays a key role in allocating capital towards green investments, such as energy-efficient infrastructure, renewable energy projects, and waste reduction programs, which can mitigate environmental risks and yield long-term cost savings.

The CFO also has a significant role in the valuation of social responsibility initiatives. They must quantify the financial benefits of programs aimed at improving labor practices, community engagement, and diversity and inclusion efforts. The CFO balances the immediate costs of these programs against the anticipated returns, such as enhanced brand reputation, customer loyalty, and the attraction and retention of top talent. These social investments are not merely ethical choices but strategic moves that drive shareholder value and create a competitive edge.

A critical aspect of the CFO's role is in sustainability reporting and disclosure. As stakeholders demand greater transparency, the CFO must ensure that the company's financial reports reflect its sustainability performance.

This involves developing metrics and key performance indicators (KPIs) that convey the organization's progress in environmental and social domains. The CFO must navigate the complexities of sustainability accounting, often working with cross-functional teams to capture and report data that accurately reflects the company's sustainable practices.

Given the increasing focus on Environmental, Social, and Governance (ESG) criteria among investors, the CFO acts as the linchpin in communicating the company's ESG narrative to the investment community. They must articulate how sustainability initiatives contribute to risk mitigation and value creation, positioning the company as a responsible investment. The CFO's adeptness in financial storytelling is crucial in aligning investor expectations with the company's sustainability journey.

The CFO's engagement with sustainability extends to capital raising and financing. They explore innovative financial instruments, such as green bonds and sustainability-linked loans, that cater to the growing market for responsible investment. These financial products often come with favorable terms, reflecting the reduced risk profile associated with sustainable business practices.

In playing an active role in the governance of sustainability initiatives, the CFO ensures that the organization's approach to sustainability is both strategic and operational. They work closely with the Chief Sustainability Officer (CSO), if one is present, to integrate sustainability goals into the business's operational fabric. This collaboration is vital for aligning financial objectives with sustainability targets and for embedding responsible practices into every level of the organization.

By leading from a position of financial acumen and strategic insight, the CFO transforms the traditional financial leadership role into one that is future-forward and ethically grounded. Through their influence, the CFO fosters a culture where sustainability and social responsibility become not just moral imperatives but integral components of the company's identity and drivers of long-term business success.

The integration of sustainability into the financial ethos represents a paradigm shift in corporate governance, with the CFO at the helm, guiding the organization towards a future where fiscal prudence and ethical stewardship coalesce to create enduring value for all stakeholders.

Preparing for the Future of Work and Organizational Design

The landscape of work is undergoing a profound transformation, driven by technological innovation, demographic shifts, and evolving cultural norms. As companies navigate this terrain, the Chief Financial Officer (CFO) is instrumental in preparing for the future of work and reimagining organizational design. This section unpacks the theoretical underpinnings of this pivotal role and outlines strategies to thrive in an emergent corporate epoch.

The CFO's role is no longer confined to ledger lines and fiscal reporting; it has expanded to encompass architecting an organization agile enough to embrace the future of work. This forward-looking posture requires the CFO to adopt a dual lens—focusing internally on operational design and externally on market dynamics and technological trends.

Internally, the CFO must reevaluate traditional organizational structures and hierarchies. Hierarchical models, often characterized by rigidity, are yielding to more fluid and dynamic forms—networks of teams that foster innovation and adaptability. In this vein, the CFO must anticipate and support changes in workforce allocation, championing a shift towards a matrixed environment where cross-functional teams collaborate on project-based work.

The CFO also needs to ensure that the organization's financial model can accommodate new ways of working. This entails developing budgeting practices and financial controls that support remote work, flexible hours, and gig economy partnerships. By doing so, the CFO ensures not only that the organization is financially sustainable but also that it is attractive to a more diverse and globalized talent pool.

Externally, the CFO must stay abreast of technological advancements that could disrupt industry norms and create new opportunities. Artificial intelligence (AI), robotics, and machine learning portend significant implications for productivity and workforce configuration. The CFO's strategic planning must account for these technologies' potential to automate processes, alter job functions, and spawn novel business models.

One of the main theoretical constructs guiding the CFO in this journey is the Resource-Based View (RBV) of the firm, which posits that a company's competitive advantage stems from the unique resources and capabilities it controls. The future of work demands that the CFO, through the lens of RBV, identifies and nurtures the organization's human capital as a key resource. This implies investing in upskilling initiatives, fostering a learning culture, and enabling knowledge sharing across the organization.

Another core theoretical perspective is the Dynamic Capabilities Framework, which stresses the importance of an organization's ability to integrate, build, and reconfigure internal and external competencies to address rapidly changing environments. The CFO, therefore, must champion strategic agility, ensuring that the organization's design is not static but continually evolves in response to external stimuli.

In preparing for the future of work, the CFO must also consider the implications for the company's culture and values. Organizational culture shapes workforce engagement and retention, and the CFO should advocate for a culture of inclusivity, innovation, and ethical practice that aligns with the broader transformations taking place in the working world.

The CFO's input is paramount in designing incentive structures that reflect the values and goals of the future-oriented organization. Performance metrics and reward systems will increasingly need to measure collaborative achievements, creativity, and adaptability, in addition to traditional financial outcomes.

Finally, the CFO should lead by example in embracing organizational change. By implementing new financial technologies, leveraging data analytics for strategic insight, and cultivating a transparent and communicative leadership style, the CFO sets the tone for the company's adaptive journey.

This section has explored the intricate theoretical

frameworks that underpin the CFO's role in preparing for the future of work and redesigning organizational structures. By embracing change, fostering a culture of perpetual learning, and ensuring strategic flexibility, the CFO enables the organization to harness the transformative potential of work's next horizon.

Breakthroughs in Analytics and Predictive Modeling

In the data-rich environment of modern finance, breakthroughs in analytics and predictive modeling stand as the vanguard of decision-making tools for the Chief Financial Officer (CFO). Fueling this revolution are the exponential growth in computational power, the proliferation of data, and advanced algorithmic innovations. This section delves into the intricacies of these breakthroughs and their transformative impact on financial planning and analysis (FP&A).

The theoretical bedrock of predictive analytics in finance is the combination of statistical methods, machine learning, and data mining. These methodologies enable CFOs to transcend traditional reactive strategies and to forecast future trends with remarkable precision. Predictive models help in identifying patterns within large datasets, interpreting complex relationships among multiple financial indicators, and predicting the probabilities of future events.

One of the most significant advancements in this domain is the introduction of machine learning (ML) techniques to financial modeling. ML algorithms, particularly deep learning models, have the capacity to learn from data iteratively and to improve their accuracy over time. These models can uncover non-linear dynamics in financial data that are often invisible to human analysts or traditional statistical models.

The application of ML in FP&A extends from credit scoring and fraud detection to algorithmic trading and risk management. For instance, the deployment of neural networks—a form of deep learning—has considerably enhanced the ability to model credit risk by analyzing vast amounts of unstructured data, such as social media activity and transaction histories, along with traditional credit information.

Another notable evolution in analytics is the rise of prescriptive analytics. While predictive analytics forecasts what is likely to happen, prescriptive analytics suggests actions to achieve desired outcomes. By leveraging optimization and simulation algorithms, CFOs can weigh various decision paths and strategize under uncertainty, effectively navigating through a multitude of financial scenarios and market conditions.

The integration of Big Data analytics into FP&A is also revolutionizing the field. With Big Data, CFOs can harness real-time insights from an expansive array of data sources, including market feeds, customer transactions, and IoT devices. This abundance of data empowers more granular and dynamic analyses, driving enhanced decision support systems.

Geospatial analytics has emerged as a potent tool, particularly in the realm of market expansion and operational efficiency. By mapping financial performance data to geographic locations, CFOs can visualize market penetration, optimize supply chains, and identify new growth opportunities.

The theoretical advancement that underpins this analytical progress is the Data-Information-Knowledge-Wisdom (DIKW) hierarchy. This model posits that raw data can be processed into information, which can then be interpreted into knowledge and eventually synthesized into strategic wisdom. This progression encapsulates the journey that a CFO seeks to navigate, leveraging cutting-edge analytical tools to transform data into actionable business intelligence.

As analytics and predictive modeling evolve, ethical considerations and governance of AI steadily gain prominence. CFOs are accountable for ensuring that models are transparent, fair, and compliant with regulatory standards. This oversight includes addressing biases in data and algorithms, safeguarding data privacy, and upholding the highest levels of data integrity.

Moreover, the increasing accessibility of cloud computing resources has democratized advanced analytics, enabling organizations of all sizes to deploy sophisticated predictive models without the need for substantial in-house infrastructure. This shift is leading to greater scalability and agility in FP&A functions.

In synthesizing these breakthroughs, CFOs can establish a more predictive and resilient FP&A function—one that is capable of harnessing the predictive power of analytics to inform strategic decisions. This section has examined the intricate theoretical constructs and practical applications that are shaping the future of analytics and predictive modeling in finance. As these technologies continue to mature, they promise to be a cornerstone of strategic financial management, offering unparalleled foresight and competitive edge in an ever-changing business landscape.

Next-generation AI Applications in FP&A

In the evolutionary arc of financial planning and analysis (FP&A), next-generation artificial intelligence (AI) applications represent a quantum leap forward. The fusion of FP&A with AI is a burgeoning frontier, poised to redefine the paradigms of financial forecasting, risk assessment, and strategic planning. This section explores the avant-garde applications of AI that are set to redefine the FP&A landscape.

Central to the integration of AI within FP&A is the transition from descriptive and diagnostic analytics towards more predictive and prescriptive capabilities. AI ushers in a new era of cognitive augmentation, where algorithms not only provide insights but also anticipate future states and prescribe optimal courses of action.

One of the most promising areas is the deployment of AI-driven forecasting models. Equipped with the ability to process vast datasets and learn from historical trends, these models refine forecasting accuracy. They can discern subtle patterns and signals amidst the noise of financial data, accounting for variables that range from consumer sentiment to macroeconomic indicators.

The adoption of AI in scenario planning empowers CFOs to construct and evaluate an extensive array of financial outcomes based on varying assumptions and external factors. Using generative adversarial networks (GANs), FP&A teams can simulate adversarial economic conditions and test the resilience of their financial strategies, thereby stress-testing plans against potential disruptions.

Robotic Process Automation (RPA), an AI facet, is transforming FP&A by automating routine tasks such as data entry, report generation, and compliance checks. This automation extends the bandwidth of financial analysts, allowing them to focus on more strategic activities. RPA, coupled with AI, enables the continuous updating of financial models in real-time, ensuring that FP&A outputs stay relevant and timely.

Natural Language Processing (NLP), a subset of AI, is revolutionizing how financial data is interpreted and synthesized. NLP enables the extraction of actionable insights from unstructured data such as news articles, earnings call transcripts, and social media posts. This capability vastly improves market intelligence and provides a more nuanced understanding of the factors influencing financial performance.

The integration of AI with advanced visualization tools is enhancing the interpretability of complex financial analyses. Through interactive dashboards and augmented reality interfaces, CFOs and stakeholders can engage with financial data in more intuitive and insightful ways, facilitating better-informed decision-making.

As AI applications in FP&A advance, ethical considerations and algorithmic accountability gain heightened significance. The responsible deployment of AI entails ensuring algorithmic transparency, avoiding biased decision-making, and keeping rigorous data privacy standards. To this end, explainable AI (XAI) is gaining traction, providing stakeholders with clarity on how AI models reach their conclusions.

The ongoing development of quantum computing presents tantalizing prospects for FP&A. Quantum algorithms have the potential to solve complex financial optimization problems exponentially faster than classical computers, offering new horizons in asset allocation, portfolio optimization, and risk management.

In practice, the implementation of AI in FP&A requires a robust technological infrastructure and a skilled workforce adept in data science and analytics. The cultivation of interdisciplinary teams that blend financial acumen with AI expertise is becoming indispensable for organizations looking to capitalize on these next-generation applications.

Looking ahead, next-generation AI applications hold the promise of a more predictive, responsive, and strategic FP&A function. This section has mapped out the theoretical underpinnings and practical implications of AI's transformative role in finance. As these technologies continue to evolve, they are set to become the linchpin of agile and forward-thinking financial departments, propelling organizations towards a future shaped by informed decisions and strategic foresight.

Quantum Computing's Potential Impact on Risk Analysis

The advent of quantum computing heralds an unprecedented era in the domain of risk analysis, an area within FP&A where the speed and complexity of computational tasks often stretch the limits of traditional computing resources. Quantum computing's potential to process data and perform calculations at speeds exponentially greater than classical computers can fundamentally transform the way risk is assessed, quantified, and managed.

Quantum computing's core principle is rooted in quantum mechanics, employing quantum bits, or qubits, which unlike binary bits that represent data as 0s or 1s, can exist in multiple states simultaneously through a phenomenon known as superposition. This attribute, along with entanglement, enables quantum computers to evaluate a multitude of possibilities concurrently, drastically reducing the time required for complex computations.

In the intricate realm of risk analysis, the application of quantum computing could revitalize traditional methodologies, providing FP&A professionals with tools to run incredibly sophisticated simulations and analyses. One such application is the Monte Carlo simulation, a technique used to understand the impact of risk and uncertainty in financial forecasting and decision-making. Quantum algorithms can perform these simulations with a degree of speed and accuracy that is currently unattainable, allowing for a near-real-time assessment of potential outcomes and their probabilities.

The potential impact of quantum computing extends to the optimization of portfolios, where it can analyze countless combinations of assets to find the most efficient frontier —balancing expected returns against associated risks. Quantum optimization algorithms could rapidly find the optimal asset mix, taking into account a complex set of constraints and interdependencies that would overwhelm classical computing processes.

Another area ripe for quantum computing's influence is in the assessment of credit risk. Quantum-enhanced machine learning models can process vast datasets, including market data, transaction records, and economic reports, to show subtle patterns that signal credit risk. These advanced models could significantly improve the accuracy of credit scoring and default prediction, thereby informing more strategic lending and investment decisions.

Quantum computing also holds promise for advancing value at risk (VaR) calculations, a critical metric used to assess and quantify the level of financial risk within a firm or investment portfolio over a specific period. The computational intensity needed for accurate VaR assessments, particularly for large, diversified portfolios with nonlinear risk profiles, makes it an ideal candidate for the application of quantum algorithms.

However, while the potential of quantum computing in risk analysis is immense, it is not without challenges. The nascent state of quantum technology means that practical and scalable applications in FP&A remain on the horizon, with ongoing research dedicated to overcoming current limitations such as qubit stability and error correction.

Further, the integration of quantum computing into existing risk analysis frameworks will need a paradigm shift in both technology infrastructure and workforce competencies. FP&A professionals will need to develop new skill sets to use quantum computing capabilities effectively, including familiarity with quantum algorithms and the nuances of quantum mechanics as they pertain to financial data.

The ethical and security considerations surrounding quantum computing are paramount, particularly as quantum algorithms could potentially decrypt the encryption standards that currently safeguard financial data. As such, anticipatory measures in cybersecurity must be a foundational element of the quantum computing dialogue within the FP&A community.

Quantum computing stands at the vanguard of a revolution in risk analysis, offering tools of unparalleled computational power that could reshape the financial landscape. This section has delved into the theoretical details of quantum computing's potential, painting a picture of a future where FP&A professionals can navigate the complexities of risk with a clarity and precision that transcends the capabilities of today's computing paradigms. As the quantum era approaches, it beckons FP&A to prepare for a transformative leap in risk analysis efficacy and sophistication.

Advancements in Prescriptive Analytics

The progression of prescriptive analytics is a testament to the evolution of data-driven decision-making within the sphere of financial planning and analysis (FP&A). It signifies an analytical leap beyond the predictive, offering a forward-looking vista that not only forecasts but also suggests multiple courses of action and their potential implications for the business. This section explores the nuances of prescriptive analytics advancements, proving its transformative potential for FP&A operations.

At its core, prescriptive analytics synthesizes big data, mathematical sciences, and automated machine learning algorithms to recommend actions that can lead to desired outcomes. It is the confluence of data-driven insights and pragmatic decision-making, delivering a roadmap for organizations to achieve their strategic aims while mitigating risk.

Recent advancements in this area have been catalyzed by the exponential growth in computational power and data storage capabilities, coupled with substantial refinements in algorithms and data processing techniques. One significant development is the integration of artificial intelligence (AI) and machine learning (ML) within prescriptive models, which enables them to learn from new data, adapt to changing conditions, and improve recommendations over time. This self-optimizing characteristic ensures that FP&A teams are equipped with dynamic and contextually relevant decision-support tools.

The sophistication of prescriptive analytics is further enhanced by the inclusion of simulation and optimization techniques. For instance, stochastic optimization models incorporate randomness and uncertainty directly into the decision-making process, allowing FP&A professionals to evaluate a multitude of scenarios and determine the most robust strategy in the face of volatility. This approach is particularly beneficial when dealing with financial markets, supply chain disruptions, or investment decisions under uncertainty.

Additionally, advancements in prescriptive analytics have led to the ability to process and analyze unstructured data—ranging from social media sentiment to regulatory updates—which can contain valuable signals for market movements or emerging risks. Natural Language Processing (NLP) techniques enable the extraction of actionable insights from such data, providing a more comprehensive risk profile and a deeper understanding of external factors that could impact financial outcomes.

The interactivity and user-friendliness of prescriptive analytics tools have also seen remarkable improvements. Intuitive interfaces and visualization dashboards now allow non-technical FP&A stakeholders to engage with complex analytical models, making data-driven recommendations accessible throughout the organization. This democratization of analytics empowers cross-functional teams to collaborate more effectively on strategic planning and risk management initiatives.

Moreover, advancements in edge computing and the Internet of Things (IoT) are beginning to intersect with prescriptive analytics. By harnessing real-time data directly from the source, FP&A teams can make quicker and more informed decisions on the fly, responding with agility to operational risks or market changes.

Despite these advancements, the implementation of prescriptive analytics within an organization's FP&A function is not without challenges. Ensuring data quality and integrity is paramount, as the outputs of prescriptive models are only as reliable as the inputs. There is also the need for continuous monitoring and validation of the models to prevent biases or errors from influencing the recommended actions.

The ethical implications of automated decision-making must also be carefully considered. As algorithms take on more complex decision-making roles, FP&A leaders must establish governance frameworks that ensure transparency, accountability, and ethical considerations are embedded within prescriptive analytics practices.

In conclusion, the advancements in prescriptive analytics have paved the way for a new era in FP&A—one where strategic decisions are informed by deep analytical rigor and a synthesis of data-driven recommendations. This section has provided a detailed exploration of how these advancements are reshaping the analytical landscape, offering FP&A practitioners sophisticated tools to navigate the complexities of financial decision-making and strategic risk management. As prescriptive analytics continues to evolve, it promises to unlock new horizons of efficiency and strategic advantage for organizations that embrace its potential.

Real-Time Adaptive Forecasting Methods

In an era where volatility is the only constant, the ability to anticipate and promptly respond to financial shifts is not just advantageous, but imperative. Real-time adaptive forecasting methods stand at the vanguard of this dynamic, offering FP&A professionals the tools to navigate the unpredictable flows of market currents. This section delves into the intricate mechanisms and groundbreaking advancements that characterize real-time adaptive forecasting, underscoring its pivotal role in contemporary financial strategy.

The premise of real-time adaptive forecasting is the continuous assimilation and analysis of data to update forecasts in response to new financial signals. Unlike static models that rely on periodic adjustments, these methods adjust their forecasts automatically as fresh data streams in, providing an up-to-the-minute reflection of expected financial outcomes. This agility is crucial for FP&A operations, where decisions must often be made on the fly and predicated on the latest available insights.

Central to these forecasting methods is the deployment of advanced analytics and machine learning algorithms capable of parsing vast and complex datasets. These algorithms are designed to detect patterns and correlations within the data, learning and evolving as they digest more information. The use of time-series forecasting models, such as ARIMA (AutoRegressive Integrated Moving Average) and its derivatives, has been bolstered by machine learning to enhance their predictive accuracy and responsiveness to change.

Another key feature of real-time adaptive forecasting is the integration of event-based triggers. These triggers are predefined conditions or thresholds that, when met, prompt an immediate re-evaluation of the forecast. For example, if a currency's value hits a certain level, or a stock's trading volume spikes unexpectedly, the forecasting model can recalibrate its predictions to reflect these market movements instantly.

Incorporating external data sources also enriches the forecasting model's contextual awareness. By tapping into real-time economic indicators, social media trends, geopolitical events, and even weather patterns, FP&A teams can factor in a broader spectrum of influences on financial performance. The confluence of internal financial metrics with external situational data yields a more holistic and anticipatory approach to forecasting.

The practical applications of real-time adaptive forecasting are vast—ranging from short-term liquidity management to long-term strategic planning. It allows organizations to perform what-if analyses on-the-go, testing various scenarios and their financial implications swiftly. This capability proves invaluable in stress-testing strategies against potential future states, ensuring financial resilience and preparedness.

From a technological standpoint, the implementation of cloud computing platforms has been instrumental in advancing real-time adaptive forecasting. The scalability and computational power of the cloud facilitate the handling of heavy data workloads and complex calculations, all while delivering the computational results at speed. Furthermore, the cloud enables seamless collaboration among FP&A teams, regardless of geographic dispersion, fostering a unified analytical effort.

Despite the promise of real-time adaptive forecasting, adoption is not without its challenges. The accuracy of these models is contingent on the quality of data ingested; thus, stringent data governance and validation protocols are essential. Organizations must also invest in the upskilling of their FP&A workforce, ensuring that team members possess the requisite analytical skills to interpret and act upon the models' outputs effectively.

Moreover, with the increased reliance on algorithmic forecasting, ethical concerns regarding transparency and bias mitigation come to the fore. It is crucial that FP&A leaders institute rigorous oversight mechanisms to maintain the integrity of the forecasting process and safeguard against opaque or discriminatory practices.

Real-time adaptive forecasting represents a quantum leap in the domain of financial prognostication. It equips FP&A professionals with a dynamic, intelligent, and multifaceted toolkit to cut through the fog of economic uncertainty. By embracing these contemporary forecasting methods, organizations can empower their financial decision-making with unparalleled immediacy and foresight, positioning themselves to thrive amidst the unpredictable tides of the global market.

Adapting to a Changing Regulatory Landscape

As the financial world whirls within a maelic hurricane of change—where market disruptions are matched by regulatory upheavals—FP&A leaders are tasked with a Sisyphean challenge: to stay ahead of the regulatory curve. This section articulates the strategies and insights required for FP&A teams to not merely comply with changing regulations but to leverage them as catalysts for strategic advantage.

In the financial sector, the regulatory landscape is as shifting as the dunes of the Sahara, with new legislation emerging with dizzying rapidity. This fluidity is driven by a multitude of factors: the aftershocks of financial crises, advancements in technology, and evolving societal values, all converging to shape the regulatory frameworks governing financial practices.

Navigating this terrain demands a proactive and forward-looking approach. FP&A professionals must cultivate a deep understanding of both the spirit and the letter of new regulations, dissecting their implications for all facets of business operations. This begins with a robust monitoring system, one that scans the horizon for legislative shifts across jurisdictions and sectors. Whether it's the advent of GDPR affecting data handling practices or the changing tides of digital asset regulation, staying informed is the first line of defense—and opportunity.

To adapt to regulatory changes, FP&A teams must ensure their financial models and forecasting tools are as malleable as the regulations themselves. This requires building in modularity and adaptability at the core of financial systems, allowing for swift recalibration in response to compliance demands. For instance, if a new tax legislation alters capital gain calculations, the financial models must be capable of incorporating these changes without a system overhaul.

The role of technology, once again, comes to the forefront as an enabler of compliance and adaptation. The proliferation of regulatory technology (RegTech) solutions—driven by AI and machine learning—can automate the tracking and reporting of compliance data, thereby reducing the manual burden on FP&A teams. By employing these sophisticated tools, organizations can achieve real-time visibility into their compliance status and receive predictive alerts on potential breaches before they occur.

However, technology is but one piece of the regulatory puzzle. The human element—specifically, the cultivation of a compliance-oriented culture—is equally vital. FP&A professionals must be instilled with a mindset that views regulatory compliance not as a hindrance but as an intrinsic component of corporate stewardship. Training programs and workshops can reinforce this perspective, equipping team members with the knowledge and ethical framework to make decisions through a compliance-conscious lens.

Collaboration with legal and compliance departments is also paramount. These interdisciplinary partnerships foster a cross-pollination of expertise, ensuring that FP&A initiatives are vetted for regulatory soundness. Such alliances also facilitate the development of contingency plans, preparing the organization to pivot gracefully in the face of regulatory shifts.

Beyond compliance, there lies the strategic realm where regulation can be a source of differentiation. FP&A leaders can turn regulatory foresight into competitive advantage by anticipating market changes that regulations might herald. For example, if tightening environmental regulations signal a shift towards green technologies, FP&A can guide the organization to invest in sustainable practices and projects proactively, capturing market share as the industry pivots.

In embracing this proactive stance, FP&A professionals must not lose sight of the global nature of today's regulatory environment. With cross-border trade and international operations being the norm, a multidimensional understanding of regional regulatory landscapes is indispensable. This global acumen ensures that multinational organizations harmonize their practices with a mosaic of local and international standards, avoiding the pitfalls of non-compliance.

As the regulatory landscape continues to morph with each passing day, FP&A teams must stand ready to adapt, innovate, and derive strategic insight from the complexities of compliance. By fostering agility, technology adoption, cross-functional collaboration, and a culture of regulatory literacy, organizations can not only navigate but thrive in the ever-shifting sands of global financial regulation.

Navigating New Financial Regulations Post-Crisis

The global financial crisis of 2008 served as a stark wake-up call, highlighting the glaring deficiencies within regulatory frameworks and the need for sweeping reform. In this intricate exploration of navigating new financial regulations post-crisis, we delve into the FP&A leader's role in steering their organization through a labyrinth of enhanced supervisory measures and compliance mandates designed to fortify the financial system against future shocks.

The introduction of regulations such as the Dodd-Frank Act in the United States and the European Market Infrastructure Regulation (EMIR) in the EU, has redefined the operational landscape for financial entities. These statutes have ushered in an era of increased transparency, stringent capital requirements, and robust consumer protection mechanisms, all intricately interwoven into the fabric of financial governance.

The post-crisis regulatory environment has seen the birth of the Consumer Financial Protection Bureau (CFP and the institutionalization of the Volcker Rule, which significantly curtailed proprietary trading by banks. For FP&A professionals, understanding these shifts is critical. They must dissect and interpret how each clause impacts their organization's fiscal strategies, from altering investment portfolios to reshaping hedging practices in light of these regulations' risk-retention rules.

One of the most pivotal aspects to navigate in this post-crisis world involves the intricate dance of liquidity management. With regulations like Basel III emphasizing liquidity coverage ratios and net stable funding ratios, FP&A teams are compelled to maintain a delicate balance between liquid assets and long-term stability. This involves a granular analysis of cash flows, a reassessment of credit lines, and an ongoing evaluation of financial instruments' contributions to overall liquidity.

Another dimension that requires meticulous attention is the 'stress testing' mandates. These regulatory-driven scenarios compel organizations to test their financial mettle against hypothetical adverse conditions, thus mandating FP&A leaders to craft financial models that can weather extreme economic downturns. Such models must be both resilient and flexible, incorporating a spectrum of variables from market crashes to geopolitical upheavals.

As FP&A teams navigate this new terrain, they also encounter the challenge of data management and reporting. Post-crisis regulations often require comprehensive reporting on risk exposure, capital adequacy, and trading activities. FP&A professionals must therefore ensure that data collection and reporting systems are not only compliant with regulations like the Foreign Account Tax Compliance Act (FATCA) and Markets in Financial Instruments Directive (MiFID II) but also optimized for accuracy and efficiency.

Interpreting the implications of regulations requires a forward-looking approach. Beyond compliance, there lies the strategic dimension where FP&A teams must align new regulatory requirements with corporate strategy. This involves evaluating the long-term impact of regulations on business growth, competitive positioning, and shareholder value. It is a balancing act between mitigating risk and seizing opportunities that arise from regulatory-induced market shifts.

Technology plays a critical role in this adaptive journey. Cutting-edge software and analytical tools enable FP&A departments to simulate regulatory impacts on financial projections, optimize data for reporting, and facilitate real-time decision-making. Automation becomes a stalwart ally, streamlining compliance processes and fortifying the organization's defenses against regulatory penalties.

However, even the most advanced tools are insufficient without a culture of compliance. Embedding a risk-aware mindset across all levels of an organization is essential. This involves training, open dialogues on regulatory changes, and the cultivation of an environment where compliance is viewed not as a burden but as a joint responsibility.

Navigating new financial regulations post-crisis demands a multifaceted approach. It requires an intricate understanding of the rules, a strategic application of their implications, and the deployment of robust technological systems. Above all, it calls for a cultural shift towards proactive compliance, ensuring that organizations not only survive in the post-crisis world but thrive amidst its complexities.

Preparing for Regulatory Changes in Digital Assets

In the wake of burgeoning digital asset markets, regulatory bodies worldwide are racing to establish frameworks to govern the issuance, trade, and management of these novel asset classes. FP&A leaders are tasked with the monumental responsibility of guiding their organizations through the nascent and evolving landscape of digital asset regulation.

The theoretical underpinnings of digital assets—a term encompassing cryptocurrencies, tokens, and various forms of digital securities—challenge traditional regulatory paradigms. Unlike conventional financial instruments, digital assets operate on decentralized networks and often lack a central authority, making regulatory oversight particularly complex.

To prepare for impending regulatory changes, FP&A teams must first cultivate a robust understanding of the foundational technology: blockchain. This distributed ledger technology not only underpins cryptocurrencies like Bitcoin but also enables the creation of 'smart contracts'—self-executing contracts with terms directly written into code. These innovations necessitate a reevaluation of existing financial reporting and compliance measures, as blockchain's inherent transparency and immutability promise to redefine audit processes and transaction verification methods.

-

Another critical focus area lies in the valuation and accounting for digital assets. Regulatory authorities, including the International Financial Reporting Standards (IFRS) Foundation and the Financial Accounting Standards Board (FAS, are contemplating the appropriate classification and valuation methodologies for digital assets. FP&A teams must be prepared to integrate these emerging standards into their financial reporting practices, ensuring accurate reflection of digital asset holdings and activities in financial statements.

In the realm of taxation, digital assets present a new frontier for regulatory authorities. FP&A leaders must navigate a labyrinth of tax implications arising from cryptocurrency transactions, token issuance, and asset transfers. This task is compounded by the international nature of digital assets, which may trigger cross-border tax considerations and necessitate a keen understanding of tax treaties and jurisdiction-specific regulations.

Regulatory preparedness also extends to risk management practices. The volatility and liquidity risks associated with digital assets, coupled with the potential for cybersecurity breaches, demand that FP&A departments incorporate digital asset-specific risk factors into their overall risk assessment and mitigation strategies.

Preparing for regulatory changes in digital assets mandates a proactive, informed approach. FP&A leaders must establish cross-functional teams, bringing together legal, compliance, and technology experts to craft a comprehensive digital asset strategy. Such strategies should be flexible enough to adapt to regulatory developments and resilient enough to safeguard the organization against the inherent risks of this innovative asset class.

Cross-border Regulatory Challenges

Navigating the labyrinthine complexity of cross-border regulatory challenges is an intricate ballet performed on the world stage by FP&A leaders. As businesses expand their operations and influence across international boundaries, they encounter a mosaic of legal frameworks, each with its own nuances, demanding scrupulous attention to detail and strategic foresight.

The genesis of cross-border regulatory challenges arises from the disparate financial regulations that govern different jurisdictions. A multinational corporation might find itself straddling various legal systems, each with specific requirements pertaining to financial reporting, corporate governance, capital requirements, and anti-money laundering protocols. The intricacy lies not only in understanding and complying with these regulations but also in harmonizing them in a way that does not stifle the organization's global strategy.

For instance, the extraterritorial reach of laws like the U.S. Foreign Account Tax Compliance Act (FATCA) and the EU's General Data Protection Regulation (GDPR) has far-reaching implications for FP&A activities. FATCA requires foreign financial institutions to report on assets held by U.S. taxpayers, while GDPR imposes strict rules on data privacy and cross-border data transfer. Navigating these regulations requires a nuanced approach to ensure that financial planning aligns with global tax strategies whilst upholding the sanctity of data privacy across borders.

Another aspect of cross-border regulatory challenges lies in transaction reporting and compliance with international accounting standards. Organizations must not only ensure the accurate representation of their financial position but also reconcile differing accounting practices to present a coherent financial narrative to stakeholders worldwide. This necessitates a robust infrastructure capable of consolidating financial data from various sources, applying the correct accounting standards, and generating transparent reports that satisfy the stipulations of diverse regulatory bodies.

Compounding these challenges is the rapid evolution of international trade agreements and tariffs, which can dramatically alter the financial landscape without warning. FP&A professionals must stay vigilant, tracking geopolitical shifts and trade negotiations to forecast their potential impact on the organization's financial health and adapt their strategies accordingly.

Furthermore, FP&A leaders must exercise agility in managing currency risk, given the fluctuating exchange rates that can significantly affect the financial performance of global operations. Hedging strategies must be devised and executed with precision, considering not only the economic factors but also the compliance aspect of cross-jurisdictional financial regulations.

The endeavor to tackle cross-border regulatory challenges is not solely a matter of compliance; it is a strategic exercise in risk management. The interplay of regulations across jurisdictions can present both opportunities and obstacles. For instance, regulatory arbitrage may offer competitive advantages in certain areas, but it also carries the risk of regulatory backlash if not managed with the utmost care and ethical consideration.

The Growing Influence of ESG Reporting Standards

In the modern tableau of global finance, the emergence of Environmental, Social, and Governance (ESG) reporting standards represents a significant paradigm shift, heralding a new era where sustainability intertwines with corporate performance. As stakeholders increasingly prioritize not only financial returns but also social and environmental impact, ESG standards have become a critical component of a comprehensive investment analysis and corporate reporting.

This intensifying focus on ESG factors is driven by a recognition of the long-term risks and opportunities that sustainability presents to businesses. Environmental challenges, such as climate change and resource depletion, social concerns, including labor practices and community impact, and governance issues like corporate ethics and transparency, are now seen as pivotal elements that can affect an organization's ability to generate value over time.

Against this backdrop, the importance of ESG reporting standards cannot be overstated. These standards provide a framework for companies to disclose material information related to their sustainability practices, offering investors and other stakeholders a lens through which to assess the non-financial dimensions of corporate performance. The maturation of ESG reporting standards, such as the Global Reporting Initiative (GRI), the Sustainability Accounting Standards Board (SAS, and the Task Force on Climate-related Financial Disclosures (TCFD), has led to an increasing harmonization of ESG reporting, enhancing comparability and reliability of the data provided.

For FP&A leaders, the growing influence of ESG standards necessitates an adept integration of sustainability metrics into financial planning and analysis. This convergence presents a complex challenge: quantifying the financial implications of ESG factors and embedding them into traditional financial models. The inclusion of ESG considerations in investment decisions and risk assessments requires a deep dive into the potential cost implications of environmental risks, the financial impact of social responsibility initiatives, and the valuation adjustments due to governance practices.

One critical element in addressing ESG reporting standards is the development of a robust data collection and reporting infrastructure. FP&A professionals must ensure that their organizations have the systems and processes in place to accurately track and report on ESG metrics. This may involve cross-departmental collaboration to gather relevant data, the implementation of advanced analytics to measure and interpret ESG performance, and the development of reporting tools that align with recognized ESG frameworks.

As regulatory pressures mount and investor scrutiny intensifies, the role of FP&A in ESG reporting has expanded beyond compliance. Proactive engagement with ESG issues can lead to identifying strategic opportunities for cost savings, revenue generation, and risk mitigation. For example, energy efficiency initiatives can reduce operational costs, socially responsible supply chain practices can enhance brand reputation and customer loyalty, and strong governance can mitigate legal and regulatory risks.

Moreover, the integration of ESG factors into FP&A practices is not a one-off exercise but a continuous process of improvement and adaptation. Organizations must remain vigilant to the evolving landscape of ESG reporting standards and investor expectations. This may involve ongoing monitoring of regulatory developments, participation in industry forums and ESG-related initiatives, and regular updates to internal reporting practices to reflect the latest standards.

The growing influence of ESG reporting standards represents both a challenge and an opportunity for FP&A leaders. Those who can adeptly navigate this new landscape, leveraging ESG insights to inform financial strategies and communicate corporate values, will position their organizations at the forefront of sustainable business practices, ready to meet the demands of a rapidly evolving global market.

EPILOGUE: TOWARD THE HORIZON OF PRUDENT STEWARDSHIP

As you close the final pages of " CFO Playbook ", you are no longer the steward of finance you once were. Through the multitude of frameworks, strategies, and spotlights on innovation within these chapters, a transformation has taken place. No longer are you wading through the morass of uncertainty that encumbers the average financial navigator; instead, you are now equipped to chart a course through the most turbulent economic seas with confidence and foresight.

Throughout this journey, we have explored the intricacies of risk management—a discipline once seen as the dry obligation of due diligence, now revealed as the artful dance of anticipation and adaptability. We have crossed the chasm that separates reactive firefighting from proactive risk architecture, understanding that the true power of FP&A lies within its ability to predict, prepare, and pivot.

As advanced CFOs and financial leaders, you have learned that risk is not a foe to be vanquished but a constant companion on the road to corporate growth and resilience. The key message of our shared expedition has been clear: embrace risk, understand it, and transform it from a source of anxiety to a wellspring of opportunity.

Let the insights gathered here serve as your compass. The environment you navigate is fraught with both peril and promise—the volatility of markets, the innovation of competitors, and the uncertainties of a global economy. But now, these are not merely challenges; they are the forging ground for your strategic acumen.

Remember the tenet that has coursed through each chapter: dynamic risk management is at the heart of prudent financial planning and analysis. It is the beacon that guides the ship, not by avoiding every storm, but by knowing when to sail through it, when to circumvent it, and when to harness the wind that it brings.

As you continue your journey, let this book be a reminder of the progress you've made and the exciting path that lies ahead. Your role extends beyond the numbers. You are the architect of your company's future, the sentinel who watches over its assets, and the visionary who anticipates its potential.

It is your hands, armed with the tools and wisdom encapsulated in these pages, that will mold the fiscal landscape of tomorrow. Your leadership holds the power to inspire, the decisions you make echo throughout the halls of your enterprise, and the risks you manage shape the success of your stakeholders.

Take heart in the knowledge that with every step forward,

with every risk navigated, you are part of a community of financial leaders who are not only safeguarding their organizations but are also paving the way for innovation and strategic excellence.

As you set down this guide, remember that the future is not to be feared but to be fashioned, with the mastery of the CFO as the craftsman and the unpredictable nature of business as the canvas. Go forth with the courage to confront uncertainty, the wisdom to recognize opportunity, and the conviction to act with integrity.

May you be steadfast in your commitment to excellence, emboldened by the prospects that lie ahead, and always aware that, with risk comes reward. Here's to the path you will forge and the legacy you will leave—an odyssey of strategic foresight, unyielding integrity, and enlightened stewardship.

Onward to a future where risk is not a gamble but a calculated stride toward greatness.

ADDITIONAL RESOURCES

Books:

1. "Value at Risk: The New Benchmark for Managing Financial Risk" by Philippe Jorion

2. "Financial Risk Manager Handbook" by Philippe Jorion and GARP (Global Association of Risk Professionals)

3. "Risk Takers: Uses and Abuses of Financial Derivatives" by John E. Marthinsen

4. "The Failure of Risk Management: Why It's Broken and How to Fix It" by Douglas W. Hubbard

5. "Against the Gods: The Remarkable Story of Risk" by Peter L. Bernstein

Articles and Research Papers:

1. "Financial Risk Management: A Practitioner's Guide to Managing Market and Credit Risk" by Steve L. Allen

2. "Enterprise Risk Management: Today's Leading Research and Best Practices for Tomorrow's Executives" by John Fraser and Betty Simkins

3. "Integrating Risk and Performance in Management Reporting" (Research articles from Chartered Institute of Management Accountants - CIMA)

4. Scholarly articles on risk management can also be found in the Journal of Risk and Insurance, and the Journal of Financial Risk Management.

Websites:

1. GARP (Global Association of Risk Professionals) - https://www.garp.org/

2. PRMIA (Professional Risk Managers' International Association) - https://www.prmia.org/

3. FRM (Financial Risk Management) – Resources Page: Khan Academy - https://www.khanacademy.org/

4. CFA Institute - https://www.cfainstitute.org/

5. Risk.net - https://www.risk.net/

Organizations:

1. The Risk Management Association (RMA) - https://www.rmahq.org/

2. Society of Actuaries (SOA) - https://www.soa.org/

3. Casualty Actuarial Society (CAS) - https://www.casact.org/

4. The Institute of Internal Auditors (IIA) - https://www.theiia.org/

Tools and Software:

1. @RISK (Palisade) - Simulation software for risk analysis and decision making under uncertainty.

2. Riskturn – Risk-based financial planning software.

3. Oracle Risk Management Cloud - Enterprise solution for managing financial risk.

4. SAS Risk Management - A suite of tools to identify, assess, and prioritize risks.

5. Moody's Analytics – Tools for credit risk management, economic research, and financial risk management.

Courses and Certifications:

1. Certified Financial Risk Management (FRM) by GARP

2. Professional Risk Management Certification (PRM) by PRMIA

3. Risk Management Certificate – Offered by various continuing education providers such as Coursera or edX featuring courses from Stanford University, New York University, and others.

4. CFA Program – While focused on investment management, also covers comprehensive risk management principals.

RISK MANAGEMENT PLAN

1. **Risk Identification Section:**
   - **Risk Category:** Classify risks into categories like market risk, credit risk, operational risk, liquidity risk, strategic risk, etc.

   - **Risk Description:** A detailed description of each identified risk.

   - **Risk Source:** Identify the source or cause of the risk.

2. **Risk Assessment Section:**
   - **Probability of Occurrence:** Assess how likely each risk is to occur (e.g., high, medium, low).

   - **Impact Assessment:** Evaluate the potential impact on the business if the risk materializes (e.g., high, medium, low).

   - **Risk Rating:** Combine probability and impact to rate the overall risk level (e.g., critical, high, moderate, low).

3. **Risk Mitigation Strategies Section:**
   - **Mitigation Measures:** Outline specific actions or strategies to manage or mitigate each risk.

- **Responsible Person/Team:** Identify who is responsible for implementing the mitigation measures.
- **Resources Required:** Specify any resources (financial, human, technological) needed for mitigation.

4. **Monitoring and Review Section:**
   - **Monitoring Plan:** Describe how each risk will be monitored (e.g., through KPIs, regular reports).
   - **Review Frequency:** State how often the risk management plan will be reviewed and updated.
   - **Contingency Plans:** Outline plans for responding to the risk if it materializes.

5. **Financial Impact Analysis Section:**
   - **Estimated Financial Impact:** Quantify the potential financial impact of each risk (e.g., in terms of revenue, costs, cash flow).
   - **Budget Contingency:** Allocate a contingency budget for risk mitigation and unexpected occurrences.

6. **Reporting and Documentation Section:**
   - **Reporting Procedure:** Define how risks and mitigation efforts will be reported to management and stakeholders.
   - **Documentation Storage:** Specify where and how documentation related to risk management will be stored and accessed.

7. **Compliance and Regulatory Considerations Section:**
   - **Regulatory Requirements:** Identify any legal or regulatory requirements related to

each risk.

- ○ **Compliance Measures:** Outline measures in place to ensure compliance with these requirements.

8. **Appendices and Support Documents:**
   - ○ Include any relevant documents, historical data, industry benchmarks, or additional resources that support the risk management plan.

AFTERWORD

As we turn the final pages of "The CFO playbook", it is fitting to take a moment to reflect on the expansive journey we have undertaken together. This book has not only equipped you with the theoretical knowledge necessary to navigate the often-turbulent waters of financial planning and analysis but has also provided practical tools to implement robust risk management strategies that are crucial for a forward-thinking Chief Financial Officer.

Throughout the chapters, we delved deep into the myriad risks that modern businesses face—from market uncertainties and cybersecurity threats to regulatory changes and geopolitical upheaval. We have seen how the role of the CFO has evolved, from mere custodian of numbers to strategic partner and anticipator of the unseen. Risk management, we have learned, is not about the avoidance of risk altogether but about understanding and mitigating it to a level that aligns with the company's overall appetite and strategic objectives.

Perhaps one of the most resonant themes of this guide has been the emphasis on the need for a proactive stance. In the realm of financial planning and analysis, anticipation and preparation are the keys to resilience. Instead of reacting to events as they unfold, the advanced CFO must cultivate a forward-looking approach, leveraging data analytics, AI-driven projections, and scenario-planning to navigate potential futures with confidence and agility.

The discussions on technology's role in risk management have underscored an inevitable truth of our times—the CFO who shies away from digital transformation does so at their peril. We have explored sophisticated models and software that enable the integration of real-time data into risk assessments, ensuring that the FP&A function can pivot and adapt with unprecedented precision. This digital evolution, in turn, has been shown to demand a symbiotic relationship with a human perspective—the keen insight and ethical compass of the CFO.

We have also considered the importance of fostering a risk-aware culture throughout the organization. As financial leaders, CFOs have a unique opportunity to champion policies and practices that imbue a sense of shared responsibility for risk management. By encouraging open communication, learning, and cross-functional collaboration, CFOs create an environment where knowledge is power, and that power is dispersed across the entire spectrum of the organization, fostering both innovation and vigilance.

In closing, if there is a single takeaway from this comprehensive guide, it may be the understanding that risk management is not a static endeavor but a dynamic process that demands continuous refinement. The role of the CFO in this process is both challenging and vital, requiring an all-encompassing view of both the financial landscape and the broader spectrum of factors that influence a company's success.

As we bid farewell, it is my hope that the insights and

strategies outlined in this guide have not just informed you, but inspired you. May the pages you have perused serve as a springboard for further exploration and as a trusted companion in the enduring pursuit of excellence within the risk management sphere.

With the themes presented in mind, I leave you with the encouragement to embrace the changing tides of risk with anticipation, innovate boldly in the face of uncertainty, and lead with the wisdom that marries analytic acumen with the human touch.

Thank you for allowing this book to be part of your professional journey, and may it drive you to new heights of effectiveness, strategy, and leadership in your role as a pioneering CFO within the dynamic discipline of financial planning and analysis.